ABOUT THE AUTHOR

Bernadette Brady is a professional astrologer who holds a Masters degree in Cultural Astronomy and Astrology from Bath Spa University, England. Her research work in fixed stars is a journey she has been travelling since the mid 1980s. Her first work in this area is contained in her innovative book *Brady's Book of Fixed Stars* (Samuel Weiser, 1998) in which she suggests a return to the visual use of stars. From these ideas Bernadette co-authored the visual astrology software package *Starlight* (Zyntara Publications 2002) which is designed to enable astrologers to work with and research the sky in a visual manner. Her fixed star journey has continued through her work in the *Visual Astrology Newsletter* a publication dedicated to fixed stars and visual astrology that has been produced monthly since January 2005. Bernadette's journey continues in this new book.

Her other books are: *Predictive Astrology: The Eagle and the Lark* (Samuel Weiser, 1992 & 1998), now heralded as a classic, and *Astrology, a place in chaos* (The Wessex Astrologer 2006) which is her Masters dissertation, on the mapping of chaos theory and complexity science to astrology. Bernadette is also the co-author of research astrological software *Jigsaw* (Astrolabe 1994, 1999).

Her personal web site is: www.BernadetteBrady.com

STAR AND PLANET COMBINATIONS

Bernadette Brady

The Wessex Astrologer

Published in 2008 by
The Wessex Astrologer Ltd
4A Woodside Road
Bournemouth
BH5 2AZ
England

www.wessexastrologer.com

Copyright © Bernadette Brady

ISBN 9781902405308

A catalogue record of this book is available at The British Library

Cover design by Iris de Leeuw

Printed and bound in the UK by Biddles Ltd, Kings Lynn, Norfolk.

All rights reserved. No part of this work may be used or reproduced in any manner without written permission. A reviewer may quote brief passages.

For Gillian Helfgott

who many years ago started
me on this journey.

Acknowledgements

I am indebted to Sarah Ashton who played a vital part of the development of the software, Starlight, which embodies the techniques contained in my earlier book on fixed stars in 1998. Sarah's remarkable skills, not only in mathematics, but also in being able to take my ensouled world of the sky and place it into a software package, have opened the door wider for research into this field. It is her skills and devotion to the sky that have enabled me to continue my research into the stars and without her contribution to the subject this book would not have been possible.

I also want to thank Ysha de Donna co-aurthor of *Pulses and Impulses*, (Townsend, G. & De Donna, Y., *Pulses and Impulses*, A practitioner's guide to a unique new pulse diagnosis technique, Wellingbourough: Thorsons Publishers, 1990.) for her help in compiling the physiological correspondences listed for every star. Also for her many generous hours of editing on the manuscript.

Contents

Section 1 Working with the Sky and the Stars   1
    Parans, the Original Method   2
    Parans and the Outer Planets   6
    The Heliacal Rising and Setting Stars, the Psychopomps   7
    The Heliacal Rising Star, the Resurrection Star   9
    The Heliacal Setting star – Salvation in a Star   10
    Working with the Star and Planet Combinations   11

Section 2 The Star Tables   15
    Finding your Heliacal Rising and Heliacal Setting Stars   15
    Star Tables   19
    Finding your Natal Star and Planet Parans   41
    Star Upper or Lower Culminating – Career and Prime Years   44
    Star Rise – the Parans of your Youth   45
    Star Set – the Parans of your Latter Years   45
    A Star at a Pivot Point at your Moment of Birth   46
    Star Paran Tables   49

Section 3 Star and Planet combinations   63
    The Delineated Stars - an Overview   64
    Achernar, *Erindanus*   67
    Acrux, *Crux*   70
    Acubens, *Cancer*   73
    Aculeus, *Scorpio*   76
    Acumen, *Scorpio*   79
    Agena, *Centaurus*   82
    Al Rescha, *Pisces*   85
    Alcyone, *The Pleiades in Taurus*   88
    Aldebaran, *Taurus*   91
    Alderamin, *Cepheus*   94
    Algol, *Perseus*   97
    Alhena, *Gemini*   100
    Alkes, *The Crater*   103
    Alnilam, *Orion*   106
    Alphard, *The Hydra*   109
    Alphecca, *Corona Borealis*   112
    Alpheratz, *Andromeda*   115

Altair, *Aquila*	118
Ankaa, *The Phoenix*	121
Antares, *Scorpio*	124
Arcturus, *Bootes*	127
Bellatrix, *Orion*	130
Betelgeuse, *Orion*	133
Canopus, *Carinae*	136
Capella, *Aurigae*	139
Capulus, *Perseus*	142
Castor, *Gemini*	145
Deneb Adige, *Cygnus*	148
Deneb Algedi, *Capricorn*	151
Denebola, *Leo*	154
Diadem, *Coma Berenices*	157
Dubhe, *Ursa Major*	160
El Nath, *Taurus*	163
Facies, *Sagittarius*	166
Fomalhaut, *Piscis Australis*	169
Hamal, *Aries*	172
Markab, *Pegasus*	175
Menkar, *Cetus*	178
Mirach, *Andromeda*	181
Mirfak, *Perseus*	184
Murzims, *Canis Major*	187
Phact, *Columba*	190
Polaris, *Ursa Minor*	193
Pollux, *Gemini*	196
Procyon, *Canis Minor*	199
Ras Algethi, *Hercules*	202
Ras Alhague, *Ophiuchus*	205
Regulus, *Leo*	208
Rigel, *Orion*	211
Rukbat, *Sagittarius*	214
Sadalmelek, *Aquarius*	217
Sadalsuud, *Aquarius*	220
Scheat, *Pegasus*	223
Schedar, *Cassiopeia*	225
Sirius, *Canis Major*	228
Spica, *Virgo*	231
Sualocin, *Delphinus*	234

Thuban, *Draco*	237
Toliman, *Centaurus*	240
Vega, *Lyra*	243
Vindemiatrix, *Virgo*	247
Zosma, *Leo*	250
Zuben Elgenubi, *Libra*	253
Zuben Eschamali, *Libra*	256

Section 1

Working with the Sky and the Stars

It has been a long time since astrologers really reached for the sky. The vault of the heavens with its lace-work of stars has been abandoned by most astrologers for nearly two millennia. Yet despite the dust of this neglect I think most astrologers do look up at the starry night sky and feel a yearning, a desire to reach out and embrace the sky, allowing it a place in their astrological souls.

If you are one of these astrologers, aware of the sky but feeling disconnected from it, then you have probably found that the sky does not easily reveal itself and its knowledge. Yet this gap between the sky and the astrologer has, I believe, more to do with our ignorance than the sky's reluctance. It has been, after all nearly 2000 years since our astrology moved its focus from sky to books, and as a result we no longer "see" the stars, we see books and charts instead. We have forgotten how the sky moves, how stars touch the earth and then fly to the heavens, we have forgotten how a star can die but then burst forward with life again in its own personal act of divine resurrection; we have, in fact, removed their identities, their stories and their divinity. Through our love of books rather than sky, the stars have been reduced to simple lists of ecliptical degrees; cut out of their constellations, and removed from their star phases. Nineteen centuries ago Ptolemy wrote on star phases and a star's special earth-sky-planet relationship; once this was so important but now it is largely forgotten.

For this reason you have to "think" yourself back into the sky, you have to work at it. Our modern western mind has been moulded by reductionism: the pursuit of truth by the technique of breaking everything down to its simplest units in order to gain understanding. This methodology has produced great benefits in our modern world of technology and machines, but this approach is not easily applied to the sky. Our attempts to apply reductionism to the stars has resulted in the astrological tradition of seeing the stars firstly as pseudo planet combinations and then as separate isolated units which can be collapsed onto the line of the ecliptic, making them more easily tabulated, standardised, and organised. I know that many astrologers prefer this method of working with fixed stars but I am deeply uncomfortable with it; for me it is like loving butterflies by sticking them onto blotting paper. I want my stars to be free, I want to rejoice at their rebirth, marvel at their resurrections and most importantly I want to honour their stories.

The sky is not a single line, the ecliptic, but a great dome of wonder that surrounds us, wrapping us in a cloak of mythology, stories and constant narratives. I personally do not want to be limited to the shoelace of the ecliptic as my only contact with the sky; I want to experience the wonder of the heavens in their entirety.

Parans, the Original Method

To work with the whole sky one must return to the original method of working with fixed stars. The full name of the technique as used by Vetius Valens in the 1st century CE is paranatellontato[1] and it was used to talk of constellations that rose, culminated or set at the same time and thus formed a sky narrative[2]. The astrologer known as Anonymous of 379 also wrote of star and planet parans suggesting that it may only be acceptable to collapse stars onto the ecliptic if they were located close to it, but one should work with the parans for all other stars[3]. Ptolemy also wrote his work, *The Phases of the Fixed Stars* in the 1st century CE, which deals with the individual star's unique pattern of rising and setting for a particular location.[4] So parans are not new; they are in fact very old, and are the original method used by the astrologer/priests of the Babylonians and the astrologer/scribes and astrologer/researchers of the earlier Hellenistic era. Parans are visually very simple but because they are affected by the observer's latitude they resist being reduced to a simple universal list of ecliptical degrees.

Parans belong in the visual world, not the tabulated one. If you go outside to watch the sky and you notice that a bright star is setting and, let us say, Jupiter is culminating, then you have noticed a paran. A paran is simply the simultaneous rising, setting, or crossing of the meridian (above or below) of planets and/or stars.

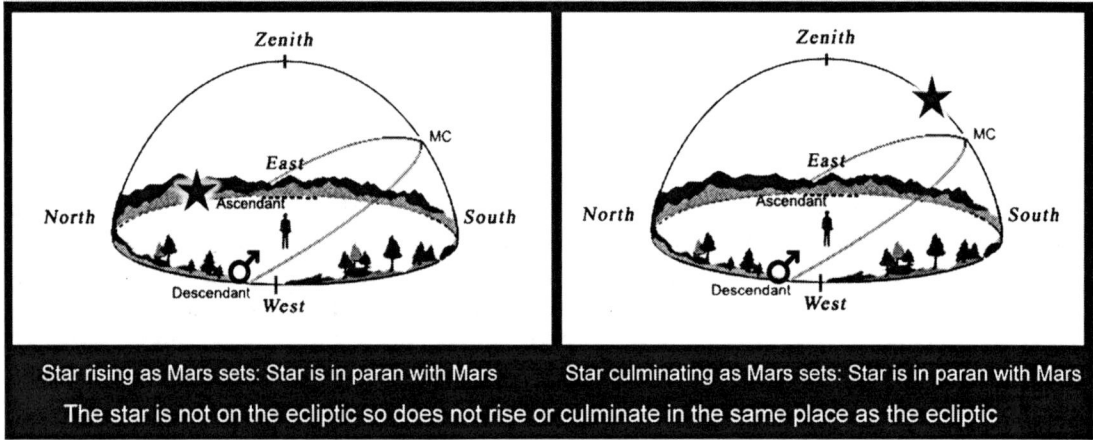

Figure 1 - Parans

In *figure 1 left*, a star is rising as Mars is setting below the western horizon. They are both on the line of the horizon at the same time and this places them in a paran relationship. In *figure 1 right*, a star is on its upper culminating pivot point, reaching its highest position in the sky, as Mars is on the western horizon. This is also a paran relationship between Mars and the star.

When a star forms a paran relationship to a planet then it is a unique sky-earth-planet combination – a union specific not only to the time of the event but also the place of the event. Additionally, it is a three way union which respects the location of all three members; the earth, the planet in its exact location in the sky, and the star, its location in the celestial sphere and relationship to its constellation.

Anonymous 379, the Greek astrologer named after the year in which he wrote his work on fixed stars, gives meanings for some star and planet parans. For example, in talking about Spica, the bright star in the wheat sheaf of Virgo, when in paran to Saturn, he says, " ... those experienced in medicine and prognostic will be made highly learned in secret matters and books of initiations." He goes on to talk of Spica in paran with Jupiter by saying ... "he furnishes greater good fortune, renown, dominion, hegemony."[5]

In his delineation we can clearly see the blending of the nature of the planet with another influence, that of the star. He has done this, of course, within the tradition of his astrology. In our practice we may choose not to be so absolute with our statements and instead use the fixed stars within our own astrological traditions to help us reduce some of the options that our modern approach to astrology produces.

For most of us a planetary aspect within a chart will have a range of expressions and a spectrum of potentials. When we combine planets in a horoscope we relate these to large collective patterns and suggest, via the art of astrology, how the individual may find a way to reveal these patterns in their life. Hence a Mercury-Pluto combination, to use just one example, is a pattern of mental intensity, idiosyncratic behaviour or neurotic tendency; if seen in a person's horoscope it indicates the potential for this motif to emerge in their life.

But to delineate a chart one must first develop the skill of identifying these collective archetypes or issues and then (and most certainly the hardest part of the process) to synthesise the unique blend into a meaningful life story or life-expression. Consequently, the question that plays around the edge of the astrologer's mind as one stirs the soup of aspects, planets and houses is that, although one can see the basic qualities and issues in the chart, just how strong will be each flavour and what will be the final nature of the mix? There are never definitive answers to these questions, but if we begin to notice the sky-earth-planet relationships that are embedded in the chart rather than focusing solely on the earth-planet part of the equation, then we can, I believe, gain real insight into how to slant our delineation of a chart.

Let us take an example of two people both with Mercury ruling their Ascendant, both with Mercury in their 2nd house and both with Mercury lightly aspected. The first is Agatha Christie, the famous crime writer, whose Mercury in Libra has no tight aspects *(see figure 2)*, and the second is Alan Turing, the genius of World War II who broke the German codes and built the first recognised computer. Turing has Mercury in Cancer, forming a quincunx to Jupiter and a wide conjunction to the Sun and a wide square to the Moon *(see figure 3)*.

4 Star and Planet Combinations

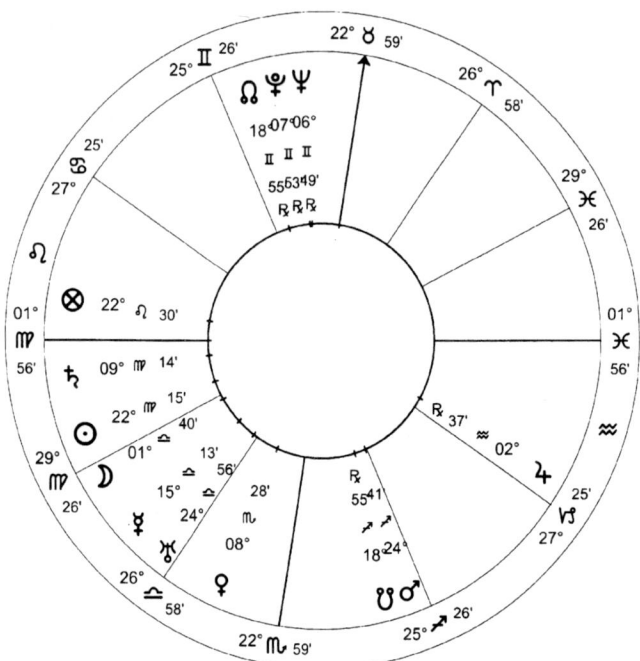

Figure 2
Agatha Christie born 15th September, 1890. 4.00 am GMT, Torquay, UK. Blackwell's database. Alcabitius house system.

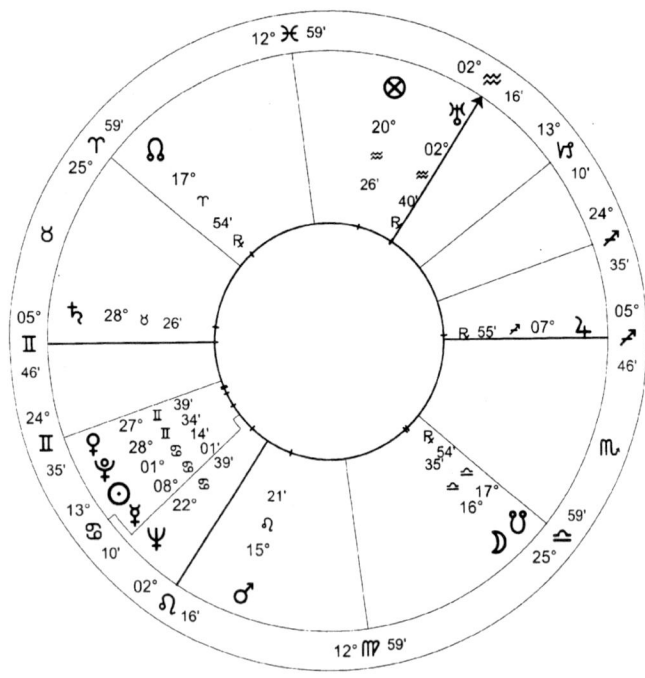

Figure 3
Alan Turing born 23rd June, 1912. 2.15 am GMT. London, UK. Blackwell's database. Alcabitius house system.

It is clear that these people have quite different charts, which would have an impact on the astrologer's delineation of their natal Mercurys. Nevertheless, we can draw considerable insight into the nature of their interests and their approach and attitude to their mental endeavours by looking at the stars that are in paran with their natal Mercurys.

For Alan Turing *(see figure 3)*, with his Cancer Mercury and Gemini rising, we would read a love of ideas, a natural curiosity but an emotional flavour to his thinking. We would expect him to go with his instincts more than follow the rules, and as Mercury is the ruler of his Ascendant and in his second house we would expect this love of ideas to be a major part of his life. We would also consider him to be mentally creative as his Mercury rules his 5th house. This is a simplistic delineation but one with which I think most astrologers would agree.

The following stars are also in paran to his Mercury[6] and the delineation has been taken from those given later in this book:

Mercury rising when Regulus is at its lower culmination:
To have a grand design, to inspire people with an idea. To receive recognition for noble ideas but the need to avoid revenge and refuse to be baited by gossip.

Mercury at its upper culmination when Alkes is rising:
To undertake detailed and precise work. A careful thinker who is at their best when allowed to plan, think and execute all in their own time.

Mercury at its upper culmination when Facies is at its lower culmination:
A gift of prolonged and intense mental focus. A pessimistic attitude, or one who is judged, or speaks, harshly.

Mercury setting when Mirach is rising:
The translator, a person who builds rapport between ideas or languages. The sales person or counsellor.

Mercury setting when Menkar is at its lower culmination:
An inspirational thinker. An uncanny nose for solving a problem or understanding what is needed. To find solutions to life problems in one's dreams.

Mercury at its lower culmination when Vega is at its upper culmination:
A visionary with a very persuasive voice and/or charismatic ideas. To be interested in the secrets, fantasy writing or the mythology of different cultures.

Alan Turing was not given any recognition for his work due to its secret nature. Even after the war the British government did not want the world to know that they had broken the code of the Enigma machines, as they had issued them to Commonwealth countries and wanted to be able to spy on those nations. The warning of the need to *"refuse to be baited by gossip"* with his Regulus paran is blatant. Turing, despite being the genius who deciphered codes, created new ways of thinking, and built the first problem solving machines, eventually committed suicide because of the social bias against him and the medical treatment he received in an endeavour to cure his homosexuality. He has now, many years after his death, received the recognition for his work promised by Regulus. If you look at the other star parans to his Mercury you can see that they speak for themselves for they show us his genius and even his desire to explore secrets and other cultures.

In contrast we have the other Mercury-strong chart of Agatha Christie. Her Mercury is in Libra with Virgo rising *(see figure 2)*. Such a Mercury will also love detail but located in Libra will give a more artistic emphasis, with an interest in and understanding of human relationship, rather than a mathematical, scientific orientation. With its location in her second house and ruling her Ascendant, like Turing, it is one of her key resources and its rulership of her 11th house shows the fluent use of her communication skills to reach or link up with many people. Christie's parans are quite different to Turing's and are as follows:

Mercury rising when Scheat is setting:
The innovator, gifted with ideas, words or rhythm; far-sighted. To be able to think outside the square. To actively seek the "truth".

Mercury at its upper culmination when Antares is rising:
Mental obsession with a subject or a person. The bane of subjective and fearful thinking. The need for objectivity.

So Christie is obsessive but gifted with her Libra Mercury, and she uses this to become a prolific crime writer as the Antares paran would be too intense to allow her to tolerate the idea of the romantic novel.

These are quite simple examples. I have not even explored the constellational meanings of these stars. But the key point here is that the star parans have not displaced or overpowered the meaning of the planetary combination. Instead they have simply, effectively and easily focused it, allowing the astrologer to give a far more detailed delineation of the chart.

Stars do not swamp a planet; they act like a foundation sitting underneath a chart, like the roots of a great tree. Knowledge of the star mythology that is tied to a planet helps us to focus our delineations.

Parans and the Outer Planets

Both Alan Turing and Agatha Christie belong to the Pluto in Gemini generation and although we can separate their individual Plutos by house and aspect, we do not tend to delineate Pluto in its sign for a single individual. However, when an outer planet forms a paran with a star it does so along one thin band of latitude and will only be applicable for twelve months or so. Thus the star and outer planet paran relationships do enable us to give some personal meanings to these generational planets.

For example Alan Turing's Pluto is at 28° Gemini and in a paran relationship to Hamal, the alpha star of the constellation Aries. Once again I quote from the text later in this book:

Hamal with Pluto:
Single mindedness, willing to engage in life and death issues. To be drawn towards tragic or powerful figures; to desire to explore the underworld.

Compare this with Agatha Christie's Pluto at 7° Gemini in a paran relationship to Deneb Algedi, the alpha star of Capricorn.

Deneb Algedi with Pluto:
Interest in the fabric of the law, to want to understand the workings of society. To wrestle with the legal system.

Turing is the man who cracks the secret code of the Germans in World War II and then suicides under the pressure of social punishment resulting from the conflict between his sexual orientation and the social mores of his time. Christie is a famous crime writer whose characters are always trying to find the murderer and uphold the law while at the same time wrestling with questions of human behaviour in society.

By using star and planet parans, we therefore gain many different versions of Uranus, Neptune and Pluto - 64 of which are given in this work.

The Stars Delineated in this Book

There are over 9,000 stars in the sky visible to the naked eye and one is always faced with the question of which stars to use. When I first started working with fixed stars I assumed that only the brightest stars would be important, but although all the bright stars with magnitudes 1 or brighter[7] are important so too are stars which are quite faint and hard to see even on a good night. Another approach was the idea that possibly only the stars in the zodiac belt were important for astrologers, but this also proved to be incorrect.

What I have found is that the stars that seem to contribute a consistent and reliable symbolism across diverse groups, from the famous and celebrated, to one's clients' – and even to one's pets' – charts, are the stars that are mythologically "bright". The stars that hold, for different reasons, a great deal of mythology. Like, for example, Alkes, the small star in The Crater with a magnitude of only 4.08. For reasons not totally clear, it carries the mythology of the grail, or the cauldron, with all its stories and mysticism. And it carries this rich symbolism to every planet it touches.

Thus the 64 stars given here are the set that I have worked with over the last fifteen years, and I have only allowed a star membership in the group if it shows a consistent symbolic application. Other astrologers may of course choose to work with more or less stars. If you are new to fixed star work then you may want to start with just the bright stars (each star's magnitude is listed with its other details) to help you first to become familiar with a smaller group.

The Heliacal Rising and Setting Stars, the Psychopomps

The idea, desire and methodology of the ascent of the soul has been a predominant, ever-present theme in the thinking of humanity. From the Egyptian Pyramid texts of the Old Kingdom (2650 – 2152 BCE) we see in some of the first writings that the sky is considered to be divine and the soul, after death, moving upwards towards a perfect, immortal life.

Thousands of years later, Plato (c.427– c.347 BCE) attempts to describe the soul's ascent in *The Republic* where he suggests that we live in a cave outside of which there is a brighter light which he defines as the World Soul, a concept of a great collective spiritual being into which we all seek entry[8]. Later the neo-Platonist, Plotinus (c.205 – 270) expands Plato's thinking by describing the soul in his *Enneads* where he talks of the moment of the heavens being reflected in our individual souls. He states that our personal souls have been captured and held down "by the clay it bears with it" while all the time:

> "even in us the Spirit which dwells with the Soul does thus circle about the divinity. For since God is omnipresent, the Soul desiring perfect union must take the circular course: God is not stationed."[9]

Here Plotinus, like the earlier Egyptians, links the soul directly to the moment of the heavens and notes that our own souls mirror this moment in a desire to rejoin with the divine. These ideas have been carried through the ages and yet, surprisingly, in the traditions of twentieth century astrology there is little evidence of this long established sky/earth/soul concept. However, when we work with the full dome of the heavens, we can once again think about the great movements of divine circles of Plotinus and weave them into our astrological thinking.

When we actually watch the sky a few things become obvious. Some stars are circumpolar, meaning they never set and are visible for the whole night throughout the entire year. To the Egyptians such stars were deemed to be immortal and god-like if not gods themselves, for they *never* travelled below the earth to the underworld. However some stars were only visitors to the place of the immortals. For most nights such a star would be seen to rise or set during the night, but there would come a time in the year when the star was seen to rise *just after* sunset. Then at the following sunset the star would already be in the night sky. From that time forward for days or months, the star would be visible for the whole night and thus be imitating the immortal stars. Eventually there would be a sunrise where the star would be seen very close to the western horizon and as a few days passed it would finally be seen to set *just before* sunrise. This marked the star's return to the land of the mortals and such a star, which was the most recent star to return from such a visit, is known as the heliacal setting star (setting just before the sunrise).

Similarly there is a group of stars which, after a time of rising or setting during the night will be seen to set just after sunset and then not reappear again the next night. They may be absent from the sky for many nights or months. Such stars were considered divine beings that had died and were travelling through the underworld. These stars would eventually resurrect and on emerging from the underworld would claim the title of the heliacal rising star (rising just before or with the rising sun). A star's return from the underworld was a source of religious celebration and joy for the Egyptians as well as the Greeks, who both built temples aligned to the points on the horizon where certain stars would be reborn[10].

There are many philosophical and theological implications of a star's ability to move from the realm of the gods to the realm of humankind and then, after a time of "mortality", ascend back to the gods. Or for a star to be a god, appear to "die" but then return, as promised, on a set date, having been reborn again from the deeps of the underworld. The Christian celebrations of the Nativity (God being born in the mortal world) and Easter (God resurrecting from the dead) being only two obvious expressions of these theological concepts.

The Heliacal Rising Star, the Resurrection Star

The heliacal rising star is, in a non-enchanted world, simply a star that has disappeared from view as a result of the sun moving into the part of the sky occupied by the star.[11] For example, here is a pattern for the year 1000 BCE in Cairo, Egypt, for Sirius the brightest star in the sky.

> In any given year in that era it would be last seen to set just after sunset around 6 May.
> The exact setting with the sun occurs on 21 May. (This is the acronychal setting of the star).
> It is then not visible at any time during the night. (This is what Ptolemy called the star's period of arising and lying hidden).
> It then rises with the sun (so technically not visible but called its cosmic heliacal rising) on 6 July. (This is the end of the period of arising and lying hidden).
> It would eventually be seen around the morning of 21 July, rising as a tiny point of light in the pre-dawn light. This is the apparent heliacal rising of the star.

A star will only act in this fashion if its celestial latitude is in the opposite hemisphere to that of the observer. Cairo is located north of the ecliptic and Sirius is south.

This pattern, when viewed in a world where the stars are divine, is one where the divine entity known as Sirius dies around 6 May each year and is then absent from one's religious and spiritual life. However around 21 July each year Sirius resurrects, emerges from the underworld, and shows us once again that there is life after death.

The Star's Resurrection

The heliacal rising star for any one period was, in fact, the god who had most recently resurrected. When a star did return from the underworld it was considered to govern that time period until the next star returned from the underworld. The Egyptians used a set of 28 stars spaced around the year but it is uncertain exactly which stars they used. However, we can adapt this thinking to our modern astrology. For the time and place of your birth there would have been a star which was the most recent star to return from the underworld, and in the ancient Egyptian tradition this star would contribute to the quality of that place and time. It is, I believe, a significant background endowment to your natal chart; part of the soil into which your chart is seeded and one of the ways that it reaches out to touch the divine.

The heliacal rising star is a link, a psychopomp, between you and the "other place"; the divine or the enchanted. As this star resurrects by emerging from the underworld, its endowment to your chart is not concerned with the daily chatter of a busy life. Rather, it is focused into the realm of one's soul, one's spiritual pathway. This star and its mythic symbolism provide a deep sense of one's inherent nature, one's gifts, and the unseen ancestral issues that are pushing or pulling one through life. To ponder on the heliacal rising star, and explore its mythology, is to achieve insights into your life mission and abilities, and the gifts from your inner being that you have been given to help complete the mission. It seems to pull you or steer you through your life. You can find your heliacal rising star using the tables in the next section.

The Heliacal Setting Star – Salvation in a Star
The heliacal setting star is, in a non-enchanted world, simply a star that is normally seen to rise or set during the night, becoming visible for the entire night as a result of the sun's movement around the ecliptic. For example here is a pattern for the year 1000 BCE in Cairo, Egypt, for Vega the bright star in the constellation Lyra.

> In any given year in that era Vega would be last seen to rise just after sunset around the 26 April. The exact rising at sunset would occur on 11 May (This is known as the acronychal rising of the star).
> After this date the star is then visible for the entire night, not being seen to either rise or set. (Known as its period of curtailed passage).
> It then sets as the sun rises on the 28 July. (Cosmic or true heliacal setting which is the ending to its period of curtailed passage).
> It would however eventually be *seen* around the 12 August, to be appearing as a tiny light low in the west at sunrise and just as the light of the sun flooded the sky the star would be seen to set. (Apparent heliacal setting).

A star will only act in this fashion if its celestial latitude is in the same hemisphere to that of the observer. Cairo is located north of the ecliptic and so too is Vega.

This pattern, when viewed in a world where the stars are divine, is one where the divine entity known as Vega leaves the mortal earth and travels to the realm of the immortals around 26 April each year. Vega is then visible for the entire night and is not seen to "touch the earth". Consequently the star is unavailable for one's religious and spiritual life; however around 12 August each year Vega rejoins the earth and is thus incarnated once again, showing us the birth of a living god.

At the time of your birth this star is the 'divine being' which has most recently returned to earth and is offering you a gift. However, recognition of these gifts comes slowly to one's consciousness. As you struggle with the inner pressure of the "demands" of your heliacal rising star, the ups and downs of your life, you slowly discover the gifts of your heliacal setting star, and once found these are the very skills that become central to the journey of your life.

Both of these stars talk of your soul's journey as you deal with your mortal life. You can find your heliacal setting star in the tables in the next section. When you find both this and your heliacal rising star, think about them, study their constellations, learn to see them in the sky if you can, and try and step back to see the bigger picture of your life. This pair of stars will be common for all people born for your calendar date and latitude of birth, so you will share them with many other people. However they are not generational like the zodiac signs of the outer planets, they are instead an unnamed bond you share with a small group of people; a bond between a calendar date, a latitude and a person.

These two stars are, as a pair, one of the most important contributions that the sky has to offer astrologers. Their return to the astrologer's awareness is, I believe, one of the most important reasons for working with the stars in this ancient way, for they give us an insight into the individual's soul.

Working with the Star and Planet Combinations

Once you have found your star and planet parans from the Star Tables you are ready to start to work with the individual stars.

For each star two images are given, firstly of the star's position in its constellation reflective of Ptolemy's star catalogue, and secondly its position on the celestial sphere.

The celestial sphere is shown with the 0° Aries point on the ecliptic (where it crosses the equator) aligned with 0° longitude. The globe of the world is also shown although it will only be in this particular orientation once every 24 hours; it is shown here to help you understand the location of the stars on the celestial sphere.

Star – General Information
Under the celestial sphere is a list of information concerning the star, its constellation, magnitude (the smaller this number the brighter the star) and the star's position as for 1 January, 2000. The BV Colour is also listed for general interest and for possible personal research work into potential correlations between a star's colour and its astrological use.

A brief introduction to the constellation follows, designed to give you background information about the history behind the star and its constellation. I have covered the constellation mythology in far more detail in my first work on this subject[12] so, since this book is designed as a companion to that, I have given just a brief overview.

Next is the star's astrological meaning which, linked with the constellation image and history, should enable you to begin to build a picture in your mind of the themes, issues and nature of the star in question.

Finally, the World Cities section is a list of major cities over which the star will pass directly every day. As the earth rotates a star appears to circle the globe fixed on a band of latitude. Understanding this relationship between the stars and the globe will begin to give you an insight into how a place can be embedded with a star's mythology and thus have its own star-earth relationship.

The Images of the Constellations

The images of the constellations displayed with each star are all presented in the classical or "internal" view, that of seeing the stars from the earth. The stick figures are those from *Starlight* software. The location of the stars within each constellation matches the location given to the stars by Ptolemy in the *Almagest*. However, there are other ways of representing constellation images and their stars.

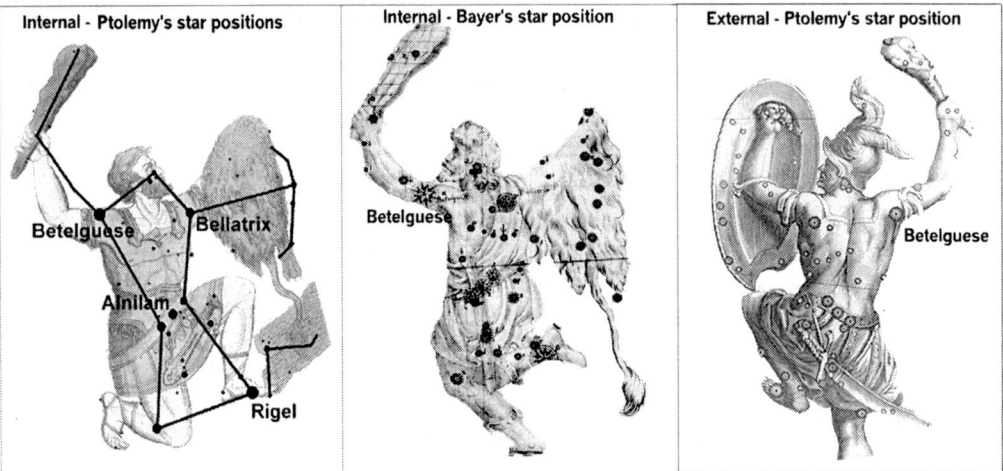

Figure 4 - Three different representations of Orion. The figure on the left is an internal view using Ptolemy's star positions. The figure in the middle is from Johann Bayer's *Uranometria*, and that on the right is from Johannes Hevelius' *Firmanentum Sobiescianum sive Uranographia*.

Figure 4 shows three representations of the constellation Orion. The figure on the left is an internal view using Ptolemy's star positions which locate the bright star Betelguese in the right shoulder of Orion and is reflective of how you would see the stars. The figure in the middle is from Johann Bayer's *Uranometria* published in 1603. He also maintained the internal view but drew his constellation images from behind, thereby reversing Ptolemy's star positions and placing Betelgeuse in the left shoulder of Orion. The figure on the right is from Johannes Hevelius' *Uranographia* published in 1690. He displayed the figure as an external view, as if looking from outside the celestial sphere down to the earth. This is what is used on celestial globes. Hevelius shows us the back of Orion and thus he maintains Ptolemy's star positions by placing Betelguese in the right shoulder of Orion. This style was also used by the Mesopotamian cartographers in the first millennia BCE. Consequently, when looking at a celestial map or constellation images one always needs to be aware of the view the cartographer has chosen to portray. As already stated in this work, all the images are of an internal view using Ptolemy's star positions.

List of image sources
Aquarius, Bootes, Cancer, Canis Minor and Major, Capricorn, Hydra, Ophiuchus, Orion, Pegasus, Perseus, Pisces, Scorpio, Taurus and Virgo are all based on the standard cartography designs which were made popular by the 19th century English artist Sydney Hall with varying degrees of modifications.

Andromeda, Auriga, Coma Berenices, Cygnus and Hercules are modified from John Flamsteed, *Atlas Coelestis* published in 1729.

Altair, Aries and Ursa Major have all been created using actual photographs of those animals while Gemini is based on my own photographs of two different statues.

The Argo, Cassiopeia, Columbia, Delphinus and Phoenix are based on versions by Johannes Hevelius' *Firmanentum Sobiescianum sive Uranographia*, published 1690 and reversed to maintain the internal perspective.

The Centaur is based on a photograph I took of the centaurs of the Elgin Marbles in the British Museum, while Leo is a modified photograph of the lions in Trafalgar Square, London.

Cepheus is based on a German 19th century print listed with the name of Krieger and titled "Jewish King".

Cetus is a modified version of the images in Johann Leonard Rost's *Atlas Portcetillis Coelestis* published 1723.

Corona Borealis, Crux, Eridanus and Lyra are my own designs.

Draco is a combination of different dragon images and shows the constellation in its original form with wings. (These wings now form the constellation Ursa Minor).

Libra is based on a set of 1st century Roman scales found in England.

Sagittarius is based on an image on the reverse of a 2-rupee Russian coin.

Ursa Minor was inspired by an Inuit sculpture of a polar bear.

Star – Personalised Information

For each star a delineation is given for:

- The star as the heliacal rising or setting star, as discussed earlier.
- The star if it is on one of its pivot points at the time of birth

As stars are not limited to the ecliptic, their diurnal rotation inscribes their own circles. If a star is at one of its own pivot points (that is it may be rising on the eastern horizon or setting on the western horizon, or it may have just reached the point of its upper culmination or the point of its lower culmination in its diurnal cycle) at the time when you were born, then it is "On a pivot point at the time of birth".

- The star's physiological correspondence – this is the physiological association that I feel, in consideration of a star's attributes, is linked with the star.

Following this, each star is delineated when it is in a paran relationship to the sun, moon and the planets and including the mean node.

Each planet and star text is divided into two parts. The first is the delineation for the star and planet paran in a natal chart; the text, after the marker "♦", is for mundane or predictive work. For example when considering the star Alphard, which is the Heart of the Serpent, in paran with the Sun, the following text is given:

Sun: To have strong passions, to be a victim of or a perpetrator of violent or aggressive actions. To feel angry at injustices, or be subject to mistreatment by authority figures. ♦ An occasion of apparent ruthlessness. *Voltaire, 18th century French author who is held in worldwide repute as a courageous crusader against tyranny, bigotry and cruelty.*

The first information would apply to a natal Sun in paran with Alphard, but if by transit the Sun moved into paran with Alphard for a particular latitude you could find that some news stories about unusual ruthlessness were being featured. Or, your progressed Sun may move into a paran with Alphard, in which case you may be subject to some ruthless dealings in your work or with your associates.

After each delineation I have given an example. These examples are not suggested as proofs but rather as illustrations. They are people who have this star and planet paran in their chart and whose public life seems to capture the essence of the star and planet relationship. They are offered here to help give an additional view of the combinations.

And finally, before you dive into the tables and all the delineations, if this is your first encounter with the idea of an enchanted sky I would like to bid you a very warm welcome to what I have found to be one of the most beautiful and rewarding areas of astrology.

NOTES

1. Giorgio de Santillana and Hertha von Dechend, *Hamlet's Mill* (Boston: Non-pareil, 1977), p.256.
2. Vettius Valens, *The Anthology Book I*, trans. Robert Schmidt (Berkeley Springs, WV: The Golden Hind Press, 1993), pp. 7-17.
3. See editorial by Robert Hand in Anonymous of 397, *The Treaties on the Bright Fixed Stars*, trans. Robert Schmidt (Berkeley Springs, WV: The Golden Hind Press, 1993).
4. Claudius Ptolemy, *The Phases of the Fixed Stars*, trans. Robert Schmidt (Berkeley Springs, WV: The Golden Hind Press, 1993).
5. Anonymous 397, *The Treaties on the Bright Fixed Stars*, p.5.
6. The following star and planet parans were calculated using the software *Starlight*, available from www.zyntara.com.
7. A magnitude of 1 is bright, –1 is very bright, a full moon is about –12.6 and a positive value of 5 is on the edge of being visible to the human eye.
8. Plato, "Republic," in *Plato Complete Works*, ed. John M. Cooper (Cambridge: Hackett Publishing Company, 1997), Book VII (514a-20a).
9. *Plotinus, Plotinus, the Enneads*, trans. Stephen MacKenna (New York, USA: Larson Publications, 1992), II.2.
10. See Norman Lockyer, *The Dawn of Astronomy* (Kila, MT: Kessinger, 1892).
11. For a full description of the mechanics and meaning of star phase I refer the reader to my earlier work on this subject: Bernadette Brady, *Brady's Book of Fixed Stars* (Maine, USA: Samuel Weiser Inc., 1998).
12. *Brady's Book of Fixed Stars* (Maine USA: Samuel Wieser Inc.,1998).

Section 2

The Star Tables

Finding your Heliacal Rising and Heliacal Setting Stars

As discussed earlier, for your date and place of birth you will have both a heliacal rising star, and a heliacal setting star.

The heliacal rising star is the star that rises with or before the sun on the day of your birth and in doing so is the most recent star to have returned from its journey through the underworld. This star is associated with the theological themes of resurrection and governs the time period until another star returns from the underworld to claim the title of heliacal rising star. This time period is a consequence of the location of a star in the sky, the latitude of your birth place and the time of the year; it could be just one day or it could last for several months.

You will also have a heliacal setting star, which is the star which has "fallen to earth", the star that is seen to set before sun rise which is the most recent star to begin to touch the earth after a period of curtailed passage when it was visiting the "immortals". It has, in a mythological sense, been visiting with the immortal pole stars. At sunrise, on your day of birth, this star is seen to set just before the sun rises and thus links the divine realm of the gods with the earth. Such a star carries the theological themes of the Nativity, the birth of a god amongst humankind. It will carry this symbolism for your latitude of birth until another star "falls to earth", which, again could be for just a day or for several months.

As discussed earlier, both stars are a form of psychopomp in your life acting as a bridge between the mortal earth and the divine sky; their mythology, therefore, is interwoven with your life journey and spiritual path. But before you can personally begin to explore this area of star lore you need to determine which stars are filling these roles for you.

Using the Tables

Following you will find a set of 21 tables. These tables are constructed for the star positions of 1 January, 2000 and for a time of midnight GMT. They show the particular day of the year when a star will rise (or set) when it is the same degree as the rising sun. They will be affected by precession and shift about a day per seventy-two years, so they are not designed to be used for historical charts.

Each table is labelled with a latitude, starting with a table for 45° South and moving in 5° increments to a table for the latitude 60° North. Your first step in finding your psychopomp stars is to find the table that is closest to your latitude of birth.

You can see that each table lists the dates for both a star returning from the underworld - the heliacal rising star and labelled "HR", and the star that has just begun to touch the earth after a period of time with the immortals (circumpolar stars) - the heliacal setting star labelled "HS".

Find the date that is either your GMT date of birth, or a date listed which is the first date that precedes your date of birth. That date will list a star with a label of either HR (heliacal rising) or HS (heliacal setting). Once you have found that star look back to find the next listing for the other star - that is to say if you have found a HR star then look back to find the next HS star, or vice versa.

For example, if you were born in London then you need to turn to the table for 50° North, the closest to London's latitude of 51° North 30' (see *figure 5*). If you were born on 13 July (any year in the last 72 or so) you would see that the closest date *before* your date of birth is given as 10 July. You can also see that on 10 July Betelgeuse became the heliacal rising star (HR). You then look back from that date to find the first star listed to be a heliacal setting star (HS) and discover that for you this star is Arcturus on 21 June.

Heliacal Rising and Setting Stars for latitude 50⁰ North (1 January 2000)

04-Jan	Aculeus	HR	21-Jun	Arcturus	HS	01-Sep	Sualocin	HS
16-Jan	Acumen	HR	05-Jul	Bellatrix	HR	02-Sep	Sadalmelek	HS
01-Feb	Pollux	HS	09-Jul	Alhena	HR	03-Sep	Alphard	HR
11-Feb	Castor	HS	10-Jul	Betelgeuse	HR	17-Sep	Vega	HS
21-Feb	Regulus	HS	14-Jul	Alnilam	HR	27-Sep	Markab	HS
21-Feb	Deneb Algedi	HR	17-Jul	Rigel	HR	29-Sep	Alkes	HR
22-Apr	Zosma	HS	18-Jul	Alphecca	HS	12-Oct	Scheat	HS
23-Apr	Denebola	HS	23-Jul	Ras Algethi	HS	8-Oct	Spica	HR
07-May	Zuben Elgen	HS	25-Jul	Ras Alhague	HS	2-Oct	Alpheratz	HS

Heliacal Rising Star is Betelgeuse

Heliacal Setting Star is Arcturus

Figure 5 – Finding the heliacal rising and heliacal setting stars for a person born on 13 July, in London, UK.

So for you, with a birth in London, UK on 13 July, your stars are:

Heliacal rising = Betelgeuse
Heliacal setting = Arcturus

You can now look up these two stars in the star and planet combination section and begin to explore the meanings of these two key stars in your life.

If there is more than one star listed on either your date of birth or on the date immediately listed in the table before your date of birth then use both stars. For example, in *figure 6*, if you were born on 6 July, in Jersey City, New Jersey, USA, you would use the table for 40° North (Jersey City is at latitude 40° N 43'). Upon checking this table you would note that there are two stars listed for 6 July and both are heliacal rising stars, Alnilam and Alhena. Your heliacal setting star would be Alphecca as it is the first star listed as "HS" before your birth day.

Heliacal Rising and Setting Stars for latitude 40° North (1 January 2000)

04-Jan	Acumen	HR	07-Jun	Aldebaran	HR	24-Aug	Sualocin	HS
16-Jan	Mirfak	HS	09-Jun	Ankaa	HR	29-Aug	Alphard	HR
20-Jan	Capella	HS	28-Jun	Bellatrix	HR	30-Aug	Sadalmelek	HS
24-Jan	Pollux	HS	01-Jul	Alphecca	HS	22-Sep	Markab	HS
27-Jan	Castor	HS	04-Jul	Betelgeuse	HR	24-Sep	Alkes	HR
12-Feb	Rukbat	HR	06-Jul	Alhena	HR	30-Sep	Deneb Adige	HS
18-Feb	Deneb Algedi	HR	06-Jul	Alnilam	HR	03-Oct	Scheat	HS
20-Feb	Regulus	HS	07-Jul	Rigel	HR	17-Oct	Alpheratz	HS
01-Apr	Zosma	HS	12-Jul	Ras Algethi	HS	18-Oct	Spica	HR
06-Apr	Denebola	HS	15-Jul	Ras Alhague	HS	04-Nov	Hamal	HS
12-Apr	Fomalhaut	HR	28-Jul	Procyon	HR	05-Nov	Mirach	HS

**Two Heliacal Rising Stars
Alnilam and Alhena**

Figure 6 – A person born in Jersey City, NJ on 6 July would have two heliacal rising stars, Alnilam and Alhena, and their heliacal setting star would be Alphecca.

Thus for such a birth there would be two heliacal rising stars, Alnilam and Alhena, as both stars returned to the earth on the same day, and the heliacal setting star would be Alphecca.

If you were born early in the year, let us say on 10 January, once again in Jersey City, NJ, you will note from *figure 6* that your heliacal rising star is Acumen on 4 January, but you would need to look back into December to find your heliacal setting star which would be El Nath (not shown in *figure 6*) on 20 December.

If you were born in the southern hemisphere make sure you use the southern latitude tables. You may also find it interesting to follow a star through the 5° increments in latitude to start to understand the impact that latitude has on a star's rising or setting. Additionally you can see that stars which become the heliacal rising in the northern hemisphere become the heliacal setting stars in the southern hemisphere and vice versa. There is also no table for the equator as all stars at this latitude will at some time become the heliacal rising star for a few days.

Star Tables

The Heliacal Rising and Setting
Latitudes 45° South to 60° North

Star Paran Tables
Latitudes
Latitudes 50° South to 65° North

20 Star and Planet Combinations

Heliacal Rising and Setting Stars for latitude 45° South (1 January 2000)

Date	Star	H	Date	Star	H	Date	Star	H
06-Jan	Betelgeuse	HS	29-Feb	Vega	HR	23-Aug	Deneb Algedi	HS
07-Jan	Alhena	HS	22-Mar	Markab	HR	24-Aug	Regulus	HR
08-Jan	Alphecca	HR	24-Mar	Alkes	HS	04-Sep	Rukbat	HS
09-Jan	Alnilam	HS	04-Apr	Scheat	HR	13-Oct	Zosma	HR
11-Jan	Rigel	HS	15-Apr	Spica	HS	17-Oct	Denebola	HR
16-Jan	Ras Algethi	HR	17-Apr	Alpheratz	HR	28-Oct	Fomalhaut	HS
18-Jan	Ras Alhague	HR	04-May	Hamal	HR	08-Nov	Zuben Elgen.	HR
28-Jan	Procyon	HS	08-May	Mirach	HR	09-Nov	Vindemiatrix	HR
31-Jan	Murzims	HS	24-May	Alcyone	HR	11-Nov	Al Rescha	HS
04-Feb	Sirius	HS	05-Jun	Antares	HS	22-Nov	Diadem	HR
06-Feb	Acubens	HS	13-Jun	Algol	HR	27-Nov	Zuben Escham.	HR
09-Feb	Altair	HR	20-Jun	El Nath	HR	29-Nov	Menkar	HS
10-Feb	Phact	HS	30-Jun	Aculeus	HS	10-Dec	Aldebaran	HS
17-Feb	Sadalsuud	HR	01-Jul	Facies	HS	12-Dec	Arcturus	HR
24-Feb	Sualocin	HR	09-Jul	Acumen	HS	29-Dec	Ankaa	HS
27-Feb	Alphard	HS	29-Jul	Pollux	HR	31-Dec	Bellatrix	HS
28-Feb	Sadalmelek	HR	04-Aug	Castor	HR			

Heliacal Rising and Setting Stars for latitude 40° South (1 January 2000)

Date	Star	H	Date	Star	H	Date	Star	H
04-Jan	Betelgeuse	HS	21-Mar	Alkes	HS	15-Aug	Rukbat	HS
06-Jan	Alhena	HS	27-Mar	Deneb Adige	HR	21-Aug	Deneb Algedi	HS
06-Jan	Alnilam	HS	31-Mar	Scheat	HR	24-Aug	Regulus	HR
06-Jan	Rigel	HS	14-Apr	Alpheratz	HR	05-Oct	Zosma	HR
11-Jan	Ras Algethi	HR	14-Apr	Spica	HS	10-Oct	Denebola	HR
13-Jan	Ras Alhague	HR	02-May	Hamal	HR	15-Oct	Fomalhaut	HS
26-Jan	Procyon	HS	03-May	Mirach	HR	03-Nov	Vindemiatrix	HR
27-Jan	Murzims	HS	24-May	Alcyone	HR	07-Nov	Al Rescha	HS
30-Jan	Sirius	HS	04-Jun	Antares	HS	08-Nov	Zuben Elgen.	HR
02-Feb	Phact	HS	05-Jun	Algol	HR	14-Nov	Diadem	HR
06-Feb	Acubens	HS	19-Jun	El Nath	HR	24-Nov	Zuben Escham.	HR
06-Feb	Altair	HR	27-Jun	Aculeus	HS	25-Nov	Menkar	HS
16-Feb	Sadalsuud	HR	01-Jul	Facies	HS	05-Dec	Arcturus	HR
19-Feb	Vega	HR	04-Jul	Acumen	HS	08-Dec	Aldebaran	HS
21-Feb	Sualocin	HR	17-Jul	Mirfak	HR	10-Dec	Ankaa	HS
25-Feb	Alphard	HS	22-Jul	Capella	HR	28-Dec	Bellatrix	HS
27-Feb	Sadalmelek	HR	26-Jul	Pollux	HR	31-Dec	Alphecca	HR
20-Mar	Markab	HR	29-Jul	Castor	HR			

Heliacal Rising and Setting Stars for latitude 35° South (1 January 2000)

Date	Star	H/R/S	Date	Star	H/R/S	Date	Star	H/R/S
01-Jan	Betelgeuse	HS	17-Mar	Deneb Adige	HR	26-Jul	Castor	HR
02-Jan	Rigel	HS	18-Mar	Markab	HR	05-Aug	Rukbat	HS
03-Jan	Alnilam	HS	19-Mar	Alkes	HS	20-Aug	Deneb Algedi	HS
05-Jan	Alhena	HS	27-Mar	Scheat	HR	24-Aug	Regulus	HR
06-Jan	Ras Algethi	HR	11-Apr	Alpheratz	HR	29-Sep	Zosma	HR
09-Jan	Ras Alhague	HR	14-Apr	Spica	HS	05-Oct	Denebola	HR
22-Jan	Murzims	HS	30-Apr	Mirach	HR	05-Oct	Fomalhaut	HS
24-Jan	Procyon	HS	01-May	Hamal	HR	28-Oct	Vindemiatrix	HR
26-Jan	Phact	HS	23-May	Alcyone	HR	05-Nov	Al Rescha	HS
26-Jan	Sirius	HS	31-May	Algol	HR	07-Nov	Diadem	HR
03-Feb	Altair	HR	03-Jun	Antares	HS	08-Nov	Zuben Elgen.	HR
05-Feb	Acubens	HS	18-Jun	El Nath	HR	22-Nov	Zuben Escham.	HR
11-Feb	Vega	HR	21-Jun	Mirfak	HR	22-Nov	Menkar	HS
16-Feb	Sadalsuud	HR	25-Jun	Aculeus	HS	26-Nov	Ankaa	HS
18-Feb	Sualocin	HR	01-Jul	Facies	HS	28-Nov	Arcturus	HR
23-Feb	Alphard	HS	01-Jul	Acumen	HS	07-Dec	Aldebaran	HS
26-Feb	Sadalmelek	HR	10-Jul	Capella	HR	24-Dec	Alphecca	HR
06-Mar	Canopus	HS	24-Jul	Pollux	HR	26-Dec	Bellatrix	HS

Heliacal Rising and Setting Stars for latitude 30° South (1 January 2000)

Date	Star	H	Date	Star	H	Date	Star	H
02-Jan	Ras Algethi	HR	24-Mar	Scheat	HR	20-Aug	Deneb Algedi	HS
03-Jan	Achernar	HS	08-Apr	Alpheratz	HR	23-Aug	Regulus	HR
04-Jan	Alhena	HS	14-Apr	Spica	HS	24-Sep	Zosma	HR
05-Jan	Ras Alhague	HR	26-Apr	Mirach	HR	28-Sep	Fomalhaut	HS
18-Jan	Murzims	HS	30-Apr	Hamal	HR	02-Oct	Denebola	HR
19-Jan	Phact	HS	22-May	Schedar	HR	24-Oct	Vindemiatrix	HR
22-Jan	Sirius	HS	23-May	Alcyone	HR	01-Nov	Diadem	HR
23-Jan	Procyon	HS	27-May	Algol	HR	03-Nov	Al Rescha	HS
01-Feb	Altair	HR	02-Jun	Antares	HS	08-Nov	Zuben Elgen.	HR
04-Feb	Vega	HR	12-Jun	Mirfak	HR	14-Nov	Ankaa	HS
05-Feb	Acubens	HS	15-Jun	Capulus	HR	20-Nov	Menkar	HS
15-Feb	Sadalsuud	HR	17-Jun	El Nath	HR	20-Nov	Zuben Escham.	HR
15-Feb	Sualocin	HR	23-Jun	Aculeus	HS	22-Nov	Arcturus	HR
20-Feb	Canopus	HS	29-Jun	Acumen	HS	06-Dec	Aldebaran	HS
21-Feb	Alphard	HS	01-Jul	Facies	HS	17-Dec	Alphecca	HR
25-Feb	Sadalmelek	HR	03-Jul	Capella	HR	24-Dec	Bellatrix	HS
08-Mar	Deneb Adige	HR	23-Jul	Pollux	HR	29-Dec	Rigel	HS
16-Mar	Markab	HR	23-Jul	Castor	HR	30-Dec	Alnilam	HS
17-Mar	Alkes	HS	30-Jul	Rukbat	HS	30-Dec	Betelgeuse	HS

Star and Plant Combinations

Heliacal Rising and Setting Stars for latitude 25° South (1 January 2000)

Date	Star	H	Date	Star	H	Date	Star	H
02-Jan	Ras Alhague	HR	14-Apr	Spica	HS	23-Aug	Regulus	HR
03-Jan	Alhena	HS	23-Apr	Mirach	HR	21-Sep	Zosma	HR
13-Jan	Phact	HS	29-Apr	Hamal	HR	23-Sep	Fomalhaut	HS
14-Jan	Murzims	HS	10-May	Schedar	HR	29-Sep	Denebola	HR
17-Jan	Thuban	HR	22-May	Alcyone	HR	21-Oct	Vindemiatrix	HR
18-Jan	Sirius	HS	24-May	Algol	HR	28-Oct	Diadem	HR
21-Jan	Procyon	HS	26-May	Acrux	HS	01-Nov	Al Rescha	HS
29-Jan	Altair	HR	02-Jun	Antares	HS	04-Nov	Ankaa	HS
29-Jan	Vega	HR	02-Jun	Capulus	HR	08-Nov	Zuben Elgen.	HR
04-Feb	Acubens	HS	05-Jun	Mirfak	HR	17-Nov	Arcturus	HR
08-Feb	Canopus	HS	07-Jun	Agena	HS	18-Nov	Menkar	HS
12-Feb	Sualocin	HR	16-Jun	Toliman	HS	19-Nov	Zuben Escham.	HR
14-Feb	Sadalsuud	HR	16-Jun	El Nath	HR	20-Nov	Dubhe	HR
19-Feb	Alphard	HS	22-Jun	Aculeus	HS	06-Dec	Aldebaran	HS
24-Feb	Sadalmelek	HR	27-Jun	Acumen	HS	12-Dec	Alphecca	HR
01-Mar	Deneb Adige	HR	28-Jun	Capella	HR	15-Dec	Achernar	HS
15-Mar	Markab	HR	30-Jun	Facies	HS	22-Dec	Bellatrix	HS
25-Mar	Alkes	HS	21-Jul	Pollux	HR	26-Dec	Rigel	HS
21-Mar	Scheat	HR	21-Jul	Castor	HR	27-Dec	Alnilam	HS
05-Apr	Alpheratz	HR	26-Jul	Rukbat	HS	28-Dec	Ras Algethi	HR
11-Apr	Alderamin	HR	19-Aug	Deneb Algedi	HS	28-Dec	Betelgeuse	HS

Heliacal Rising and Setting Stars for latitude 20° South (1 January 2000)

Date	Star	Type	Date	Star	Type
03-Jan	Alhena	HS	28-Apr	Hamal	HR
08-Jan	Phact	HS	01-May	Schedar	HR
07-Jan	Murzims	HS	09-May	Acrux	HS
15-Jan	Sirius	HS	21-May	Algol	HR
20-Jan	Procyon	HS	22-May	Alcyone	HR
23-Jan	Vega	HR	24-May	Capulus	HR
27-Jan	Altair	HR	26-May	Agena	HS
30-Jan	Canopus	HS	31-May	Mirfak	HR
04-Feb	Acubens	HS	01-Jun	Antares	HS
09-Feb	Sualocin	HR	04-Jun	Toliman	HS
13-Feb	Sadalsuud	HR	16-Jun	El Nath	HR
17-Feb	Alphard	HS	21-Jun	Aculeus	HS
23-Feb	Sadalmelek	HR	23-Jun	Capella	HR
23-Feb	Deneb Adige	HR	25-Jun	Acumen	HS
13-Mar	Alkes	HS	30-Jun	Facies	HS
13-Mar	Markab	HR	19-Jul	Castor	HR
18-Mar	Scheat	HR	20-Jul	Pollux	HR
25-Mar	Alderamin	HR	22-Jul	Rukbat	HS
03-Apr	Alpheratz	HR	19-Aug	Deneb Algedi	HS
14-Apr	Spica	HS	23-Aug	Regulus	HR
20-Apr	Mirach	HR	18-Sep	Zosma	HR
			18-Sep	Fomalhaut	HS
			27-Sep	Denebola	HR
			18-Oct	Vindemiatrix	HR
			24-Oct	Diadem	HR
			26-Oct	Ankaa	HS
			29-Oct	Dubhe	HR
			30-Oct	Al Rescha	HS
			08-Nov	Zuben Elgen.	HR
			13-Nov	Arcturus	HR
			16-Nov	Menkar	HS
			18-Nov	Zuben Escham.	HR
			01-Dec	Achernar	HS
			05-Dec	Aldebaran	HS
			06-Dec	Alphecca	HR
			20-Dec	Bellatrix	HS
			21-Dec	Thuban	HR
			22-Dec	Rigel	HS
			25-Dec	Ras Algethi	HR
			25-Dec	Alnilam	HS
			26-Dec	Betelgeuse	HS
			28-Dec	Ras Alhague	HR

Heliacal Rising and Setting Stars for latitude 15° South (1 January 2000)

Date	Star	H	Date	Star	H	Date	Star	H
02-Jan	Phact	HS	23-Apr	Schedar	HR	16-Sep	Zosma	HR
02-Jan	Alhena	HS	27-Apr	Acrux	HS	25-Sep	Denebola	HR
07-Jan	Murzims	HS	27-Apr	Hamal	HR	13-Oct	Dubhe	HR
12-Jan	Sirius	HS	17-May	Agena	HS	16-Oct	Vindemiatrix	HR
17-Jan	Vega	HR	17-May	Capulus	HR	19-Oct	Ankaa	HS
18-Jan	Procyon	HS	18-May	Algol	HR	21-Oct	Diadem	HR
21-Jan	Canopus	HS	21-May	Alcyone	HR	29-Oct	Al Rescha	HS
24-Jan	Altair	HR	26-May	Toliman	HS	08-Nov	Zuben Elgen.	HR
03-Feb	Acubens	HS	27-May	Mirfak	HR	09-Nov	Arcturus	HR
06-Feb	Sualocin	HR	01-Jun	Antares	HS	14-Nov	Menkar	HS
13-Feb	Sadalsuud	HR	15-Jun	El Nath	HR	17-Nov	Zuben Escham.	HR
15-Feb	Alphard	HS	19-Jun	Aculeus	HS	19-Nov	Achernar	HS
17-Feb	Deneb Adige	HR	20-Jun	Capella	HR	01-Dec	Alphecca	HR
22-Feb	Sadalmelek	HR	24-Jun	Acumen	HS	04-Dec	Aldebaran	HS
11-Mar	Alderamin	HR	30-Jun	Facies	HS	05-Dec	Thuban	HR
11-Mar	Markab	HR	18-Jul	Castor	HR	18-Dec	Bellatrix	HS
11-Mar	Alkes	HS	19-Jul	Rukbat	HS	20-Dec	Rigel	HS
15-Mar	Scheat	HR	19-Jul	Pollux	HR	21-Dec	Ras Algethi	HR
31-Mar	Alpheratz	HR	18-Aug	Deneb Algedi	HS	23-Dec	Alnilam	HS
13-Apr	Spica	HS	23-Aug	Regulus	HR	25-Dec	Betelgeuse	HS
18-Apr	Mirach	HR	14-Sep	Fomalhaut	HS	25-Dec	Ras Alhague	HR

Heliacal Rising and Setting Stars for latitude 10° South (1 January 2000)

Date	Star	H	Date	Star	H	Date	Star	H
01-Jan	Alhena	HS	17-Apr	Acrux	HS	23-Sep	Denebola	HR
04-Jan	Murzims	HS	26-Apr	Hamal	HR	29-Sep	Dubhe	HR
08-Jan	Sirius	HS	09-May	Agena	HS	12-Oct	Ankaa	HS
11-Jan	Vega	HR	10-May	Capulus	HR	14-Oct	Vindemiatrix	HR
13-Jan	Canopus	HS	16-May	Algol	HR	17-Oct	Diadem	HR
17-Jan	Procyon	HS	18-May	Toliman	HS	28-Oct	Al Rescha	HS
22-Jan	Altair	HR	21-May	Alcyone	HR	05-Nov	Arcturus	HR
03-Feb	Acubens	HS	23-May	Mirfak	HR	08-Nov	Achernar	HS
03-Feb	Sualocin	HR	31-May	Antares	HS	08-Nov	Zuben Elgen.	HR
11-Feb	Deneb Adige	HR	14-Jun	El Nath	HR	13-Nov	Menkar	HS
12-Feb	Sadalsuud	HR	17-Jun	Capella	HR	16-Nov	Zuben Escham.	HR
13-Feb	Alphard	HS	18-Jun	Aculeus	HS	21-Nov	Thuban	HR
21-Feb	Sadalmelek	HR	22-Jun	Acumen	HS	27-Nov	Alphecca	HR
29-Feb	Alderamin	HR	30-Jun	Facies	HS	04-Dec	Aldebaran	HS
09-Mar	Markab	HR	16-Jul	Rukbat	HS	17-Dec	Bellatrix	HS
09-Mar	Alkes	HS	17-Jul	Castor	HR	17-Dec	Rigel	HS
12-Mar	Scheat	HR	18-Jul	Pollux	HR	18-Dec	Ras Algethi	HR
28-Mar	Alpheratz	HR	18-Aug	Deneb Algedi	HS	21-Dec	Alnilam	HS
13-Apr	Spica	HS	23-Aug	Regulus	HR	22-Dec	Ras Alhague	HR
15-Apr	Mirach	HR	11-Sep	Fomalhaut	HS	24-Dec	Betelgeuse	HS
16-Apr	Schedar	HR	14-Sep	Zosma	HR	27-Dec	Phact	HS

Heliacal Rising and Setting Stars for latitude 05° South (1 January 2000)

Date	Star	H	Date	Star	H
05-Jan	Vega	HR	01-May	Agena	HS
05-Jan	Sirius	HS	04-May	Capulus	HR
05-Jan	Canopus	HS	10-May	Toliman	HS
16-Jan	Procyon	HS	13-May	Algol	HR
19-Jan	Altair	HR	18-May	Mirfak	HR
31-Jan	Sualocin	HR	20-May	Alcyone	HR
02-Feb	Acubens	HS	31-May	Antares	HS
04-Feb	Deneb Adige	HR	14-Jun	El Nath	HR
11-Feb	Sadalsuud	HR	14-Jun	Capella	HR
11-Feb	Alphard	HS	17-Jun	Aculeus	HS
18-Feb	Alderamin	HR	21-Jun	Acumen	HS
20-Feb	Sadalmelek	HR	30-Jun	Facies	HS
06-Mar	Alkes	HS	14-Jul	Rukbat	HS
07-Mar	Markab	HR	15-Jul	Castor	HR
09-Mar	Scheat	HR	18-Jul	Pollux	HR
26-Mar	Alpheratz	HR	18-Aug	Deneb Algedi	HS
07-Apr	Acrux	HS	23-Aug	Regulus	HR
08-Apr	Schedar	HR	08-Sep	Fomalhaut	HS
12-Apr	Mirach	HR	12-Sep	Zosma	HR
13-Apr	Spica	HS	18-Sep	Dubhe	HR
25-Apr	Hamal	HR	21-Sep	Denebola	HS
			06-Oct	Ankaa	HS
			12-Oct	Vindemiatrix	HR
			15-Oct	Diadem	HR
			27-Oct	Al Rescha	HS
			29-Oct	Achernar	HS
			02-Nov	Arcturus	HR
			08-Nov	Zuben Elgen.	HR
			08-Nov	Thuban	HR
			12-Nov	Menkar	HS
			15-Nov	Zuben Escham.	HR
			22-Nov	Alphecca	HR
			03-Dec	Aldebaran	HS
			14-Dec	Rigel	HS
			15-Dec	Ras Algethi	HR
			15-Dec	Bellatrix	HS
			19-Dec	Alnilam	HS
			19-Dec	Ras Alhague	HR
			22-Dec	Betelgeuse	HS
			22-Dec	Phact	HS
			30-Dec	Murzims	HS
			31-Dec	Alhena	HS

Heliacal Rising and Setting Stars for latitude 05° North (1 January 2000)

Date	Star	H/R or H/S	Date	Star	H/R or H/S	Date	Star	H/R or H/S
13-Jan	Rukbat	HR	13-Jun	Rigel	HR	09-Sep	Alkes	HR
14-Jan	Castor	HS	14-Jun	Bellatrix	HR	10-Sep	Markab	HS
16-Jan	Pollux	HS	14-Jun	Ras Algethi	HS	11-Sep	Scheat	HS
14-Feb	Deneb Algedi	HR	18-Jun	Ras Alhague	HS	28-Sep	Alpheratz	HS
20-Feb	Regulus	HS	18-Jun	Alnilam	HR	11-Oct	Acrux	HR
06-Mar	Fomalhaut	HR	22-Jun	Betelgeuse	HR	12-Oct	Schedar	HS
10-Mar	Zosma	HS	22-Jun	Phact	HR	15-Oct	Mirach	HS
15-Mar	Dubhe	HS	30-Jun	Murzims	HR	17-Oct	Spica	HR
19-Mar	Denebola	HS	01-Jul	Alhena	HR	28-Oct	Hamal	HS
02-Apr	Ankaa	HR	06-Jul	Vega	HS	03-Nov	Agena	HR
08-Apr	Vindemiatrix	HS	06-Jul	Sirius	HR	06-Nov	Capulus	HS
11-Apr	Diadem	HS	06-Jul	Canopus	HR	12-Nov	Toliman	HR
24-Apr	Al Rescha	HR	17-Jul	Procyon	HR	14-Nov	Algol	HS
26-Apr	Achernar	HR	21-Jul	Altair	HS	20-Nov	Mirfak	HS
30-Apr	Arcturus	HS	03-Aug	Sualocin	HS	22-Nov	Alcyone	HS
06-May	Thuban	HS	05-Aug	Acubens	HR	02-Dec	Antares	HR
06-May	Zuben Elgen.	HS	07-Aug	Deneb Adige	HS	15-Dec	El Nath	HS
10-May	Menkar	HR	14-Aug	Sadalsuud	HS	15-Dec	Capella	HS
13-May	Zuben Escham.	HS	14-Aug	Alphard	HR	18-Dec	Aculeus	HR
21-May	Alphecca	HS	21-Aug	Alderamin	HS	22-Dec	Acumen	HR
02-Jun	Aldebaran	HR	23-Aug	Sadalmelek	HS	30-Dec	Facies	HR

Heliacal Rising and Setting Stars for latitude 10° North (1 January 2000)

Date	Star	H	Date	Star	H	Date	Star	H
15-Jan	Rukbat	HR	16-Jun	Bellatrix	HR	11-Sep	Alkes	HR
15-Jan	Castor	HS	16-Jun	Rigel	HR	12-Sep	Markab	HS
17-Jan	Pollux	HS	17-Jun	Ras Algethi	HS	14-Sep	Scheat	HS
15-Feb	Deneb Algedi	HR	20-Jun	Alnilam	HR	01-Oct	Alpheratz	HS
20-Feb	Regulus	HS	22-Jun	Ras Alhague	HS	17-Oct	Spica	HR
09-Mar	Fomalhaut	HR	23-Jun	Betelgeuse	HR	18-Oct	Mirach	HS
11-Mar	Zosma	HS	27-Jun	Phact	HR	19-Oct	Schedar	HS
20-Mar	Denebola	HS	02-Jul	Alhena	HR	20-Oct	Acrux	HR
27-Mar	Dubhe	HS	04-Jul	Murzims	HR	29-Oct	Hamal	HS
08-Apr	Ankaa	HR	09-Jul	Sirius	HR	11-Nov	Agena	HR
10-Apr	Vindemiatrix	HS	12-Jul	Vega	HS	12-Nov	Capulus	HS
14-Apr	Diadem	HS	14-Jul	Canopus	HR	17-Nov	Algol	HS
25-Apr	Al Rescha	HR	18-Jul	Procyon	HR	19-Nov	Toliman	HR
03-May	Arcturus	HS	24-Jul	Altair	HS	22-Nov	Alcyone	HS
06-May	Zuben Elgen.	HS	05-Aug	Acubens	HR	24-Nov	Mirfak	HS
06-May	Achernar	HR	06-Aug	Sualocin	HS	02-Dec	Antares	HR
11-May	Menkar	HR	14-Aug	Deneb Adige	HS	15-Dec	El Nath	HS
14-May	Zuben Escham.	HS	15-Aug	Sadalsuud	HS	18-Dec	Capella	HS
19-May	Thuban	HS	16-Aug	Alphard	HR	19-Dec	Aculeus	HR
26-May	Alphecca	HS	24-Aug	Sadalmelek	HS	23-Dec	Acumen	HR
02-Jun	Aldebaran	HR	02-Sep	Alderamin	HS	30-Dec	Facies	HR

Heliacal Rising and Setting Stars for latitude 15° North (1 January 2000)

Date	Star	Type	Date	Star	Type	Date	Star	Type
16-Jan	Castor	HS	18-Jun	Bellatrix	HR	13-Sep	Alkes	HR
17-Jan	Rukbat	HR	19-Jun	Rigel	HR	14-Sep	Alderamin	HS
18-Jan	Pollux	HS	21-Jun	Ras Algethi	HS	17-Sep	Scheat	HS
15-Feb	Deneb Algedi	HR	22-Jun	Alnilam	HR	04-Oct	Alpheratz	HS
20-Feb	Regulus	HS	25-Jun	Betelgeuse	HR	17-Oct	Spica	HR
12-Mar	Fomalhaut	HR	25-Jun	Ras Alhague	HS	21-Oct	Mirach	HS
13-Mar	Zosma	HS	02-Jul	Alhena	HR	26-Oct	Schedar	HS
22-Mar	Denebola	HS	03-Jul	Phact	HR	30-Oct	Acrux	HR
09-Apr	Dubhe	HS	08-Jul	Murzims	HR	30-Oct	Hamal	HS
12-Apr	Vindemiatrix	HS	13-Jul	Sirius	HR	18-Nov	Capulus	HS
15-Apr	Ankaa	HR	18-Jul	Vega	HS	18-Nov	Agena	HR
17-Apr	Diadem	HS	20-Jul	Procyon	HR	20-Nov	Algol	HS
26-Apr	Al Rescha	HR	23-Jul	Canopus	HR	23-Nov	Alcyone	HS
06-May	Zuben Elgen.	HS	26-Jul	Altair	HS	27-Nov	Toliman	HR
07-May	Arcturus	HS	06-Aug	Acubens	HR	28-Nov	Mirfak	HS
13-May	Menkar	HR	09-Aug	Sualocin	HS	03-Dec	Antares	HR
15-May	Zuben Escham.	HS	16-Aug	Sadalsuud	HS	16-Dec	El Nath	HS
18-May	Achernar	HR	18-Aug	Alphard	HR	20-Dec	Aculeus	HR
31-May	Alphecca	HS	20-Aug	Deneb Adige	HS	21-Dec	Capella	HS
03-Jun	Aldebaran	HR	25-Aug	Sadalmelek	HS	24-Dec	Acumen	HR
03-Jun	Thuban	HS	13-Sep	Markab	HS	30-Dec	Facies	HR

Heliacal Rising and Setting Stars for latitude 20° North (1 January 2000)

Date	Star	H	Date	Star	H	Date	Star	H
18-Jan	Castor	HS	21-Jun	Thuban	HS	15-Sep	Alkes	HR
19-Jan	Pollux	HS	22-Jun	Rigel	HR	20-Sep	Scheat	HS
20-Jan	Rukbat	HR	24-Jun	Ras Algethi	HS	27-Sep	Alderamin	HS
15-Feb	Deneb Algedi	HR	25-Jun	Alnilam	HR	06-Oct	Alpheratz	HS
20-Feb	Regulus	HS	26-Jun	Betelgeuse	HR	17-Oct	Spica	HR
16-Mar	Zosma	HS	28-Jun	Ras Alhague	HS	24-Oct	Mirach	HS
16-Mar	Fomalhaut	HR	03-Jul	Alhena	HR	31-Oct	Hamal	HS
24-Mar	Denebola	HS	09-Jul	Phact	HR	03-Nov	Schedar	HS
15-Apr	Vindemiatrix	HS	12-Jul	Murzims	HR	11-Nov	Acrux	HR
21-Apr	Diadem	HS	16-Jul	Sirius	HR	22-Nov	Algol	HS
23-Apr	Ankaa	HR	21-Jul	Procyon	HR	23-Nov	Alcyone	HS
26-Apr	Dubhe	HS	24-Jul	Vega	HS	25-Nov	Capulus	HS
27-Apr	Al Rescha	HR	29-Jul	Altair	HS	27-Nov	Agena	HR
06-May	Zuben Elgen.	HS	01-Aug	Canopus	HR	02-Dec	Mirfak	HS
11-May	Arcturus	HS	06-Aug	Acubens	HR	03-Dec	Antares	HR
14-May	Menkar	HR	12-Aug	Sualocin	HS	05-Dec	Toliman	HR
16-May	Zuben Escham.	HS	16-Aug	Sadalsuud	HS	16-Dec	El Nath	HS
30-May	Achernar	HR	20-Aug	Alphard	HR	21-Dec	Aculeus	HR
03-Jun	Aldebaran	HR	26-Aug	Sadalmelek	HS	24-Dec	Capella	HS
05-Jun	Alphecca	HS	27-Aug	Deneb Adige	HS	25-Dec	Acumen	HR
19-Jun	Bellatrix	HR	15-Sep	Markab	HS	30-Dec	Facies	HR

Heliacal Rising and Setting Stars for latitude 25° North (1 January 2000)

Date	Star	H	Date	Star	H	Date	Star	H
19-Jan	Castor	HS	25-Jun	Rigel	HR	17-Sep	Markab	HS
20-Jan	Pollux	HS	27-Jun	Alnilam	HR	23-Sep	Scheat	HS
24-Jan	Rukbat	HR	28-Jun	Betelgeuse	HR	09-Oct	Alpheratz	HS
16-Feb	Deneb Algedi	HR	28-Jun	Ras Algethi	HS	15-Oct	Alderamin	HS
20-Feb	Regulus	HS	02-Jul	Ras Alhague	HS	17-Oct	Spica	HR
19-Mar	Zosma	HS	04-Jul	Alhena	HR	27-Oct	Mirach	HS
20-Mar	Fomalhaut	HR	15-Jul	Phact	HR	01-Nov	Hamal	HS
26-Mar	Denebola	HS	16-Jul	Murzims	HR	11-Nov	Schedar	HS
18-Apr	Vindemiatrix	HS	18-Jul	Thuban	HS	23-Nov	Alcyone	HS
25-Apr	Diadem	HS	20-Jul	Sirius	HR	25-Nov	Algol	HS
29-Apr	Al Rescha	HR	23-Jul	Procyon	HR	27-Nov	Acrux	HR
02-May	Ankaa	HR	31-Jul	Altair	HS	03-Dec	Antares	HR
06-May	Zuben Elgen.	HS	31-Jul	Vega	HS	04-Dec	Capulus	HS
16-May	Arcturus	HS	07-Aug	Acubens	HR	07-Dec	Mirfak	HS
16-May	Menkar	HR	11-Aug	Canopus	HR	08-Dec	Agena	HR
17-May	Zuben Escham.	HS	15-Aug	Sualocin	HS	17-Dec	Toliman	HR
19-May	Dubhe	HS	17-Aug	Sadalsuud	HS	17-Dec	El Nath	HS
04-Jun	Aldebaran	HR	22-Aug	Alphard	HR	22-Dec	Aculeus	HR
10-Jun	Alphecca	HS	27-Aug	Sadalmelek	HS	27-Dec	Acumen	HR
14-Jun	Achernar	HR	03-Sep	Deneb Adige	HS	28-Dec	Capella	HS
21-Jun	Bellatrix	HR	17-Sep	Alkes	HR	30-Dec	Facies	HR

Heliacal Rising and Setting Stars for latitude 30° North (1 January 2000)

Date	Star	R/S	Date	Star	R/S	Date	Star	R/S
02-Jan	Capella	HS	23-Jun	Bellatrix	HR	28-Aug	Sadalmelek	HS
21-Jan	Pollux	HS	29-Jun	Rigel	HR	10-Sep	Deneb Adige	HS
21-Jan	Castor	HS	30-Jun	Betelgeuse	HR	19-Sep	Alkes	HR
28-Jan	Rukbat	HR	30-Jun	Alnilam	HR	19-Sep	Markab	HS
16-Feb	Deneb Algedi	HR	02-Jul	Ras Algethi	HS	26-Sep	Scheat	HS
20-Feb	Regulus	HS	03-Jul	Achernar	HR	11-Oct	Alpheratz	HS
22-Mar	Zosma	HS	05-Jul	Alhena	HR	17-Oct	Spica	HR
26-Mar	Fomalhaut	HR	06-Jul	Ras Alhague	HS	30-Oct	Mirach	HS
29-Mar	Denebola	HS	20-Jul	Murzims	HR	02-Nov	Hamal	HS
21-Apr	Vindemiatrix	HS	21-Jul	Phact	HR	23-Nov	Schedar	HS
29-Apr	Diadem	HS	24-Jul	Procyon	HR	24-Nov	Alcyone	HS
30-Apr	Al Rescha	HR	24-Jul	Sirius	HR	28-Nov	Algol	HS
06-May	Zuben Elgen.	HS	03-Aug	Altair	HS	04-Dec	Antares	HR
12-May	Ankaa	HR	07-Aug	Vega	HS	13-Dec	Mirfak	HS
18-May	Menkar	HR	07-Aug	Acubens	HR	16-Dec	Capulus	HS
19-May	Zuben Escham.	HS	18-Aug	Sualocin	HS	18-Dec	El Nath	HS
21-May	Arcturus	HS	18-Aug	Sadalsuud	HS	23-Dec	Aculeus	HR
05-Jun	Aldebaran	HR	23-Aug	Canopus	HR	29-Dec	Acumen	HR
17-Jun	Alphecca	HS	24-Aug	Alphard	HR	30-Dec	Facies	HR

Finding your Heliacal Rising and Heliacal Setting Stars   35

Heliacal Rising and Setting Stars for latitude 35° North (1 January 2000)

Date	Star	H	Date	Star	H	Date	Star	H
09-Jan	Capella	HS	23-Jun	Alphecca	HS	29-Aug	Sadalmelek	HS
22-Jan	Pollux	HS	26-Jun	Bellatrix	HR	08-Sep	Canopus	HR
24-Jan	Castor	HS	02-Jul	Betelgeuse	HR	19-Sep	Deneb Adige	HS
03-Feb	Rukbat	HR	03-Jul	Rigel	HR	21-Sep	Markab	HS
17-Feb	Deneb Algedi	HR	03-Jul	Alnilam	HR	22-Sep	Alkes	HR
20-Feb	Regulus	HS	05-Jul	Alhena	HR	30-Sep	Scheat	HS
26-Mar	Zosma	HS	07-Jul	Ras Algethi	HS	14-Oct	Alpheratz	HS
02-Apr	Denebola	HS	10-Jul	Ras Alhague	HS	18-Oct	Spica	HR
02-Apr	Fomalhaut	HR	24-Jul	Murzims	HR	02-Nov	Mirach	HS
25-Apr	Vindemiatrix	HS	26-Jul	Procyon	HR	03-Nov	Hamal	HS
03-May	Al Rescha	HR	28-Jul	Sirius	HR	24-Nov	Alcyone	HS
05-May	Diadem	HS	28-Jul	Phact	HR	02-Dec	Algol	HS
06-May	Zuben Elgen.	HS	06-Aug	Altair	HS	05-Dec	Antares	HR
21-May	Zuben Escham.	HS	08-Aug	Acubens	HR	19-Dec	El Nath	HS
21-May	Menkar	HR	14-Aug	Vega	HS	21-Dec	Mirfak	HS
25-May	Ankaa	HR	19-Aug	Sadalsuud	HS	25-Dec	Aculeus	HR
27-May	Arcturus	HS	21-Aug	Sualocin	HS	31-Dec	Facies	HR
06-Jun	Aldebaran	HR	27-Aug	Alphard	HR	31-Dec	Acumen	HR

Heliacal Rising and Setting Stars for latitude 40° North (1 January 2000)

Date	Star	H/R	Date	Star	H/R
04-Jan	Acumen	HR	07-Jun	Aldebaran	HR	24-Aug	Sualocin	HS
16-Jan	Mirfak	HS	09-Jun	Ankaa	HR	29-Aug	Alphard	HR
20-Jan	Capella	HS	28-Jun	Bellatrix	HR	30-Aug	Sadalmelek	HS
24-Jan	Pollux	HS	01-Jul	Alphecca	HS	22-Sep	Markab	HS
27-Jan	Castor	HS	04-Jul	Betelgeuse	HR	24-Sep	Alkes	HR
12-Feb	Rukbat	HR	06-Jul	Alhena	HR	30-Sep	Deneb Adige	HS
18-Feb	Deneb Algedi	HR	06-Jul	Alnilam	HR	03-Oct	Scheat	HS
20-Feb	Regulus	HS	07-Jul	Rigel	HR	17-Oct	Alpheratz	HS
01-Apr	Zosma	HS	12-Jul	Ras Algethi	HS	18-Oct	Spica	HR
06-Apr	Denebola	HS	15-Jul	Ras Alhague	HS	04-Nov	Hamal	HS
12-Apr	Fomalhaut	HR	28-Jul	Procyon	HR	05-Nov	Mirach	HS
01-May	Vindemiatrix	HS	29-Jul	Murzims	HR	25-Nov	Alcyone	HS
05-May	Al Rescha	HR	01-Aug	Sirius	HR	05-Dec	Antares	HR
06-May	Zuben Elgen.	HS	04-Aug	Phact	HR	07-Dec	Algol	HS
12-May	Diadem	HS	09-Aug	Acubens	HR	20-Dec	El Nath	HS
23-May	Zuben Escham.	HS	09-Aug	Altair	HS	27-Dec	Aculeus	HR
24-May	Menkar	HR	20-Aug	Sadalsuud	HS	31-Dec	Facies	HR
03-Jun	Arcturus	HS	23-Aug	Vega	HS			

Heliacal Rising and Setting Stars for latitude 45° North (1 January 2000)

Date	Star	H	Date	Star	H
08-Jan	Acumen	HR	29-Jun	Ankaa	HR	31-Aug	Alphard	HR
27-Jan	Pollux	HS	01-Jul	Bellatrix	HR	31-Aug	Sadalmelek	HS
01-Feb	Castor	HS	07-Jul	Betelgeuse	HR	02-Sep	Vega	HS
19-Feb	Deneb Algedi	HR	08-Jul	Alhena	HR	24-Sep	Markab	HS
20-Feb	Regulus	HS	09-Jul	Alphecca	HS	26-Sep	Alkes	HR
02-Mar	Rukbat	HR	10-Jul	Alnilam	HR	07-Oct	Scheat	HS
10-Apr	Zosma	HS	12-Jul	Rigel	HR	18-Oct	Spica	HR
13-Apr	Denebola	HS	17-Jul	Ras Algethi	HS	21-Oct	Alpheratz	HS
25-Apr	Fomalhaut	HR	20-Jul	Ras Alhague	HS	06-Nov	Hamal	HS
06-May	Zuben Elgen.	HS	30-Jul	Procyon	HR	10-Nov	Mirach	HS
07-May	Vindemiatrix	HS	03-Aug	Murzims	HR	25-Nov	Alcyone	HS
09-May	Al Rescha	HR	06-Aug	Sirius	HR	06-Dec	Antares	HR
21-May	Diadem	HS	09-Aug	Acubens	HR	14-Dec	Algol	HS
26-May	Zuben Escham.	HS	12-Aug	Altair	HS	21-Dec	El Nath	HS
28-May	Menkar	HR	13-Aug	Phact	HR	30-Dec	Aculeus	HR
09-Jun	Aldebaran	HR	21-Aug	Sadalsuud	HS	31-Dec	Facies	HR
11-Jun	Arcturus	HS	28-Aug	Sualocin	HS			

Heliacal Rising and Setting Stars for latitude 50° North (1 January 2000)

04-Jan	Aculeus	HR	21-Jun	Arcturus	HS	
16-Jan	Acumen	HR	05-Jul	Bellatrix	HR	
01-Feb	Pollux	HS	09-Jul	Alhena	HR	
11-Feb	Castor	HS	10-Jul	Betelgeuse	HR	
21-Feb	Regulus	HS	14-Jul	Alnilam	HR	
21-Feb	Deneb Algedi	HR	17-Jul	Rigel	HR	
22-Apr	Zosma	HS	18-Jul	Alphecca	HS	
23-Apr	Denebola	HS	23-Jul	Ras Algethi	HS	
07-May	Zuben Elgen.	HS	25-Jul	Ras Alhague	HS	
14-May	Al Rescha	HR	01-Aug	Procyon	HR	
14-May	Fomalhaut	HR	09-Aug	Murzims	HR	
17-May	Vindemiatrix	HS	10-Aug	Acubens	HR	
29-May	Zuben Escham.	HS	11-Aug	Sirius	HR	
31-May	Diadem	HS	16-Aug	Altair	HS	
02-Jun	Menkar	HR	22-Aug	Sadalsuud	HS	
11-Jun	Aldebaran	HR	24-Aug	Phact	HR	
			01-Sep	Sualocin	HS	
			02-Sep	Sadalmelek	HS	
			03-Sep	Alphard	HR	
			17-Sep	Vega	HS	
			27-Sep	Markab	HS	
			29-Sep	Alkes	HR	
			12-Oct	Scheat	HS	
			18-Oct	Spica	HR	
			25-Oct	Alpheratz	HS	
			07-Nov	Hamal	HS	
			17-Nov	Mirach	HS	
			26-Nov	Alcyone	HS	
			07-Dec	Antares	HR	
			23-Dec	El Nath	HS	
			31-Dec	Facies	HR	

Heliacal Rising and Setting Stars for latitude 55° North (1 January 2000)

01-Jan	Facies	HR	13-Jun	Aldebaran	HR	20-Aug	Altair	HS
14-Jan	Aculeus	HR	14-Jun	Diadem	HS	23-Aug	Sadalsuud	HS
12-Feb	Pollux	HS	02-Jul	Arcturus	HS	03-Sep	Sadalmelek	HS
21-Feb	Regulus	HS	09-Jul	Bellatrix	HR	05-Sep	Alphard	HR
25-Feb	Deneb Algedi	HR	11-Jul	Alhena	HR	05-Sep	Sualocin	HS
27-Feb	Acumen	HR	14-Jul	Betelgeuse	HR	09-Sep	Phact	HR
10-Mar	Castor	HS	19-Jul	Alnilam	HR	29-Sep	Markab	HS
07-May	Zuben Elgen.	HS	23-Jul	Rigel	HR	02-Oct	Alkes	HR
08-May	Denebola	HS	29-Jul	Alphecca	HS	17-Oct	Scheat	HS
12-May	Zosma	HS	30-Jul	Ras Algethi	HS	19-Oct	Spica	HR
22-May	Al Rescha	HR	31-Jul	Ras Alhague	HS	30-Oct	Alpheratz	HS
29-May	Vindemiatrix	HS	04-Aug	Procyon	HR	09-Nov	Hamal	HS
04-Jun	Zuben Escham.	HS	11-Aug	Acubens	HR	27-Nov	Alcyone	HS
08-Jun	Fomalhaut	HR	15-Aug	Murzims	HR	09-Dec	Antares	HR
09-Jun	Menkar	HR	17-Aug	Sirius	HR	26-Dec	El Nath	HS

Heliacal Rising and Setting Stars for latitude 60° North (1 January 2000)

Date	Star	H	Date	Star	H	Date	Star	H
02-Jan	Facies	HR	10-Jul	Fomalhaut	HR	24-Aug	Sirius	HR
06-Jan	El Nath	HS	13-Jul	Alhena	HR	24-Aug	Sadalsuud	HS
23-Feb	Regulus	HS	14-Jul	Bellatrix	HR	04-Sep	Sadalmelek	HS
07-Mar	Deneb Algedi	HR	15-Jul	Arcturus	HS	08-Sep	Alphard	HR
05-Apr	Pollux	HS	18-Jul	Betelgeuse	HR	10-Sep	Sualocin	HS
08-May	Zuben Elgen.	HS	25-Jul	Alnilam	HR	02-Oct	Markab	HS
31-May	Denebola	HS	30-Jul	Rigel	HR	06-Oct	Alkes	HR
03-Jun	Al Rescha	HR	06-Aug	Ras Algethi	HS	19-Oct	Spica	HR
08-Jun	Zosma	HS	07-Aug	Ras Alhague	HS	26-Oct	Scheat	HS
12-Jun	Zuben Escham.	HS	07-Aug	Procyon	HR	09-Nov	Alpheratz	HS
15-Jun	Vindemiatrix	HS	12-Aug	Acubens	HR	12-Nov	Hamal	HS
08-Jun	Aldebaran	HR	12-Aug	Alphecca	HS	29-Nov	Alcyone	HS
19-Jun	Menkar	HR	22-Aug	Murzims	HR	12-Dec	Antares	HR
30-Jun	Diadem	HS	24-Aug	Altair	HS			

Finding your natal star and planet parans

Parans, or rather *paranatellontato* as they were known by Vetius Valens in the 1st century CE, are a simple concept when one is standing outside under the sky, but unfortunately they do not lend themselves to our modern desire for linear tables. The right computer software can produce a full list of the natal star and planet parans, and it can recreate the sky for the moment of birth and measure the times for when both stars and planets cross over the horizon – east or west – and the points of upper culmination and lower culmination[1]. If you do not have this then you can discover quite a few, if not all, of your natal star and planet parans from the following tables.

Basically (see Section 1 for more details), a paran relationship exists between a planet and a star when they have the *potential* to be on a pivot point at the same time, the planet on one of its pivot points (rising, setting, upper culmination or lower culmination) and the star on one of its pivot points. The time of this joining between planet and star may happen later on the day of your birth but in effect you are born into a time when the said star and planet were involved in this special sky-planet-earth relationship.

The limitations of these paran tables

The parans formed when a star and planet are on different types of pivot points cannot be located using just these tables. So, for example, if a planet (or star) is on the horizon – east or west – while the star (or planet) is at its upper or lower culmination in the course of its diurnal movement you will not find them in the following tables. This restriction is because the number of degrees that exist between the point of culmination and the horizon not only varies throughout any given 24 hour period but is also affected by the latitude.

Additionally, these tables cannot take into account any possible celestial latitude of your natal planets. Celestial latitude is the distance between the planet and the ecliptic, although astrologers tend to disregard it and simply locate all planets on the ecliptic regardless of the planets' actual position in the sky. In working with star parans, however, one needs to use its true location, as a planet may actually rise (or set) not when its ecliptic degree rises or sets but a little time earlier or later.

For example, if you were born on 1 March, 1965 in New York you would have, in your natal chart, Pluto at 15° Virgo. Now if you were born when 15° Virgo was rising your drawn up chart would display Pluto sitting right on your Ascendant. However, because Pluto was not actually on the ecliptic (it had a celestial latitude of 14° 39' north) it really rose when 10° Virgo was on the Ascendant.

To further complicate this picture, with the faster moving planets they will be moving as they transcribe their diurnal arc in the sky. A planets' ecliptical degree at the time of its upper culmination may be different to its degree when it is setting. This is especially true for the Moon, but is of less importance for the slower moving planets. When looking for your natal Moon's star parans you will get a clearer picture if you find the degree of the Moon on your day of birth when it rises, reaches its upper culmination, sets and is at its lower culmination. (Use the Egyptian or Roman definition of a day, which is from the dawn before you were born – even if it is the day before – to the next dawn).

Finally, it would be preferable to have paran tables for every degree of latitude, as at times a shift of one degree of latitude can change a star's rising or setting position (if it is at high declination north or south) by four or five degrees. However, given the limitations already caused by ignoring celestial latitude, such extensive paran tables are not warranted.

As you can see, parans do not comfortably lend themselves to the hard fixed corners of tables, but nevertheless the following tables will enable you to begin your journey of working in what I consider to be one of the most rewarding and informative areas of astrology - one that has laid neglected for over 2000 years. Happy paran hunting.

Note: You can obtain a full listing of your natal star and planet parans sent to you free of charge if you visit www.Zyntara.com

Working with the Paran Tables

The tables cover, in steps of 5° the latitudes from 50° South to 65° North, and for each band of latitude the following information is given for the 64 stars delineated in this book.

The Co-culminating degree

After the name of each star is a column that lists its co-culminating ecliptical degree. This is the degree on the ecliptic which would be culminating (on the MC) when the star is on its point of upper culmination. It is important to understand that the star itself will not be actually on the ecliptic but may be well below or above it in the sky. The degree of co-culmination of a star is constant regardless of the latitude of the observer, so the table sorts the stars via their co-culminating degree starting from Aries and moving through to Pisces.

Because the majority of stars are not actually located on the ecliptic they do not rise and set with the same ecliptical degrees so you will notice two columns of figures labelled Co-Rise and Co-Set.

Co-Rise

This is the degree of the ecliptic that will be rising when the star is also rising. Once again the star will probably not be on the ecliptic but will be rising in the eastern side of the plane of the horizon, either north or south of the actual position of the ecliptic.

Co-Set

This is the degree of the ecliptic that will be setting when the star is also setting. Once again the star will probably not be on the ecliptic but will be setting in the western side of the plane of the horizon, either north or south of the actual position of the ecliptic.

Not Visible – NotVis

When a star will not rise for a particular latitude, it is listed as "NotVis" in the first latitude table for the page, after which there is a blank line through the tables. If a star fails to rise above the plane of the horizon it cannot engage in the star-planet-earth relationships which are central to this fixed star work. Thus if a star is not visible for your latitude of birth do not use its co-culminating degree as it is not part of the star-earth-planet relationship for your latitude.

Circumpolar – Cpole

When a star will not set for a particular latitude it is listed as "Cpole" in the first latitude table for the page, after which there is a blank line through the tables. If a star is circumpolar it will not set at that latitude and thus not touch the plane of the horizon. The only information you can use with such a star is its co-culminating degree.

If you follow a star through the latitude tables you will notice how stars which have southern declination (see the star in its delineation section to find its location on the celestial sphere) will move towards NotVis as the latitude becomes further north, while those in high northern declinations will become circumpolar. Stars of northern declination will move towards NotVis as the latitude becomes further south, while those in high southern declinations will become circumpolar.

To find your star and planet parans you will need to know firstly your latitude of birth and secondly the degrees of your four angles (Ascendant, MC, Descendant and IC) as well as the degrees of each of your natal planets. The first step is to locate the table which is the closest to the latitude of your birth place.

Finding your Planet and Star Parans

Make a list of the degree positions of your natal planets and the ecliptical degrees which are opposite. Part of your list may look something like this:

Cincinnati, Ohio – Latitude 39°N 06, using table for 40°North				
Planet	Opposite degree	Co culmination /lower culmination	Co Rise - Star Rise Planet rise or set	Co Set - Star Set Planet rise or set
Sun 13/53 ♈	13/53 ♎			
Mars 17/33 ♑	17/33 ♋			
Jupiter 19/54 ♐	19/54 ♊			
… rest of your planets				

Special Note on Timing: Stars that are forming a paran to a planet as they reach their upper culmination tend to be more strongly focused into the middle years of a person life. This concept of the pivot point the star is on is discussed in detail in the companion to this book, *Brady's Book of Fixed Stars*, (Samuel Weiser Inc. 1998). In brief, if a star is rising its influence begins in one's childhood, upper culmination stars begin to be expressed in the years of adulthood and setting stars tend to express themselves in the latter years of one's life. The stars at their lower culmination are those which are foundation stars, active from the start but more obvious as one grows older.

Stars at Upper Culmination or at their Lower Culmination – the prime years
Scan the Co-Culminating degrees of *all* the stars, ignoring those stars marked as not visible, to see if any listed degree is either the same as or is in opposition to one of your natal planets.

Use an orb of no more than 2° and make a note of any star parans that you find. In star parans one normally uses only an orb of 1° but here you are not sure of the impact of a planet's celestial latitude upon its star parans so the slightly larger orb helps compensate for this uncertainty.

Any match that you find will be the star forming a paran to your planet while it is either at its upper culmination or at its lower culmination. Your partial table will now, using a 2° orb, look like this – showing you four star and planet parans that were active on the day of your birth.

Cincinnati, Ohio – Latitude 39°N 06, using table for 40°North				
Planet	Opposite degree	Co culmination /lower culmination	Co Rise -Star Rise Planet rise or set	Co Set -Star Set Planet rise or set
Sun 13/53 ♈	13/53 ♎	No stars		
Mars 17/33 ♑	17/33 ♋	Rukbat		
Jupiter 19/54 ♐	19/54 ♊	Ras Algethi Rigel Capella		
… rest of your planets	…	…	…	…

Stars forming parans to planets when they are on their upper culmination pivot point will relate to your career and middle years of life, while stars on their lower culmination will be themes throughout your life which become more obvious in the years of your prime. For example the delineation for Rukbat, which is the foot of Sagittarius with Mars, is:

> To be motivated to provide a base for others. To build an idea, institution or object to be used as a foundation. ◆ A group makes a stand, a project is begun. *Michel Gauquelin, 20th century French psychologist and statistician who, in the 1950s, conducted statistical research on astrology.*

This suggests that in the prime of your life, possibly between 30 to 65 years of age, your motivation, or what you are enthusiastic about as this is your Mars, will be to work for a foundation, or try and create a club, or association. You are motivated to support something or build something.

Star Rise – the parans of your youth

Once you have finished scanning the co-culminating degrees then do the same for the Co-Rise column and note any combinations which are the same degree. This will give you the stars that rose when your planet rose. Now look at the degree opposite your planet in the Co-Rising column to find if any star was rising when your planet was setting. Your partial table would look like this:

Cincinnati, Ohio – Latitude 39° N 06, using table for 40° North				
Planet	Opposite degree	Co culmination /lower culmination	Co Rise -Star Rise Planet rise or set	Co Set -Star Set Planet rise or set
Sun 13/53 ♈	13/53 ♎	No stars	Arcturus	
Mars 17/33 ♑	17/33 ♋	Rukbat	Pollux	
Jupiter 19/54 ♐	19/54 ♊	Ras Algethi Rigel Capella	Ankaa	
… rest of your planets	…	…	…	…

As a rule of thumb, these star parans tend to have a strong influence in your youth or first third of your life. So, for example, the parans to your Sun or Moon will be reflective of your view of your father and mother as well as about yourself.

For the above chart the Sun is setting as Arcturus, the bright red star in the constellation Bootes, was rising, and the delineation of this star and the Sun is:

> A pathfinder, to break new ground and be willing to explore unheard-of options. One who will either embody this spirit of adventure or be drawn to those who do. ♦ Strong or new leadership emerges. *Jan Riebeeck, 17th century Dutch merchant who was the founder of Cape Town and white settlement in South Africa.*

Hence, if this is your chart, it suggests that your view of your father was as an adventurer and what you learnt from him was to be adventurous, firstly in your youth and then through the rest of your life.

Star Set – the parans of your latter years

Once you have finished scanning the Co-Rise degrees do the same for the Co-Set column and note any combinations which are the same degree or the degree opposite. This will give you the stars that set when your planet set, or, when looking at the degree opposite the planet, a star that set when your natal planet rose. Your table would now look like this:

Cincinnati, Ohio – Latitude 39°N 06, using table for 40°North				
Planet	Opposite degree	Co culmination /lower culmination	Co Rise -Star Rise Planet rise or set	Co Set -Star Set Planet rise or set
Sun 13/53 ♈	13/53 ♎	No stars	Arcturus	No stars
Mars 17/33 ♑	17/33 ♋	Rukbat	Pollux	Ras Algethi
Jupiter 19/54 ♐	19/54 ♊	Ras Algethi Rigel Capella	Ankaa	No stars
… rest of your planets	…	…	…	…

As a rule of thumb, these star parans tend to have a strong influence in your older age, or last third of your life. In this example we have located Ras Algethi setting as Mars set. The delineation of this combination is as follows:

> Wanting to live by a moral code; strong principles and sense of justice. A tendency to take a simplistic view of social issues. ◆ Justice is done, what is natural and correct comes to pass. *Giovanni Pico della Mirandola, 15th century Italian philosopher known for his treatise on the enemies of the Catholic Church, which included an exposition of the deficiencies of astrology.*

Which suggests that as you get older – mid to late 60s – you adopt a personal moral code which becomes central to your way of life. You may feel this in your prime years but this paran suggests that it becomes more important in your later years.

A star on its pivot point at your moment of birth
Once you have completed your star and planet parans consider the four points of your natal chart's angles and build another table (see example on the next page) listing the four degrees in the following manner:

> a) Look up the degree of your MC in the Co-culminating column ONLY
>
> b) Look up the degree of your IC in the Co-culminating column ONLY
>
> b) Look up the degree of your Ascendant in the Co-Rising column ONLY
>
> c) Look up the degree of your Descendant in the Co-Setting column ONLY

These stars are strongly focused into your physical life, your preferred lifestyle, and are with you for your whole life. For example to be born at the moment when Phact, the star in the bow of the Argo, is at its upper culmination is delineated as:

A risk taker, a person who wants to explore new horizons. To have restlessness as one's shadow. ◆ Needing the "new" on a daily level. *Walt Disney, 20th century American entrepreneur who was an innovator in animation and theme park design.*

Cincinnati, Ohio – Latitude 39 °N 06, using table for 40° North.			
Angle	Co-culminate column natal MC/IC axis ONLY	Co Rise - natal Ascendant ONLY	Co Set - Star Set
Ascendant 25/56 ♍	Do not use this column	No stars	Do not use
Descendant 25/65 ♓		Do not use	No stars
M.C. 25/22 ♊	Alnilam Phact	Do not use these columns	
I.C. 25/22 ♐	Aculeus		

Now combine this with the above statement concerning the Aries Sun in paran to Arcturus and you start to see a picture of a bold adventurous person who is willing to take risks.

At the end of scanning your chart you will have:

1) Your heliacal rising and setting stars.
2) A short list of star and planet parans – it will not be complete – but it will be a beginning.
3) The stars on the angles at the moment of your birth.

Once you have completed your table, keep it as a page in this book so that you can refer to it as you need to.

You can now look up the meanings of these star and planet combinations and begin the wondrous journey of rediscovering the sky myths in your chart. Remember, these combinations do not override the interpretations you already know about your chart but rather they add to their meanings by focusing a planetary expression into a particular theme.

NOTES

1. The software that has been especially designed to find these parans is *Starlight* and is available from www.Zyntara.com

STAR PARAN

TABLES

Star and Planet Combinations

Star	Co-Culm	50° South Co-Rise	50° South Co-Set	45° South Co-Rise	45° South Co-Set	40° South Co-Rise	40° South Co-Set	35° South Co-Rise	35° South Co-Set
Alpheratz	02°♈17'	01°♉14'	20°♉16'	27°♈12'	06°♒04'	23°♈50'	18°♒37'	20°♈52'	28°♒26'
Ankaa	07°♈09'	Cpole		15°♒27'	06°♋57'	25°♒39'	18°♊10'	02°♓31'	03°♊40'
Schedar	11°♈01'	NotVis							
Mirach	18°♈54'	24°♉24'	18°♉10'	17°♉43'	10°♒49'	13°♉08'	27°♒49'	09°♉25'	10°♓24'
Achernar	26°♈20'	Cpole							
Al Rescha	02°♉43'	24°♈14'	23°♉13'	25°♈13'	18°♉20'	26°♈08'	14°♉51'	27°♈00'	12°♉13'
Hamal	04°♉03'	14°♉58'	01°♈27'	13°♉27'	11°♈37'	12°♉09'	17°♈40'	11°♉00'	21°♈44'
Capulus	07°♉06'	NotVis							
Polaris	10°♉37'	NotVis							
Menkar	18°♉02'	06°♉05'	11°♊13'	07°♉33'	06°♊22'	08°♉54'	02°♊40'	10°♉09'	29°♉44'
Algol	19°♉30'	NotVis		22°♊31'	05°♓18'	14°♊41'	00°♈31'	09°♊46'	14°♈56'
Mirfak	23°♉28'	NotVis				24°♋29'	08°♒20'	29°♊35'	22°♓06'
Alcyone	29°♉05'	03°♊58'	19°♉13'	03°♊10'	21°♉59'	02°♊32'	23°♉42'	02°♊00'	24°♉55'
Aldebaran	10°♊35'	04°♊23'	19°♊39'	05°♊20'	17°♊46'	06°♊08'	16°♊21'	06°♊50'	15°♊14'
Rigel	19°♊33'	19°♉07'	24°♋16'	23°♉08'	19°♋15'	26°♉46'	14°♋47'	00°♊07'	10°♋47'
Capella	20°♊03'	NotVis				29°♋16'	01°♉09'	17°♋30'	17°♉35'
Bellatrix	22°♊00'	03°♊49'	12°♋41'	06°♊28'	09°♋20'	08°♊47'	06°♋31'	10°♊50'	04°♋04'
El Nath	22°♊16'	00°♋56'	11°♊38'	29°♊02'	14°♊21'	27°♊42'	16°♊06'	26°♊41'	17°♊22'
Alnilam	24°♊33'	29°♉10'	21°♋57'	02°♊43'	17°♋54'	05°♊52'	14°♋21'	08°♊43'	11°♋11'
Phact	25°♊20'	22°♈22'	00°♍23'	02°♊03'	20°♌19'	09°♊56'	12°♌04'	16°♊51'	04°♌50'
Betelgeuse	28°♊54'	10°♊30'	17°♋38'	13°♊20'	14°♋42'	15°♊45'	12°♋13'	17°♊53'	10°♋02'
Murzim	05°♋13'	22°♉09'	15°♌59'	28°♉01'	10°♌36'	03°♊19'	05°♌44'	08°♊10'	01°♌14'
Canopus	05°♋30'	Cpole							
Alhena	08°♋40'	28°♊57'	16°♋52'	00°♋47'	15°♋31'	02°♋13'	14°♋24'	03°♋23'	13°♋28'
Sirius	10°♋23'	27°♉29'	18°♊44'	03°♋27'	13°♌45'	08°♋50'	09°♌13'	13°♋43'	05°♌02'
Castor	21°♋54'	21°♌18'	06°♋08'	11°♌28'	09°♋35'	06°♌13'	11°♋55'	02°♌49'	13°♋42'
Procyon	23°♋00'	29°♊59'	08°♌57'	04°♋06'	06°♌49'	07°♋27'	04°♌55'	10°♋16'	03°♌10'
Pollux	24°♋25'	11°♌21'	15°♋20'	06°♋20'	17°♋01'	03°♌22'	18°♋18'	01°♌20'	19°♋20'
Acubens	12°♌10'	01°♌24'	17°♌13'	03°♌58'	16°♌34'	05°♌47'	15°♋59'	07°♌08'	15°♋27'
Alphard	19°♌29'	10°♋05'	10°♍10'	17°♋28'	07°♍45'	23°♋31'	05°♍30'	28°♋31'	03°♍23'
Regulus	00°♍00'	01°♍16'	29°♌33'	00°♍55'	29°♌36'	00°♍41'	29°♌39'	00°♍32'	29°♌42'
Alkes	13°♍40'	21°♋42'	05°♎51'	02°♌30'	03°♎14'	11°♌06'	00°♎50'	17°♌58'	28°♍36'
Dubhe	14°♍43'	NotVis							

Finding your Heliacal Rising and Heliacal Setting Stars 51

Star	Co-Culm	50° South Co-Rise	50° South Co-Set	45° South Co-Rise	45° South Co-Set	40° South Co-Rise	40° South Co-Set	35° South Co-Rise	35° South Co-Set
Zosma	17° ♍ 31'	02° ♍ 10'	02° ♍ 48'	19° ♌ 53'	04° ♍ 38'	11° ♌ 39'	06° ♍ 16'	05° ♌ 49'	07° ♍ 46'
Denebola	27° ♍ 01'	02° ♍ 43'	15° ♍ 05'	23° ♌ 11'	16° ♍ 29'	16° ♌ 43'	17° ♍ 45'	12° ♌ 04'	18° ♍ 57'
Acrux	07° ♎ 14'	Cpole							
Vindemiatrix	16° ♌ 52'	25° ♍ 43'	01° ♎ 35'	16° ♍ 49'	03° ♎ 20'	10° ♍ 10'	04° ♎ 57'	05° ♍ 05'	06° ♎ 29'
Diadem	18° ♌ 57'	09° ♐ 56'	26° ♍ 41'	29° ♏ 30'	29° ♍ 18'	21° ♏ 09'	01° ♎ 42'	14° ♏ 27'	03° ♎ 56'
Spica	23° ♌ 01'	17° ♎ 06'	25° ♎ 00'	18° ♎ 48'	24° ♎ 46'	19° ♎ 52'	24° ♎ 33'	20° ♎ 37'	24° ♎ 21'
Agena	03° ♏ 10'	Cpole							
Thuban	03° ♏ 19'	Cpole							
Arcturus	06° ♏ 14'	29° ♐ 33'	06° ♎ 46'	20° ♐ 21'	10° ♎ 18'	12° ♐ 28'	13° ♎ 31'	05° ♐ 43'	16° ♎ 32'
Toliman	12° ♏ 20'	Cpole							
Zuben Elgen.	15° ♏ 11'	15° ♏ 59'	14° ♏ 50'	15° ♏ 46'	14° ♏ 53'	15° ♏ 38'	14° ♏ 55'	15° ♏ 32'	14° ♏ 57'
Zuben Esch.	21° ♏ 40'	07° ♐ 51'	13° ♏ 18'	04° ♐ 17'	14° ♏ 23'	01° ♐ 40'	15° ♏ 21'	29° ♏ 37'	16° ♏ 14'
Alphecca	25° ♏ 59'	25° ♉ 45'	12° ♎ 04'	16° ♉ 47'	17° ♎ 48'	08° ♉ 52'	22° ♎ 51'	01° ♉ 48'	27° ♎ 29'
Antares	09° ♐ 03'	28° ♏ 47'	15° ♐ 10'	01° ♐ 35'	14° ♐ 03'	03° ♐ 20'	13° ♐ 12'	04° ♐ 35'	12° ♐ 30'
Ras Algethi	19° ♐ 34'	00° ♒ 09'	13° ♏ 29'	24° ♑ 28'	18° ♏ 10'	19° ♑ 21'	22° ♏ 26'	14° ♑ 43'	26° ♏ 23'
Ras Alhague	24° ♐ 14'	02° ♒ 06'	18° ♏ 49'	26° ♑ 52'	23° ♏ 31'	22° ♑ 09'	27° ♏ 46'	17° ♑ 51'	01° ♐ 41'
Aculeus	25° ♐ 25'	05° ♐ 48'	12° ♑ 32'	11° ♐ 28'	08° ♑ 03'	14° ♐ 45'	05° ♑ 17'	17° ♐ 03'	03° ♑ 18'
Acumen	28° ♐ 35'	00° ♐ 50'	25° ♑ 05'	09° ♐ 47'	16° ♑ 47'	14° ♐ 28'	12° ♑ 22'	17° ♐ 34'	09° ♑ 24'
Facies	08° ♑ 21'	07° ♑ 20'	09° ♑ 35'	07° ♑ 32'	09° ♑ 19'	07° ♑ 40'	09° ♑ 07'	07° ♑ 48'	08° ♑ 58'
Vega	08° ♑ 29'	24° ♓ 36'	23° ♉ 00'	09° ♓ 17'	04° ♍ 37'	29° ♒ 29'	15° ♏ 03'	21° ♒ 25'	23° ♏ 40'
Rukbat	19° ♑ 22'	Cpole		17° ♑ 56'	11° ♓ 04'	26° ♑ 32'	22° ♒ 34'	01° ♒ 34'	13° ♒ 08'
Altair	25° ♑ 42'	23° ♒ 06'	17° ♐ 50'	19° ♒ 42'	23° ♐ 46'	16° ♒ 34'	28° ♐ 56'	13° ♒ 39'	03° ♑ 28'
Sualocin	07° ♒ 30'	08° ♓ 19'	20° ♐ 21'	04° ♓ 35'	27° ♐ 52'	01° ♓ 09'	04° ♑ 25'	27° ♒ 56'	10° ♑ 10'
Deneb Adige	07° ♒ 56'	NotVis				06° ♈ 37'	27° ♏ 21'	26° ♓ 07'	10° ♐ 30'
Alderamin	17° ♒ 11'	NotVis							
Sadalsuud	20° ♒ 29'	28° ♒ 39'	02° ♒ 02'	27° ♒ 40'	06° ♒ 19'	26° ♒ 46'	09° ♒ 25'	25° ♒ 55'	11° ♒ 47'
Deneb Algedi	24° ♒ 27'	21° ♒ 49'	01° ♓ 39'	22° ♒ 09'	29° ♒ 36'	22° ♒ 27'	28° ♒ 18'	22° ♒ 44'	27° ♒ 24'
Sadalmelek	29° ♒ 19'	09° ♓ 15'	05° ♒ 20'	08° ♓ 06'	10° ♒ 57'	07° ♓ 02'	15° ♒ 01'	06° ♓ 01'	18° ♒ 06'
Fomalhaut	13° ♓ 05'	18° ♒ 22'	23° ♉ 00'	22° ♒ 00'	04° ♉ 50'	24° ♒ 58'	21° ♈ 44'	27° ♒ 33'	12° ♈ 15'
Scheat	14° ♓ 44'	18° ♈ 14'	05° ♉ 03'	13° ♈ 49'	18° ♉ 05'	10° ♈ 01'	29° ♉ 04'	06° ♈ 35'	08° ♒ 16'
Markab	15° ♓ 00'	03° ♈ 39'	28° ♉ 52'	01° ♈ 29'	09° ♒ 01'	29° ♓ 30'	16° ♒ 49'	27° ♓ 37'	22° ♒ 54'

52 Star and Planet Combinations

Star	Co-Culm	30° South		25° South		20° South		15° South	
		Co-Rise	Co-Set	Co-Rise	Co-Set	Co-Rise	Co-Set	Co-Rise	Co-Set
Alpheratz	02°♈17'	18°♈07'	06°♓12'	15°♈30'	12°♓28'	12°♈57'	17°♓38'	10°♈24'	22°♓01'
Ankaa	07°♈09'	08°♓10'	21°♉37'	13°♓13'	11°♉25'	17°♓59'	02°♉43'	22°♓38'	25°♈10'
Schedar	11°♈01'	00°♊49'	24°♉22'	19°♉01'	14°♒55'	10°♉23'	00°♓28'	02°♉51'	13°♓06'
Mirach	18°♈54'	06°♉10'	19°♓51'	03°♉12'	27°♓09'	00°♉22'	03°♈00'	27°♈36'	07°♈50'
Achernar	26°♈20'	25°♒57'	11°♋24'	10°♓06'	23°♊03'	20°♓34'	08°♊57'	29°♓49'	26°♉46'
Al Rescha	02°♉43'	27°♈50'	10°♉08'	28°♈38'	08°♉26'	29°♈25'	07°♉00'	00°♉13'	05°♉45'
Hamal	04°♉03'	09°♉56'	24°♈41'	08°♉56'	26°♈58'	07°♉59'	28°♈49'	07°♉01'	00°♉22'
Capulus	07°♉06'	24°♊16'	20°♒12'	11°♊34'	14°♓24'	03°♊10'	00°♈34'	26°♉12'	12°♈34'
Polaris	10°♉37'	NotVis							
Menkar	18°♉02'	11°♉19'	27°♋19'	12°♉27'	25°♋17'	13°♉34'	23°♉31'	14°♉39'	21°♉58'
Algol	19°♉30'	05°♊59'	24°♈15'	02°♊49'	00°♉53'	29°♉58'	05°♉57'	27°♉19'	10°♉05'
Mirfak	23°♉28'	20°♊50'	11°♈24'	14°♊47'	23°♈34'	09°♊53'	02°♉13'	05°♊33'	08°♉54'
Alcyone	29°♉05'	01°♊31'	25°♊50'	01°♊05'	26°♉35'	00°♊40'	27°♉12'	00°♊16'	27°♉45'
Aldebaran	10°♊35'	07°♊27'	14°♊19'	08°♊02'	13°♊31'	08°♊34'	12°♊50'	09°♊05'	12°♊12'
Rigel	19°♊33'	03°♊14'	07°♋08'	06°♊10'	03°♋47'	08°♊58'	00°♋40'	11°♊40'	27°♊43'
Capella	20°♊03'	10°♋46'	26°♉29'	05°♋56'	02°♊30'	02°♋04'	07°♊06'	28°♊44'	10°♊53'
Bellatrix	22°♊00'	12°♊42'	01°♋55'	14°♊26'	29°♊59'	16°♊03'	28°♊12'	17°♊35'	26°♊33'
El Nath	22°♊16'	25°♊51'	18°♊22'	25°♊08'	19°♊12'	24°♊29'	19°♊55'	23°♊54'	20°♊34'
Alnilam	24°♊33'	11°♊19'	08°♋19'	13°♊46'	05°♋42'	16°♊03'	03°♋16'	18°♊15'	00°♋58'
Phact	25°♊20'	23°♉09'	28°♋16'	29°♉01'	22°♋10'	04°♊34'	16°♋25'	09°♊55'	10°♋56'
Betelgeuse	28°♊54'	19°♊47'	08°♋06'	21°♊31'	06°♋20'	23°♊07'	04°♋42'	24°♊38'	03°♋10'
Murzim	05°♋13'	12°♊39'	27°♋03'	16°♊50'	23°♋06'	20°♊47'	19°♋20'	24°♊33'	15°♋42'
Canopus	05°♋30'	10°♉18'	29°♌55'	21°♊51'	18°♌36'	01°♋44'	08°♌54'	10°♋46'	00°♌03'
Alhena	08°♋40'	04°♋23'	12°♋38'	05°♋15'	11°♋52'	06°♋01'	11°♋11'	06°♋44'	10°♋31'
Sirius	10°♋23'	18°♊12'	01°♌07'	22°♊23'	27°♋25'	26°♋17'	23°♋52'	00°♋00'	20°♋25'
Castor	21°♋54'	00°♌19'	15°♋12'	28°♋22'	16°♋29'	26°♋45'	17°♋40'	25°♋22'	18°♌45'
Procyon	23°♋00'	12°♋41'	01°♌34'	14°♋48'	00°♌03'	16°♋42'	28°♋36'	18°♋26'	27°♋11'
Pollux	24°♋25'	29°♋48'	20°♋13'	28°♋34'	21°♋00'	27°♋33'	21°♋44'	26°♋39'	22°♋25'
Acubens	12°♌10'	08°♌13'	14°♌57'	09°♌06'	14°♌28'	09°♌52'	14°♌01'	10°♌31'	13°♌33'
Alphard	19°♌29'	02°♌45'	01°♍21'	06°♌22'	29°♌23'	09°♌33'	27°♌27'	12°♌22'	25°♌31'
Regulus	00°♍00'	00°♍25'	29°♌45'	00°♍19'	29°♌47'	00°♍14'	29°♌50'	00°♍10'	29°♌52'
Alkes	13°♍40'	23°♌32'	26°♍28'	28°♌10'	24°♍24'	02°♍05'	22°♍20'	05°♍29'	20°♍16'
Dubhe	14°♍43'	NotVis		28°♏00'	24°♋17'	05°♏53'	07°♌48'	19°♎22'	17°♌50'

Finding your Heliacal Rising and Heliacal Setting Stars   53

Star	Co-Culm	30° South Co-Rise	30° South Co-Set	25° South Co-Rise	25° South Co-Set	20° South Co-Rise	20° South Co-Set	15° South Co-Rise	15° South Co-Set
Zosma	17° ♍ 31'	01° ♌ 28'	09° ♍ 11'	28° ♌ 03'	10° ♍ 33'	25° ♍ 17'	11° ♍ 53'	22° ♍ 57'	13° ♍ 14'
Denebola	27° ♍ 01'	08° ♌ 33'	20° ♍ 06'	05° ♌ 46'	21° ♍ 13'	03° ♌ 29'	22° ♍ 19'	01° ♌ 33'	23° ♍ 26'
Acrux	07° ♎ 14'	Cpole		17° ♋ 24'	04° ♐ 58'	11° ♌ 53'	18° ♏ 25'	29° ♌ 30'	07° ♏ 04'
Vindemiatrix	16° ♌ 52'	01° ♏ 03'	07° ♌ 57'	27° ♌ 45'	09° ♌ 23'	24° ♌ 58'	10° ♌ 49'	22° ♌ 35'	12° ♌ 15'
Diadem	18° ♌ 57'	08° ♏ 58'	06° ♌ 05'	04° ♏ 24'	08° ♌ 11'	00° ♏ 31'	10° ♌ 14'	27° ♌ 08'	12° ♌ 19'
Spica	23° ♌ 01'	21° ♌ 10'	24° ♌ 09'	21° ♌ 37'	23° ♌ 58'	21° ♌ 59'	23° ♌ 47'	22° ♌ 17'	23° ♌ 36'
Agena	03° ♏ 10'	Cpole		27° ♌ 56'	15° ♌ 58'	18° ♍ 36'	04° ♐ 38'	03° ♌ 31'	26° ♏ 00'
Thuban	03° ♏ 19'	NotVis		25° ♑ 50'	19° ♌ 25'	29° ♐ 34'	12° ♍ 51'	12° ♐ 48'	27° ♍ 12'
Arcturus	06° ♏ 14'	29° ♏ 54'	19° ♑ 24'	24° ♏ 50'	22° ♌ 11'	20° ♏ 21'	24° ♌ 55'	16° ♏ 21'	27° ♌ 39'
Toliman	12° ♏ 20'	Cpole		07° ♍ 24'	25° ♐ 21'	28° ♍ 58'	13° ♐ 22'	13° ♌ 46'	04° ♐ 37'
Zuben Elgen.	15° ♏ 11'	15° ♏ 27'	14° ♏ 59'	15° ♏ 23'	15° ♏ 01'	15° ♏ 20'	15° ♏ 03'	15° ♏ 17'	15° ♏ 05'
Zuben Esch.	21° ♏ 40'	27° ♏ 58'	17° ♏ 04'	26° ♏ 35'	17° ♏ 51'	25° ♏ 23'	18° ♏ 37'	24° ♏ 19'	19° ♏ 22'
Alphecca	25° ♏ 59'	25° ♐ 24'	01° ♏ 50'	19° ♐ 35'	05° ♏ 58'	14° ♐ 14'	10° ♏ 00'	09° ♐ 16'	13° ♏ 57'
Antares	09° ♐ 03'	05° ♐ 32'	11° ♐ 53'	06° ♐ 19'	11° ♐ 21'	06° ♐ 59'	10° ♐ 52'	07° ♐ 34'	10° ♐ 23'
Ras Algethi	19° ♐ 34'	10° ♑ 28'	00° ♐ 04'	06° ♑ 31'	03° ♐ 34'	02° ♑ 49'	06° ♐ 54'	29° ♐ 20'	10° ♐ 08'
Ras Alhague	24° ♐ 14'	13° ♑ 54'	05° ♐ 20'	10° ♑ 14'	08° ♐ 45'	06° ♑ 47'	12° ♐ 01'	03° ♑ 29'	15° ♐ 10'
Aculeus	25° ♐ 25'	18° ♐ 48'	01° ♑ 44'	20° ♐ 13'	00° ♑ 25'	21° ♐ 27'	29° ♐ 17'	22° ♐ 33'	28° ♐ 14'
Acumen	28° ♐ 35'	19° ♐ 54'	07° ♑ 08'	21° ♐ 47'	05° ♑ 18'	23° ♐ 24'	03° ♑ 44'	24° ♐ 50'	02° ♑ 20'
Facies	08° ♑ 21'	07° ♑ 54'	08° ♑ 51'	07° ♑ 59'	08° ♑ 45'	08° ♑ 04'	08° ♑ 39'	08° ♑ 08'	08° ♑ 34'
Vega	08° ♑ 29'	14° ♐ 17'	01° ♒ 18'	07° ♒ 43'	08° ♐ 17'	01° ♒ 32'	14° ♐ 49'	25° ♐ 36'	21° ♐ 01'
Rukbat	19° ♑ 22'	05° ♑ 14'	07° ♒ 06'	08° ♑ 11'	02° ♒ 43'	10° ♑ 43'	29° ♑ 15'	13° ♑ 01'	26° ♑ 22'
Altair	25° ♑ 42'	10° ♒ 53'	07° ♑ 30'	08° ♒ 16'	11° ♑ 08'	05° ♒ 43'	14° ♑ 27'	03° ♒ 13'	17° ♑ 31'
Sualocin	07° ♒ 30'	24° ♒ 53'	15° ♒ 15'	21° ♒ 57'	19° ♒ 47'	19° ♒ 04'	23° ♒ 54'	16° ♒ 13'	27° ♒ 39'
Deneb Adige	07° ♒ 56'	17° ♓ 49'	21° ♑ 10'	10° ♓ 31'	00° ♑ 33'	03° ♓ 44'	09° ♑ 02'	27° ♒ 14'	16° ♑ 54'
Alderamin	17° ♒ 11'	NotVis		21° ♈ 23'	06° ♑ 52'	03° ♈ 58'	26° ♑ 20'	20° ♓ 58'	11° ♑ 02'
Sadalsuud	20° ♒ 29'	25° ♒ 07'	13° ♒ 39'	24° ♒ 21'	15° ♒ 12'	23° ♒ 36'	16° ♒ 31'	22° ♒ 50'	17° ♒ 40'
Deneb Algedi	24° ♒ 27'	22° ♒ 59'	26° ♒ 43'	23° ♒ 14'	26° ♒ 11'	23° ♒ 28'	25° ♒ 44'	23° ♒ 42'	25° ♒ 22'
Sadalmelek	29° ♒ 19'	05° ♓ 03'	20° ♒ 33'	04° ♓ 07'	22° ♒ 34'	03° ♓ 12'	24° ♒ 16'	02° ♓ 16'	25° ♒ 44'
Fomalhaut	13° ♓ 05'	29° ♒ 54'	05° ♈ 11'	02° ♓ 06'	29° ♓ 42'	04° ♓ 15'	25° ♓ 17'	06° ♓ 22'	21° ♓ 35'
Scheat	14° ♓ 44'	03° ♈ 23'	15° ♒ 59'	00° ♈ 19'	22° ♒ 30'	27° ♓ 18'	28° ♒ 05'	24° ♓ 18'	02° ♓ 57'
Markab	15° ♓ 00'	25° ♓ 50'	27° ♒ 47'	24° ♓ 05'	01° ♓ 46'	22° ♓ 21'	05° ♓ 08'	20° ♓ 36'	08° ♓ 02'

Star and Planet Combinations

Star	Co-Culm	10° South		05° South		The Equator		05° North	
		Co-Rise	Co-Set	Co-Rise	Co-Set	Co-Rise	Co-Set	Co-Rise	Co-Set
Alpheratz	02°♈17'	07°♈49'	25°♓50'	05°♈08'	29°♓13'	02°♈17'	02°♈17'	29°♓13'	05°♈08'
Ankaa	07°♈09'	27°♓18'	18°♈32'	02°♈06'	12°♈35'	07°♈09'	07°♈09'	12°♈35'	02°♈06'
Schedar	11°♈01'	25°♈42'	23°♓42'	18°♈32'	02°♈51'	11°♈01'	11°♈01'	02°♈51'	18°♈32'
Mirach	18°♈54'	24°♈48'	11°♈58'	21°♈56'	15°♈37'	18°♈54'	18°♈54'	15°♈37'	21°♈56'
Achernar	26°♈20'	08°♈37'	15°♉48'	17°♈22'	05°♉45'	26°♈20'	26°♈20'	05°♉45'	17°♈22'
Al Rescha	02°♉43'	01°♉01'	04°♉38'	01°♉51'	03°♉38'	02°♉43'	02°♉43'	03°♉38'	01°♉51'
Hamal	04°♉03'	06°♉04'	01°♉44'	05°♉05'	02°♉56'	04°♉03'	04°♉03'	02°♉56'	05°♉05'
Capulus	07°♉06'	19°♉49'	22°♈06'	13°♉34'	00°♉05'	07°♉06'	07°♉06'	00°♉05'	13°♉34'
Polaris	10°♉37'	NotVis				10°♉37'	10°♉37'	Cpole	
Menkar	18°♉02'	15°♉45'	20°♉33'	16°♉52'	19°♉15'	18°♉02'	18°♉02'	19°♉15'	16°♉52'
Algol	19°♉30'	24°♉44'	13°♉35'	22°♉09'	16°♉40'	19°♉30'	19°♉30'	16°♉40'	22°♉09'
Mirfak	23°♉28'	01°♊30'	14°♉24'	27°♉32'	19°♉10'	23°♉28'	23°♉28'	19°♉10'	27°♉32'
Alcyone	29°♉05'	29°♉53'	28°♉14'	29°♉29'	28°♉40'	29°♉05'	29°♉05'	28°♉40'	29°♉29'
Aldebaran	10°♊35'	09°♊35'	11°♊38'	10°♊05'	11°♊06'	10°♊35'	10°♊35'	11°♊06'	10°♊05'
Rigel	19°♊33'	14°♊19'	24°♊55'	16°♊56'	22°♊12'	19°♊33'	19°♊33'	22°♊12'	16°♊56'
Capella	20°♊03'	25°♊43'	14°♊11'	22°♊51'	17°♊12'	20°♊03'	20°♊03'	17°♊12'	22°♊51'
Bellatrix	22°♊00'	19°♊04'	24°♊58'	20°♊32'	23°♊28'	22°♊00'	22°♊00'	23°♊28'	20°♊32'
El Nath	22°♊16'	23°♊20'	21°♊10'	22°♊48'	21°♊43'	22°♊16'	22°♊16'	21°♊43'	22°♊48'
Alnilam	24°♊33'	20°♊23'	28°♊46'	22°♊28'	26°♊38'	24°♊33'	24°♊33'	26°♊38'	22°♊28'
Phact	25°♊20'	15°♊08'	05°♋37'	20°♊15'	00°♋27'	25°♊20'	25°♊20'	00°♋27'	20°♊15'
Betelgeuse	28°♊54'	26°♊05'	01°♋43'	27°♊30'	00°♋17'	28°♊54'	28°♊54'	00°♋17'	27°♊30'
Murzim	05°♋13'	28°♊11'	12°♋10'	01°♋44'	08°♋41'	05°♋13'	05°♋13'	08°♋41'	01°♋44'
Canopus	05°♋30'	19°♊16'	21°♋39'	27°♊28'	13°♋32'	05°♋30'	05°♋30'	13°♋32'	27°♊28'
Alhena	08°♋40'	07°♋24'	09°♋54'	08°♋03'	09°♋17'	08°♋40'	08°♋40'	09°♋17'	08°♋03'
Sirius	10°♋23'	03°♋34'	17°♋03'	07°♋00'	13°♋43'	10°♋23'	10°♋23'	13°♋43'	07°♋00'
Castor	21°♋54'	24°♋07'	19°♋49'	22°♋58'	20°♋51'	21°♋54'	21°♋54'	20°♋51'	22°♋58'
Procyon	23°♋00'	20°♋02'	25°♋48'	21°♋33'	24°♋24'	23°♋00'	23°♋00'	24°♋24'	21°♋33'
Pollux	24°♋25'	25°♋51'	23°♋05'	25°♋07'	23°♋45'	24°♋25'	24°♋25'	23°♋45'	25°♋07'
Acubens	12°♌10'	11°♌07'	13°♌06'	11°♌39'	12°♌38'	12°♌10'	12°♌10'	12°♌38'	11°♌39'
Alphard	19°♌29'	14°♌56'	23°♌34'	17°♌17'	21°♌34'	19°♌29'	19°♌29'	21°♌34'	17°♌17'
Regulus	00°♍00'	29°♌06'	29°♌55'	00°♍03'	29°♌57'	00°♍00'	00°♍00'	29°♌57'	00°♍03'
Alkes	13°♍40'	08°♍29'	18°♍10'	11°♍11'	15°♍58'	13°♍40'	13°♍40'	15°♍58'	11°♍11'
Dubhe	14°♍43'	06°♎00'	26°♍49'	24°♍41'	05°♍36'	14°♍43'	14°♍43'	24°♍41'	05°♍36'

Finding your Heliacal Rising and Heliacal Setting Stars   55

Star	Co-Culm	10° South Co-Rise	10° South Co-Set	05° South Co-Rise	05° South Co-Set	The Equator Co-Rise	The Equator Co-Set	05° North Co-Rise	05° North Co-Set
Zosma	17°♌31'	20°♍56'	14°♍36'	19°♍09'	16°♍01'	17°♍31'	17°♍31'	16°♍01'	19°♍09'
Denebola	27°♌01'	29°♍52'	24°♍34'	28°♍22'	25°♍45'	27°♍01'	27°♍01'	25°♍45'	28°♍22'
Acrux	07°♌14'	13°♍56'	27°♌04'	26°♍17'	17°♌20'	07°♌14'	07°♌14'	17°♌20'	26°♍17'
Vindemiatrix	16°♌52'	20°♌29'	13°♌43'	18°♌36'	15°♌15'	16°♌52'	16°♌52'	15°♌15'	18°♌36'
Diadem	18°♌57'	24°♌08'	14°♌26'	21°♌26'	16°♌38'	18°♌57'	18°♌57'	16°♌38'	21°♌26'
Spica	23°♌01'	22°♌33'	23°♌25'	22°♌48'	23°♌13'	23°♌01'	23°♌01'	23°♌13'	22°♌48'
Agena	03°♍10'	15°♌09'	18°♍19'	24°♌46'	10°♍52'	03°♍10'	03°♍10'	10°♍52'	24°♌46'
Thuban	03°♍19'	28°♍32'	09°♌38'	15°♏33'	21°♌28'	03°♍19'	03°♍19'	21°♌28'	15°♏33'
Arcturus	06°♍14'	12°♏42'	00°♍25'	09°♍21'	03°♍16'	06°♍14'	06°♍14'	03°♍16'	09°♍21'
Toliman	12°♍20'	25°♌03'	27°♍01'	04°♏17'	19°♍45'	12°♍20'	12°♍20'	19°♍45'	04°♏17'
Zuben Elgen.	15°♏11'	15°♏15'	15°♏07'	15°♏13'	15°♏09'	15°♏11'	15°♏11'	15°♏09'	15°♏13'
Zuben Esch.	21°♏40'	23°♏22'	20°♏07'	22°♏29'	20°♏53'	21°♏40'	21°♏40'	20°♏53'	22°♏29'
Alphecca	25°♏59'	04°♐37'	17°♏55'	00°♐12'	21°♏54'	25°♏59'	25°♏59'	21°♏54'	00°♐12'
Antares	09°♐03'	08°♐05'	09°♐56'	08°♐35'	09°♐30'	09°♐03'	09°♐03'	09°♐30'	08°♐35'
Ras Algethi	19°♐34'	25°♐59'	13°♐18'	22°♐44'	16°♐26'	19°♐34'	19°♐34'	16°♐26'	22°♐44'
Ras Alhague	24°♐14'	00°♑20'	18°♐13'	27°♐16'	21°♐14'	24°♐14'	24°♐14'	21°♐14'	27°♐16'
Aculeus	25°♐25'	23°♐33'	27°♐16'	24°♐30'	26°♐20'	25°♐25'	25°♐25'	26°♐20'	24°♐30'
Acumen	28°♐35'	26°♐08'	01°♑02'	27°♐23'	29°♐48'	28°♐35'	28°♐35'	29°♐48'	27°♐23'
Facies	08°♑21'	08°♑13'	08°♑30'	08°♑17'	08°♑25'	08°♑21'	08°♑21'	08°♑25'	08°♑17'
Vega	08°♑29'	19°♑49'	26°♐58'	14°♑08'	02°♑46'	08°♑29'	08°♑29'	02°♑46'	14°♑08'
Rukbat	19°♑22'	15°♑10'	23°♑50'	17°♑16'	21°♑32'	19°♑22'	19°♑22'	21°♑32'	17°♑16'
Altair	25°♑42'	00°♒44'	20°♑23'	28°♑14'	23°♑06'	25°♑42'	25°♑42'	23°♑06'	28°♑14'
Sualocin	07°♒30'	13°♒22'	01°♒08'	10°♒28'	04°♒24'	07°♒30'	07°♒30'	04°♒24'	10°♒28'
Deneb Adige	07°♒56'	20°♒50'	24°♑15'	14°♒26'	01°♒14'	07°♒56'	07°♒56'	01°♒14'	14°♒26'
Alderamin	17°♒11'	09°♓22'	23°♑56'	28°♒15'	05°♒51'	17°♒11'	17°♒11'	05°♒51'	28°♒15'
Sadalsuud	20°♒29'	22°♒05'	18°♒41'	21°♒18'	19°♒37'	20°♒29'	20°♒29'	19°♒37'	21°♒18'
Deneb Algedi	24°♒27'	23°♒57'	25°♒02'	24°♒12'	24°♒44'	24°♒27'	24°♒27'	24°♒44'	24°♒12'
Sadalmelek	29°♒19'	01°♓19'	27°♒03'	00°♓21'	28°♒14'	29°♒19'	29°♒19'	28°♒14'	00°♓21'
Fomalhaut	13°♓05'	08°♓31'	18°♓25'	10°♓44'	15°♓37'	13°♓05'	13°♓05'	15°♓37'	10°♓44'
Scheat	14°♓44'	21°♓14'	07°♓16'	18°♓04'	11°♓09'	14°♓44'	14°♓44'	11°♓09'	18°♓04'
Markab	15°♓00'	18°♓49'	10°♓36'	16°♓57'	12°♓54'	15°♓00'	15°♓00'	12°♓54'	16°♓57'

56 Star and Planet Combinations

Star	Co-Culm	10° North Co-Rise	10° North Co-Set	15° North Co-Rise	15° North Co-Set	20° North Co-Rise	20° North Co-Set	25° North Co-Rise	25° North Co-Set
Alpheratz	02°♈17'	25°♓50'	07°♈49'	22°♓01'	10°♈24'	17°♓38'	12°♈57'	12°♓28'	15°♈30'
Ankaa	07°♈09'	18°♈32'	27°♓18'	25°♈10'	22°♓38'	02°♉43'	17°♓59'	11°♉25'	13°♓13'
Schedar	11°♈01'	23°♈42'	25°♈42'	13°♓06'	02°♉51'	00°♓28'	10°♉23'	14°♒55'	19°♉01'
Mirach	18°♈54'	11°♈58'	24°♈48'	07°♈50'	27°♈36'	03°♈00'	00°♉22'	27°♓09'	03°♉12'
Achernar	26°♈20'	15°♈48'	08°♈37'	26°♉46'	29°♓49'	08°♊57'	20°♓34'	23°♊03'	10°♓06'
Al Rescha	02°♉43'	04°♉38'	01°♉01'	05°♉45'	00°♉13'	07°♉00'	29°♈25'	08°♉26'	28°♈38'
Hamal	04°♉03'	01°♉44'	06°♉04'	00°♉22'	07°♉01'	28°♈49'	07°♉59'	26°♈58'	08°♉56'
Capulus	07°♉06'	22°♈06'	19°♉49'	12°♈34'	26°♉12'	00°♈34'	03°♊10'	14°♓24'	11°♊34'
Polaris	10°♉37'	Cpole							
Menkar	18°♉02'	20°♉33'	15°♉45'	21°♉58'	14°♉39'	23°♉31'	13°♉34'	25°♉17'	12°♉27'
Algol	19°♉30'	13°♉35'	24°♉44'	10°♉05'	27°♉19'	05°♉57'	29°♉58'	00°♉53'	02°♊49'
Mirfak	23°♉28'	14°♉24'	01°♊30'	08°♉54'	05°♊33'	02°♉13'	09°♊53'	23°♈34'	14°♊47'
Alcyone	29°♉05'	28°♉14'	29°♉53'	27°♉45'	00°♊16'	27°♉12'	00°♊40'	26°♉35'	01°♊05'
Aldebaran	10°♊35'	11°♊38'	09°♊35'	12°♊12'	09°♊05'	12°♊50'	08°♊34'	13°♊31'	08°♊02'
Rigel	19°♊33'	24°♊55'	14°♊19'	27°♊43'	11°♊40'	00°♋40'	08°♊58'	03°♋47'	06°♊10'
Capella	20°♊03'	14°♊11'	25°♊43'	10°♊53'	28°♊44'	07°♊06'	02°♋04'	02°♊30'	05°♋56'
Bellatrix	22°♊00'	24°♊58'	19°♊04'	26°♊33'	17°♊35'	28°♊12'	16°♊03'	29°♊59'	14°♊26'
El Nath	22°♊16'	21°♊10'	23°♊20'	20°♊34'	23°♊54'	19°♊55'	24°♊29'	19°♊12'	25°♊08'
Alnilam	24°♊33'	28°♊46'	20°♊23'	00°♋58'	18°♊15'	03°♋16'	16°♊03'	05°♋42'	13°♊46'
Phact	25°♊20'	05°♋37'	15°♊08'	10°♋56'	09°♊55'	16°♋25'	04°♊34'	22°♋10'	29°♉01'
Betelgeuse	28°♊54'	01°♋43'	26°♊05'	03°♋10'	24°♊38'	04°♋42'	23°♊07'	06°♋20'	21°♊31'
Murzim	05°♋13'	12°♋10'	28°♊11'	15°♋42'	24°♊33'	19°♋20'	20°♊47'	23°♋06'	16°♊50'
Canopus	05°♋30'	21°♋39'	19°♊16'	00°♌03'	10°♊46'	08°♌54'	01°♊44'	18°♌36'	21°♉51'
Alhena	08°♋40'	09°♋54'	07°♋24'	10°♋31'	06°♋44'	11°♋11'	06°♋01'	11°♋52'	05°♋15'
Sirius	10°♋23'	17°♋03'	03°♋34'	20°♋25'	00°♋00'	23°♋52'	26°♊17'	27°♋25'	22°♊23'
Castor	21°♋54'	19°♋49'	24°♋07'	18°♋45'	25°♋22'	17°♋40'	26°♋45'	16°♋29'	28°♋22'
Procyon	23°♋00'	25°♋48'	20°♋02'	27°♋11'	18°♋26'	28°♋36'	16°♋42'	00°♌03'	14°♋48'
Pollux	24°♋25'	23°♋05'	25°♋51'	22°♋25'	26°♋39'	21°♋44'	27°♋33'	21°♋00'	28°♋34'
Acubens	12°♌10'	13°♌06'	11°♌07'	13°♌33'	10°♌31'	14°♌01'	09°♌52'	14°♌28'	09°♌06'
Alphard	19°♌29'	23°♌34'	14°♌56'	25°♌31'	12°♌22'	27°♌27'	09°♌33'	29°♌23'	06°♌22'
Regulus	00°♍00'	29°♌55'	00°♍06'	29°♌52'	00°♍10'	29°♌50'	00°♍14'	00°♍03'	14°♌48'
Alkes	13°♍40'	18°♍10'	08°♍29'	20°♍16'	05°♍29'	22°♍20'	02°♍05'	24°♍24'	28°♌10'
Dubhe	14°♍43'	26°♌49'	06°♎00'	17°♌50'	19°♎22'	07°♌48'	05°♏53'	24°♋17'	28°♍00'

Finding your Heliacal Rising and Heliacal Setting Stars   57

Star	Co-Culm	10° North Co-Rise	10° North Co-Set	15° North Co-Rise	15° North Co-Set	20° North Co-Rise	20° North Co-Set	25° North Co-Rise	25° North Co-Set
Zosma	17°♍31'	14°♍36'	20°♍56'	13°♍14'	22°♍57'	11°♍53'	25°♍17'	10°♍33'	28°♍03'
Denebola	27°♍01'	24°♍34'	29°♍52'	23°♍26'	01°♎33'	22°♍19'	03°♎29'	21°♍13'	05°♎46'
Acrux	07°♎14'	27°♎04'	13°♍56'	07°♏04'	29°♌30'	18°♏25'	11°♌53'	04°♐58'	17°♋24'
Vindemiatrix	16°♎52'	13°♎43'	20°♎29'	12°♎15'	22°♎35'	10°♎49'	24°♎58'	09°♎23'	27°♎45'
Diadem	18°♎57'	14°♎26'	24°♎08'	12°♎19'	27°♎08'	10°♎14'	00°♏31'	08°♎11'	04°♏24'
Spica	23°♎01'	23°♎25'	22°♎33'	23°♎36'	22°♎17'	23°♎47'	21°♎59'	23°♎58'	21°♎37'
Agena	03°♏10'	18°♏19'	15°♎09'	26°♏00'	03°♎31'	04°♐38'	18°♎36'	15°♐58'	27°♌56'
Thuban	03°♏19'	09°♎38'	28°♏32'	27°♎12'	12°♐48'	12°♍51'	29°♐34'	19°♌25'	25°♑50'
Arcturus	06°♏14'	00°♏25'	12°♏42'	27°♎39'	16°♏21'	24°♎55'	20°♏21'	22°♎11'	24°♏50'
Toliman	12°♏20'	27°♏01'	25°♎03'	04°♐37'	13°♎46'	13°♐22'	28°♏58'	25°♐21'	07°♍24'
Zuben Elgen.	15°♏11'	15°♏07'	15°♐15'	15°♏05'	15°♏17'	15°♏03'	15°♏20'	15°♏01'	15°♏23'
Zuben Esch.	21°♏40'	20°♏07'	23°♏22'	19°♏22'	24°♏19'	18°♏37'	25°♏23'	17°♏51'	26°♏35'
Alphecca	25°♏59'	17°♏55'	04°♐37'	13°♏57'	09°♐16'	10°♏00'	14°♐14'	05°♏58'	19°♐35'
Antares	09°♐03'	09°♐56'	08°♐05'	10°♐23'	07°♐34'	10°♐52'	06°♐59'	11°♐21'	06°♐19'
Ras Algethi	19°♐34'	13°♐18'	25°♐59'	10°♐08'	29°♐20'	06°♐54'	02°♑49'	03°♐34'	06°♑31'
Ras Alhague	24°♐14'	18°♐13'	00°♑20'	15°♐10'	03°♑29'	12°♐01'	06°♑47'	08°♐45'	10°♑14'
Aculeus	25°♐25'	27°♐16'	23°♐33'	28°♐14'	22°♐33'	29°♐17'	21°♐27'	00°♑25'	20°♐13'
Acumen	28°♐35'	01°♑02'	26°♐08'	02°♑20'	24°♐50'	03°♑44'	23°♐24'	05°♑18'	21°♐47'
Facies	08°♑21'	08°♑30'	08°♑13'	08°♑34'	08°♑08'	08°♑39'	08°♑04'	08°♑45'	07°♑59'
Vega	08°♑29'	26°♐58'	19°♑49'	21°♐01'	25°♑36'	14°♐49'	01°♒32'	08°♐17'	07°♒43'
Rukbat	19°♑22'	23°♑50'	15°♑10'	26°♑22'	13°♑01'	29°♑15'	10°♑43'	02°♒43'	08°♑11'
Altair	25°♑42'	20°♑23'	00°♒44'	17°♑31'	03°♒13'	14°♑27'	05°♒43'	11°♑08'	08°♒16'
Sualocin	07°♒30'	01°♒08'	13°♒22'	27°♑39'	16°♒13'	23°♑54'	19°♒04'	19°♑47'	21°♒57'
Deneb Adige	07°♒56'	24°♑15'	20°♒50'	16°♑54'	27°♒14'	09°♑02'	03°♓44'	00°♑33'	10°♓31'
Alderamin	17°♒11'	23°♑56'	09°♓22'	11°♑02'	20°♓58'	26°♑20'	03°♈58'	06°♑52'	21°♈23'
Sadalsuud	20°♒29'	18°♒41'	22°♒05'	17°♒40'	22°♒50'	16°♒31'	23°♒36'	15°♒12'	24°♒21'
Deneb Algedi	24°♒27'	25°♒02'	23°♒57'	25°♒22'	23°♒42'	25°♒44'	23°♒28'	26°♒11'	23°♒14'
Sadalmelek	29°♒19'	27°♒03'	01°♓19'	25°♒44'	02°♓16'	24°♒16'	03°♓12'	22°♒34'	04°♓07'
Fomalhaut	13°♓05'	18°♓25'	08°♓31'	21°♓35'	06°♓22'	25°♓17'	04°♓15'	29°♓42'	02°♓06'
Scheat	14°♓44'	07°♓16'	21°♓14'	02°♓57'	24°♓18'	28°♒05'	27°♓18'	22°♒30'	00°♈19'
Markab	15°♓00'	10°♓36'	18°♓49'	08°♓02'	20°♓36'	05°♓08'	22°♓21'	01°♓46'	24°♓05'

Star and Planet Combinations

Zodiac sign abbreviations used: Ar=Aries, Ta=Taurus, Ge=Gemini, Cn=Cancer, Le=Leo, Vi=Virgo, Li=Libra, Sc=Scorpio, Sg=Sagittarius, Cp=Capricorn, Aq=Aquarius, Pi=Pisces.

Star	Co-Culm	30° North Co-Rise	30° North Co-Set	35° North Co-Rise	35° North Co-Set	40° North Co-Rise	40° North Co-Set	45° North Co-Rise	45° North Co-Set
Alpheratz	02°Ar 17'	06°Pi 12'	18°Ar 07'	28°Aq 26'	20°Ar 52'	18°Aq 37'	23°Ar 50'	06°Aq 04'	27°Ar 12'
Ankaa	07°Ar 09'	21°Ta 37'	08°Pi 10'	03°Ge 40'	02°Pi 31'	18°Ge 10'	25°Aq 39'	06°Cn 57'	15°Aq 27'
Schedar	11°Ar 01'	24°Ta 22'	00°Ge 49'	Cpole					
Mirach	18°Ar 54'	19°Pi 51'	06°Ta 10'	10°Pi 24'	09°Ta 25'	27°Aq 49'	13°Ta 08'	10°Aq 49'	17°Ta 43'
Achernar	26°Ar 20'	11°Cn 24'	25°Aq 57'	NotVis					
Al Rescha	02°Ta 43'	10°Ta 08'	27°Ar 50'	12°Ta 13'	27°Ar 00'	14°Ta 51'	26°Ar 08'	18°Ta 20'	25°Ar 13'
Hamal	04°Ta 03'	24°Ar 41'	09°Ta 56'	21°Ar 44'	11°Ta 00'	17°Ar 40'	12°Ta 09'	11°Ar 37'	13°Ta 27'
Capulus	07°Ta 06'	20°Aq 12'	24°Ge 16'	Cpole					
Polaris	10°Ta 37'	Cpole							
Menkar	18°Ta 02'	27°Ta 19'	11°Ta 19'	29°Ta 44'	10°Ta 09'	02°Ge 40'	08°Ta 54'	06°Ge 22'	07°Ta 33'
Algol	19°Ta 30'	24°Ar 15'	05°Ge 59'	14°Ar 56'	09°Ge 46'	00°Ar 31'	14°Ge 41'	05°Pi 18'	22°Ge 31'
Mirfak	23°Ta 28'	11°Ar 24'	20°Ge 50'	22°Pi 06'	29°Ge 35'	08°Aq 20'	24°Cn 29'	Cpole	
Alcyone	29°Ta 05'	25°Ta 50'	01°Ge 31'	24°Ta 55'	02°Ge 00'	23°Ta 42'	02°Ge 32'	21°Ta 59'	03°Ge 10'
Aldebaran	10°Ge 35'	14°Ge 19'	07°Ge 27'	15°Ge 14'	06°Ge 50'	16°Ge 21'	06°Ge 08'	17°Ge 46'	05°Ge 20'
Rigel	19°Ge 33'	07°Ge 08'	03°Ge 14'	10°Cn 47'	00°Ge 07'	14°Cn 47'	26°Ta 46'	19°Cn 15'	23°Ta 08'
Capella	20°Ge 03'	26°Ta 29'	10°Cn 46'	17°Ta 35'	17°Cn 30'	01°Ta 09'	29°Cn 16'	Cpole	
Bellatrix	22°Ge 00'	01°Ge 55'	12°Ge 42'	04°Ge 04'	10°Ge 50'	06°Ge 31'	08°Ge 47'	09°Ge 20'	06°Ge 28'
El Nath	22°Ge 16'	18°Ge 22'	25°Ge 51'	17°Ge 22'	26°Ge 41'	16°Ge 06'	27°Ge 42'	14°Ge 21'	29°Ge 02'
Alnilam	24°Ge 33'	08°Ge 19'	11°Ge 19'	11°Ge 11'	08°Ge 43'	14°Ge 21'	05°Ge 52'	17°Ge 54'	02°Ge 43'
Phact	25°Ge 20'	28°Ge 16'	23°Ta 09'	04°Le 50'	16°Ta 51'	12°Le 04'	09°Ta 56'	20°Le 19'	02°Ge 03'
Betelgeuse	28°Ge 54'	08°Ge 06'	19°Ge 47'	10°Cn 02'	17°Ge 53'	12°Cn 13'	15°Ge 45'	14°Cn 42'	13°Ge 20'
Murzim	05°Cn 13'	27°Ge 03'	12°Ge 39'	01°Le 14'	08°Ge 10'	05°Le 44'	03°Ge 19'	10°Le 36'	28°Ta 01'
Canopus	05°Cn 30'	29°Le 55'	10°Ta 18'	15°Vi 38'	24°Ar 20'	NotVis			
Alhena	08°Cn 40'	12°Cn 38'	04°Cn 23'	13°Cn 28'	03°Cn 23'	14°Cn 24'	02°Cn 13'	15°Cn 31'	00°Cn 47'
Sirius	10°Cn 23'	01°Le 07'	18°Ge 12'	05°Le 02'	13°Ge 43'	09°Le 13'	08°Ge 50'	13°Le 45'	03°Ge 27'
Castor	21°Cn 54'	15°Cn 12'	00°Le 19'	13°Cn 42'	02°Le 49'	11°Cn 55'	06°Le 13'	09°Cn 35'	11°Le 28'
Procyon	23°Cn 00'	01°Le 34'	12°Cn 41'	03°Le 10'	10°Cn 16'	04°Le 55'	07°Cn 27'	06°Le 49'	04°Cn 06'
Pollux	24°Cn 25'	20°Cn 13'	29°Cn 48'	19°Cn 20'	01°Le 20'	18°Cn 18'	03°Le 22'	17°Cn 01'	06°Le 20'
Acubens	12°Le 10'	14°Le 57'	08°Le 13'	15°Le 27'	07°Le 08'	15°Le 59'	05°Le 47'	16°Le 34'	03°Le 58'
Alphard	19°Le 29'	01°Vi 21'	02°Le 45'	03°Vi 23'	28°Cn 31'	05°Vi 30'	23°Cn 31'	07°Vi 45'	17°Cn 28'
Regulus	00°Vi 00'	29°Le 45'	00°Vi 25'	29°Le 42'	00°Vi 32'	29°Le 39'	00°Vi 41'	29°Le 36'	00°Vi 55'
Alkes	13°Vi 40'	26°Vi 28'	23°Le 32'	28°Vi 36'	17°Le 58'	00°Li 50'	11°Le 06'	03°Li 14'	02°Le 30'
Dubhe	14°Vi 43'	Cpole							

Finding your Heliacal Rising and Heliacal Setting Stars 59

Star	Co-Culm	30° North Co-Rise	30° North Co-Set	35° North Co-Rise	35° North Co-Set	40° North Co-Rise	40° North Co-Set	45° North Co-Rise	45° North Co-Set
Zosma	17°♍31'	09°♍11'	01°♎28'	07°♍46'	05°♎49'	06°♍16'	11°♎39'	04°♍38'	19°♎53'
Denebola	27°♍01'	20°♍06'	08°♎33'	18°♍57'	12°♎04'	17°♍45'	16°♎43'	16°♍29'	23°♎11'
Acrux	07°♎14'	NotVis							
Vindemiatrix	16°♎52'	07°♎57'	01°♏03'	06°♎29'	05°♏05'	04°♎57'	10°♏10'	03°♎20'	16°♏49'
Diadem	18°♎57'	06°♎05'	08°♏58'	03°♎56'	14°♏27'	01°♎42'	21°♏09'	29°♍18'	29°♏30'
Spica	23°♎01'	24°♎09'	21°♎10'	24°♎21'	20°♎37'	24°♎33'	19°♎52'	24°♎46'	18°♎48'
Agena	03°♏10'	NotVis							
Thuban	03°♏19'	Cpole							
Arcturus	06°♏14'	19°♎24'	29°♏54'	16°♎32'	05°♐43'	13°♎31'	12°♐28'	10°♎18'	20°♐21'
Toliman	12°♏20'	NotVis							
Zuben Elgen.	15°♏11'	14°♏59'	15°♏27'	14°♏57'	15°♏32'	14°♏55'	15°♏38'	14°♏53'	15°♏46'
Zuben Esch.	21°♏40'	17°♏04'	27°♏58'	16°♏14'	29°♏37'	15°♏21'	01°♐40'	14°♏23'	04°♐17'
Alphecca	25°♏59'	01°♏50'	25°♐24'	27°♎29'	01°♑48'	22°♎51'	08°♑52'	17°♎48'	16°♑47'
Antares	09°♐03'	11°♐53'	05°♐32'	12°♐30'	04°♐35'	13°♐12'	03°♐20'	14°♐03'	01°♐35'
Ras Algethi	19°♐34'	00°♐04'	10°♑28'	26°♏23'	14°♑43'	22°♏26'	19°♑21'	18°♏10'	24°♑28'
Ras Alhague	24°♐14'	05°♐20'	13°♑54'	01°♐41'	17°♑51'	27°♏46'	22°♑09'	23°♏31'	26°♑52'
Aculeus	25°♐25'	01°♐44'	18°♐48'	03°♐18'	17°♐03'	05°♐17'	14°♐45'	08°♐03'	11°♐28'
Acumen	28°♐35'	07°♐08'	19°♐54'	09°♐24'	17°♐34'	12°♐22'	14°♐28'	16°♐47'	09°♐47'
Facies	08°♑21'	08°♐51'	07°♑54'	08°♐58'	07°♑48'	09°♐07'	07°♑40'	09°♐19'	07°♑32'
Vega	08°♑29'	01°♐18'	14°♒17'	23°♏40'	21°♒25'	15°♏03'	29°♒29'	04°♏37'	09°♓17'
Rukbat	19°♑22'	07°♑06'	05°♑14'	13°♒08'	01°♑34'	22°♒34'	26°♐32'	11°♓04'	17°♒56'
Altair	25°♑42'	07°♑30'	10°♒53'	03°♑28'	13°♒39'	28°♐56'	16°♒34'	23°♒46'	19°♒42'
Sualocin	07°♒30'	15°♑15'	24°♒53'	03°♑10'	27°♒56'	04°♑25'	01°♓09'	27°♒52'	04°♓35'
Deneb Adige	07°♒56'	21°♐10'	17°♓49'	10°♐30'	26°♓07'	27°♏21'	06°♈37'	Cpole	
Alderamin	17°♒11'	Cpole							
Sadalsuud	20°♒29'	13°♒39'	25°♒07'	11°♒47'	25°♒55'	09°♒25'	26°♒46'	06°♒19'	27°♒40'
Deneb Algedi	24°♒27'	26°♑43'	22°♒59'	27°♑24'	22°♒44'	28°♑18'	22°♒27'	29°♑36'	22°♒09'
Sadalmelek	29°♒19'	20°♒33'	05°♓03'	18°♒06'	06°♓01'	15°♒01'	07°♓02'	10°♒57'	08°♓06'
Fomalhaut	13°♓05'	05°♈11'	29°♒54'	12°♈15'	27°♒33'	21°♈44'	24°♒58'	04°♉50'	22°♒00'
Scheat	14°♓44'	15°♒59'	03°♈23'	08°♒16'	06°♈35'	29°♑04'	10°♈01'	18°♑05'	13°♈49'
Markab	15°♓00'	27°♒47'	25°♓50'	22°♒54'	27°♓37'	16°♒49'	29°♓30'	09°♒01'	01°♈29'

60   Star and Planet Combinations

Star	Co-Culm	50° North		55° North		60° North		65° North	
		Co-Rise	Co-Set	Co-Rise	Co-Set	Co-Rise	Co-Set	Co-Rise	Co-Set
Alpheratz	02°♈17'	20°♋16'	01°♉14'	01°♉08'	06°♉38'	06°♐38'	17°♉11'		
Ankaa	07°♈09'	NotVis							
Schedar	11°♈01'	Cpole							
Mirach	18°♈54'	18°♉10'	24°♉24'	Cpole					
Achernar	26°♈20'	NotVis							
Al Rescha	02°♉43'	23°♊13'	24°♈14'	00°♊32'	23°♈08'	12°♊24'	21°♈54'	02°♋34'	20°♈29'
Hamal	04°♉03'	01°♈27'	14°♉58'	11°♓44'	16°♉53'	02°♒55'	19°♉35'	18°♐51'	25°♉02'
Capulus	07°♉06'	Cpole							
Polaris	10°♉37'	Cpole							
Menkar	18°♉02'	11°♊13'	06°♉05'	17°♊50'	04°♉26'	27°♊17	02°♉34'	11°♋09'	00°♉22'
Algol	19°♉30'	Cpole							
Mirfak	23°♉28'	Cpole							
Alcyone	29°♉05'	19°♊13'	03°♊58'	13°♉42'	05°♊01'	25°♈20'	06°♊42'	05°♉04'	11°♊19'
Aldebaran	10°♊35'	19°♊39'	04°♊23'	22°♊24'	03°♊12'	26°♊56'	01°♊39'	06°♋19'	29°♉19'
Rigel	19°♊33'	24°♋16'	19°♉07'	29°♋58'	14°♉39'	06°♌29'	09°♉35'	14°♌00'	03°♉46'
Capella	20°♊03'	Cpole							
Bellatrix	22°♊00'	12°♋41'	03°♊49'	16°♋46'	00°♊42'	21°♋53'	26°♉56'	28°♋30'	22°♉14'
El Nath	22°♊16'	11°♊38'	00°♋56'	06°♊13'	04°♋15'	11°♉15'	15°♋01'		
Alnilam	24°♊33'	21°♋57'	29°♉10'	26°♋39'	25°♉08'	02°♌09'	20°♉28'	08°♌41'	15°♉00'
Phact	25°♊20'	00°♍23'	22°♈22'	16°♍31'	06°♈39'	NotVis			
Betelgeuse	28°♊54'	17°♋38'	10°♊30'	21°♋10'	07°♊06'	25°♋34'	02°♊53'	01°♌14'	27°♋29'
Murzim	05°♋13'	15°♌59'	22°♉09'	22°♌01'	15°♉33'	28°♌58'	07°♉58'	07°♍23'	28°♈52'
Canopus	05°♋30'	NotVis							
Alhena	08°♋40'	16°♋52'	28°♊57'	18°♋35'	26°♊27'	20°♋57'	22°♊41'	24°♋38'	15°♊59'
Sirius	10°♋23'	18°♌44'	27°♉29'	24°♌18'	20°♋46'	00°♍41'	13°♉06'	08°♍19'	04°♉05'
Castor	21°♋54'	06°♌08'	21°♌18'	29°♊17'	19°♍35'	Cpole			
Procyon	23°♋00'	08°♌57'	29°♊59'	11°♋23'	24°♊46'	14°♌14'	17°♊59'	17°♌40'	08°♊53'
Pollux	24°♋25'	15°♋20'	11°♌21'	12°♋43'	22°♌40'	06°♋41'	15°♌12'		
Acubens	12°♌10'	17°♌13'	01°♌24'	17°♌58'	27°♋23'	18°♌52'	20°♋04'	20°♌00'	02°♋57'
Alphard	19°♌29'	10°♍10'	10°♋05'	12°♍50'	01°♌00'	15°♍49'	19°♊59'	19°♍16'	07°♊04'
Regulus	00°♍00'	29°♌33'	01°♍16'	29°♌29'	01°♍55'	29°♌25'	03°♍32'	29°♌20'	16°♍41'
Alkes	13°♍40'	05°♎51'	21°♋42'	08°♎50'	08°♋20'	12°♎22'	22°♊38'	16°♎56'	05°♊24'
Dubhe	14°♍43'	Cpole							

Finding your Heliacal Rising and Heliacal Setting Stars   61

Star	Co-Culm	50° North Co-Rise	50° North Co-Set	55° North Co-Rise	55° North Co-Set	60° North Co-Rise	60° North Co-Set	65° North Co-Rise	65° North Co-Set
Zosma	17° ♍ 31'	02° ♌ 48'	02° ♏ 10'	00° ♍ 39'	20° ♏ 52'	27° ♌ 55'	16° ♐ 45'	23° ♌ 55'	14° ♑ 18'
Denebola	27° ♍ 01'	15° ♍ 05'	02° ♏ 43'	13° ♍ 31'	17° ♏ 30'	11° ♍ 41'	09° ♐ 53'	09° ♍ 26'	07° ♑ 28'
Acrux	07° ♎ 14'	NotVis							
Vindemiatrix	16° ♌ 52'	01° ♎ 35'	25° ♏ 43'	29° ♍ 39'	07° ♐ 50'	27° ♍ 28'	23° ♐ 55'	24° ♍ 55'	13° ♑ 12'
Diadem	18° ♌ 57'	26° ♍ 41'	09° ♐ 56'	23° ♍ 44'	22° ♐ 47'	20° ♍ 15'	07° ♑ 54'	15° ♍ 50'	24° ♑ 33'
Spica	23° ♎ 01'	25° ♎ 00'	17° ♎ 06'	25° ♎ 16'	13° ♎ 57'	25° ♎ 34'	05° ♎ 45'	25° ♎ 56'	13° ♌ 52'
Agena	03° ♏ 10'	NotVis							
Thuban	03° ♏ 19'	Cpole							
Arcturus	06° ♏ 14'	06° ♎ 46'	29° ♐ 33'	02° ♎ 46'	10° ♑ 13'	28° ♍ 03'	22° ♑ 24'	21° ♍ 54'	06° ♒ 18'
Toliman	12° ♏ 20'	NotVis							
Zuben Elgen.	15° ♏ 11'	14° ♏ 50'	15° ♏ 59'	14° ♏ 47'	16° ♏ 22'	14° ♏ 43'	17° ♏ 15'	14° ♏ 37'	22° ♏ 50'
Zuben Esch.	21° ♏ 40'	13° ♏ 18'	07° ♐ 51'	12° ♏ 04'	13° ♐ 00'	10° ♏ 37'	21° ♐ 09'	08° ♏ 51'	05° ♐ 35'
Alphecca	25° ♏ 59'	12° ♐ 04'	25° ♐ 45'	05° ♎ 11'	06° ♒ 11'	25° ♍ 39'	19° ♒ 30'	Cpole	
Antares	09° ♐ 03'	15° ♐ 10'	28° ♏ 47'	16° ♐ 50'	23° ♏ 11'	20° ♐ 06'	02° ♏ 06'	NotVis	
Ras Algethi	19° ♐ 34'	13° ♏ 29'	00° ♒ 09'	08° ♏ 15'	06° ♒ 33'	02° ♏ 19'	13° ♒ 50'	25° ♎ 22'	22° ♒ 15'
Ras Alhague	24° ♐ 14'	18° ♏ 49'	02° ♒ 06'	13° ♏ 35'	08° ♒ 00'	07° ♏ 40'	14° ♒ 40'	00° ♏ 48'	22° ♒ 23'
Aculeus	25° ♐ 25'	12° ♐ 32'	05° ♐ 48'	23° ♐ 24'	20° ♏ 39'	NotVis			
Acumen	28° ♐ 35'	25° ♐ 05'	00° ♐ 50'	07° ♓ 06'	14° ♎ 38'	NotVis			
Facies	08° ♑ 21'	09° ♑ 35'	07° ♑ 20'	10° ♑ 02'	07° ♑ 03'	11° ♑ 00'	06° ♑ 32'	18° ♑ 43'	04° ♑ 38'
Vega	08° ♑ 29'	18° ♎ 37'	24° ♓ 36'	Cpole					
Rukbat	19° ♑ 22'	NotVis							
Altair	25° ♑ 42'	17° ♐ 50'	23° ♒ 06'	10° ♐ 58'	26° ♒ 53'	03° ♐ 01'	01° ♓ 08'	23° ♏ 51'	06° ♓ 01'
Sualocin	07° ♒ 30'	20° ♐ 21'	08° ♓ 19'	11° ♐ 45'	12° ♓ 29'	01° ♐ 56'	17° ♓ 15'	20° ♏ 43'	23° ♓ 00'
Deneb Adige	07° ♒ 56'	Cpole							
Alderamin	17° ♓ 11'	Cpole							
Sadalsuud	20° ♒ 29'	02° ♒ 02'	28° ♒ 39'	25° ♑ 39'	29° ♒ 45'	15° ♑ 17'	01° ♓ 00'	27° ♐ 04'	02° ♑ 29'
Deneb Algedi	24° ♒ 27'	01° ♓ 39'	21° ♒ 49'	05° ♓ 33'	21° ♒ 25'	16° ♓ 14'	20° ♒ 57'	25° ♐ 29'	20° ♒ 18'
Sadalmelek	29° ♒ 19'	05° ♒ 20'	09° ♓ 15'	27° ♑ 07'	10° ♓ 30'	14° ♒ 28'	11° ♓ 55'	24° ♐ 52'	13° ♓ 32'
Fomalhaut	13° ♓ 05'	23° ♑ 00'	18° ♒ 22'	16° ♊ 42'	13° ♓ 15'	18° ♋ 01'	01° ♒ 01'	NotVis	
Scheat	14° ♓ 44'	05° ♑ 03'	18° ♈ 14'	19° ♐ 47'	23° ♈ 53'	00° ♐ 42'	03° ♑ 04'	Cpole	
Markab	15° ♓ 00'	28° ♑ 52'	03° ♈ 39'	15° ♑ 43'	06° ♈ 04'	29° ♐ 29'	08° ♈ 53'	11° ♐ 20'	12° ♈ 19'

Section 3

Star and Planet Combinations

The Delineated Stars, an Overview (positions for 1st January 2000)

Star	Constellation	Celestial Longitude	Celestial Latitude	Theme
Achernar	Eridanus	15 ♓ 18	59S23	Rapid changes
Acrux	Crux	11 ♏ 52	52S52	The material world
Acubens	Cancer	13 ♌ 39	05S05	The love of life
Aculeus	Scorpio	25 ♐ 44	08S53	Constructive Criticism
Acumen	Scorpio	28 ♐ 43	11S23	Criticism that weakens
Agena	Centaurus	23 ♏ 47	44S08	The common touch
Al Rescha	Pisces	29 ♈ 23	09S04	Joining things together
Alcyone	Taurus	00 ♊ 00	04N03	Inner vision
Aldebaran	Taurus	09 ♊ 47	05S28	Integrity at all times
Alderamin	Cepheus	12 ♈ 46	68N55	Honour and leadership
Algol	Perseus	26 ♉ 10	22N26	Intense passion
Alhena	Gemini	09 ♋ 06	06S45	Promotion of ideas
Alkes	The Crater	23 ♍ 41	22S43	To carry a precious thing
Alnilam	Orion	23 ♊ 28	24S30	To hold together
Alphard	The Hydra	27 ♌ 17	22S23	Obsession
Alphecca	Corona Borealis	12 ♏ 17	44N19	A gift with thorns
Alpheratz	Andromeda	14 ♈ 18	25N41	Speed and freedom
Altair	Aquila	01 ♒ 46	29N18	Boldness
Ankaa	The Phoenix	15 ♓ 29	40S38	Resurrection
Antares	Scorpio	09 ♐ 45	04S34	Obsessive passion
Arcturus	Bootes	24 ♎ 14	30N44	A path-finder
Bellatrix	Orion	20 ♊ 57	16S49	Success with stress
Betelgeuse	Orion	28 ♊ 45	16S02	Success with ease
Canopus	Carinae	14 ♋ 59	75S49	The dominant leader
Capella	Aurigae	21 ♊ 52	22N52	Independence
Capulus	Perseus	24 ♉ 12	40N23	Penetrating action
Castor	Gemini	20 ♋ 15	10N06	The storyteller
Deneb Adige	Cygnus	05 ♓ 19	59N55	The spiritual warrior
Deneb Algedi	Capricorn	23 ♒ 32	02S36	The law giver
Denebola	Leo	21 ♍ 37	12N16	Non-conforming
Diadem	Coma Berenices	08 ♎ 57	22N59	A sacrifice
Dubhe	Ursa Major	15 ♌ 12	49N41	Passive strength
El Nath	Taurus	22 ♊ 35	05N23	Focus attack
Facies	Sagittarius	08 ♑ 18	00S44	Penetrating vision

Name	Constellation	Longitude	Declination	Meaning
Fomalhaut	Piscis Australis	03 ♓ 51	21S08	Idealism
Hamal	Aries	07 ♉ 40	09N58	Will and determination
Markab	Pegasus	23 ♓ 29	19N24	Stability
Menkar	Cetus	14 ♉ 19	12S35	Open to the collective
Mirach	Andromeda	00 ♉ 24	25N57	Receptive, indulgent
Mirfak	Perseus	02 ♊ 05	30N08	A love of acton
Murzims	Canis Major	07 ♋ 12	41S15	To wish to speak
Phact	Columba	22 ♊ 11	57S23	To explore
Polaris	Ursa Minor	28 ♊ 35	66N06	To feel guided
Pollux	Gemini	23 ♋ 13	06N41	Insights through stress
Procyon	Canis Minor	25 ♋ 47	16S01	Things in transition
Ras Algethi	Hercules	16 ♐ 08	37N17	The natural order
Ras Alhague	Ophiuchus	22 ♐ 26	35N50	The healer
Regulus	Leo	29 ♌ 50	00N28	Success but vengeance
Rigel	Orion	16 ♊ 50	31S07	The educator, the scholar
Rukbat	Sagittarius	16 ♑ 38	18S23	Steadfastness
Sadalmelek	Aquarius	03 ♓ 21	10N40	Making one's own luck
Sadalsuud	Aquarius	23 ♒ 23	08N37	A natural rapport, luck
Scheat	Pegasus	29 ♓ 22	31N09	Searching for truth
Schedar	Cassiopeia	07 ♉ 47	46N38	Dignity
Sirius	Canis Major	14 ♋ 05	39S36	The quest for immortality
Spica	Virgo	23 ♎ 50	02S03	To be gifted
Sualocin	Delphinus	17 ♒ 22	33N01	Playfulness
Thuban	Draco	07 ♍ 28	66N21	To hoard or guard
Toliman	Centaurus	29 ♏ 28	42S36	The teacher
Vega	Lyra	15 ♑ 18	61N44	Enchantment
Vindemiatrix	Virgo	09 ♎ 56	16N12	To collect and gather
Zosma	Leo	11 ♍ 19	14N20	Victimisation
Zuben Elgenubi	Libra	15 ♏ 05	00N20	The volunteer
Zuben Eschamali	Libra	19 ♏ 22	08N30	The professional helper

Star and Planet Combinations 67

ACHERNAR

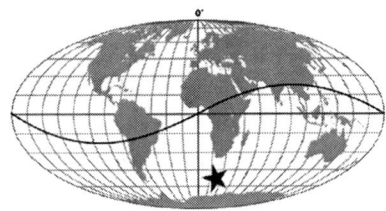

Achernar

Constellation:	Eridanus
α Eridanus, magnitude	0.46
1 January 2000 =	RA 1hr 37'42"
Declination	-57° 15'
Celestial longitude	15° ♓ 18'
Celestial latitude	59°S23'
BV Colour =	Blue-Green

Eridanus, The River

Eridanus begins at the feet of Orion at the bright star Rigel and then wanders southward down towards the South Pole area, ending by the Phoenix. This is believed to have been the river into which the great millstone of heaven fell when the earth's axis shifted by precession[2]. This great stone dislodged from the North Pole and fell into Eridanus. Other stories talk of Phaethon, the son of Apollo, falling into the river after losing control of his father's sun chariot[3].

Principle of Achernar, change through crisis, rapid endings

Achernar is a turbulent star and it can indicate crises. It will bring into a life fast-occurring events, like fire and flood – literally or symbolically – and such changes will feel like old issues which are simply swept away. All matters and events associated with Achernar will require quick and efficient action.

Heliacal Rising Star

A family or cultural background of a chaotic history which seems to be part of one's personal journey – dealing with and accepting that life contains turbulent times. A growing understanding and acceptance that life will contain unstable situations. *Terence Hanbury White, 20th century Indian-born English author who wrote "The Once and Future King". He was a conscientious objector to WWII, and his experience of the war had a profound effect on his work, which included commentaries on war and human nature via the heroic narrative.*

Heliacal Setting Star
Being placed in situations which force a person to learn how to deal with turbulence and crisis – flourishing in crisis and thus finding oneself being drawn to working, helping and or studying people or systems in upheaval, or disordered times. Seeking situations of crisis as the way to reach one's full potential. *Kahlia Chamberlain, daughter born to Lindy Chamberlain in 1982 while serving a prison sentence for the murder of her infant daughter in the Australian desert. It was eventually proven that a dingo had taken the child, and the family's story later inspired the film "Evil Angels".*

Star on one of its pivot points at the moment of birth
A lifestyle that contains sudden and rapid changes in fortune. A risk taker or one who puts themselves at risk through work, hobbies or lifestyle. A person who works in a high-risk or volatile environment. *Event: The Apollo 11 Launch, Man on the Moon.*

Physiological Correspondence: The veins and arteries – the body's circulation system.

Ptolemy's Location: The star at the end of the river[1].

World Cities: nil at latitudes between 55° to 59° south.

Achernar in paran with:

Sun: To deal with, or live in, a state of crisis, to identify oneself with crises. To be in a rapidly changing situation requiring crisis management skills.   ♦   A time of disruption. *Diego Rivera, 19th century Mexican artist whose left-wing politics caused his work to be banned in the USA.*

Moon: Self-destructive, or helping others who are self-destructive. To have difficulties with female family members.   ♦   A crisis involving a child or a loved person in one's care *Bao Dai, 20th century monarch, the last emperor of Vietnam. He initially sought to reform and modernize Vietnam but was unable to win French cooperation.*

Mercury: A worrier, with a caustic dry wit. A person comfortable with and competent in forums of debate.   ♦   A time of financial turmoil, worrying news. *Paul Keating, 20th century Australian Prime Minster known for his dry and caustic wit.*

Venus: To experience turbulence in relationships, to like change in one's personal or domestic life.   ♦   Events which offend or challenge social values. *Peter Abrahams, 20th century South African author who dealt mainly with the political struggles of black people.*

Mars: To cause, or spend one's life in, chaotic times. To be highly focussed and willing to cause change or disruption in order to achieve goals.   ♦   Accidents or turbulent events, to be in a time of uncertainty. *Bao Dai, the last emperor of Vietnam, see Moon with Achernar.*

Jupiter: To be able to succeed in the face of crisis. To have a profession which involves understanding or dealing with crises. To be able to see the silver lining that hides in storm clouds. ◆ Quick action succeeds. *Achmed Sukarno, 20th century freedom fighter and leader who was the first President of Indonesia.*

Saturn: A person who can be a leader in hard times or a dictator in good times. Needing to learn to lead with care and create with flexibility. ◆ Changes occurring in authority through crisis or upheaval. *Mao Tse-Tung, 20th century freedom fighter and co-founder of the People's Republic of China.*

Uranus: To have sudden changes in status, sudden shifts from popular to unpopular or vice versa. To work with people in crisis on a large scale. ◆ News of fresh perspectives or inventions that bring change. *Anthony Fokker, 20th century Indonesian born German aircraft pioneer who produced over 40 different types of aircraft during World War I.*

Neptune: To work with or deal with minority issues, to promote the unpopular cause. A person who fights for the well-being of the environment. ◆ Upheavals due to fire, floods or explosions. *Raden Adjeng (Lady) Kartini, 20th century leader who was the inspiration for Indonesian independence and Indonesian feminism.*

Pluto: Able to see or to be a victim of the darker side of a problem. Being vulnerable to the unthinking actions of others. To be in the wrong place at the wrong time. ◆ A solution found by the revelation of a deeper issue. *Azaria Chamberlain, the baby who was killed by a dingo in the Australian desert; the media attack on her parents became a landmark case in Australian legal history.*

The Moon's Node: A person who fights for a political idea, to be a popular "battler". Working for or with people who want to bring in change. To be the instigator of upheavals. ◆ A new political ideal emerges. *Jaya Pratash Narayan, 19th century Indian left-wing activist against the British in India.*

NOTES

1. It is not clear if Ptolemy means the Achernar of modern times, as Achernar simply means the end of the river and this constellation has been extended since Ptolemy's day. His Achernar could have been the star we now call Acamar, magnitude 3, which is thought to have dimmed since Ptolemy's time.
2. Giorgio de Santillana and Hertha von Dechend, *Hamlet's Mill*, Boston: Non-pareil, 1977, p.162.
3. H.A. Guerber, *The Myths of Greece and Rome*, London: Harrap, 1991, p.53.

ACRUX

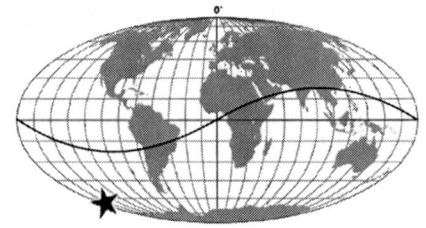

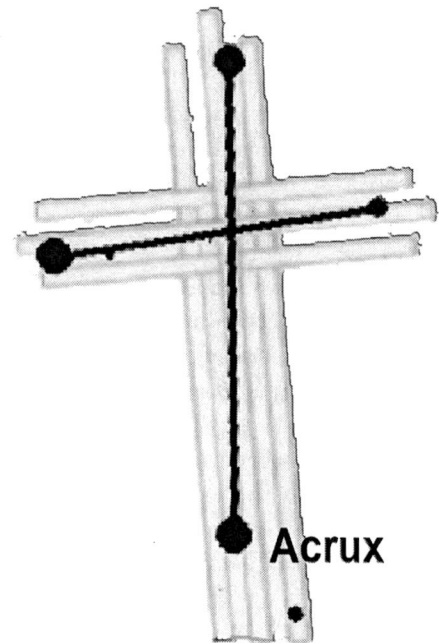

Acrux

Constellation	Crux
α1 Crucis, magnitude	1.33
1 January 2000 =	RA 12hr 26'36"
Declination	-63° 06'
Celestial longitude	11° ♏ 52'
Celestial latitude	52°S52'
BV Colour =	Blue-Green

Crux, the Southern Cross
This is the smallest constellation in the sky. Originally it was part of the Centaur, being located between his front and back legs. Crux was named in the 16th century by Amerigo Vespucci and would have been visible to Ptolemy but due to precession slipped from European view around 400 CE.

Principle of Acrux, making things happen, understanding the material world
The cross is considered here in an astrological context rather than in the light of its religious. The cross in astrology is the Cross of Matter (the axis of the Ascendant/Descendant and the MC/IC), its expression being to give things substance, to bring into form. It is the centre of every chart and, from this perspective, talks about the soul or spirit of the individual grappling with the physical world into which it has been born. Thus Acrux is concerned with the physical world and established regimes. Its symbolism embraces the art of making money and bringing things into form.

Heliacal Rising Star
Instinctually knowing and understanding the world of money and power. To seek the pleasures of power and money, or to be able to achieve goals on a physical and practical level. A member of the establishment. *Bao Dai, 20th century monarch, the last emperor of Vietnam.*

Heliacal Setting Star
Finding that one has a skill for handling money or property for other people. Learning how to use money and power to help, heal or even to divide. An unexpected solution to a practical problem. *Country: South Africa – became a republic on 31st May 1961; this meant separation from the British monarchy and the use of apartheid as an instrument of social order.*

Star on one of its pivot points at the moment of birth
A lifestyle that embraces the material world of money or power. A love of the market place, to work with valuable goods or manage real estate. *Country: The national chart of Singapore – 9 August, 1965.*

Physiological Correspondence: The stomach, cauldron of material nourishment, foundation of physical well-being.

Ptolemy's location: The star in the Centaur's foot and at the base of the Cross.

World Cities: nil at latitudes between 61° to 65° south.

Acrux in paran with:

Sun: Wanting to be a successful member of the establishment. An achiever, to be able to work within the system for personal gain. ♦ A period when the establishment prevails. *Tung-Po Su, 11th century Chinese poet and essayist, considered one of China's greatest literary figures and reformers.*

Moon: A love of money or, conversely, a social conscience which desires that the established order provides the material needs of life for others. ♦ A period when people need help and support. *Mohandas K. Gandhi, 19th century Indian leader who fought for Indian independence from Britain and become the first Prime Minster of India.*

Mercury: A person who is a practical thinker and takes decisive action in solving problems. To love logic and scientific methodologies. ♦ A time when money makes a difference. *Jaya Prakash, 19th century Indian revolutionary who demanded that land be distributed among the landless.*

Venus: To view art or society in a monetary way. To place a monetary value on relationships or art. ♦ Money matters overrule social issues. *John Howard, 20th century Australian conservative Prime Minister who considered a balanced budget a method of creating social well-being.*

Mars: Assertiveness and holding focus on money, power or military force. To deal with life's problems in an assertive manner. ♦ Those in power win the day. *Pancho Villa, 19th century Mexican revolutionary and guerrilla leader.*

Jupiter: To find success in the mainstream world, whether in business or through associations. To find that one gains from fortunate turns of events. ♦ Those who have power gain more power. *Ann Haddy, Australian actor who starred in 2,965 episodes of "Neighbours".*

Saturn: A reformer within the established order. One who works from within the system to bring change. A person who seeks change but without too much disruption. ♦ Reform in laws and money matters. *U Thant, 20th century Burmese academic, public servant and third Secretary General of the UN.*

Uranus: Subject to jealousy, to be concerned with the rights and property of the individual either politically or personally. ♦ A time of greed or a time of coveting one's neighbour's goods. *Luc Jouret, 20th century leader of the right-wing pan-European nationalist political party and involved with the Knights Templar movements.*

Neptune: The negotiator or embezzler, to seek money honestly or dishonestly from large corporate enterprises. ♦ A period when big business struggles with corruption or collapse. *Sir Thomas Raffles, 18th century founder of Singapore and responsible for the creation of Britain's Far East empire.*

Pluto: A person who can cross a divide, making a non-issue an issue, bringing money or power into areas where it was not expected. ♦ A time of success in business, or success in marketing an idea. *Poppy King, Australian business woman who at age 18 created a cosmetics company which rapidly became one of the leaders in its field, her idea was a better type of lipstick.*

The Node: The voice of the establishment, wanting to speak out and represent people but in a conservative manner. ♦ Events which reinforce the conventional point of view. *Liliuokalani, the 19th century Hawaiian monarch of the islands, who fought, unsuccessfully, to regain her throne after annexation by the USA.*

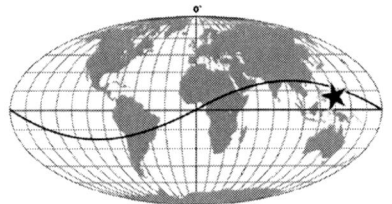

ACUBENS

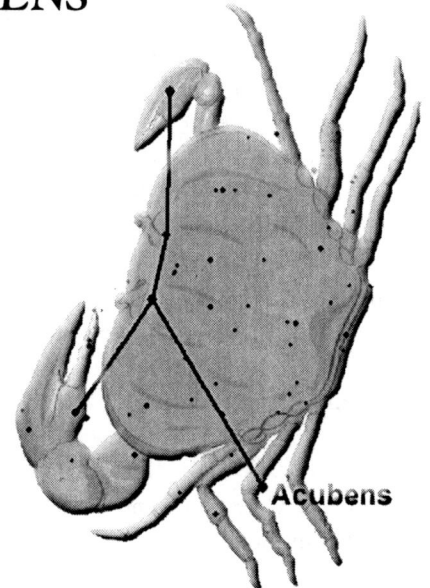

Constellation	Cancer
α Cancri, magnitude	4.25
1 January 2000 =	RA 8hr 58'29"
Declination	+11° 51'
Celestial longitude	13° ♌ 39'
Celestial latitude	05°S05'
BV Colour =	White

Cancer, the Scarab Beetle of Life

By about 2,000 BCE the stars of Cancer rose before the dawn at the time of the summer solstice. The Sun, having reached its southernmost point of rising on the horizon, would then turn on its path and begin its journey northward. It was the Chaldeans who officially linked this constellation to the crab apparently because of this sideways movement of the Sun as it entered the constellation[1]. The Egyptians, however, linked the constellation to the Scarab Beetle, a symbol of immortality, rising from the dead and settling "... upon the empty throne in the boat of Ra"[2]. A place where the Sun god was born again. This may well be the source for the later belief that this group of stars was the source of all life and a portal for the souls of men – called the Gate of Men, the place where souls entered into the earth's material realms.

Principle of Acubens, the love of life

Acubens can shape one's spiritual attitudes and arouse a belief in the concept of resurrection, whether in a religious way or simply as an optimistic outlook on life. It can also attract a person to the profession of, or at least stimulate an interest in, the bringing in of new life; or, conversely, helping in the process of death. This star's themes are those of life and resurrection, a gatekeeper, a midwife of incoming or outgoing, the cycle of life.

Heliacal Rising Star

A love of life and a respect for life, from a spiritual, biological or even historical viewpoint. Holding strong beliefs about the correct way to give life to an idea, community or environment.

Believing in the sacredness of life and seeking to breathe life into an idea or a living being. *Gene Roddenberry, the creator of the TV series Star Trek.*

Heliacal Setting Star
Learning the skills that bring life to ideas or situations, discovering how to nurture ideas and people to bring forth new concepts. Seeking to place oneself in the centre of new ideas, and wanting to be involved with the creation of new projects. *Neil Kerley, Australian football star and later involved with the development of football on a national level.*

Star on one of its pivot points at the moment of birth
A lifestyle that embraces the importance of giving life to people or ideas. Working with gateway situations – birth, death, endings and beginnings; working in unusual areas. *Michel Gauquelin, 20th century French psychologist and statistician who, in the 1950s, conducted statistical research on astrology.*

Physiological Correspondence: Reproductive system. The power of generativity, and the future of one's family line.

Ptolemy's location: The star in the southern claw.

World Cities: Bangkok, Thailand; Caracas, Venezuela at latitudes between 10° to14° north.

Acubens in paran with:

Sun: The Healer, a person who sees life as sacred. To identify oneself with the perspective that life and its many expressions is sacred.   ♦   Matters of the protection or sacredness of life take centre stage. *Francis Xavier, 16th century priest considered to be the greatest Roman Catholic missionary of modern times.*

Moon: A paternal instinct; trying to make people's lives more fruitful. A joy in seeing people, planets, animals, or even ideas, blossom and grow.   ♦   A period when children and welfare are central issues. *Carl Jung, 20th century Swiss psychiatrist, one of the founding fathers of modern depth psychology.*

Mercury: To have an interest in the ways of life; to explore how life works, whether socially or physically. To record, discuss and reveal in any way the diversity and mystery of life.   ♦   Issues of education become important to the community. *Joy Adamson, Czech author of a series of books about a lioness, her most famous being 'Elsa: Born Free'.*

Venus: To have happy relationships and to be blessed with good friends. A good networker, skilled in being able to bring people or ideas together in a way that revitalises them.   ♦   Events which bring people together, a strong sense of community. *Richard Outcault, early 20th century US author responsible for the development of the comic strip.*

Mars: The craftsperson; to create or build ideas or objects. A person who is able to bring ideas into practical expression.   ♦   Art and architecture take the focus. *Sir Christopher Wren, 17th century architect, designer, and astronomer described as the greatest English architect of his time.*

Jupiter: To take joy from one's children; to be blessed with fruitfulness and vitality. A Midas touch, to be successful in one's endeavours.   ♦   The most creative plan succeeds. *Sir Thomas Raffles, 18th century founder of Singapore and responsible for the creation of Britain's Far East empire.*

Saturn: The cartographer; one who maps, records or collects people, events, or things. A person who seeks to document life.   ♦   A historic time, unfolding events become part of the nation's history. *Galileo Galilei, 16th century Italian mathematician and the father of the experimental method and physics.*

Uranus: A person whose creations are popular – stories, art, ideas or inventions. To have an interest in the natural sciences, biology, medicine or the environment.   ♦   Public attention on lives lost, or saved. *Jules Verne, 19th century French author considered the father of science fiction.*

Neptune: To have a vision and to seek to fulfil one's dreams; to have high expectations of other people, or to be naïve.   ♦   Ethics, or human rights called into question. *Shah Jahan, the Mogul emperor who built the Taj Mahal in 1631.*

Pluto: To be un-accepting of religion or commonly held beliefs. To seek a new view on life, whether in philosophy or in art.   ♦   A time when events unfold which disregard the sacredness of life. *Rene Descartes, French philosopher who, in 1619, formulated his idea of a universal science.*

The Node: To be involved with public heath or fitness, or interested in the welfare of others. The anthropologist, or one who works for their own community.   ♦   Public health and wellbeing are making the news. *John Pringle, English physician credited with writing, in the 18th century, the manual outlining the procedures for the establishment of military hospitals.*

NOTES

1. Gertude Jobes and James Jobes, *Outer Space: Myths, Name Meanings, Calendars,* New York: Scarecrow, 1964, p.131.
2. Wallis E. A. Budge, *The Gods of the Egyptians* vol. I, New York: Dover, 1969, p.356.

ACULEUS

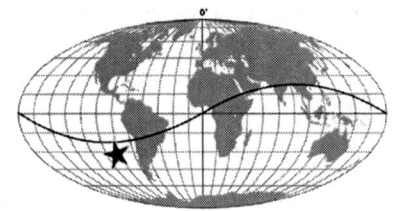

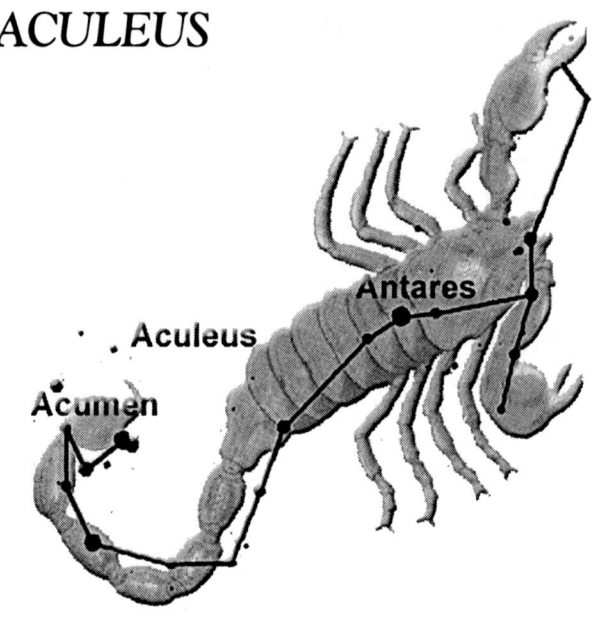

Constellation	Scorpius
Nebula, magnitude	4.20
1 January 2000 =	RA 17hr 40' 03"
Declination	-32° 15'
Celestial longitude	25° ♐ 44'
Celestial latitude	08°S53'
BV Colour =	White

Scorpio, the Scorpion

From 5,000 BCE to approximately 1,000 BCE in the northern hemisphere, the Sun was amongst the stars of the Great Scorpion, Scorpio and Libra, for the Autumn equinox. Being one of the signs of an equinox, it was considered one of the four gateways to the other world. It was known as a bringer of darkness for, as the Sun entered this constellation, it moved into the southern hemisphere and this marked the beginning of the dark part of the year. (For more information see also Acumen and Antares).

Principle of Aculeus, constructive criticism

This is one of a pair of nebulae, its twin being Acumen. Aculeus and Acumen, the tail of Scorpio, the sting, are linked to attacks, physical, mental, verbal or spiritual. Aculeus brings the less damaging attack, the kind an individual can endure and use to harden or strengthen themselves. It is the concept of strengthening in the forge of criticism.

Heliacal Rising Star

The philosophy of life that rough stones can be polished by life's difficulties. Acceptance of the ups and downs of life as part of the process of growing and learning. An embracing of difficulties as a feature of one's life. *Stephen Hawking, renowned 20th century English physicist who suffers from a degenerative neuromuscular disease.*

Heliacal Setting Star
To learn how to weather the storm, and roll with the punches. A person who becomes stronger as they get older, who has confidence that they can cope with most of life's difficulties; even a tendency to seek such difficulties as a way of honing one's life skills. *Kenneth Coles, 20th century Australian businessman who was the founder of Coles retail empire.*

Star on one of its pivot points at the moment of birth
A lifestyle where wisdom is learned in the school-of-hard-knocks. To laugh or make light of difficulties but at the same time have a "get one's hands dirty" approach to life. To work in comedy or to work in repairs – people or things. *Julie Andrews, English actress whose most famous roles were in "The Sound of Music" and "Mary Poppins".*

Physiological Correspondence: The peritoneum – the abdominal membrane that covers and protects the viscera.

Ptolemy's location: Nebula in the tail of the scorpion.

World Cities: Cape Town, South Africa; Cordoba, Argentina; Perth and Sydney, Australia; Santiago, Chile at latitudes between 30^0 to 34^0 south.

Aculeus in paran with:

Sun: To grow in strength through attacks or difficulties. A person who is a battler and able to negotiate the rocky roads of life. To benefit from dealing with these difficulties. ♦ Society gains by being challenged. *Gustave Eiffel, 19th century French architect who is remembered for building the tower that bears his name.*

Moon: To become compassionate person due to hardships suffered. Possible difficulties with women, whether lover, sister, friend, mother or workmate. ♦ Welfare philosophies challenged. *Joseph Pulitzer, journalist who established the Pulitzer Prizes for fiction, poetry, drama, music and various categories of newspaper work.*

Mercury: A person who can be mentally focused, dealing with hard problems, or a person who struggles with financial issues. Willingly working with challenging subjects. ♦ A time when difficult financial decisions are made. *Michelangelo Buonarroti, 15th century Italian artist, sculptor, poet and architect who painted the Sistine Chapel.*

Venus: One who moves from hardship to a more noble life. Being able to pull oneself up by one's own boot-straps. ♦ A time of greater social awareness through noticing people in need. *William Penn, a Quaker leader whose strength of belief led him to oversee the founding of the colony of the Commonwealth of Pennsylvania.*

Mars: To find frequent hardships in pursuing one's dreams. A person who is not afraid of hard physical or mental toil in pursuit of success. ♦ The public becoming aware of the hardships endured by people. *Wolfgang Amadeus Mozart, 18th century Austrian composer who is considered the greatest musical genius of modern times, however he died in poverty.*

Jupiter: The outsider; to take a different point of view. To feel optimistic in the face of hard challenge and willingly enter into tense, stressful or even dangerous situations. To have the courage to stand by one's beliefs. ♦ A person suggests coming at a problem from a different angle. *Nelson Mandela, 19th century freedom fighter and the first Prime Minister of South Africa.*

Saturn: The researcher, a person who seeks practical solutions to problems. One who deals with the material world in a manner that solves or alleviates problems. ♦ A new practical policy is revealed. *Hermann Rorschach, 19th century Swiss psychiatrist who developed the inkblot test that is used for diagnosing psychopathological illnesses.*

Uranus: A person who tries to give voice to the difficulties of life within their culture or community. To worry about one's community. ♦ A time when there is action against a culture or a community. *John Keats, 18th century English poet who wrote many works, one of his most famous being "Ode to Melancholy".*

Neptune: Being able to see the weakness within an ideal or the fault of an argument. Interest in all matters to do with defence, be it in health, commerce or military matters. A desire to help the weak. ♦ An ill-planned attack unfolds. *St Vincent de Paul, 16th century French saint who worked to help the poor.*

Pluto: Being able to see a weakness in a system, making the best of a observed opportunity, be it in one's social or business network – a trader. ♦ A challenge to a person or a group. *Duke of Wellington, British Army commander during the Napoleonic Wars.*

The Node: A person who wants to help. Wanting to represent a group as a battler or sports figure, wanting to take action on behalf of a group. ♦ A hard won victory. *Manfred Baron von Richthofen (the Red Baron) a WWI German flying ace.*

ACUMEN

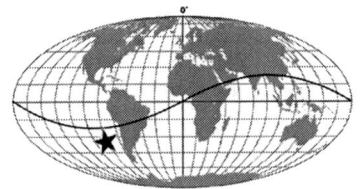

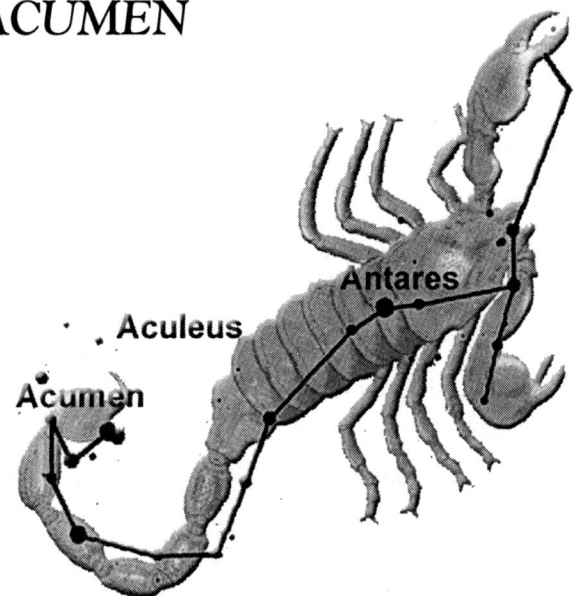

Constellation	Scorpius
Nebula, magnitude	3.00
1 January 2000 =	RA 17hr 53'51"
Declination	-34° 49'
Celestial longitude	28° ♐ 43'
Celestial latitude	11°S23'
BV Colour =	White

Scorpio, the Scorpion

From 5,000 BCE to approximately 1,000 BCE in the northern hemisphere, the Sun was amongst the stars of the Great Scorpion, Scorpio and Libra, for the Autumn equinox. To the Egyptians the Scorpion showed the way into the underworld, the time when the sun moved into the land of the dead. To the Celts the sun's entry into these stars was the feast of Samhain[1] when the souls of the dead would roam the earth. Holding one of the signs of an equinox, the scorpion was considered one of the four gateways to the other world and was known as a bringer of darkness, for as the Sun entered this constellation, it moved into the southern hemisphere and this marked the beginning of the dark part of the year. (For more information see Aculeus and Antares).

Principle of Acumen, criticism which can weaken

This is one of a pair of nebulae, its twin being Aculeus. Both of these stars, Aculeus and Acumen, in the tail of Scorpio, the sting, tend to be linked to attacks, not only physical but also mental, verbal or spiritual. Acumen carries the negative or shadow side, so there are attacks that weaken, attacks that can slowly but surely erode the person.

Heliacal Rising Star

A sense that life is filled with attacks or hindrance so a need to learn, as a part of one's life lesson, to overcome obstacles. A feeling that one has suffered at the hands of others or has been subject to rumours. A life journey struggling against criticism. *Wolfgang Amadeus Mozart, 18th century Austrian composer who is considered the greatest musical genius of modern times, howver he died in poverty.*

Heliacal Setting Star
One who has to face challenges, and find that difficult or hostile situations fuels one personal drive. Needing to pit one's wits against another or a situation. *Sir Edmund Hillary, 20th century New Zealand mountaineer who together with his Tibetan guide, Tenzing Norgay, were the first to climb Mount Everest.*

Star on one of its pivot points at the moment of birth
A life that is constantly challenged by others. To hold views which are contra those of the mainstream. Working in challenging situations where one can test oneself against the odds. *Paul Newman, US actor who also loves car racing.*

Physiological Correspondence: The Pericardium – the sac that contains the heart: protects the heart against not only physical but also emotional shock.

Ptolemy's location: Nebula in the tail of the scorpion.

World Cities: Adelaide and Sydney, Australia; Auckland, New Zealand; Buenos Aires, Argentina; Santiago, Chile at latitudes between 33^0 to 37^0 south.

Acumen in paran with:

Sun: Subject to attacks on one's credibility. To experience small challenges which can slowly weaken one's defences. Needing to learn to allow time to sort out issues, needing to learn how to bend and flow with the times.   ♦   A time when a leader is challenged. *Queen Elizabeth I, the English queen who survived assassination attempts and the pressure of the court on her to marry.*

Moon: Experiencing, dealing with, or creating, hardships. A person who needs to maintain an optimistic attitude, a person who works hard to try and make a difference.   ♦   A loved one suffers difficulties. *Albert Einstein, 20th century German physicist known for his work in energy and matter.*

Mercury: Difficult or tedious mental endeavours; stressful financial dealings. Beliefs or ideas which place one at a disadvantage in the establishment.   ♦   A time when persistence is needed to overcome a challenge. *John Harrison, 17th century English clock maker who developed the chronometer but fought for many years to be paid for his invention.*

Venus: An activist, or an artist – one who works in unusual or unpopular media. To take the unpopular social position in relationship or friendships, or to befriend social outcasts.
   ♦   Unpopular people take centre stage. *Alan Turing, 20th century mathematical genius and inventor who developed the early computer that cracked the German Enigma code of WWII, but was driven to suicide because of his homosexuality.*

Mars: A person who is motivated to act even in the face of hardship or negative social opinion. Seeking the difficult undertaking or the stimulating challenge. One who needs a challenge.
• Actions against social opinion. *Florence Nightingale, 19th century English reformer who was the founder of the modern profession of nursing.*

Jupiter: To put oneself at risk in response to one's social conscience. Feeling lucky or blessed and being able to steer through difficult waters. • A risky endeavour is suggested. *Ida Wells-Barnett, black journalist who led an anti-lynching crusade in the United States in the 1890s.*

Saturn: To suffer hardships which fuel personal motivation or anger. Striving to help those in hardship, or facing hardship to fulfil one's passions. • Bitterness and anger at hardships endured by others. *Vincent van Gogh, 19th century Dutch artist who painted peasants at their work.*

Uranus: To fight against discrimination, to resist or challenge biased attacks on a group.
• A time when racial or social discrimination predominates. *Annie Besant, 19th century reformer known for her work with the Theosophical Society as well as her promotion of self-rule for India.*

Neptune: A tendency to let one's imagination outweigh reason. To learn to grow in wisdom by challenging one's own beliefs or physical limits. • Religious zeal used against a group. *Roberto Ridolfi, who conspired to assassinate Elizabeth I of England and restore Catholic rule to England.*

Pluto: One's strengths are one's weakness and one's weaknesses are one's strength. To look for solutions where others thinks there are none. • A time when systems fail. *Percival Lowell, the 19th century US astronomer who predicted the existence of the planet Pluto and started the search which led to its discovery.*

The Node: To voice the unpopular opinion, to represent a difficult position and be prepared to take the hard path for the benefit of both oneself and others. • A contra-argument is put forward. *Peter Lalor, a 19th century rebel who is best known for his leadership of the most famous, though unsuccessful, insurrection in Australian history at the Eureka Stockade.*

NOTES

1. Miranda J. Green, *Dictionary of Celtic Myth and Legend*, London: Thames & Hudson, 1992, p.187.

AGENA

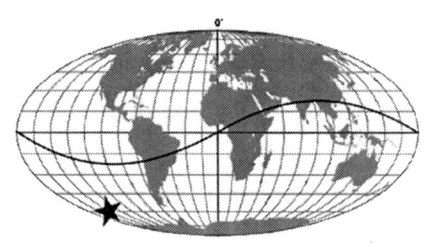

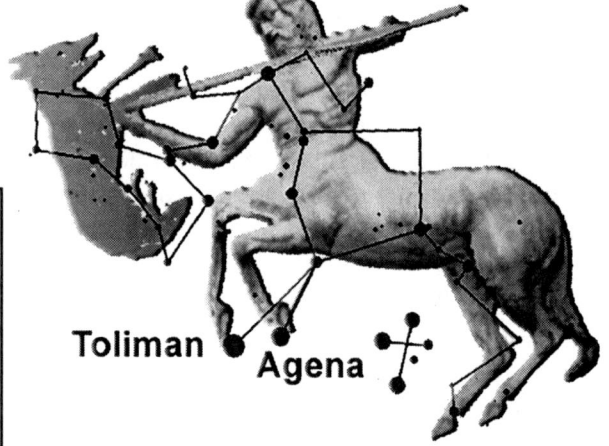

Constellation	Centaurus
β Centauri, magnitude	0.61
1 January 2000 =	RA 14hr 03'48"
Declination	-60° 22'
Celestial longitude	23° ♏ 47'
Celestial latitude	44°S08'
BV Colour =	Blue-Green

Centaurus, Chiron the Centaur

Centaurus the Centaur, Lupus the Wolf and Ara the Altar are a group of three constellations that are entangled in a story of worship and devotion. The Centaur is a large constellation covering an area between 30° and 60° of southern declination and is said to be holding Lupus, the wolf, in his out-stretched hand. He is thought, by both the Greeks and the Arabs, to be making his way to Ara, the Altar to make a sacrifice[1]. To that end he is often shown carrying a water canteen for the necessary libation. He is associated with being a healer and a teacher, but he also carries a wound. (For more information see Toliman).

Principle of Agena, to have the common touch

Agena, in the Centaur's foot, is symbolic of the sacrifices required for growth. This star is associated with concern for some cause, or issue that needs to be corrected or healed, either privately or collectively. Yet the sacrifice Chiron makes is the everyday ritual of his life and, in this way, Agena talks of the everyday things which, if attended to, will lead to success. Agena is about the common touch, to understand what people need or want. The repeating ordinariness of life.

Heliacal Rising Star

A natural ability in dealing with the ordinary, everyday things, and finding that this path leads to success or fulfilment. The gift of the common touch; a feeling or intuition for what people want or need, which can be of great benefit both to oneself and others. *Bette Midler, the US comedian renowned for her common touch.*

Heliacal Setting Star
To learn though life's ups and downs that the most obvious solution is often the best, to find answers to difficulties through simple uncomplicated solutions. To discover that one has a natural skill at untangling difficult situations. *Jose B de Andrada e Silva, 18th century Brazilian freedom fighter who was the chief architect of Brazil's independence from Portugal.*

Star on one of its pivot points at the moment of birth
To follow one's common sense, even if this is the hardest path and goes against what is accepted and normal in the context of one's society. To be involved with sport, TV, daily tabloids and the like. *Jaya Prakash Narayan, Indian freedom fighter who was initially a defender of the use of physical force, but was won over to Gandhi's position of nonviolence.*

Physiological Correspondence: The muscles of the feet.

Ptolemy's location: The star below the knee in the left foot.

World Cities: nil at latitudes between 58^0 to 64^0 south.

Agena in paran with:

Sun: To have the common touch; to be in step with the masses. To be raised in a working class world and feel proud of it, and, or to have skills in dealing with the public in any profession.
• Matters to do with a popular person. *Sidney Nolan, 20th century Australian artist whose most famous painting depicts Ned Kelly (bushranger).*

Moon: To enjoy the ordinary things of life – sport, TV, daily papers; and to work hard or receive the help of another in order to gain an education or to improve one's life. To help others advance who are marginalised.   • The compassionate individual wins the day. *Chiang Kai-Shek, Chinese statesman who, in 1934, launched the "New Life Movement" to inculcate Confucian morals into the country and to promote Western hygiene.*

Mercury: One who works for the people or the public. To have a strong political slant to one's thinking.   • News stories which deal with the basic laws of society. *Rabindranath Tagore, Bengali poet who was awarded the Nobel Prize for Literature in 1913. His sympathy for the poverty of the Bengali people and their backwardness became the keynote of much of his writing.*

Venus: An individual whose ideas are accepted by many people. A natural popularity; to be considered good company, a bit of a rogue.   • Taking the popular, conforming pathway. *Sidney Nolan, see Agena in paran with the Sun.*

Mars: To be one who is geared to the needs and interests of ordinary people: the athlete in a popular sport; or the person who simply enjoys activities which are loved by many. ◆ A time when a single event can obsess the populace. *Azaria Chamberlain, the infant killed by a dingo in the Australian desert in 1980. Her death totally consumed the Australian people regarding the possible guilt of her mother.*

Jupiter: A person who gains nobility through simple, rural, or common folk, issues. To find pleasure in the simple things of life. ◆ A time when success can be gained by being "ordinary". *C.S. Forester, 19th century Egyptian born British author known for his novels "Horatio Hornblower" and "The African Queen".*

Saturn: A desire to influence the everyday lives of people. A desire to build something lasting, to pull together loose ends and make a lasting contribution. ◆ A leader emerges who has the common touch. *Achmed Sukarno, the first president of Indonesia (1945-66).*

Uranus: To have a political interest in helping one's community. Seeking to make a difference on a large social issue, to give the common folk a voice or to represent their ideas. ◆ A time when the community is gripped by sport or political issues. *Jane Doyle, a highly respected news presenter in Australian television.*

Neptune: A person who helps others or experiences times of hopelessness, dealing with seemingly lost causes but having the vision to see a way forward. Being drawn to religious beliefs which are based in simplicity of life. ◆ Leaders uphold the religion of the people. *Ramakrishna, a 19th century Indian holy man who, through his religious experiences, demonstrated the essential unity of all religions.*

Pluto: To influence the opinion of a large number of people, to want to help to change society's attitude to a subject through politics or demonstrations. ◆ A dramatic event changes the political or social attitudes of a nation. *Corazon Aquino, 20th century Philippine President who led a non-violent "people power" campaign that succeeded in overthrowing Marcos.*

The Node: To voice the dissatisfaction of the common folk. To see oneself as part of a struggle for greater rights for the silent majority. ◆ The popular opinion wins through. *Mohandas K. Gandhi, 20th century Indian leader whose pacifism swayed the population of India into unity.*

NOTES

1. Aratus, "Phaenomena," in *Callimachus, Hymns and Epigrams Lycohpron, Aratus*, Cambridge: Harvard University Press, 1989, p.241.

AL RESCHA

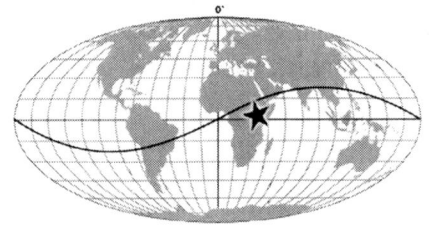

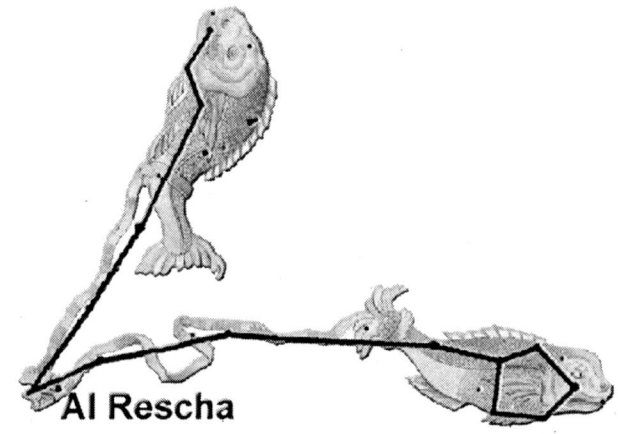

Constellation	Pisces
α Piscium, magnitude	4.33
1 January 2000 =	RA 2hr 02'02"
Declination	+02° 46'
Celestial longitude	29° ♈ 23'
Celestial latitude	09°S04'
BV Colour =	White

Pisces, the two fishes

Pisces began to receive the lead position in the zodiac around 2,000 years ago when the spring equinox heliacal rising stars slipped from Aries the Ram to Pisces the Fishes. However, this was never a clear distinction as Pisces is such a large constellation, and its two fish actually encompass the stars of Aries. The fish was an ancient symbol and the Greeks incorporated it as a form of Aphrodite *Salacia*, the fish-goddess. She was depicted as a fertile mother nursing a child and her temples always contained ponds of fish. Her followers would eat fish on her holy day which was Friday, a custom later adopted by the Catholic Church. To the Mesopotamians this was the area in the sky known as the Swallows (or the Tails) and Anunitu[1] the Babylonian goddess associated with childbirth.

Principle of Al Rescha, the Sacred Knot, the pulling together of ideas

This star takes its major symbolism from the concept of the knot. This is the joining point of the two fish of Pisces. It represents the point of contact between two types of knowledge: the joining of different ideas to create wisdom and understanding, or the marrying of two concepts to create a greater concept. This is a gentle star that indicates a tendency to seek different connections, to look at things in a different light, to join separate concepts in search of a greater understanding.

Heliacal Rising Star
To have the skill of being able to bring ideas and/or people together. A life-path which seeks different connections, to look at things in a different light. Being able to join separate concepts to gain a greater understanding. *Florence Nightingale, 19th century English reformer who created the nursing profession that we know today.*

Heliacal Setting Star
A person who finds solutions to old problems by making unusual connections; learning, through life's experience, that the answers are found by looking outside of the assumed area of the problem. To develop a skill for finding the perfect mix or blend. *Sir James Hardy, notable 20th century Australian wine maker.*

Star on one of its pivot points at the moment of birth
The everyday need to bring things together, whether people or ideas. To be interested in history or pursuing an interest in how things work. *Manning Clark, historian and author of the best-known general history of Australia, 'History of Australia', published between 1962 and 1987.*

Physiological Correspondence: The tendons and ligaments of the body, enabling agility and flexibility.

Ptolemy's location: The star marking the knot in the cord binding the two fishes.

World Cities: Kuala Lumpur, Malaysia; Singapore at latitudes between 0^0 to 4^0 north.

Al Rescha in paran with:

Sun: One who can solve problems by finding unusual or creative solutions. One who can be a mediator between groups.   ◆   A focus on a person who either unites or polarizes. *Henri Dunant, the founder of the Red Cross and the Young Men's Christian Association [YMCA].*

Moon: A love of diversity amongst one's friends. To seek enjoyment of a wide variety of foods, and of pleasures. Finding oneself acting as the bridge between different groups of friends.
◆   A period when one encounters a diversity of people and ideas. *Hans Christian Andersen, 19th century Danish author of children's fairy stories, considered one of the world's best story-tellers.*

Mercury: To take ideas from one world and use them in another; a lover of languages and being able to work with diverse groups.   ◆   Foreign news or policies affecting the domestic situation. *Matteo Ricci, 16th century Italian missionary who introduced Christianity to the Chinese empire and pioneered the beginnings of mutual understanding between China and the West.*

Venus: Insight into the hidden patterns of society, ideas, or places. A talent with financial markets, or simply a perceptive understanding of people.   ◆   A relationship problem is finally understood. *Maria Montessori, the originator of the educational system which bears her name, based on a child's creativity and natural willingness to learn.*

Mars: Being able to find unusual resources in order to achieve one's goals. To strive to achieve what others consider is impossible; to gain success by approaching the problem from a different angle. ◆ A time of linking two different ideas, objects or places. *Immanuel Velikovsky, 20th century American writer and proponent of controversial theories of cosmogony and history.*

Jupiter: An innovative thinker who sets a standard for others to follow. Being able to envision what can be achieved and find solutions to difficult problems in an unusual way. ◆ The success of the innovative idea. *Carl Jung, 20th century Swiss psychiatrist, one of the founding fathers of modern depth psychology.*

Saturn: A talent for putting one's ideas and dreams into practice. To be seen as a wise, spiritual or creative leader. ◆ A time where a leader needs to present the image of the wise old man or woman. *John Wesley, 18th century Anglican clergyman, evangelist, and founder of the Methodist movement in the Church of England.*

Uranus: To form unconventional relationships, to always have one eye on an escape route. A love of sociology or subjects focused on how society works. ◆ Rapid changes in the physical world, explosion or collapse. *Henry VIII, the Tudor king of England noted for the number of his wives and for the establishment of the Church of England.*

Neptune: A person who seeks their own "tribe", seeking to join together with others to help with the realization of a dream. ◆ People coming together for prayer or ritual. *Ivar Aasen, a fervent 19th century nationalist who created the "national language" called "Landsmal", later known as New Norwegian.*

Pluto: A person who is willing to confront or challenge the established ways, who wants to mix with different cultures. A person who takes a contra attitude. ◆ Groups joined together due to hardship or aggressive attacks. *George Eliot, 19th century female author who pushed against the social restrictions placed on women.*

The Node: To seek to give voice to perfection, to look for the elegant and beautiful, to try to bridge distances physically or mentally in one's life, to find a balance. ◆ An event brings unity. *John Keats, 19th century English poet who is best known for his lyrical verse and his search for perfection in poetry.*

NOTES

1. Black and Green, *Gods, Demons and Symbols of Ancient Mesopotamia*, p. 190.

ALCYONE

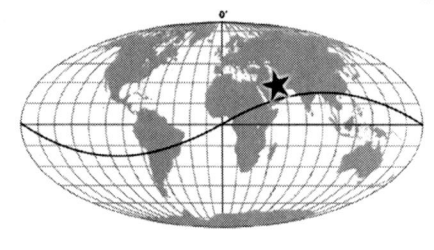
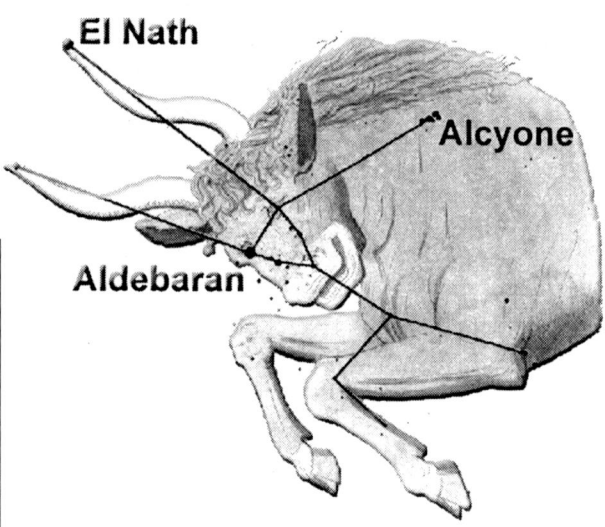

Constellation   Taurus
η Tauri, magnitude   2.87
1 January 2000 =   RA 3hr 47'29"
Declination   +24° 06'
Celestial longitude   00° Ⅱ 00'
Celestial latitude   04°N03'
BV Colour =   Blue-Green

The Pleiades, in Taurus, The Third Eye

The Pleiades is a cluster of seven stars in the shoulder of the Bull. These stars have had many names from "a bevy of Maidens" as described by Manlius[1], to the Chinese "Seven Sisters of Industry" and even a "Hen with her Chickens"[2]. To the Babylonians this group was known as "the Stars", as well as "the Seven Gods" who had the power to work against evil through magical incantations[3]. This cluster of stars was also used to mark the month of mourning for the dead, with prayers being said as it was seen to rise at sunset (acronychal rising); and this has been enshrined in All Hallows Eve (31 October), All Saints Day (1 November) and All Souls Day (2 November). In modern times many countries still use a set date in November for remembering those who die in war. (For more information see El-Nath and Aldebaran).

Principle of Alcyone, inner vision but judgemental

This star seeks the inner eye, the third eye. Alcyone is associated with a desire to seek inner knowledge and is linked to the Fates and the judgment of the dead. It is a star which suggests visionary and mystical abilities, but also a potential for ruthlessness or judgmental anger. It can be associated with great insight, but also narrow-mindedness.

Heliacal Rising Star

To have strong spiritual and visionary skills that weave through the very fabric of one's life. To have artistic or intuitive vision, but recognising that such vision has the shadow side of giving or receiving harsh judgment. To seek inner knowledge; the mystic who can be ruthless. *Colleen*

McCullough, 20th century New Zealand author and scientist noted for the depth of her research and intense style.

Heliacal Setting Star
Life's journey draws one into drama; to discover that one has a skill for handling intensity; to seek emotionally fraught situations as a way of fueling one's creativity. To experience moments of great insight under pressure. To become a critic. *Ludwig Van Beethoven, 18th century German composer renowned for the passion and drama of his music.*

Star on one of its pivot points at the moment of birth
A strong sense of knowing, a strong sense of destiny, a desire to walk the correct, if not the popular, pathway. An inner vision that can lead to a judgmental attitude. To work in areas charged with judgment or human drama. *Abraham Lincoln, the sixteenth US president, who was assassinated because of his anti-slavery views.*

Physiological Correspondence: The liver, stores the body's energy and filters out toxins.

Ptolemy's location: The brightest star of the Pleiades.

World Cities: Calcutta, India; Canton and Hong Kong, China; Havana, Cuba; Mazatlan, Mexico; at latitudes between 22° to 26° north.

Alcyone in paran with:

Sun: The ruthless visionary, a passionate but potentially arrogant person. A tendency to be harsh in the judgement of others, and thus a need to balance one's insights with compassion.   ♦   A ruthless situation, no mercy, no compassion. *Martin Luther, 15th century German reformer whose attacks on the abuses of the clergy precipitated the Protestant Reformation.*

Moon: Insightful into the darker side of life. A gift of insight and mysticism, but leading to encounters with both the best and the worst in human nature.   ♦   A crime of passion. *John Lennon, assassinated by a crazed fan, was the Beatles' rhythm guitarist and vocalist and a partner in the Lennon-McCartney song writing team.*

Mercury: To be insightful and brilliant, but struggling with the darker side of human nature. A ruthless entrepreneur, a persuasive orator.   ♦   A time of blind or angry obsession. *Peter Ilyich Tchaikovsky, leading 19th century Russian composer whose works are notable for their melodic inspiration and their orchestration.*

Venus: A love of theatre, art or rituals: the poetic soul. Seeking enchantment and wanting to make it part of the fabric of one's daily life. A poetic soul who will look for a life with mystical or magical meaning. ♦ A time of ritual. *Sun Myung Moon, 20th century founder of the Holy Spirit Association for the Unification of World Christianity. Moon's disciples are known as Moonies.*

Mars: To be aware and sensitive to difficult social issues. The critic, the commentator on social ills, one who is motivated to address the imbalances in the world. ♦ People become angry at injustices. *John Lennon – see Alcyone in paran with the Moon.*

Jupiter: A person who is passionate about human rights. To want to improve the world by promoting different practices or inventions. To seek the big solution, to watch the big picture. ♦ A time when brave reform is suggested. *Susan Anthony, 19th century English social reformer who was active in temperance and anti-slavery movements, and who later became a champion of women's rights.*

Saturn: The desire to re-shape the theological or political ideas of others. A need to place one's ideas, beliefs or visions into a satisfying shape or form. ♦ The law judges harshly a section of the community. *Gerardus Mercator, 16th century Flemish cartographer, geographer and mathematician best known for his mapping work in charting the globe.*

Uranus: To be judgemental of the establishment, or conversely, to be judgemental of those who challenge the establishment. ♦ An angry group in the community. *Charles I, 17th century English monarch whose autocratic rule and disputes with Parliament led to a civil war and his execution.*

Neptune: To have strong opinions on religious or artistic expression, to seek to correct imbalances within society. ♦ A time when those in need are treated harshly. *Sir Christopher Wren, 17th century English architect, who designed St Paul's Cathedral in the way he wished rather than acquiescing to the desires of the monarchy.*

Pluto: To act prematurely, to live with little regard for the law or the customs of one's culture; or to seek to change the laws. ♦ A fight against organised crime. *Jesse James, 19th century outlaw who, together with his brother Frank, became the most notorious outlaw of the American West.*

The Node: The political satirist, or commentator; to criticise one's own culture or to comment on the actions of those in power. ♦ The voice of disagreement. *Savinien Cyrano de Bergerac, 17th century French author who satirised the religious and scientific views of his era.*

NOTES

1. Marcus Manilius, *Astronomica*. Translated by G.P. Goold, Loeb Classical Library. (London: Harvard University Press. 1977) 4:518-520.
2. Richard Hinckley Allen, *Star Names Their Lore and Meaning*, New York: Dover Publications, Inc., 1963, p.393.
3. Black and Green, *Gods, Demons and Symbols of Ancient Mesopotamia*, p.162.

ALDEBARAN

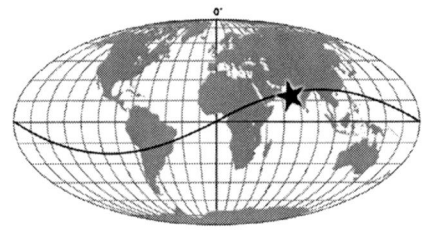

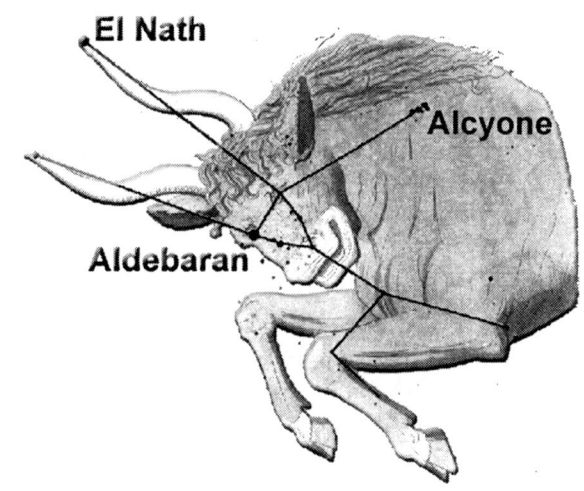

Constellation	Taurus
α Tauri, magnitude	0.85
1 January 2000 =	RA 4hr 35'56"
Declination	+16° 30'
Celestial longitude	09° II 47'
Celestial latitude	05°S28'
BV Colour =	Red

Taurus, the Bull

Taurus marked the vernal equinox from about 4,000 to 1700 BCE. To the Mesopotamians this was the Great Bull of Heaven, and was depicted in a winged form[1]. The bull was also sacred to the Egyptians who celebrated the birth of an Apis bull, a calf born with particular markings, seeing the animal as a living god. However, after two thousand years the spring equinox slipped from the stars of Taurus, the Bull, into the stars of Aries, The Ram, and the cults of the bull and the sacred calf slipped into history while another god, that of the ram or the lamb emerged. The Israelites distinguished their beliefs from other forms worship by using the blood of the lamb as a sacred fluid and symbol. In later mythology, the image of the bull took on a more negative essence as shown in the Greek myth of Jason, who had to tame a fiery bull in order to pass one of the tests towards claiming the Golden Fleece of Aries[2] (symbolic of the new incoming god). (For more information see Alcyone and El-Nath).

Principle of Aldebaran, the Eye of the Bull, integrity at all times

Aldebaran is one of the great stars in the sky. It is considered one of the Royal Stars of Persia, being the Watcher in the East, the cornerstone marking the spring equinox. In this capacity Aldebaran was the god Mithra, or Ahura Mazda, the slayer of the Cosmic Bull. Mithra was a military god who gave victories to his followers, but only if they followed the strictest procedure in his worship. Aldebaran's connection to Mithra, and the beliefs and customs linked to the god, imply that success will come but only through ethical integrity. Mithra also wore the title "lord of contracts". He considered all exchanges as sacred and oversaw the business of his followers, insisting on their honesty and purity. If they failed, they would be condemned to an ordeal of fire.

Heliacal Rising Star
To hold strong principles, ethics, and beliefs which will, however, be challenged. Success and personal strength coming from the ability to live by one's principles. To be guided by one's principles and integrity. *William Butler Yeats, 19th century Irish poet, who maintained his commitment to Irish literature.*

Heliacal Setting Star
To reject one's family beliefs and seek one's own. To look for and eventually find a set of principles to which one can dedicate one's life, whether political, religious, scientific or sociological. *Robert Menzies, longest serving Australian Prime Minister (1939-41, 1949-66) who founded the Australian conservative party (Liberals).*

Star on one of its pivot points at the moment of birth
To face moral dilemmas which challenge one's integrity and honesty on a daily basis. To depend on one's principles and integrity as the compass and foundation of life. To be the noble warrior. *Bruce Lee, 20th century US martial arts master who bought martial arts into western awareness.*

Physiological Correspondence: The hypothalamus – controller of bodily temperature and fluid balance.

Ptolemy's location: The bright red star in the Hyades in the southern eye.

World Cities: Dakar, Senegal; Guatemala City, Guatemala; Kingston, Jamaica; Manila, Philippines; Rangoon, Myanmar at latitudes between 14° to 18° north.

Aldebaran in paran with:

Sun: To gain success, respect, and a reputation for one's honesty. A person who will maintain honour and integrity at all costs.   ♦   A military event. *Abraham Lincoln, 16th US President considered to have established the values of that republic.*

Moon: Physically gifted, or a lover of nature. Emotionally drawn to causes which one sees as noble and just.   ♦   Environmental concerns, people needing to look after each other and the land. *John James Audubon, 19th century US ornithologist and bird artist whose work promoted the conservation of bird life around the world.*

Mercury: The noble thinker, the person with integrity, one who will take on noble projects. A naturalist with a strong sense of faith in themselves.   ♦   News of environmental issues. *Johann Voss, 18th century German poet remembered chiefly for his translations of Homer.*

Venus: The social commentator, or creative person who is accepted by society. A background in the arts, or an appreciation of the nature and needs of society. ◆ A time of community awareness on social and/or environmental issues. *Auguste Rodin, 19th century French sculptor; his massive statues, including "The Thinker", contributed to his reputation as the greatest portraitist in the history of sculpture.*

Mars: The successful craftsperson; to gain success through decisive action. To appreciate physical talent, and to understand that clear, focused action produces one's best results. ◆ A person is portrayed as the noble soldier. *Neil Armstrong, first man to walk on the Moon, on 21 July 1969.*

Jupiter: Success in large and noble projects. To dedicate oneself to the big picture for the good of one's culture or society. ◆ The success of a noble project. *William Penn, 17th century English Quaker leader who oversaw the founding of the colony of the Commonwealth of Pennsylvania.*

Saturn: To be politically aware, to make comment. Dedicated to putting one's ideas into practice, to make things happen and bring about lasting change. ◆ A planned military action revealed. *George Stephenson, 18th century English engineer and principal inventor of the railroad locomotive.*

Uranus: To defend a social issue, to work towards maintaining the integrity of one's cultural heritage, to feel spiritually linked to the principles that hold one's society together. ◆ The people are asked to act with dignity and social awareness. *Leonie Adams, 20th century US poet whose verse interprets emotions and nature with an almost mystical vision.*

Neptune: To have strong social ideals centred on minority groups, or minority issues. To dedicate one's life to a seemingly hopeless but noble cause. ◆ A natural disaster. *Mao Tse-Tung, 20th century Chinese statesman who was a founding member of the Chinese Communist Party.*

Pluto: To believe that strong action is required to maintain one's beliefs. To defend one's principles in battle, physically or mentally. ◆ Aggressive military action. *Manfred Baron von Richthofen (The Red Baron), WWI German flying ace.*

The Node: To feel that one is the symbol, voice or representative of an idea. To preach or act in a way to promote an idea. ◆ A time of strong leadership. *Matteo Ricci, 16th century Italian missionary who introduced Christianity to the Chinese empire and lived there for 30 years.*

NOTES

1. Black and Green, *Gods, Demons and Symbols of Ancient Mesopotamia*, p.49.
2. Thomas Bulfinch, *Myths of Greece and Rome*, New York: Penguin, 1979, p.153.

ALDERAMIN

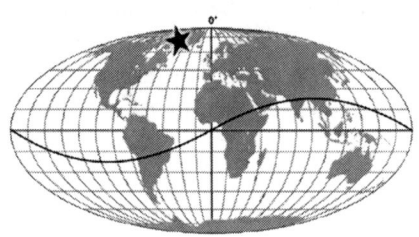

Constellation	Cepheus
α Cepheii, magnitude	2.44
1 January 2000 =	
RA	21hr 18' 33"
Declination	+62° 35'
Celestial longitude	12° ♈ 46'
Celestial latitude	68°N55'
BV Colour =	White

Cepheus, The King

Cepheus is a member of the royal family which orbits close to the North Pole. Its origins are lost in prehistory. Aratus, in the 4th century BCE, along with the general belief of the day, considered this king to be of Euphratean origin[1]. In this way the constellation filled the role of "the King" in many cultures. The Chinese allocated this area of the sky to the "Inner Throne of the Five Emperors"[2]. The medieval Christians called him King Solomon. Cepheus occupied the pole star position between 21,000 and 19,000 BCE and more than likely gained its leadership role in that period. It will not return to that predominant role until around 7,500 CE.

Principle of Alderamin, the King, honour and good leadership

Alderamin symbolizes a balanced male energy, in harmony with the feminine and the earth, but within the context of the focused, concentrated energy of masculinity, rather than the more passive, intuitive energy of the feminine. It is the version of kingship represented in Celtic myths of the king who willingly returns his body to the soil in order to fertilise his culture. Strong but in harmony with life. This star is associated with gentle power, focused and forceful but not aggressive.

Heliacal Rising Star

To be a source of peaceful strength which becomes one of the foundations of life. To know that the greatest benefits and success coming through gentle determination, rather than undertaking dramatic aggressive action. *Antonio Crespo, 19th century Brazilian poet who is known for seeking intellectual perfection without falling into romantic sentimentality.*

Heliacal Setting Star
To learn that strength and dignity provides the most productive pathway. To model oneself on examples of dignity and strength in history or literature, to find success when one acts with dignity. *Mohandas K. Gandhi, 19th century Indian statesman who advocated pacifism and the sanctity of all living things.*

Star on one of its pivot points at the moment of birth
A lifestyle based on quiet dignity and the firm but gentle use of power. To work in a way that uses strong power but through gentle hands. *Julie Newmar, US actress who played Cat Woman in the Batman movies.*

Physiological Correspondence: The eliminative organs, their essential role in clearing waste from the body.

Ptolemy's location: The star in the right shoulder.

World Cities: Helsinki, Finland; Reykjavik, Iceland at latitudes between $60°$ to $64°$ north.

Alderamin in paran with:

Sun: To be a person which identifies themselves with an idea and works toward its protection or propagation. To be noted for one's dignity and honour. ◆ A time to act with dignity. *Anne Frank, child author who is known for the diary she kept for two years while in hiding from Nazi persecution.*

Moon: To be a leader of people or a promoter of ideals. To care about or work for those who are disempowered. To earn respect for one's dedication. ◆ The natural leader emerges. *Henry Ford, US industrialist who revolutionized factory production by introducing the assembly line as well as welfare for his workforce.*

Mercury: To have quiet confidence, to maintain integrity in business dealings. To bring a quiet confidence, dignity and gentle, persistent determination to one's work. ◆ A period when honour and dignity matter. *Ayn Rand, 20th century US writer (born in Russia) noted for presenting her philosophy of objectivism which emphasises that all real achievement is the product of individual ability and effort.*

Venus: A person with a self-confident attitude; talented in design, the arts, or movement. To look for dignity and loyalty in one's relationships. ◆ A focus on the self-made person. *Bjorn Borg, Swedish tennis champion renowned for his calm focused control.*

Mars: To want to be involved in a noble cause; to play the game with dignity. To want to act in a dignified manner and to be the noble warrior. ◆ A noble sportsman or performer speaks out.

Florenz Ziegfeld, 19th century American theatrical producer who brought the revue to spectacular heights under the slogan "Glorifying the American Girl."

Jupiter: A tendency to glorify the past or to have an idealist illusion of the future. One who can create illusions by using a profile of dignity and believability. ♦ The moral high ground is promoted. *Jean Eugene Robert-Houdin, 19th century French performer considered to be the father of modern conjuring and established the idea and image of the stage magician.*

Saturn: A person with a conservative nature who prefers to move forward in established ways. A tendency for pessimism. ♦ The traditional conservative attitude prevails. *Thomas Hardy, 19th century English author whose main works were all tragedies increasingly pessimistic in tone.*

Uranus: To link oneself with community or social causes, to be able to represent the common people, to see the dignity in commonly held beliefs. ♦ A popular leader emerges, a leader of the people. *Gustave Eiffel, 19th century French engineer who built the, now iconic, Eiffel Tower.*

Neptune: A pacifist, to treat others with dignity. To maintain dignity in the face of corruption. ♦ A time when a leader falls from grace or a noble hero emerges. *Harriet Beecher Stowe, 19th century US author whose work, Uncle Tom's Cabin, contributed much to popular feeling against slavery.*

Pluto: To do everything in one's power to bring nobility to a time in history, an invention, a future ideal or an idea. To give honour to those who bring forth the noble idea. ♦ A period when a strong focus is needed. *Sir Leonard Woolley, 19th century British archaeologist whose excavation of the ancient Sumerian city of Ur (in modern Iraq) greatly advanced knowledge of ancient Mesopotamian civilization.*

The Node: To be a spokesperson for the need for dignity in one's society, to endeavour to instil in others the noble pathway, to believe that one is in a superior position. ♦ A leader plays the king. *Oliver Cromwell, the leader of the parliamentary forces during the English Civil Wars, and Lord Protector during the period of the Commonwealth from 1653-1658.*

NOTES

1. Aratus, "Phaenomena," p.221.
2. Jobes and Jobes, *Outer Space: Myths, Name Meanings, Calendars*, p.149.

ALGOL

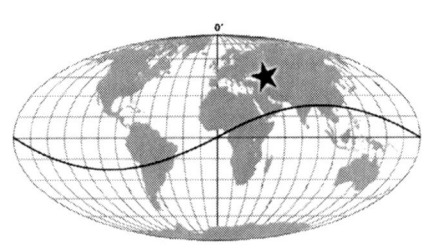

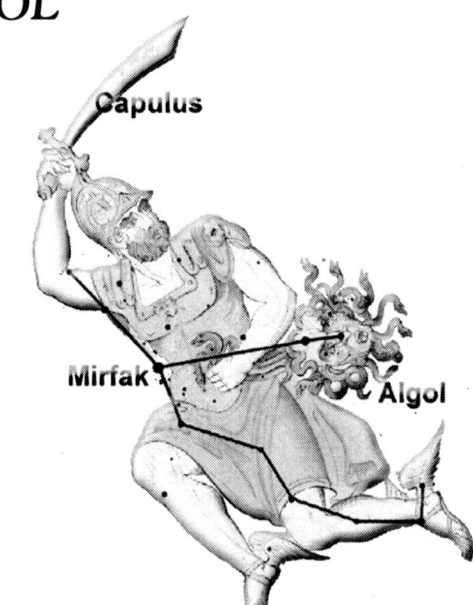

Constellation	Perseus
β Persei, magnitude	2.12
1 January 2000 =	RA 3hr 08' 10"
Declination	+40° 57'
Celestial longitude	26° ♉ 10'
Celestial latitude	22°N26'
BV Colour =	Blue-Green

Perseus, who holds the Head of the Beast

Placed just south of Andromeda, he stands facing Andromeda with his foot on the Milky Way. In the Mesopotamian sky he was known as "the old man"[1]. To the Hebrews he was known as Ham, son of Noah. But in Egyptian cosmology he is Khem, the young black son of Cepheus the king[2]. Perseus can also be seen in the Greek mould as the conquering hero saving the damsel in distress (Andromeda), with his raised sword and holding his prize of Medusa's head. Or we can see him as part of the natural balance of the celestial royal family: Andromeda's suitor, young, masculine, full of male energy symbolised by his raised sword like a huge phallus, holding in his hand the head of an animal or the head of an enemy as his offering, his hunting prize. (For more information see Capulus and Mirfak).

Principle of Algol, the head of the beast, intense focused passion

Algol was called Ras al Ghul by the Arabs (the Head of the Demon), and they considered this demon to be the wife of the Devil. The Chinese called the star *Tseih She,* meaning Piled-up Corpses[3]. In Talmudic Law she is the first wife of Adam, Lilith, who left him because she refused to be submissive to his needs. Lilith then fled Paradise and became a demon of the wind. She was considered a curse, as she contained sexual pleasure and was the cause of all male wet dreams. Algol came to embody everything that men feared in the feminine. She is not the mother face of the goddess but rather the passionate lover or the whore. She is female kundalini energy. This star contains immense female passion and power, or the potential power of Mother Nature, strong but not evil.

Heliacal Rising Star
To take the path of intensity and drama, to follow the road that contains the most passion, to seek strong emotional relationships as a way of life. *Errol Flynn, Australian actor who was the dashing hero on screen in 1930s and 40s and led a freewheeling, hedonistic lifestyle off screen.*

Heliacal Setting Star
To find oneself in passionate or intense situations, to learn that in times of human crisis one has the skills to stay calm. In later life to involve oneself in intense situations in pursuit of one's needs. *George Armstrong Custer, 19th century US Military office who led his men to their death in one of the most controversial battles against the native people in the history of the USA.*

Star on one of its pivot points at the moment of birth
Embracing a hard physical life where one pits oneself against the elements, constantly seeking challenges; the athletic or physical person or a life of fighting against injustice, either for oneself or for others. *Mark Spitz, US swimming champion who won seven gold medals in the 1972 Olympics.*

Physiological Correspondence: The endocrine system and its hormones, one's moods.

Ptolemy's location: The bright star in the head of the Gorgon.

World Cities: Ankara, Turkey; Barcelona and Madrid, Spain; Beijing, China; Naples and Rome, Italy; Sofia, Bulgaria at latitudes between $39°$ to $43°$ north.

Algol in paran with:

Sun: To passionately link oneself to an idea or cause, to destroy or create, to seek the edge of change. Knowing no limits to one's desire for intensity.   ♦   Passion that can inspire or destroy. *Adolf Hitler, as negative example, but also Gregor Mendel, 19th century Czech monk whose work with peas allowed him to discover the basis of genetics.*

Moon: Plagued by personal tragedies, one's own, or other people's. To have a strong social conscience.   ♦   A time of melancholy, sadness or loss. *Mary Wollstonecraft, 18th century English writer, noted for being a passionate advocate of educational and social equality for women.*

Mercury: Forthright, empathic, emotionally pondering. A tendency to be brooding and possessive of others, while at the same time a deep interest in different cultures. The passionate, intense writer or communicator.   ♦   Emotional issues abound. *Isabelle Allende, 20th century Chilean novelist who deals with intense human emotional issues.*

Venus: A turbulent personal life which leads to an interest in other people and their problems. Social reform; to be a victim or a saviour.   ♦   Rumours or slander abound. *Marie Stopes, advocate of birth control who, in 1921, founded the United Kingdom's first instructional clinic for contraception.*

Mars: Encountering crisis situations through actions motivated by one's intense passion. An obsession which may lead to a destructive situation but can also yield great creativity. ♦ A constructive, but also destructive, situation emerges. *Horace Wells, American dentist who pioneered anaesthesia for surgery. He was ridiculed for his work and eventually committed suicide.*

Jupiter: To move towards the fulfilment of one's beliefs with little regard for social subtleties, niceties or protocol. An obsession with power, whether political, physical or spiritual. ♦ A time when an unpopular but truthful voice is head. *Jeanne d'Arc, 15th century woman who commanded the French army in the defeat of the English.*

Saturn: A person who establishing new boundaries through a desire to undertake difficult tasks. Having the courage to ask the hard questions. ♦ The law needing to concern itself with ethical issues. *Hanna Reitsch, the leading female German pilot of WWII and the first woman to be awarded the Iron Cross.*

Uranus: To be upset at injustices towards those who have no power. To seek to help in some way people or animals who have suffered. ♦ A person tries to take or claim power over a community. *Billy Graham, US career evangelist, considered the most influential spiritual advisor of US 20th century society.*

Neptune: To have a strong belief or a spiritual passion; an artistic or creative drive which is an obsession and a willingness to take on large projects. ♦ People are uplifted in body and soul. *Raffaello Sanzio (Raphael), Italian artist who was one of the master painters and architects of the Italian Renaissance.*

Pluto: One who is prepared to work with or encounter the more shadowy side of society. Willing to engage in unfashionable subjects. ♦ Assassination, to kill one's enemies. *Henri Toulouse-Lautrec, 19th century French artist who painted the activities in the brothels of Paris.*

The Node: To represent the intense or the sexual elements within one's community. To give voice to the passion of the common people; to be interested in the sexual, passionate life of society. ♦ Sexuality or scandal in the news. *Susan Anthony, 19th century US social reformer active in temperance and anti-slavery movements and a champion of women's rights.*

NOTES

1. Hermann Hunger, *Astrological Reports to Assyrian Kings*, Helsinki: Helsinki University Press, 1992, p.121.
2. Jobes and Jobes, *Outer Space: Myths, Name Meanings, Calendars*, p.227.
3. Allen, *Star Names Their Lore and Meaning*, p.332.

ALHENA

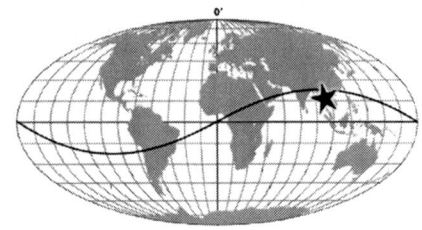

Constellation	Gemini
γ Geminorum, magnitude	1.93
1 January 2000 =	RA 6hr 37' 43"
Declination	+16° 24'
Celestial longitude	09° ♋ 06'
Celestial latitude	06°S45'
BV Colour =	White

Gemini, the Twins
Known as the twins in most ancient writings, these two companion stars and their resulting constellation embody the wonder of twins in the human psyche. Dylan and Lleu, twin powers of dark and light, were born from Arianhrod the Celtic goddess of the Star Wheel[1]. Ahura Mazda and Ahriman were God and Devil born simultaneously from Zurvan's womb in Zoroastrian mythology. In the bible it is Cain and Abel. For the Egyptians, the god of the Morning Star and light was Horus and the God of the Evening Star was his evil brother Set, who was darkness and was also connected to the never-setting circumpolar stars[2]. (For more information see Castor and Pollux).

Principle of Alhena, the One Who Marches, to promote an idea
This star carries both the concept of the *Proudly Marching One* and the tradition of the god with the wounded heel[3]. The Egyptians believed that, at the solstice and equinox, the Sun god touched the earth and thus connected himself to the physical world wounding his heel in the process. Alhena came to represent the heel of an immortal or sacred one who touches the earth with great pride. It is associated with the following of a cause, a belief for which one will "march". This marching may bring pain at some level, but it is a pain embraced with the pride and love associated with the desire to link oneself to an ideal.

Heliacal Rising Star
To person born with a strong sense of purpose, to align oneself with a mission or an idea, to have a vocation which guides one's life. To have a talent in speaking out. *Ida Wells-Barnet, a black American journalist who led an anti-lynching crusade in the United States in the 1890s.*

Heliacal Setting Star
To be propelled by circumstances to take action and to learn to speak out. Finding that one cannot ignore a situation and feeling thus "pushed" into taking a stand. *Samuel Alexander, 19th century philosopher whose growing concern for the situation of European Jewry led him to be involved with the idea of a Jewish homeland.*

Star on one of its pivot points at the moment of birth
To be wounded by words, to physically embody, or become the embodiment of, one's beliefs. To work in a field that requires one to speak out. *Martin Luther, 15th century religious reformer whose beliefs established the Lutheran Church.*

Physiological Correspondence: The heel, the feet – the quality of one's gait.

Ptolemy's location: The star in the heel of the left foot of the western twin, Pollux.

World Cities: Dakar, Senegal; Guatemala City, Guatemala; Kingston, Jamacia; Manila, Philippines; Rangoon, Myanmar at latitudes between 14° to 18° north.

Alhena in paran with:

Sun: A person who has a desire for a mission, to be seek to be identified with a cause. To lead a life engaged in large or difficult tasks; to feel lost without a goal or purposeful journey.   ◆   A leader with a mission is revealed. *Margaret Thatcher, first woman to become British Prime Minister, who unflinchingly reformed British industry and society.*

Moon: To have a vocation or desire to guide or help people. To be motivated by humanitarian issues rather than one's own personal needs.   ◆   A common mission or goal emerges. *Madame Blavatsky, 19th century spiritualist who brought a new religious message and was the founder of the Theosophical Society.*

Mercury: To have a voice, to demand the right to be heard. A natural business sense in service to the realisation of ideas, philosophies and concepts.   ◆   Some injustice or swindle comes to light. *Emily Balch, American leader of the women's movement for peace during and after World War I.*

Venus: A unique attitude to beauty or fashion, to have individual taste and not following general fashions or social values.   ◆   Matters of social reform are in the news. *Margaret Sanger, 19th century social reformer, founder of the birth control movement in the USA.*

Mars: To believe that action speaks louder than words; to have strong politically ideas and/or to be one who leads others into action. ◆ A time of political activists. *Jeanne d'Arc, 15th century woman who commanded the French army in defeating the English.*

Jupiter: The scholar or explorer. A desire to explore the world intellectually or physically. To seek insights into spiritual beliefs. To be an avid reader or information gatherer. ◆ A person acts with strong belief. *Henry the Navigator, 14th century Portuguese patron noted for his support of voyages of discovery to the New World.*

Saturn: A social architect, one who can create new social systems. A person who seeks practical solutions to social problems or the expression of ideas. ◆ New ideas or policies for social reform. *Peter the Great, 17th century Russian Czar who was responsible for extending Russian borders and engaging Russia in the wider European world.*

Uranus: A person who takes the position of a contra; to protest, actively or intellectually, against the established system. To be involved in public parades, meetings and marches, or to work outside of the system. ◆ A time of protest. *Bugsy Siegel, 20th century US gangster and crime boss who initially developed Las Vegas as a gambling Mecca.*

Neptune: To shake the status quo in art, literature or popular culture. To have a strong desire to express different opinions through art and poetry, or in virtual communities or media. ◆ Ground-shaking times. *Giacomo Torelli, 17th century Italian designer whose development of theatre machinery provided the basis for modern theatrical devices.*

Pluto: To have the ability to shift the very foundations of a people's belief structure. The one who brings in change and new systems to their family or community. ◆ A shift of foundations, people take a different path of action. *Rene Descartes, 17th century philosopher, known as the "Father of Modern Philosophy".*

The Node: A person who is an instrument of change, willing or unwilling. To find oneself being swept along by the tide of circumstances. ◆ A key point in time and place, where the events have a lasting effect. *James Naismith, 19th century Canadian credited with inventing the game of basketball.*

NOTES

1. Green, *Dictionary of Celtic Myth and Legend*, p.34.
2. Norman Lockyer, *The Dawn of Astronomy*, Kila, MT: Kessinger, 1892, p.146.
3. Allen, *Star Names Their Lore and Meaning*, p.234.

ALKES

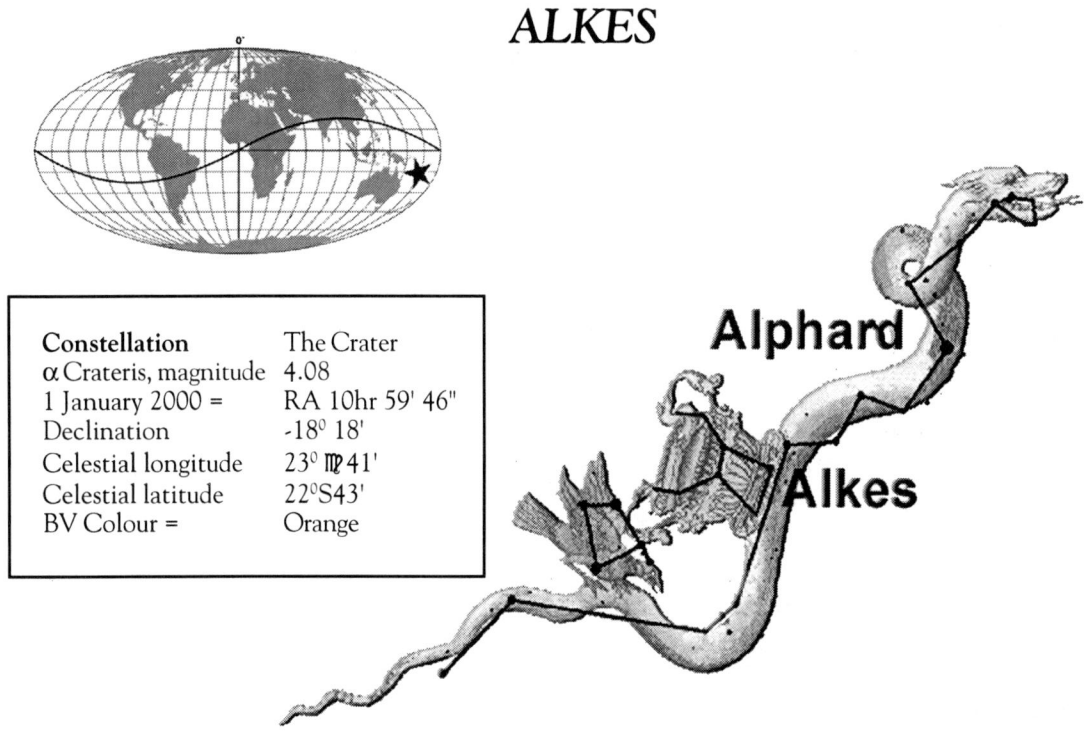

Constellation	The Crater
α Crateris, magnitude	4.08
1 January 2000 =	RA 10hr 59' 46"
Declination	-18° 18'
Celestial longitude	23° ♍ 41'
Celestial latitude	22°S43'
BV Colour =	Orange

Crater, the Crater or the Cup

The cup sits on the back of the Hydra, who guards it from the ever-thirsty Corvus the Raven. Historically considered the constellation Hydra et Corvus et Crater, but modern cataloguing has broken it into its three asterisms. The Greeks thought of it as the Cup in which Icarus stored his sacred wine and also the prophetic Well of Apollo[1]. In this sense the constellation of the Cup represented for many cultures the concept of the Sacred or Holy Cup, be it the Well of Apollo, the skull as a prophetic drinking vessel to the Celts, the Cauldron of Bran, the Holy Grail of Christian mythology or the Lamp of Aladdin. It is the "Cup" with all its symbolism. The vessel that holds life and is therefore sacred.

Principle of Alkes, the cup, to carry something precious

Alkes is the alpha star of the crater, and carries the symbolism of the sacred cup. It is thus associated with people who have a spiritual, mystical and even prophetic nature. It implies that something precious is being carried by the individual and this can be an idea, a vocation, a philosophy, artistic expression or even the individual's family genes. The presence of Alkes in a chart indicates that one is the inheritor of something precious.

Heliacal Rising Star
To be the living vessel of a sacred body of knowledge or philosophy and to know that your life is about the "precious" thing you carry. This may be an idea, a talent or even a prophetic gift. To feel born into an idea or situation. *Annie Besant, 19th century UK reformer who is best known for her work with the Theosophical Society, as well as her promotion of self-rule for India.*

Heliacal Setting Star
To be given a precious gift which will prove to be both a joy and a responsibility. A discovered talent, or to be handed another person's work needing completion. *Sir Robert Helpmann, 20th century Australian ballet dancer and choreographer who began his career by working with both Pavlova and later Margot Fonteyn.*

Star on one of its pivot points at the moment of birth
To be seen as representing a concept or archetype and so to carry a projection for others. To struggle to be seen as oneself. One's work can overpower one's life. *Albert Einstein, 19th century German physicist who produced the theory of relativity.*

Physiological Correspondence: The ovaries or testes – the quality of one's genetic material.

Ptolemy's location: The bright star in the base of the Cup, common with the Water-snake.

World Cities: La Paz, Bolivia; Tananarive, Madagascar at latitudes between 16^0 to 20^0 south.

Alkes in paran with:

Sun: A person who is a vessel, one who caries something for others. To hold something for others, be it story-telling, art, music, insights, or visions.   ♦   A national treasure is revealed. *Charles Perrault, French author known for his collection of stories for children, first published in French and then in English in 1729 as "Tales of Mother Goose".*

Moon: A love and empathy for life and nature. Being drawn to biology, anthropology or any subject which explores the wonders of life.   ♦   A time when one must focus on what can be saved. *Betty Williams, Northern Irish peace activist who co- founded the Community for Peace People and shared the 1976 Nobel Prize for Peace.*

Mercury: To undertake detailed and precise work. A careful thinker who is at their best when allowed to plan, think and execute all in their own time.   ♦   A far reaching news item. *Charles Darwin, 19th century naturalist who established and documented the theory of evolution which eventually became known as "Darwinism".*

Venus: Someone with strong social values whose opinions can influence others. To be interested in fashion, art or social customs. A unique way of seeing human life; to champion human rights and to contribute insights as well as reform.   ◆   A time of looking to the future needs of others. *Queen Elizabeth II, current English monarch who has upheld the dignity and tradition of the monarchy in changing times.*

Mars: To take action to achieve and protect one's ideals. To want to give safety or to build security, not just for oneself but also for loved ones. To support different charities which align with one's philosophies.   ◆   The protection of an idea. *Germane Greer, 20th century leading feminist writer and educator.*

Jupiter: To be the physical representation of an ideal. A desire to provide a safe haven for people or ideas.   ◆   A time when the popular or cherished wins through. *Charles Atlas, body builder who became popularly known as "America's Most Perfectly Developed Man".*

Saturn: To be the source of new methods or doctrines. One's actions become a foundation onto which others can build.   ◆   A vessel is broken, the laws, or leaders, are changed. *Robert de Sorbon, 13th century French theologian, who was the founder of the Sorbonne, now identified with the University of Paris.*

Uranus: To hold a special place in people's hearts or carry a popular message aimed at challenging the establishment.   ◆   A period where the popular rather than the powerful win through. *J.K Rowling, 20th century UK author of the best-selling Harry Potter series of books.*

Neptune: To be handed both a sweet and bitter cup. To gain something magical and at other times to lose something precious. To be able to bring magic to others, in the real or virtual world.   ◆   A time of fantasy. *Anna Pavlova, 19th century Russian dancer who was a prima ballerina in 1906.*

Pluto: To be awed and humbled by the emerging story of life. To lose oneself to a larger theme in history: to be a part of a story, rather then being the story.   ◆   A perpetual flame is lit, to remember fallen heroes. *Billie Holiday, 20th century US Jazz singer, whose work reflected the struggle with race issues and her personal struggle with drugs.*

The Node: To align oneself in order to represent a sacred issue, to carry the flame of an idea, to seek to inspire others to carry an idea forward in time, noble or not.   ◆   A person is seen to represent many. *George Washington, 18th century American statesman and first president of the United States.*

NOTES

1.   Jobes and Jobes, *Outer Space: Myths, Name Meanings, Calendars*, p.161.

ALNILAM

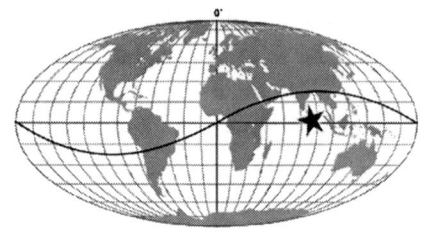

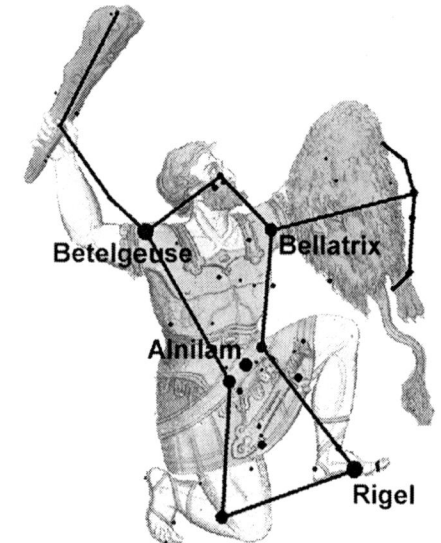

Constellation	Orion
ε Orionis, magnitude	1.70
1 January 2000 =	RA 5hr 36' 13"
Declination	-01° 12'
Celestial longitude	23° ♊ 28'
Celestial latitude	24°S30'
BV Colour =	Blue-Green

Orion, the Hunter

The Egyptians considered this constellation to be a divine being, with the Pharaohs being his physical incarnation. However, the effects of precession caused Orion to slip lower and lower in the sky at the time of the commencement of the Egyptian year and, to account for these observations, the Egyptians developed the concept of an immortal god dying and passing on his throne to his son[1]. For the Mesopotamians this was the Great Shepherd of Anu, guarding the great flocks of the sky[2]. However, several thousand years or so later the Greeks took Orion and turned him into a giant, an unwelcome admirer of Artemis. Artemis in turn created a giant Scorpion who stung him on the foot, causing him to go blind. But he regained his sight by watching the sunrise[3]. (For more information see Bellatrix, Betelgeuse and Rigel).

Principle of Alnilam, the Belt of Orion, to hold things together

This is the bright buckle of the belt of the god or great shepherd and the star is symbolically linked with pulling things together. This is the skill of taking what is already known, and improving and/or expanding the subject in such a way that a new foundation is laid. Alnilam is not associated with fame or recognition but is linked rather with the steady, reliable plod that can produce well-grounded, long lasting work.

Heliacal Rising Star

To understand that one's life is linked to healing something or completing something. To fill a gap, and thus having a desire to compete a story. To want to join things together to make something larger then its parts. *Richard Branson, 20th century English entrepreneur whose success is grounded in exploiting market gaps.*

Heliacal Setting Star
Being compelled by life events to find solutions to problems in unusual places, being able to think "outside the square". Finding fulfilment by placing oneself in alien situations. *Henry Handel Richardson, 19th century female Australian author who wrote "The Getting of Wisdom" which focuses on the theme of an outsider trying to come to terms with an alien culture.*

Star on one of its pivot points at the moment of birth
To be a living bridge between one world and another, one life and another. To find success through attention to detail, and use this success to portray an idea, or another person – the actor. *Marlon Brando, US actor who is widely regarded as one of the most influential actors of all time and renowned for his meticulously detailed "system" acting.*

Physiological Correspondence: Hips and pelvis – strength and stability of lower back.

Ptolemy's location: The middle star in Orion's belt.

World Cities: Belem, Brazil; Guayaquil, Ecuador; Nairobi, Kenya, at latitudes between $1°$ north to $3°$ south.

Alnilam in paran with:

Sun: A person who builds bridges between ideas or people. To have an ability to see or understand problems in a new light. ◆ A team leader steps forward. *Ludwig Zamenhof, Russian physician who created the international artificial language, Esperanto.*

Moon: One who can solve life's everyday problems. To look for unique solutions to daily problems. To build a reputation for providing new approaches to old problems. ◆ A time when the fabric of society is stressed. *John Montagu 4th Earl of Sandwich, who created the idea of the sandwich.*

Mercury: An intellectual desire to understand ways by which ideas or philosophies can be linked together. The desire to establish links between disparate ideas. ◆ An original thinker emerges. *H.G. Wells, English novelist, journalist, sociologist, and historian, best known for science fiction such as "The Time Machine" and "The War of the Worlds".*

Venus: A strong sense of rhythm and timing, whether physically or socially, a good negotiator or mediator. To understand the creative nature of connections between different ideas or groups of people. ◆ A time when the combining of different resources is done for the common good. *Alfred Bernhard Nobel, 19th century industrialist who is better known for his establishment of the Nobel Prize.*

Mars: To love physical challenges and to actively seek mental or physical gaps to be bridged. A proactive problem-solver. ◆ A group endeavour to solve a problem. *Gasparo Angiolini, 18th century Italian ballet master who was one of the first to integrate dance, music and plot in dramatic ballets.*

Jupiter: A person who can successfully bridge the gap between one social status and another. ◆ A time of cultural exchange. *Mack Sennett, US film maker who created the Keystone Cops and developed slapstick comedy for film.*

Saturn: The ability to find different physical or practical solutions to problems; to excel where others may not even see that a solution is possible. Being able to hold things together where others fail. ◆ Victory to those with the most resources. *Boris Spassky, Soviet chess master, world champion from 1969 to 1972.*

Uranus: To work in a field that helps establish better communication between different ideas or cultures. To be good at solving people problems – work or social needs. ◆ Developments in popular culture. *Oliver Evans, 19th century US industrialist who created the first fully operational production line.*

Neptune: Being able to bring dreams into reality, to move from the magical realm to the practical, the impossible to the possible. A person who can give a dream a practical expression. ◆ Groups disband. *Jules Verne, 19th century French author whose writings laid much of the foundation for modern science fiction.*

Pluto: A person who can polarize a group; someone who is aware of the power, for creativity or destructiveness, of the inherent differences in or between groups. To separate things. ◆ A polarizing time, us versus them. *Cyrus McCormick, 19th century US farmer known as the inventor of the mechanical reaper.*

The Node: To involve one's life with the differences between groups, either by being different oneself or by helping those who struggle to deal with differences. ◆ A time when differences are being highlighted. *Dorothea Dix, 19th century US social reformer who was dedicated to the plight of those with a mental illness.*

NOTES

1. J.B. Sellers, *The Death of Gods in Ancient Egypt*, London: Penguin, 1992, p.170.
2. Black and Green, *Gods, Demons and Symbols of Ancient Mesopotamia*, p.190.
3. Bulfinch, *Myths of Greece and Rome*, p.238.

ALPHARD

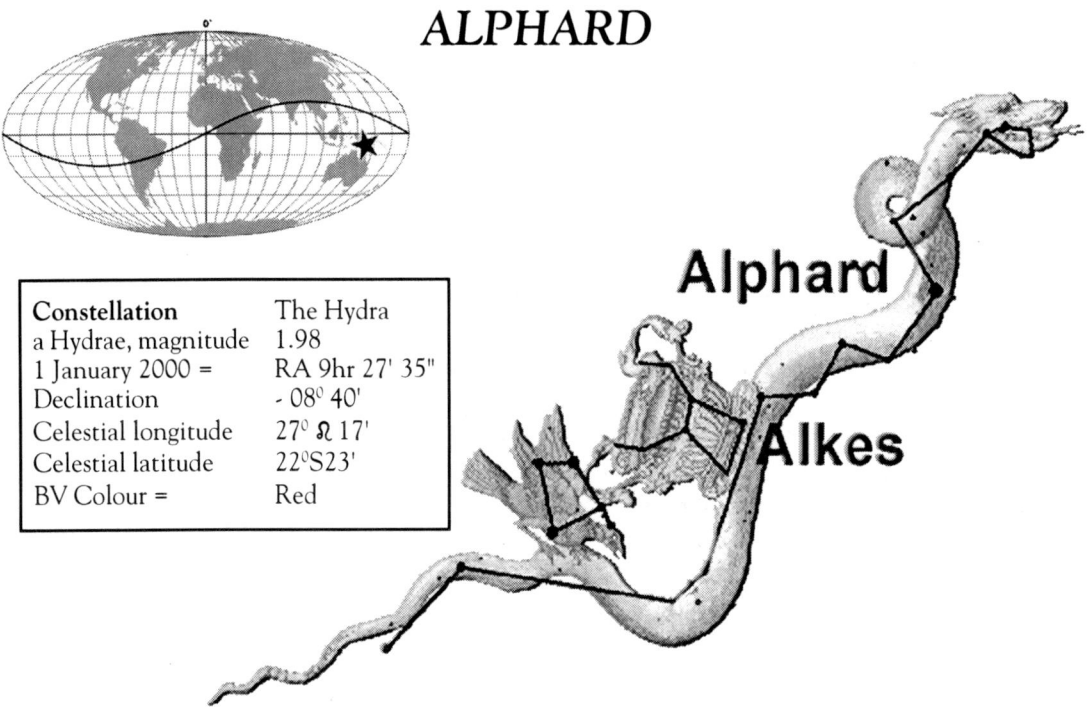

Constellation	The Hydra
α Hydrae, magnitude	1.98
1 January 2000 =	RA 9hr 27' 35"
Declination	- 08° 40'
Celestial longitude	27° ♌ 17'
Celestial latitude	22°S23'
BV Colour =	Red

The Hydra – the Serpent

Hydra is the largest constellation in the sky, stretching for nearly 95° across the heavens from Cancer to Scorpio. It has gone through many names but through most cultures it has been a snake, a serpent or a water snake. The Greeks claimed that this snake was the creature that attacked the heroes of the Argo. Hydra is also considered to be the constellation on an uranographic stone from the Euphrates of 1200 BCE showing it as the source of the "great deep" and thus to the great dragon Tiamat[1]. Many cultures have such snake or serpent connected with their creation myths in some way. The Hydra is symbolically the ancient female energy in one of its original forms and has probably occupied the sky for tens of thousands of years.

The principle of Alphard the Heart of the Serpent, obsession

Alphard, as the Heart of the Serpent, carries the symbolism of the great serpent of creation and thus can easily manifest in our turbulent world as violent, untamed energy and/or emotional outbursts and even chaos. Nevertheless, to think of Alphard in this purely violent way is misleading, for only when its driving force is submerged in the unconscious will its expression be murderous and violent. Its preferred expression is through conscious passion focused, even obsessively, on a desired goal with strength and determination. It is the creative emergent energy of the void or chaos.

Heliacal Rising Star
To live one's life passionately, to prefer the intense to the calm, to admire and seek to emulate the creative passion of others. Being drawn, intentionally or not, to intense emotional encounters. *Hiram Revels, 19th century US politician who was the first African-American citizen elected to the US Senate.*

Heliacal Setting Star
To learn through life's lessons that obsession and perhaps even ruthlessness can be the path to success. To act with passion and to discover that a strong focus will bring the desired results. *Rupert Murdoch, 20th century Australian-born newspaper magnate who owns a large number of the world's major English-language newspapers.*

Star on one of its pivot points at the moment of birth
A direct, no-nonsense, hard-hitting approach to life, which will cascade into one's physical world. At times ruthless, at other times sexual, and in worst case situations even vengeful. Physically assertive and forthright. *Peter Sellers, best known for his comic-genius roles in "Doctor Strangelove" and "The Pink Panther", he struggled all his life with his own darker side.*

Physiological Correspondence: The sexual organs, and the libido – erotic energy.

Ptolemy's location: The bright star of the two in the south [of the hydra].

World Cities: Jakarta, Indonesia, Port Moresby, Papua New Guinea at latitudes between 6^0 to 10^0 south.

Alphard in paran with:

Sun: To have strong passions, to be a victim of or a perpetrator of violent or aggressive actions. To feel angry at injustices, or be subject to mistreatment by authority figures. ♦ An occasion of apparent ruthlessness. *Voltaire, 18th century French author who is held in worldwide repute as a courageous crusader against tyranny, bigotry and cruelty.*

Moon: Difficulties with receiving love and nurturing, a tragic mother figure. A ruthless attitude to life, a passion for one's own pursuits. ♦ A period when the safety of the home or homeland is at risk. *Richard Gatling, 19th century US inventor of the machine gun.*

Mercury: The one who reveals or is the holder of secrets, an investigating mind, a sharp tongue. A lover of rituals. ♦ Secrets are revealed or a vitriolic outburst. *Dorothy Sayers, 20th century English author known for her detective novels featuring the debonnaire Lord Peter Wimsey.*

Venus: To be harshly judged or treated in matters of money, relationships or social attitudes. A desire for strong, intense, passionate relationships. ♦ A minority group treated ruthlessly.

Juan Valdes, painter and the major figure in Sevillian painting for many years, known for his dramatic, inventive, and often violent paintings.

Mars: To have an aggressive attitude in achieving one's goals. A passionate environmentalist whose desire to help can lead to damaging other groups.   ♦   The ruthless action of an individual or group. *Bram Stoker, 19th century Irish author of the popular horror tale "Dracula".*

Jupiter: An explorer of places or people. The ability to probe deeply into the bigger issues and problems of life. An explorer willing to go into taboo areas in order to find answers.   ♦   Dark events are revealed. *Nostradamus, 16th century French astrologer and physician well known for his "Centuries", a collection of prophecies.*

Saturn: A person who will fight the system, one who becomes engaged in a long struggle. To clash with the law and become bitter at the status-quo.   ♦   A time of struggle against those in power. *John Almon, 18th century English journalist who struggled with Parliament for the right to publish reports of debates.*

Uranus: The desire to help the common folk, to be involved with projects which will better the every day lives of people. A defender of children and those in need.   ♦   A group feels threatened. *Milton Hershey, 19th century US industrialist who founded the corporation which popularized chocolate candy throughout the world.*

Neptune: A desire to improve the spiritual or creative life of others, holding strong religious views, a tendency to proselytise.   ♦   A sad, but natural, disaster. *Joseph Smith, 19th century US religious reformer who is known as the founder of the Church of Jesus Christ of Latter-day Saints (Mormons).*

Pluto: To look for a noble challenge, or to be ruthless and to seek retribution. Willing to be involved in the lives of many people.   ♦   A time of seeking retribution. *Cecil Rhodes, 19th century British statesman whose personal and professional empire encompassed British South Africa.*

The Node: To be interested in all things to do with life and the environment, to be concerned with balance and order, to seek the overall picture.   ♦   An environmental issue. *Gregory Mendel, 19th century botanist, who was the first to lay a mathematical foundation for the science of genetics.*

NOTES

1.   Allen, *Star Names Their Lore and Meaning*, p.248.

ALPHECCA

Constellation	Corona Borealis
α Corona Borealis, magnitude	2.23
1 January 2000 =	
RA	15hr 34' 39"
Declination	+26° 43'
Celestial longitude	12° ♏ 17'
Celestial latitude	44°N19'
BV Colour =	White

Corona Borealis – A crown of flowers

One of three crowns in the sky, the other two crowns being Coma Berenice the head of hair, also in the northern sky, and Corona Australis in the southern sky. Called by many names, the early Greeks called it a Wreath, as well as Ariadnaea Corona, Ariadne's Tiara and sometimes even the Coiled Hair of Ariadne[1]. The imagery of this crown has predominantly been that of a woman's head piece, a crown or garland of flowers. The Greeks saw it as the wedding garland of flowers given to Ariadne by Venus to celebrate her marriage to Dionysus after she was deserted by Theseus[2]. The constellation was also known by the Persians as The Broken Platter, for the circle of stars is incomplete.

The principle of Alphecca, the star of the flower crown, a gift with thorns

This star is associated with a woman's crown and thus symbolic of achievements in a quiet, passive way. Yet this crown of flowers also contains thorns and, although there are advancements through life which are not necessarily through one's own efforts, there is always a price to pay. Alphecca's presence can indicate that one is offered a change in social status or community standing, but this advancement is not gained through hard work but rather through love or luck. This gift, like all gifts, has a price attached, and thus all possible advancement indicated by Alphecca should be considered with awareness of likely consequences.

Heliacal Rising Star

To be guided by a strong belief in one's own abilities while deeply believing that success will only come, or is only of value, if one has paid the price with a physical or emotional sacrifice. To be a fertile person with ideas and life. *Robert Brown, 20th century Australian politician who was the inaugural Parliamentary Leader of the Australian Greens and the first openly gay member of the Parliament of Australia.*

Heliacal Setting Star
Discovering that good emerges from difficult times, learning that sacrifice brings rewards and even fruitfulness. Interest in the physical side of life, medicine or other forms of physical healing. *Alexander Fleming, 19th century Scottish bacteriologist who is credited with the discovery of penicillin.*

Star on one of its pivot points at the moment of birth
To be handed a gift in life, then to discover that it demands a physical price. Struggling to achieve the most you can, while learning that the difficult times are also followed by periods of success. Teaching others how to deal with the vagaries of life. *Marlene Dietrich, German-born actress of the early 20th century renowned for her dark and haunting singing voice.*

Physiological Correspondence: The skull, particularly the cranium and sinus cavities.

Ptolemy's location: The bright star in the Crown.

World Cities: New Delhi, India at latitudes between 25° to 29° north.

Alphecca in paran with:

Sun: To be talented and hold a special gift which yields a fruitful life, embracing the good with the difficulties or hardship.   •   A leader emerges out of hardship. *Joshua Slocum, 19th century Canadian who was the first man in recorded history to sail solo around the world.*

Moon: A desire to leave a legacy in the more creative and emotional side of life. An interest in children, religion, song, poetry and/or theatre.   •   A person's life is seen as a legacy. *Hans Christian Andersen, 19th century Danish author considered to be one of the world's great story-tellers.*

Mercury: A successful merchant or trader. To have fruitful and successful ideas. Blessed with communication skills whether through writing, talking or in the virtual world.   •   The success of a new business venture. *Rene Lalique, French jeweller who is best known for his original jewellery designs which became a feature of the Art Nouveau movement.*

Venus: Seeking strong social bonds, and being intolerant of superficial relationships. An ability to see what the social issues really are, rather than being blinded by mainstream views.
•   Central social issues are revealed. *Dorothea Dix, US social reformer whose dedication to the plight of those with a mental illness saw reforms instituted in the USA and Europe.*

Mars: To learn that hard toil will lead to success. To know that one's potential success lies in the wisdom of examining one's failures. ♦ An impasse, a time of a stuck state. *Alfred Dreyfus, French Jew who was tried for treason and sent to Devil's Island. This divided France into anti-Semitic factions versus left wing, anti-military factions.*

Jupiter: The gift of endurance, mentally or physically. Fortunate events grow from hardship or difficulties. One's leadership skills are polished by abrasive life events. ♦ The hard road yields the best results. *Alfred Dreyfus, see Mars and Alphecca above.*

Saturn: The desire to help remove human or animal suffering, a humanitarian quality which will be focused into one's precise field of expertise. ♦ People working together to get through difficult times. *Clara Barton, 19th century US founder of the American Red Cross.*

Uranus: Being able to reach the common people, having a good sense of what will be popular but also dealing with personal difficulties. ♦ Safety systems or security systems fail. *Elvis Presley, 20th century US rock star whose huge success led to a life of increasing isolation.*

Neptune: A person who can have successful endeavours in the virtual world, or one's who success prove to be ephemeral. Good fortune which seems to emerge with little effort, but can also disappear with little cause. ♦ Euphoria or sadness in the community. *Nostradamus, 16th century French astrologer and physician well known for his "Centuries", a collection of prophecies.*

Pluto: Being drawn to charismatic ideas or people, or to be charismatic oneself. Dependence on charismatic people leading to one's own undoing. ♦ Those who seek power come undone. *Elizabeth Taylor, 20th century British actress renowned for the abundant number of her marriages.*

The Node: A gift of seeing the magic in everyday matters. To explore social values around relationships, whether of a sexual, business or private nature. ♦ Broken relationships make the news. *Grandma Moses, 19th century US folk painter known for her simple and ingenuous painting style portraying rural life in America at the turn of the 19th century.*

NOTES

1. Adrian Room, *Dictionary of Astronomical Names*, New York: Routledge, 1988, p.76.
2. Aratus, "Phaenomena," p. 213.

ALPHERATZ

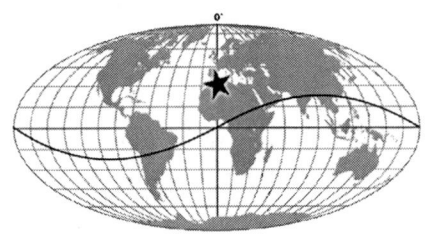

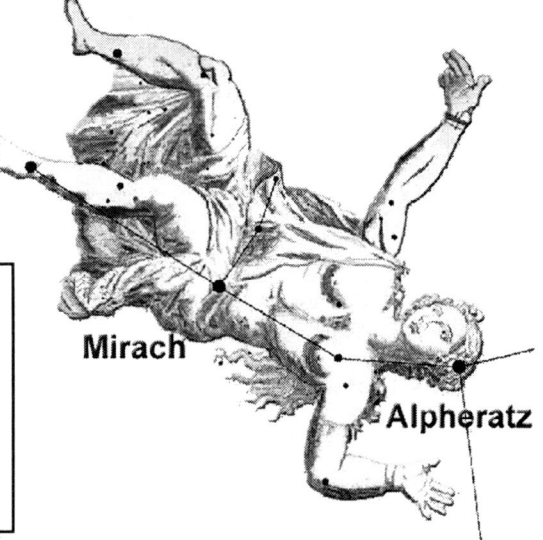

Constellation	Andromeda
α Andromedae, magnitude	2.06
1 January 2000 =	RA 00hr 08' 22"
Declination	+29° 05'
Celestial longitude	14° ♈ 18'
Celestial latitude	25°N41'
BV Colour =	Blue-Green

Andromeda, the daughter of the king

Andromeda is one member of the polar royal family consisting of Cepheus the king, Cassiopeia the queen, Andromeda the daughter or princess, and Perseus the prince. In this family she represents the young princess who is receiving the handsome prince, Perseus, who strides towards her with his sword upright in his hand. In this way the pair represents human fertility and the cycle of life in balance with the authority of the king and the queen. This receptive position of the fertile virgin ready to take a suitor was later translated by the Greeks into a chained woman needing to be saved by Perseus[1]. Regardless of her chains Andromeda is a symbol of the female desire to receive, the female desire to take pleasure in a lover and be fruitful. (For more information see Mirach).

The principle of Alpheratz, the navel of the horse, speed and freedom

Alpheratz, originally regarded as part of Pegasus[2], is now both the head of the princess and the navel of Pegasus. However, it still seems to be more strongly linked to the wonder of the flying horse and its symbolism of freedom, love of movement, speed and the sheer joy of the wind in one's hair.

Heliacal Rising Star

To lead a life based on decisive action. To have a resourceful, independent nature which propels one to reach for ever greater levels of self expression or freedom. *Anthony Fokker, German pilot and aircraft pioneer who produced over 40 different types of aircraft during World War I.*

Heliacal Setting Star
To discover through life circumstances that one works best under pressure. To find in oneself the ability to handle sudden changes and to act with speed in the development of a situation; to learn to welcome the new. *Bill Gates, 20th century US founder of Microsoft computing systems.*

Star on one of its pivot points at the moment of birth
To see oneself as independent of one's culture or society; a strong desire not to be caught in the rat-race, which can lead to lawlessness and antisocial behaviour. To work in a risk-taking situation. *Errol Flynn, 20th century Australian actor who is best known as the dashing hero of adventure films of the 1930s and 40s.*

Physiological Correspondence: The adrenal glands which produce adrenaline for bursts of energy in "fight and flight" situations.

Ptolemy's location: The star common to the Horse's navel and the head of Andromeda.

World Cities: New Delhi, India at latitudes between 25° to 29° north.

Alpheratz in paran with:

Sun: Independent and freedom-loving. Moving forward in one's chosen direction as a fundamental principle of life. To be self employed, or otherwise free to dictate the contents of one's day. • A time for independent action. *Charles I of England, English monarch whose autocratic rule and disputes with Parliament led to a civil war and his execution.*

Moon: Emotionally independent; to be self-contained or a loner. To be capable of taking actions which are contra to one's culture. • A person who stands alone takes centre stage. *Charles Sturt, Australian explorer whose expeditions (1829-30) are considered one of the greatest explorations in Australian history.*

Mercury: Outspoken, and thinking in different ways with the aim of increasing one's self-sufficiency and self-empowerment. Over confidence leading to rash action. • The radical or outspoken journalist. *Thomas Edward Lawrence, better known as "Lawrence of Arabia", who sought to unite the Arab world in WWI.*

Venus: To demand the right to follow one's own social or religious conscience, and an understanding of the impact of education on life and society in general. • News stories focused on freedom of religion. *Oliver Cromwell, leader of the parliamentary forces during the English Civil wars and Lord Protector of the Commonwealth from 1653-1658.*

Mars: Risk-taking, challenge-oriented or even physically reckless, a dare-devil with little regard for personal safety, a lover of sports and or speed, playing or watching.   ♦   A time of physical recklessness or bravery. *Peter Lalor, 19th century activist known for his leadership of the most famous, though unsuccessful, insurrection in Australian history, at the Eureka Stockade.*

Jupiter: The explorer, inventor and/or reformer. Finding that one's greatest success comes from the areas in life which are non-conservative.   ♦   A period when bold action and haste bring success. *Robert Peary, 19th century explorer who is acknowledged as having led the first expedition to reach the North Pole.*

Saturn: An architect, someone who creates in a physical way. To willingly take on the hard long road in order to see one's dreams come true.   ♦   An occasion when society is led into new ideas. *Michelangelo Buonarroti, 15th century Italian artist, sculptor, poet and architect who painted the famous Sistine Chapel ceiling.*

Uranus: To strive for new ideas to be accepted in society, to love or to loath technology; a desire for a better and/or different world.   ♦   New technology is released. *William Penn, 17th century English Quaker leader who founded the colony of the Commonwealth of Pennsylvania as a refuge for Quakers.*

Neptune: A lover of fantasy or science fiction, a person active in the virtual world. One who works within cyberspace communities.   ♦   A time when technology malfunctions. *Owen Wister, 20th century US novelist whose work established the cowboy as an American folk hero and stock fictional character.*

Pluto: Using new technologies for financial success, or becoming apprehensive of that which is foreign; having problems adapting to new ideas in society.   ♦   Technology brings tragedy to a group. *Samuel Sewall, 17th century judge who was a colonial merchant and a judge in the Salem witchcraft trials.*

The Node: The desire to better oneself and one's family. Willing to take risks to promote a philosophy or idea.   ♦   New political dreams announced. *Mao Tse-Tung, 19th century Chinese statesman who was the founding member of the founding member of the Chinese Communist Party.*

NOTES

1. Room, *Dictionary of Astronomical Names*, p.57.
2. Jobes and Jobes, *Outer Space: Myths, Name Meanings, Calendars*, p.300.

ALTAIR

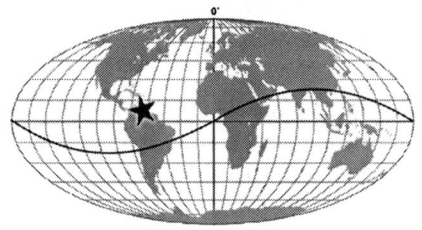

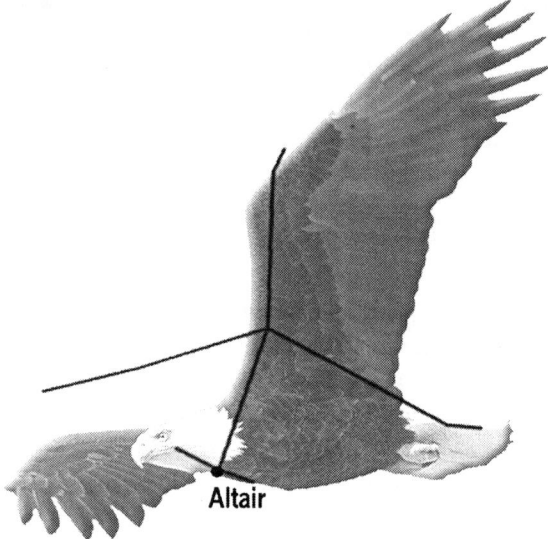

Constellation	Aquila
α Aquilae, magnitude	0.77
1 January 2000 =	RA 19hr 50' 45"
Declination	+08° 52'
Celestial longitude	01° ♒ 46'
Celestial latitude	29°N18'
BV Colour =	White

Aquila, the Eagle
Aquila is one of three birds who were known to the Greeks as the Stymphalian Birds killed by Hercules as his sixth labour. Aratus however called this constellation the storm bird, for in the northern hemisphere it rises in winter[1]. The constellation has been recognised as a bird for the last 3,500 years and has been associated with fire, lightning and sun gods, so the Greeks claimed this eagle as a form of Zeus, god of thunder and lightning. It was also a Roman custom to release eagles over the funeral pyres of emperors, for they believed the eagle would carry the soul of the warrior to the land of the immortals[2]. The eagle was seen as the instrument for calling fire down from heaven; and the spirit or soul, having passed through the sacrificial fire, was borne away by the eagle. This symbolism is reflected in the Old Testament with the fires sent down by Yahweh to consume the son of Abraham. Because of its connection with fire, the eagle was often confused with the phoenix. The eagle was the royal bird of Rome and a symbol of male sovereignty.

The principle of Altair, the Eagle, boldness and military power
Altair is associated with boldness and action but this boldness is also connected to human relationships and caring. This star carries the divine fire of inspiration which transforms into determination, the ability to achieve through risk-taking or through dogged determination. This is a star of action and strength and so will naturally seek action rather than inaction. At the same time this quest for action is not just for its own sake but also to serve others.

Heliacal Rising Star
To use boldness and bravery as the guiding principles of one's life, to value this type of action above all else. To seek inspiration and to have the ability to soar to places others have not been. *Max Theiler, South African scientist who won the 1951 Nobel Prize for Physiology or Medicine for his research and development of a vaccine for yellow fever.*

Heliacal Setting Star
To be thrown into situations that demand fast action, finding leadership skills by inspiring others. Seeking difficult situations as a pathway to success. *Napoleon Bonaparte, 18th century French military leader who became the French Emperor.*

Star on one of its pivot points at the moment of birth
The lifestyle of the warrior class, bold and independent, one who wants to live life by their wits. The need to express bold, brave, daredevil energy, in one's daily life. To love a challenge. *Jean-Claude Van Damme, 20th century Belgian martial artist and actor who is best known for his large catalogue of action movies.*

Physiological Correspondence: The lungs and their role in oxygenating the blood and muscles.

Ptolemy's location: The bright star in the broad of the back of the eagle.

World Cities: Panama City, Panama at latitudes between 07° to 11° north.

Altair in paran with:

Sun: To be a bold and determined individual. To be reckless or a daredevil; to have a high regard for independent and decisive action.   ♦   Bold or daring actions and/or military matters. *Roald Amundsen, Norwegian explorer who, from 1903 to 1906, sailed the Northwest Passage from E-W and located the Magnetic North Pole.*

Moon: To admire bold individuals; to seek to emulate strong or independent women. Having little regard for personal safety if loved ones are threatened.   ♦   People emotionally moved by acts of courage. *Annie Oakley, 19th century Wild West star famed for her ability to shoot accurately. She was a member of "Buffalo Bill's Wild West Troop" and became a national celebrity.*

Mercury: A natural ability to think fast yielding a military mind, a brave and independent thinker. Successful in independent action.   ♦   The military take the focus. *Queen Elizabeth I, Queen of England, she reigned between 1588-1603 and maintained England's freedom against Spanish and French forces.*

Venus: The bold artisan; one who is sexually and/or sensually orientated. To challenge the sexual, social, or sporting expectations of a society. ♦ A time for successful business partnerships. *Peter Carl Faberge, 19th century Russian considered to be one of the greatest jewellers and decorative artists of his era.*

Mars: To be daring and at times take rash action. To be drawn to the military, or to use a military-style approach to problem solving. ♦ To attack, to go to war, to act bravely. *Roberto Ridolfi, conspired unsuccessfully to assassinate Queen Elizabeth I of England and restore Catholic rule with Mary, Queen of Scots.*

Jupiter: To have the courage of one's convictions; success through bold action. ♦ A focus on the military. *Charlemagne (Charles the Great), 8th century German monarch who became master of Western Europe "by the sword and the cross".*

Saturn: Building and seeking honour in daily life. The spiritual and/or physical warrior striving to express themselves. ♦ The honouring of war heroes. *Errol Flynn, actor who is best known as the dashing hero of adventure films of the 1930s and 40s.*

Uranus: To popularise bold action, to bring it down to the level of "everyman"; a fan of popular sports. ♦ Groups take matters into their own hands. *Pierre Baron de Coubertin, 19th century Frenchman who is remembered as the father of the Modern Olympic Games.*

Neptune: A love of film, photography or virtual media; to seek to be behind the lens rather than in front. A tendency to act without sufficient preparation. ♦ Ungrounded, ill planned or fanatical actions. *Christopher Reeve, US actor who played Superman but became a quadriplegic due to an accident; he then devoted his life to helping others.*

Pluto: Always trying to work from the strongest position. To seek to dominate one's field, or to support those in authority in order to grow in strength. ♦ The people are told that the end justifies the means. *Oliver Winchester, 19th century US manufacturer who developed the Winchester rifle a success resulting from the shrewd purchase and improvement of the inventions of other men.*

The Node: To seek to fight injustice, to be a warrior for the people or for an idea. To build a lifestyle around a strong social philosophy. ♦ An act of personal bravery. *Queen Victoria of England, 19th century British monarch who was the symbol of the English Victorian era of social justice.*

NOTES

1. Aratus, "Phaenomena," p.231.
2. Barbara Walker, *The Woman's Encyclopedia of Myths and Secrets*, San Francisco: HarperSanFrancisco, 1983, p.262.

ANKAA

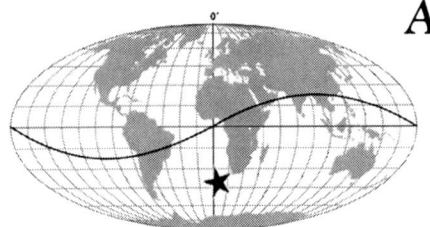
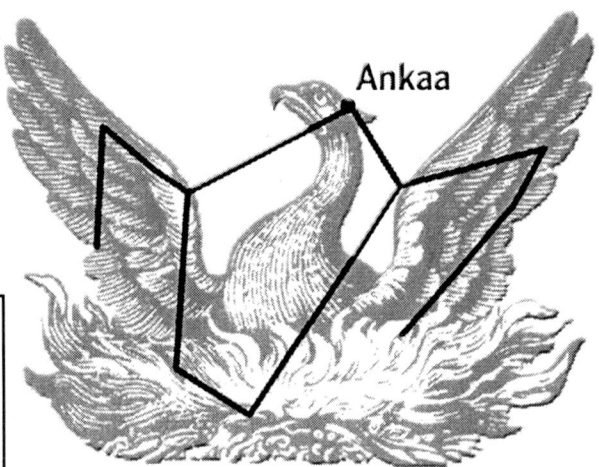

Constellation	The Phoenix
α Phoenicis, magnitude	2.39
1 January 2000 =	RA 00hr 26'16"
Declination	-42° 19'
Celestial longitude	15° ♓ 29'
Celestial latitude	40°S38'
BV Colour =	Orange

The Phoenix
This constellation was named by Johann Bayer in 1603. It lies between the Southern Fish and the river Eridanus. Although a modern constellation its name fits in with much older traditions for the Chinese, Egyptians, Indians and Persians all have myths linking with this constellation, involving a bird that symbolises some form of cyclic regeneration[1].

The principle of Ankaa, the Phoenix, resurrection
This star carries a sense of transformation or transcendence, suggesting an ability to see beyond a current problem, to consider things within the larger cycle of life and death. The star is associated with the willingness to let go of things to allow them to be transformed, or even the wilful destruction of things in order to reach for a renewed life. The ability to rise from the ashes of a situation renewed, refreshed and re-invigorated. A tendency to seek regeneration as the solution to life's problems.

Heliacal Rising Star
A natural inquisitiveness about the world and how life works. A person who can transcend their life circumstances and is able to see the potential in people or places. To have the ability to truly change or alter things via insights that go beyond the current problem. *Donald John Trump, US entrepreneur renowned for his real estate deals.*

Heliacal Setting Star
To feel forced to transcend situations; to reach for the larger solution even at the expense of one's well-being. A sense that personal sacrifice leads to salvation. *Luc Jouret, 20th century Belgian religious group leader who founded the Order of the Solar Temple, but suicided after the deaths of his followers.*

Star on one of its pivot points at the moment of birth
Resilience in life's ups and downs. Physically and mentally able to deal with the vagaries of life, being subject to transformations and alterations. Seeing endings as new beginnings. *Vivien Leigh, British actress who won two academy awards but was affected by bipolar disorder for most of her adult life.*

Physiological Correspondence: The spleen, in some traditional medicines the "transformer and transporter" of nutrients, thus its role in production of protein for building and repairing of tissues.

Ptolemy's location: Not listed by Ptolemy.

World Cities: Hobart, Australia; Wellington, New Zealand at latitudes between 40^0 to 44^0 south.

Ankaa in paran with:

Sun: One who can remake themselves, the ability to rebuild a life. To be identified with a transcending idea.   ♦   Something is rebuilt by rising from its ashes. *Matteo Ricci, introduced Christianity to the Chinese empire in the 16th century and lived there for 30 years.*

Moon: One who instigates changes in family life. Needing to adapt to frequent changes within one's family circle. To be concerned with the spiritual or physical wellbeing of others.   ♦   A child is born. *Benjamin Spock, American paediatrician whose books on child rearing changed the way children were raised throughout the western world.*

Mercury: An inventor, engineer, or one who brings order and structure. Being able to break something down to its smallest parts, even to destroying the original, to suddenly emerge with the solution or insight.   ♦   A solution is found to a long-term problem. *Albert Spalding, American professional baseball player and sporting-goods manufacturer who revolutionized sporting equipment.*

Venus: To be a trend-setter or unwilling to follow the current fashion, either in clothes, or in social or political philosophy. To have the courage to go against tradition and destroy in order to create.   ♦   A revolution, a rebirth of old issues. *Soko Yamaja, 17th century Japanese soldier, and Confucian philosopher who set forth the first systematic exposition of missions and obligations of the samurai (warrior) class.*

Mars: To see the potential of a situation or a group of people. To be motivated to either bring out the best in oneself or to help others reach their full potential in any field. ♦ A hopeful plan is put forward. *Niccolo Machiavelli, Italian statesman (1469-1527); author of "The Prince", which advocated a strong central government and argued that, in ruling people, the ends justify the means.*

Jupiter: The philanthropist, a person who strives to improve situations. One who understands the value of a well-placed action or donation to help a situation. ♦ A time of gaining success through adaptability. *Kate Barrett, American physician who directed the rescue-home movement for unwed mothers in the United States.*

Saturn: A path-maker, someone who can build new direction from chaos. To learn that difficulties are really a source of strength, a source of new beginnings. ♦ Strong leadership emerges out of chaos. *Guglielmo Marconi, Italian inventor best known as the inventor of radio telegraphy.*

Uranus: Dealing with the human drama of change or crises, helping others to see solutions to the personal problems in their life. ♦ The desire of a group to build or rebuild a public place. *Oprah Winfrey, 20th century US TV personality renowned for her talk-back shows.*

Neptune: Looking for different ways of working; being drawn to the mysterious; a love of ritual, spiritual or theatrical. Seeking to control the emerging story of life; seeking to see beyond death. ♦ An occasion of melancholy or depression. *Tennessee Williams, 20th century US playwright who wrote about his own fears of insanity and death.*

Pluto: A life saved, a second chance given; to go through darkness and find a second life. ♦ Resurrection. *Christopher Reeve, US actor who played Superman but became a quadriplegic due to an accident; he then devoted his life to helping others.*

The Node: To live or work at the edge of two worlds - life and death, east and west, beginnings and endings. ♦ A conflict of opinions. *Edward Bancroft, 18th century British spy during the American Revolution.*

NOTES

1. Allen, *Star Names Their Lore and Meaning*, p.336.

ANTARES

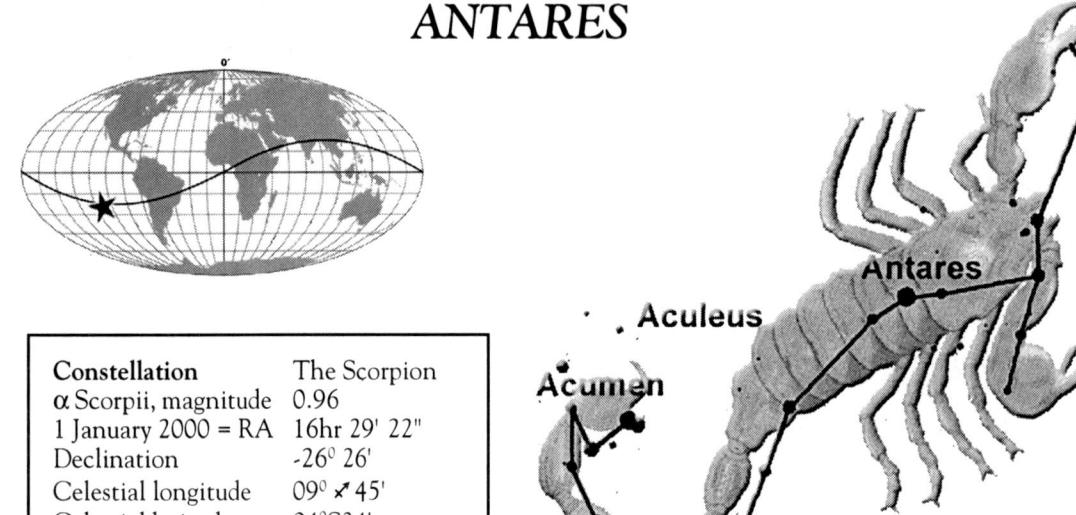

Constellation	The Scorpion
α Scorpii, magnitude	0.96
1 January 2000 = RA	16hr 29' 22"
Declination	-26° 26'
Celestial longitude	09° ♐ 45'
Celestial latitude	04°S34'
BV Colour =	Red

Scorpio, the Scorpion
Scorpio is the southern most constellation in the zodiac and it once contained the stars of Libra, known as the Claws of the Scorpion; when it lost its claws to Libra its contact with the ecliptic became minimal. From 5000 – 1000 BCE this is the part of the sky where the sun was seen to slip into the southern hemisphere, and so the constellation was associated with a gateway to the underworld, a harbinger of death or endings[1]. The Egyptians saw the Scorpion as stinging their solar god Horus and sending him to the underworld as Osiris while the Greeks retold this story in the blinding of the giant Orion by the sting of a scorpion[2]. The constellation is thus associated with transitions, life to death, birth to life, the guardian of a liminal space, a space of transitions. (For more information see Aculeus and Acumen).

The principle of Antares, the Heart of the Scorpion, obessive passion
This star is the Heart of the Scorpion and is considered one of the Royal Stars of Persia. It is the Watcher of the West. To the Persians this star was the god of the dead, Yima and, cast as one of their royal stars, it is suggestive of great success, worldly or otherwise. However, it also indicates that one can be the cause of their own undoing. The natural theme of this star is to generate success by going through a cleansing life-and-death experience. It can suggest that one seeks intensity even when not required. By its mythological symbolism its indicate extremes, whether by choice or not. The darker side of Antares is to be lost to obsession without any hope of resolution.

Heliacal Rising Star
To be driven by passion and obsession. A potential to be abrasive or even ruthless, and the need to balance obsessiveness with recognition that there can be other points of view. *Ludwig van Beethoven 18th century German composer renown for his obsessive and brilliant music.*

Heliacal Setting Star
Discovering that one's salvation lies in becoming strongly focused on a goal. A gift of intensity which gives meaning to life. *Henry Lawson, 19th century Australian poet who out of a life of deafness and hardship, became known for his writing about Australian bush life.*

Star on one of its pivot points at the moment of birth
To feel that one's life is always full of archetypal struggles between black and white; prone to obsession and being driven to deal with and even work with issues of injustice. Perpetuating, or being subjected to, polarizing events. *John F Kennedy Jr, son of the assassinated president John F Kennedy.*

Physiological Correspondence: The immune system and its ruthless approach to the protection of the body.

Ptolemy's location: The red star in the middle of the body called Antares.

World Cities: Asuncion, Paraguay; Johannesburg, South Africa at latitudes between 24⁰ to 28⁰ south.

Antares in paran with:

Sun: To be intense and focused. To attract confrontation and challenges, or to be engaged in behind-the-scenes power games.   ♦   Narrow views are aired. *Pedro Almodovar, Spanish filmmaker whose films, for example "Women on the Verge of a Nervous Breakdown", are known for their sexual themes.*

Moon: Emotional turmoil, and a willingness to face drama. Becoming obsessed with family matters or health issues.   ♦   Crimes of passion are in the news. *Isadora Duncan, US 19th century dancer who rejected formal ballet and introduced the idea of interpretative dancing based on natural rhythm.*

Mercury: Mental obsession with a subject or a person. The bane of subjective and fearful thinking. The need for objectivity.   ♦   A time of anxiety and worry. *Marquis De Sade, 18th century French author whose erotic writings gave rise to the term "sadism".*

Venus: One who breaks down social or emotional barriers. A tendency for making rash judgments, or finding it very difficult to socialise.   ♦   A period when the society is divided, extreme polarization. *Henry VIII, 16th century English monarch noted for the number of his wives and for establishing of the Church of England.*

Mars: To act, fuelled by inspiration or obsession. One who can be rash with a tendency to paint the world as black or white. A failure to see the middle ground, the need to learn to have a broader view.   ♦   *Life and death events. John of God, 16th century shepherd and soldier who was moved by Christian sermons to become the founder of the Hospitalier Order of St John of God.*

Jupiter: The engineer, to be able to envisage a structure, material or social. A talent for taking random events or problems, and seeing the way forward.   ♦   *The extremist holds power. James Watt, Scottish instrument maker and inventor whose steam engine contributed substantially to the Industrial Revolution.*

Saturn: Black versus white, a life full of the struggle with polarities. Living in a polar world which leads to resentment or gives insights into different ways of living.   ♦   *Patriotism which polarise people. Benedict Arnold, 18th century English spy in the American War of Independence.*

Uranus: Bringing the extra- ordinary into the ordinary. Seeing the remarkable in the everydayness of life.   ♦   *People are worried about the wellbeing of a group or individual. Gertrude Stein, 19th century US writer who called her work the "small hard reality" of her life.*

Neptune: The ability to see and exploit a gap; marketing or advertising. Blind focus, which can render one unaware of the danger of developing situations.   ♦   *Corruption becomes evident. Marie Antoinette, queen to Louis XVI of France, she contributed to the unrest which culminated in the French Revolution, and her execution.*

Pluto: To engage in power struggles; to struggle with one's sexuality. To have life and death experiences, and to be drawn to drama.   ♦   *Political upheavals. Peter Ilyich Tchaikovsky, Russian 19th century composer known for his drama and obsessiveness.*

The Node: To see the struggles of the masses; to understand or work with large groups. To focus on the small and in doing so reveal the larger issues.   ♦   *A tipping point, the small action that causes everything to change. Samuel Morse, 19th century US inventor of Morse code.*

NOTES

1. Lockyer, *The Dawn of Astronomy*, p.397.
2. Pierre Grimal, *The Dictionary of Classical Mythology*, trans. A. R. Maxwell-Huslop, Cambridge: Blackwell Reference, 1986, p.330.

ARCTURUS

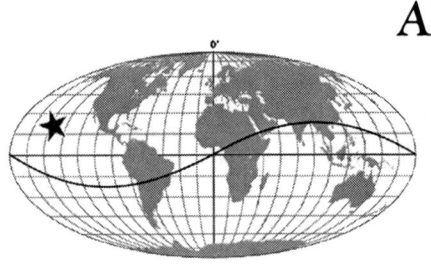

Constellation	Bootes
α Boötis, magnitude	-0.04
1 January 2000 =	RA 14hr 15' 38"
Declination	+19° 11'
Celestial longitude	24° ♎ 14'
Celestial latitude	30°N44'
BV Colour =	Orange

Bootes, the Hunter and the Farmer
The Athenians saw this constellation as the leader of a people who had fallen on difficult times. In order to help them, Bootes, their leader, invented the plow, thereby becoming one of the great benefactors of his tribe, and thus of humankind[1]. Bootes still stands in the sky holding weapons and farming tools. The alpha star of Bootes is Arcturus. This is probably one of the first stars ever named, as it appears in most ancient literature on the sky. It was used in the agricultural calendar, as its acronychal and heliacal risings once corresponded to the important dates in the farming year.

The principle of Arcturus, the hunter who now farms, a path-finder
This star symbolises the transition from the nomadic hunter-gatherer to the herder-cultivator-ploughman-villager. It appears to embody the wisdom and vision required for this fundamental shift in human consciousness from the hunter to the farmer, as it embraces the concepts of guarding, learning, teaching and leading. This star represents one who can lead the way, one who has the vision or the spirit to take the first step.

Heliacal Rising Star
One who has a strong belief in their ability to lead. To have the vision or the spirit to take the first step. A person who looks for new directions, for better or worse. *Bob Hawke, Australian Prime Minister 1983-91, renowned for his skill in negotiating with the Labour unions.*

Heliacal Setting Star
To have life events force one off the beaten track and feel compelled to find new pathways, new routes, new solutions. Learning that one's strength lies in the innovative solution, in the contra or different position. *Henry VIII, English monarch (1491-1547) who because of his conflict with the Church over issues of marriage, was pushed into the position of creating the Church of England.*

Star on one of its pivot points at the moment of birth
A life which embodies a different point of view. To have the courage to follow what one sees as the alternative or more fruitful road – for oneself and for others. *Alan Whicker, BBC journalist whose focus was not on main news stories but, for some forty years, reported on the eccentric, the ludicrous and the socially-revealing aspects of everyday life.*

Physiological Correspondence: The knees and their cartilage system – their function as the pivot of our body's versatility.

Ptolemy's location: The bright star in the fringe of the Tunic.

World Cities: Bombay, India; Kingston, Jamaica; Mexico City and Veracruz, Mexico at latitudes between 17° to 21° north.

Arcturus in paran with:

Sun: A pathfinder, to break new ground and be willing to explore unheard-of options. One who will either embody this spirit of adventure or be drawn to those who do.   ♦   Strong or new leadership emerges. *Jan Riebeeck, 17th century Dutch merchant who was the founder of Cape Town and white settlement in South Africa.*

Moon: Concerned with the health of others, physical, emotional or spiritual. Wanting to help people gain better lifestyles.   ♦   A time of concern for those in need. *Louis Pasteur, 19th century French scientist who discovered that microorganisms cause fermentation and disease. He also pioneered the process known as pasteurisation.*

Mercury: Ingenuity and cleverness which establishes new standards. A talent or ability to take bold leaps forward into new territory, to expand and break the old barriers.   ♦   A new invention, a bright idea. *Michael Ventris, cryptographer who, in 1952, deciphered the Minoan Linear B script and showed it to be Greek in its oldest known form.*

Venus: A leader in the arts or in humanist politics. A willingness to explore the difficult or unusual in friendships, art and social events.   ♦   A successful artist is profiled. *Jorn Utzon, Danish architect best known for his dynamic, imaginative but problematical design for the Sydney Opera House, Australia.*

Mars: An assertive, and at times aggressive, champion of a cause. The desire to make a difference and do things in one's own way. ♦ A time of aggression or bold action. *Bella Abzug, US Feminist Lawyer and a prominent peace campaigner who founded Women Strike for Peace and the National Women's Political Caucus.*

Jupiter: Someone who is seen as a brave or bold individual. To have courage or optimism in one's own convictions. ♦ A leader rises to the occasion and takes bold action. *Joseph-Michel Montgolfier, 18th century balloonist who was a pioneer in hot-air balloon design.*

Saturn: The engineer, the medical researcher, the explorer, the one who finds new pathways. The desire to establish and maintain better systems. ♦ A civic leader breaks with convention. *Louis Pasteur, see the Moon with Arcturus*

Uranus: An explorer, one who devises and works with their own systems, their own methods. A person who finds joy in the new. ♦ New frontiers in science, or new knowledge is revealed. *Sir William Herschel, known as the discoverer of the planet Uranus, but he also founded sidereal astronomy for the systematic observation of the heavens.*

Neptune: To work with the disadvantaged, or in an unpopular or virtual medium. To see one's work as a spiritual or artistic vocation. ♦ A leader is discredited, or a charismatic leader emerges. *Leni Riefenstahl, discrediet photographer known for her brilliant, but apparently supportive, documentary films of the Nazi movement.*

Pluto: To be headstrong and pursue one's personal opinion in the face of all challenges. To suffer from the strong opinions of others. ♦ A strong leader emerges, or prevails. *Jonathan Swift, 18th century Anglo-Irish author a prose satirist and self appointed critic of astrologers, he is best known for his satirical novel Gulliver's Travels.*

The Node: Forging new paths for one's family, tribe or society. A person who wants to make life better for all. ♦ The need for strong leadership is revealed. *Voltaire, 17th century French author held in worldwide repute as a courageous crusader against tyranny, bigotry, and cruelty.*

NOTES

1. Jobes and Jobes, *Outer Space:Myths, Name Meanings, Calendars*, p.128.

BELLATRIX

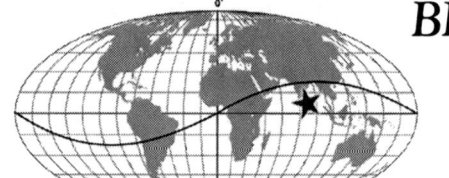

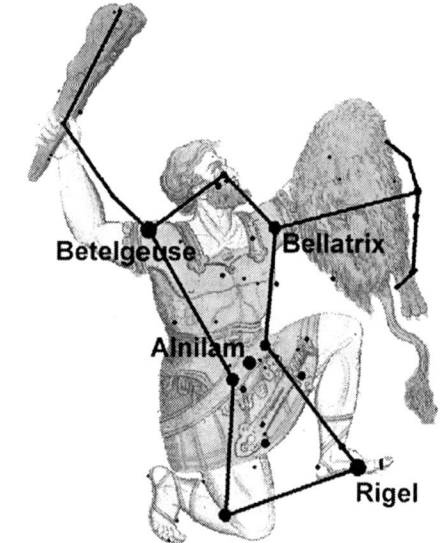

Constellation	Orionis
γ Orionis, magnitude	1.64
1 January 2000 =	RA 5hr 25' 08"
Declination	+06° 21'
Celestial longitude	20° ♊ 57'
Celestial latitude	16°S49'
BV Colour =	Blue-Green

Orion, the hero and god in the sky

Around 6,000 BCE, it was noted and celebrated by the Egyptians that Orion would rise before the sun on the morning of the spring equinox. In that era Orion was, as it of course still is, one of the brightest and most spectacular constellations of the night sky, and as it rose in the predawn light of the equinox it was scooped up into the fiery boat of the sun, thereby linking it to the divine rulership of that epoch. To the Egyptians Orion was god. The Pharaohs came from him, were his physical flesh, and upon their death they returned to him[1]. However, god on the equator was, like the gods of the ecliptic, subject to the hero's journey of the whirlpool (precession) and, as Orion slipped against the dawn rising sun of the equinox, this image, some believe, gave rise to the idea of immortal gods that can die and later be reborn. (For more information see Alnilam, Betelgeuse and Rigel.)

The principle of Bellatrix, the left arm of the god, success through the shadow

Bellatrix is the left shoulder of the god, Orion. It is called in some sources the Amazon Star or the Female Warrior and in others the Conqueror or the Roaring Conqueror. Bellatrix gives success but with a shadow, for the achievement that Bellatrix promises has a price: that of dealing with difficult aspects of the psyche. This star suggests that personal weaknesses are exposed. Personal growth and needing to face one's own demons or shadows is the price paid for success.

Heliacal Rising Star

A person who expects their success to come from struggle; to have confidence in committing to the long struggle, to believe that it is only through hard work that gains are made. *Giuseppi*

Garibaldi, 19th century Italian sea captain who became a national hero as his military campaigns brought about the formation of a unified Italy.

Heliacal Setting Star
To be born at a disadvantage, to be compelled to struggle for life and freedom, to discover one's strength under adversity. *Australia, the country (1 January 1901 chart), the nation that emerged out of its beginnings as a convict settlement.*

Star on one of its pivot points at the moment of birth
A life full of struggle but also success, to be known as a battler. No lucky breaks or free rides, victories will come only from being prepared to battle it out day by day. *David Helfgott, 20th century Australian concert pianist who has struggled with mental health and is the subject of the film "Shine"*

Physiological Correspondence: The major bones of the shoulders – e.g. scapula at the back and collarbone at the front.

Ptolemy's location: The star in the left shoulder.

World Cities: Bogota, Colombia; Cayenne, French Guiana; Georgetown, Guyana; Paramaribo, Suriname at latitudes between 04° to 08° north.

Bellatrix in paran with:

Sun: Successful, but via the harder or more physical, route. To learn that hard work and failure are a part of success. One who has skills in dealing with the physical world as an athlete or an engineer, or even a potter who can give shape to a formless mass of clay. ♦ The wounded warrior. *Mary Anne Evans, 19th century female English novelist who rebelled against the conventional role of women in society and published under the male pseudonym of "George Eliot".*

Moon: Compassionate; a person who seeks to help others. To seek improvement, for those who need it, in the basic quality of life. ♦ A desire to help others. *Daniel Hale Williams, American physician and founder of Provident Hospital in Chicago, credited with the first successful heart surgery.*

Mercury: The craftsman with alternative interests. To be skilled with one's hands, or interested in uncommon ideas. ♦ A clever plan revealed. *Paul Revere, silversmith and folk hero of the American Revolution, credited with raising the alarm on the night of 18 April 1775 to alert the people that the British were coming.*

Venus: The rogue, or the creative person who works in alternative fields. Seeking non-conventional relationships, forming associations with people that bring controversy. ♦ Dealing with a rogue. *Bugsy Siegel, US gangster and crime boss who initiated the development of Las Vegas as a gambling Mecca.*

Mars: One who takes up a common cause, whether a personal or social battle, or a fight for the environment.   ♦   The battle of the underdog; strikes and industrial turmoil. *Israel Zangwill, 19th century English author and Zionist leader, who was one of the earliest English interpreters of Jewish immigrant life.*

Jupiter: The historian or priest, to value people above material goods. A passion for teaching. To hold matters of soul and spirit as more important than money and power.   ♦   The unlikely hero wins the day. *Clare of Assisi, 12th century Italian saint who founded the Poor Clares Order.*

Saturn: A battler, to struggle against the tide. The desire to work in a difficult medium or a difficult field. One who takes on the difficult struggle.   ♦   New laws put forward focused on education and minority rights. *Deborah Sampson, 18th century US woman who joined the American War of Revolution as a soldier by assuming a man's identity, Robert Shurtleff, and enlisted in the 4th Massachusetts Regiment in 1782.*

Uranus: A popular person in alternative cultures, to suffer personal hardship due to the work one does for others.   ♦   The battler, the sports hero becomes popular. *Antonie-Joseph Sax, 19th century Belgian instrument-maker who invented the saxophone but died in poverty due to legal disputes over ownership of his invention.*

Neptune: Success in the virtual, imaginary or theatrical worlds. To find that one's resources are ephemeral.   ♦   Hard-won success slips away. *Walter Savage Landor, 18th century British writer known for his work, "Imaginary Conversations", a collection of imagined interchanges between famous people in history.*

Pluto: To be born the underdog but to find success after a long, emotional and/or bitter struggle. To live in an alien culture, or live in many different cultures.   ♦   The successful but battle-weary hero. *Galileo Galilei, 16th century Italian mathematician who is considered one of the fathers of physics but who suffered at the hands of the Church.*

The Node: One's life journey is linked with themes of personal struggle. To physically struggle with the everyday world, the fallen hero.   ♦   The battle gains the moral high ground. *John Nash, the mathematical genius of the film "A Beautiful Mind".*

NOTES

1. Leonard H. Lesko, "Ancient Egyptian Cosmogonies and Cosmology," in *Religion in Ancient Egypt*, ed. Byron E. Shafer, New York: Cornell University Press, 1991, pp. 97-103.

BETELGEUSE

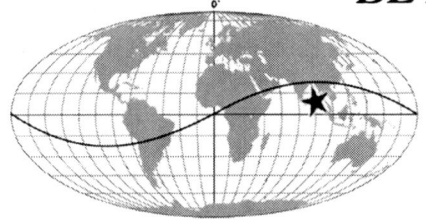

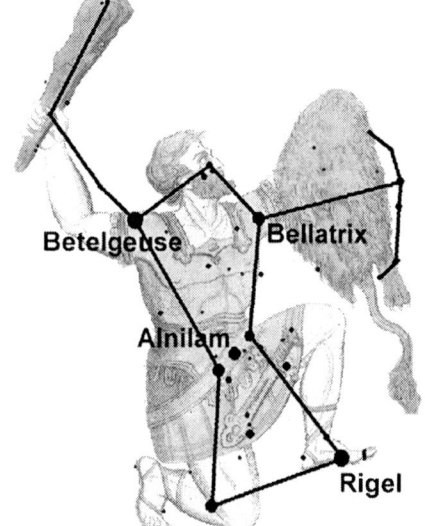

Constellation	Orionis
α Orionis, magnitude	0.50
1 January 2000 =	RA 5hr 55' 11"
Declination	+07° 24'
Celestial longitude	28° Ⅱ 45'
Celestial latitude	16°S02'
BV Colour =	Red

Orion, the hero and god in the sky

After the Egyptian association of the pharaoh with god in the sky, the Greeks took Orion and turned him into an unwelcome admirer of Artemis. Artemis in turn created a giant Scorpion who stung him on the foot, causing him to go blind[1]. This myth echoes the observation that in the north, as the Scorpion rises, Orion sets. Another version of the story was that Artemis appreciated his advances but was tricked into accidentally killing him. He swam out to sea (a metaphor for the constellation slipping into the sea through the effects of precession) where, mistaking him for driftwood, she used him as target practice[2]. These Greek stories reflect the Egyptian mythology of the death and rebirth of a hero. Indeed, Orion is the great warrior in the sky; he is a Bronze Age hero challenging the bull of heaven and as such symbolizes power and strength. (For more information see Alnilam, Bellatrix and Rigel).

The principle of Betelgeuse, the right arm of the god, success

Bright red in colour this is a star of power and worldly success. This is the right hand, armpit, or shoulder of the god, so it represents that which is clear and strong. Betelgeuse is linked with being effective, being brilliant and being successful. It amplifies talents and abilities and asks no price in return for the power and even fame that it can represent.

Heliacal Rising Star

To born with an optimistic and enthusiastic approach to life. To have a personal philosophy that action will bring success, to seek a direct approach to problems with confidence. Ambitious and a natural charisma generated through self-confidence. *Carl Lewis, 20th century US athlete who won ten Olympic medals including nine golds.*

Heliacal Setting Star
To find that success comes when one is forced to take the lead, to stand out in front or take action before one is ready. Discovering that one's strength comes to the fore when under pressure or when facing adversity. *Nicolle Dickson, Australian actor who rose unexpectedly to fame and success while trying to pay for her university education through TV work.*

Star on one of its pivot points at the moment of birth
To be empowered by a successful attitude, to expect to gain good results from one's work or one's endeavour. To gain early success or notoriety. To be seen as a larger than life figure. *Steven Spielberg, US film director and producer whose early sci-fi and adventure films are by some considered the archetype of modern Hollywood blockbuster film-making.*

Physiological Correspondence: The major muscles of the shoulders – e.g. deltoid and subscapularis.

Ptolemy's location: The bright red star in the right shoulder.

World Cities: Georgetown, Guyana; Panama City, Panama; Paramaribo, Suriname at latitudes between 05° to 09° north.

Betelgeuse in paran with:

Sun: To be confident that one has the ability to win through, to influence people and to be successful. To be considered gifted; to be persuasive. To have success in one's ventures.   ♦   The victorious warrior in the news. *Horatio Nelson, 18th century English admiral known for his courageous victories, in particular the Battle of Trafalgar which ensured the safety of Britain from invasion.*

Moon: To be concerned, from a position of power, with the quality of people's lives, a desire to help others or to help the environment.   ♦   Emotions run high concerning a popular leader. *Joyce Hall, 19th century US businessman who was the founder of Hallmark cards and helped create the modern greeting card industry.*

Mercury: To be blessed with abundant creativity. One who is skilled in oratory, writing, communications, industry, and/or commerce.   ♦   Good economic news, or a big global news story. *Frank Lloyd Wright, architect and writer, considered the most abundantly creative genius of American architecture.*

Venus: The successful artisan, or one who is socially skilled. To have an eye for fashion and be associated with society, fashion, or the arts. Relationships that can bring great financial security or provide bountiful opportunities.   ♦   Issues of opulence and wealth in the news. *Michael Todd,* *a flamboyant showman whose claims to fame are a single movie, "Around the World in 80 Days", and his marriage to Elizabeth Taylor.*

Mars: The courage to undertake large and painstaking projects. To bring precision and fine detail to one's work.   ♦   The establishment uses a heavy hand. *Neil Armstrong, first man to walk on the Moon, on 21July 1969.*

Jupiter: To have a hunger for knowledge, or adventure. A desire to travel, read, study, teach and explore, and to share this with others.   ♦   A display of confidence in actions undertaken. *John Speke, British explorer who was the first European to reach Lake Victoria in East Africa which he correctly identified as a source of the Nile.*

Saturn: Success in an arduous task or a proletarian, blue-collar field of work. To undertake projects that are demanding, tedious and even physically arduous.   ♦   Leaders focusing on proletarian issues. *Mac Wilkins, American world-record-holding discus thrower (1976-78) who was the first man ever to break the 70-metre barrier.*

Uranus: To be popular with the common folk, to seek to represent or work with everyday matters, to have the common touch.   ♦   The people seek the safety of established policies. *Katharine Hepburn, US actor who is the only person to have won four Academy Awards for Best Actress.*

Neptune: To be charismatic or to have charismatic ideas that inspire, or sometimes delude, others. The chemist, the poet or the trickster.   ♦   A time for the promotion of ideals and beliefs. *Karl Marx, 19th century Prussian philosopher, political economist, and revolutionary; known as the father of communism.*

Pluto: To achieve results in the face of large seemingly impossible obstacles. Courage to take the necessary but difficult pathway.   ♦   Benefits or breakthrough achieved in the wake of a disaster. *Sir Edmund Hilary, NZ mountain climber who climbed Mt Everest and then spent the rest of his life helping the Nepalese people.*

The Node: The need to be a successful warrior, a striving to become a larger than life figure.   ♦   A time of military action. *John F. Kennedy, thirty-fifth President of the United States, and seen as a bold reformer.*

NOTES

1. Grimal, *The Dictionary of Classical Mythology*, p.330.
2. Bulfinch, *Myths of Greece and Rome*, p.238.

CANOPUS

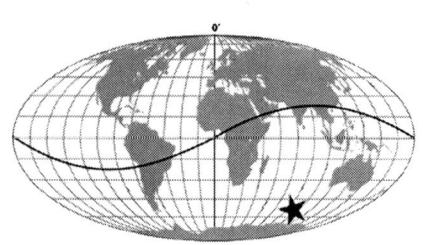

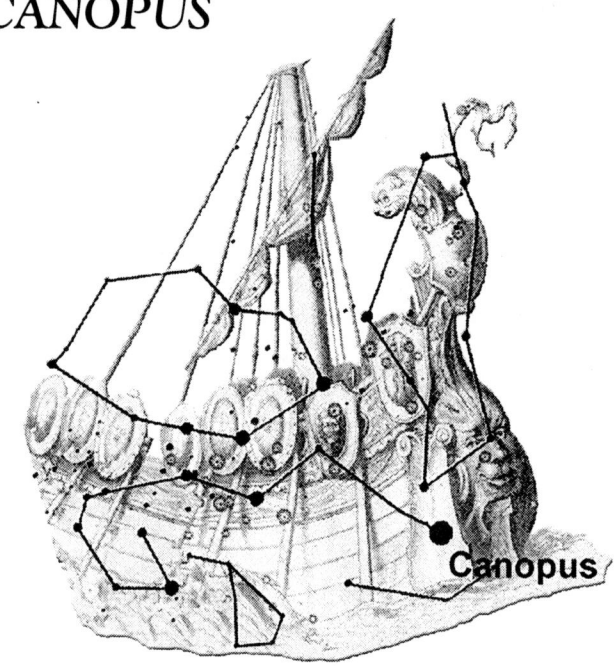

Constellation	Carinae
α Carinae, magnitude	- 0.72
1 January 2000 =	RA 6hr 23' 59"
Declination	-52° 42'
Celestial longitude	14° ♋ 59'
Celestial latitude	75°S49'
BV Colour =	White

The Argo, Carina the Keel, Puppis the Stern and Vela the Sails
At northern latitudes this southern ship rises and then stays closes to the horizon as it travels from east to west, looking like a ship sailing the ocean. In ancient times this group of stars represented such a ship which was able to sail to lands unknown. Its oldest known expression is the vessel used by Osiris and Isis after the great deluge which flooded the earth[1]. The Greeks claimed this great southern ship as the Argo, the mythical vessel that was the first great ocean-going boat, built and used by Jason to set sail "where no one has gone before" and find the Golden Fleece[2]. To the Hindus this is the vessel that Vishnu, in fish form, towed to safety during the Hindu version of one of the great floods. To the Christians this was Noah's Ark[3].

The principle of Canopus, the great navigator, a dominant leader
The Egyptians knew this star as the navigator of the great ship used to carry the dead to the afterlife. The Arabs called it The Bright One or The Wise One. It was also known as the Heavy-Weighing Canopus, a name which tells us the importance of this star, for Canopus was considered the weight at the end of the plumb-line used to define the poles[4]. The mythology of many cultures, including some American Indian tribes, saw this southern star moving northward and delineated this as the timing of the end of the world. So Canopus became linked with the concept of time, with a Saturnian theme of time eating all things. Canopus is associated with leadership, but also with matters of domination; it can destroy what it has created.

Heliacal Rising Star
To naturally seek a new way, to look for the new approach to problems. A talent for leading others into new ideas, but also a tendency to be dominating and get involved in power struggles. *Buddy Holly, 20th century US singer, songwriter, and a pioneer of rock and roll.*

Heliacal Setting Star
To do one's best work when forced to walk a different path. To have a life journey that brings success by taking the less travelled way. To be subject to criticism of one's ideas. *Manning Clark, 20th century Australian historian whose publication, History of Australia, revolutionised Australia's view of its own history.*

Star on one of its pivot points at the moment of birth
To be independent or headstrong, and seek to have total control in one's life. A strong natural leader but one who needs to dominate or control others, a person who seeks to maintain order. *Bill Clinton, 42nd president of the USA, involved in sex scandals.*

Physiological Correspondence: The sense of direction, and sense of timing.

Ptolemy's location: The bright star in the oar called Canopus.

World Cities: nil at latitudes between 50° to 54° south.

Canopus in paran with:

Sun: Leadership which can be inspirational or dictatorial. To have the confidence to pursue one's plans, but a tendency to over-dominate, over-protect.   ♦   The inspired leader or dictator wins victory. *Mao Tse-Tung, 20th century statesman who became a Marxist and a founding member of the Chinese Communist Party.*

Moon: A desire to present new philosophies in health, religion or the arts. To be drawn to professions concerned with health or social issues but to have strong ideas on how things should be done.   ♦   Disagreement concerning the needs of others. *Andrew Taylor Still, US founder of osteopathy.*

Mercury: To have strong opinions or to be heavily censored. The desire to probe the depths of subjects, and put forward new ideas and opinions.   ♦   Censorship, communication lines broken, no news. *Wole Soyinka, Nigerian playwright (Nobel Prize 1986) who wrote of West Africa's tragic history as an obstacle to human progress.*

Venus: One who has strong but inflexible social ideas. A unique but possibly dictatorial view of art, fashion or relationships.   ♦   Making judgements on social conventions, or on groups within society. *Pablo Picasso, 20th century Spanish artist who created three different movements or styles in art.*

Mars: The explorer or athlete. One who seeks to expand physical or emotional boundaries; the need to be different. ◆ Action taken with no regard for others. *Ma Rainey, US singer considered to be the "mother of the blues", the first of the black professional blues vocalists.*

Jupiter: To play the role of the hero or heroine by a determined, unswerving and inflexible attitude to achieving one's goals. ◆ A time when independent action leads to success. *Sirimavo Bandaranaike, Sri Lankan politician who was the world's first female Prime Minister.*

Saturn: To follow one's desired path even in the face of great difficulties; to be stubborn. To find leadership skills in the face of upheaval. ◆ A time of the dictator. *Peter Abrahams, South African author most of whose work was produced in exile; the impoverished township where he was born is vividly recreated in his memoir "Tell Freedom" (1954).*

Uranus: To work with the general public. To seek to either deal with common problems or help those whom society has forgotten. ◆ A single-mindedness in the mood of the general public. *Pancho Villa, 20th century Mexican revolutionary and guerrilla leader who fought against the regimes of both Porfirio Diaz and Victoriano Huerta.*

Neptune: To dare to dream; unrealistic thinking or a desire to pursue futuristic ideas. A lover of science fiction. ◆ A time of lies or falsehoods. *Piet Retief, 18th century Boer leader of the Great Trek; this was the mass migration of Boers who sought independence from British rule in South Africa.*

Pluto: Obsession with power, which can lead to downfall. To be blind to the need to change direction. Sudden changes in one's life path. ◆ Change of a long-established leader. *Michinomya Hirohito, emperor of Japan and ruler during World War II, who surrendered to the west after the bombings of Hiroshima and Nagasaki.*

The Node: To live life as a struggle, to choose the less trodden path, willing to accept difficulties in order to follow one's dreams. ◆ The establishment uses a heavy hand. *Chiang Kai-Shek, 19th century Chinese revolutionary who fought against communist rule in China and eventually created the nation of Taiwan.*

NOTES

1. Allen, *Star Names Their Lore and Meaning*, p.66.
2. Aratus, "Phaenomena," p.235.
3. Jobes and Jobes, *Outer Space: Myths, Name Meanings, Calendars*, p.120.
4. de Santillana and von Dechend, *Hamlet's Mill*, p.73.

CAPELLA

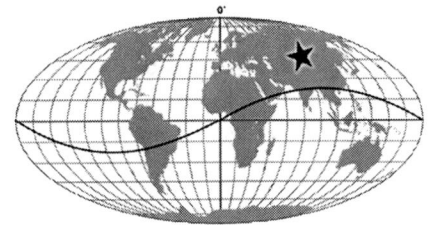

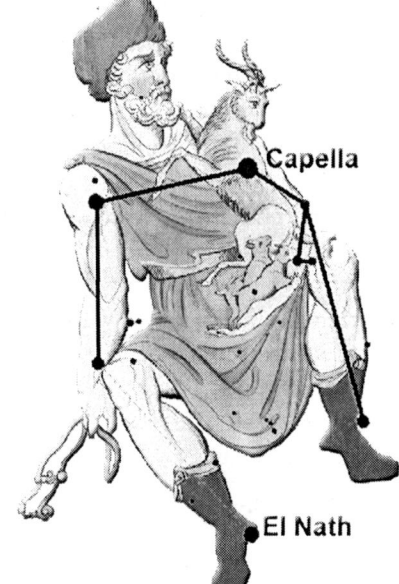

Constellation	Aurigae
α Aurigae, magnitude	0.08
1 January 2000 =	RA 5hr 16' 42"
Declination	+46° 00'
Celestial longitude	21° ♊ 52'
Celestial latitude	22°N52'
BV Colour =	Yellow

Auriga, the Charioteer

For the Babylonians the arch of the stars of the charioteer was the Crook of the great shepherd of Anu (Orion)[1], but by the time of the Greeks it has become the Charioteer[2]. Different cultures used different images for this constellation, varying from a man holding a whip and reins to a man riding in a chariot with a goat supported on his left shoulder. It is generally believed that this style of image originated in the Euphrates and that it was a well-established sky figure many millennia ago. Auriga also has an asterism of a she-goat nursing two kids. This goat was thought by the Greeks to have suckled Zeus and was therefore placed in the heavens in gratitude for her services. This asterism contains the brightest star in the constellation, Capella. In Egypt, circa 5,200 BCE, temples were aligned to its rising and setting and later in Greece it was apparently the orientation point of a temple at Eleusis dedicated to the Moon goddess, Diana[3].

The principle of Capella, the need for independence

Capella is associated with a nurturing but free-spirited flavour. The star is linked to Artemis the Greek goddess of the hunt and her Roman counterpart Diana. It is the concept of the goddess as linked to the horse and therefore embodies action and movement. Capella is therefore associated with the pursuit of freedom and independence in a non-aggressive way.

Heliacal Rising Star

To be aware of matters of freedom and fairness. To be driven by a personal philosophy that a basic right of life is to be free, whether in thinking of humans or animals. To struggle with a love of freedom in conflict with the need for personal commitments. *Nelson Mandela, 20th century revolutionary and politician who rebelled against the South African apartheid rule.*

Heliacal Setting Star
To be tested in matters of freedom, whether spiritual or physical. A need to claim the right to personal freedom, to find that only when one calms this right one able to achieve; to fight for the removal of restrictions or prejudice. *Martin Luther King, 20th century American activist who was one of the principal leaders of the American civil rights movement.*

Star on one of its pivot points at the moment of birth
A growing desire for an independent life. To try to deal with life's events in an independent, non-aggressive manner, always tilting one's decisions towards independence, while at the same time striving to balance this with domestic responsibilities. *Louisa May Alcott, 19th century US novelist who was both an abolitionist and a feminist, her most famous work being "Little Women".*

Physiological Correspondence: The diaphragm and its muscles, enabling the freely expansive and contractive action of the lungs.

Ptolemy's location: The star in the left shoulder and called Capella.

World Cities: Belgrade, Serbia; Bordeaux and Lyons, France; Bucharest, Romania; Milan and Venice, Italy; Odessa, Ukraine; Zurich, Switzerland at latitudes between 44^0 to 48^0 north.

Capella in paran with:

Sun: A desire to act as a free agent; the athlete. The need to balance the desire for independence with matters of personal responsibility. ♦ The free agent takes centre stage. *Sir Edmund Hilary, together with his Tibetan guide, Tenzing Norgay, was the first to reach the summit of the world's highest mountain, Mt Everest.*

Moon: Seeking freedom for oneself and/or others. To work in areas committed to the improvement of the quality of people's lives. A desire to demonstrate, via actions or example, that barriers can be broken. ♦ A group wants greater freedom. *Lionel Lukin, 18th century US inventor who is credited with developing the modern "unsinkable" lifeboat.*

Mercury: One who is a lateral thinker; to be far-sighted. To be able to see the connections between ideas and philosophies, or the potential in new ideas and technologies. ♦ A focus on an individual who works outside of the system, a maverick. *Marion Adams, 19th century intellectual and the first woman to develop a serious interest in photography.*

Venus: To challenge the values of society. To strive to be free of the restrictions that society can impose. ♦ A group or person goes outside of society's accepted boundaries. *Napoleon Bonaparte, 19th century French commander who revolutionised military organisation and training; also sponsored the Napoleonic Code, which became the basis for later civil law codes.*

Mars: Explorer or activist; willing to take risks. A challenge-oriented approach to life.   ◆   An action by a free-spirited group. *Ferdinand De Lesseps, 19th century diplomat who is best known for building the Suez Canal.*

Jupiter: The traveller, one who encounters new experiences. To find success and gain freedom through study, experimentation and observation.   ◆   Fast action, bold insights bring success. *John Harrison, 17th century English clockmaker who solved the problem of how to measure longitude.*

Saturn: The expert, or to challenge the status quo. One's greatest fulfilments, personally or professionally, come when one makes passionate commitments to projects.   ◆   Bold action required by civic leaders, or the law makers. *Edward Burnett Tylor, English anthropologist regarded as the founder of cultural anthropology.*

Uranus: To seek ways of working faster, or doing everyday things in a more economical manner.   ◆   The releasing of a group, the freeing up of a situation. *Ray Kroc, 20th century US restauranteur known as the founder of the fast-food industry and the McDonald's chain of restaurants.*

Neptune: A love of alternative spiritual paths; to work in leading-edge visual media, or to work for the rights of others.   ◆   Controversy over freedom and the rights of individuals. *John Dee, 16th century English astrologer who experimented with channelling angels and was astrologer to Mary Tudor and Elizabeth I.*

Pluto: To seek the freedom of one's family or tribe; to push against the system or to feel bound by the power of others.   ◆   Abrupt ending to an old conundrum. *Marie Antoinette, Queen to Louis XVI of France, she contributed to the unrest which culminated in the French Revolution, and her execution.*

The Node: A lover of speed and/or freedom; interest in physical movement and finding pleasure in fast machines, real or virtual. A supporter of ideas outside of mainstream beliefs.   ◆   A disregard for matters of physical safety; lawlessness. *Isaac Newton Lewis, US inventor known for his invention of the Lewis machine gun widely used during World War I.*

NOTES

1. Black and Green, *Gods, Demons and Symbols of Ancient Mesopotamia*, p.54.
2. Aratus, "Phaenomena," p.219.
3. Allen, *Star Names Their Lore and Meaning*, p.84.

CAPULUS

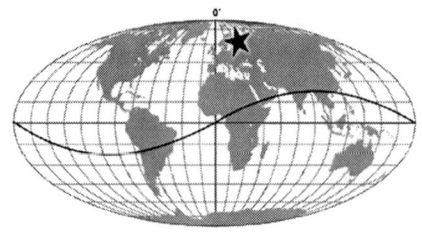

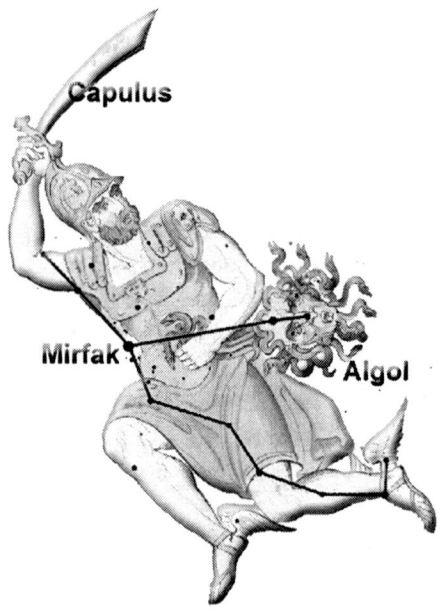

Constellation	Perseus
Nebula, magnitude	5.30
1 January 2000 =	RA 2hr 19' 00"
Declination	+57° 09'
Celestial longitude	24° ♉ 12'
Celestial latitude	40°N23'
BV Colour =	White

Perseus, the Warrior

The Old Man to the Babylonians, and to the Hebrews he was Ham, the son of Noah. But in the Egyptian cosmology he is Khem, the black son of Cepheus the king. Perseus can also be seen in the Greek mould as the conquering hero saving the damsel in distress (Andromeda), with his sword raised and holding his prize of Medusa's head. Or we can see him as part of this natural balance, the royal family: Andromeda's suitor, young, masculine, full of male energy symbolised by his raised sword, holding in his hand the head of an animal or the head of an enemy as his offering. Skilled in hunting, skill in the ways of the warrior. (For more information see Algol and Mirfak).

The principle of Capulus, the sword of the warrior, penetrating action

This star, or rather nebula, is linked to male sexual energy: concentrated, direct, penetrating action. It symbolizes being focused and passionate and therefore, at times, brutal and violent. Its energy is clear and decisive, but at times it can be ruthless, with Perseus' sword representing male kundalini energy as a counterpart to the other star in this constellation, Algol. At times it can be savage; at other times it can show single-minded, unambiguous action.

Heliacal Rising Star

To have as a personal motto "actions speak louder than words". To have a strong desire to achieve one's goals. A life filled with an unyielding determination to fulfil one's passion. *June Bronhill, leading Australian opera soprano who changed her name to reflect her birth place, Broken Hill as its citizens raised the funds for her to train as a singer.*

Heliacal Setting Star
Success gained by the seemingly reckless disregard of social or political barriers. To find that one has to fight against glass-ceilings. To enjoy playing the game of money and power. *Sarah Breedlove Walker, 20th century businesswoman and philanthropist, generally acknowledged to be the first black female millionaire in the United States.*

Star on one of its pivot points at the moment of birth
Sexual charisma, natural good looks. To live by exploiting one's sexual charms or to be strongly drawn to sexually charismatic people. A life vulnerable to aggression or recklessness. *Marilyn Monroe, US actress, model, Hollywood icon, and sex symbol who was in the end destroyed by the extremes of her life.*

Physiological Correspondence: Testosterone, the biochemical driver of sexuality in both males and females.

Ptolemy's location: The one at the end of the right hand and is misty.

World Cities: Aberdeen, Edinburgh and Glasgow, Scotland; Copenhagen, Denmark; Moscow, Russia at latitudes between 55° to 59° north.

Capulus in paran with:

Sun: To be harsh or experience harshness. To struggle with male figures, to be identified with struggle, to be involved in violence as a perpetrator or victim.   ♦   A focus on the inspired leader or dictator. *Madame Blavatsky – 19th century spiritualist and founder of the Theosophical Society, who received much criticism in her lifetime.*

Moon: To be in, or have to deal with, a hostile environment. Difficulties with women, or being concerned with the difficulties that women experience.   ♦   A hard attitude to the needs of others. *Isabel Allende, after the overthrow of Chile's coalition government she fled Chile and her first novel, "The House of Spirits" (1985) arising directly out of her exile, became a worldwide best-seller and critical success.*

Mercury: To express oneself in a confronting manner. To take on the hard intellectual fight, to struggle against attacks in order to maintain one's opinion.   ♦   Matters of censorship, or times of no news. *Raden Adjeng (Lady) Kartini – early 20th century reformer who was an inspiration for Indonesian independence and Indonesian feminism.*

Venus: Questioning society's moral standards. Drawn to relationships that restrict or block one's personal dreams. The need to rebel against family patterns.   ♦   Making judgements on social conventions. *Miguel Angel Asturias, a Guatemalan law graduate who spent many years in exile, notably in Paris, where he studied anthropology. His novels reflected the exploitation of Mayan Indians.*

Mars: Willing to deal with the difficult or macabre. The surgeon or the butcher, physically or metaphorically. ◆ Action without regard for the feelings of others. *Bram Stoker, 19th century Irish novelist and author of the popular horror tale "Dracula".*

Jupiter: One confronts problems head on. To be willing to action against the advice or conventions on one's family or community. ◆ An attack against the system. *Martin Luther, 15th century German reformer whose attacks on the abuses of the clergy precipitated the Protestant Reformation.*

Saturn: To ruthlessly fulfil one's dreams, whether positive or negative. To take the authoritarian position. ◆ Leadership in the face of difficulties. *Josef Mengele, Nazi known as the "Angel of Death", responsible for medical experimentation on inmates at Auschwitz.*

Uranus: To devote oneself to a life of service in either a political or spiritual arena. Drawn to mass spectacles of a sporting or political nature. ◆ A single-mindedness in the mood of the general public. *Mohandas K. Gandhi, 20th century Indian leader who was reared in a morally rigorous environment and promoted pacifism and the sanctity of all living things.*

Neptune: To believe that one can prosper from ideas that turn out to be self-delusory. To be subject to rumors, to suffer at the hands of slander. ◆ Lies and falsehoods abound. *Sarah Ferguson, Duchess of York and former wife of Prince Andrew of England, whose marriage ended in rumour and scandal.*

Pluto: To seek to impose one's views on others. To hold strong opinions on social order; political or religious zealotry. ◆ A mainstream leader is overthrown. *Pauline Hanson, a 20th century Australian politician who rose to fame due to her outspokenly racist right-wing beliefs.*

The Node: To embody focus and assertive action. The athlete, the successful warrior; to be seen as physically aggressive. ◆ A time of ruthlessness. *Jackie Stewart, Scottish automobile-racing driver who became the "voice" of the grand prix circuit.*

CASTOR

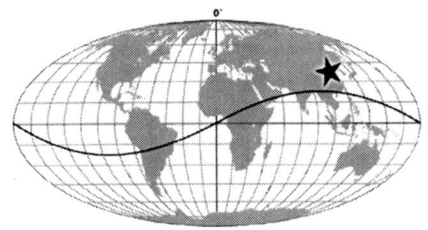

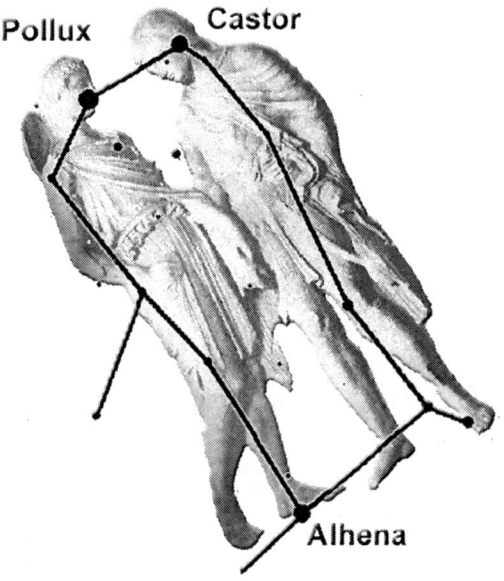

Constellation	Gemini
α Geminorum, magnitude	1.98
1 January 2000 =	RA 7hr 34' 36"
Declination	+31° 53'
Celestial longitude	20° ♋ 15'
Celestial latitude	10°N06'
BV Colour =	White

Gemini, the Twins

Known as the twins in most ancient writings this pair of stars and their constellation are linked to the wonder of twins. The myths around this constellation tend to be symbolic of the struggle of light to overcome the dark, which is also the power of the rising sun to extinguish the light of the circumpolar stars. The Morning Star (rising before the sun) was also known as Lucifer (bearing light) and the Evening Star was known as Vespers (evening). Through the effects of precession Lucifer (the morning rising star) was seen to be cast out of heaven and into the whirlpool as this star slipped into southern declinations. Twins are linked to the concept of polarity: where there is light there is dark; for every push forward there is a step that also has to be taken backwards. There are many paired stars in the heavens, each set implying one principle divided into the Civilized and the Shadow. Gemini, however, is the most well-known heavenly pair. (For more information see Alhena and Pollux).

The principle of Castor one of the Twins, the story-teller

This star seeks the bright side of the polarity, the lighter side of the story or situation. Castor allows for an understanding of the tension of polarity but gives the ability to benefit from this tension without the loss or difficulties of the shadow. It represents the exploration of ideas and their expression through research or story without the need to examine or take into account the shadowy side of life.

Heliacal Rising Star
Always seeking knowledge and wanting a voice. A lifestyle which is a journey through the hills-and-valleys of polarities. Having to learn to live with polarities, juggling two lifestyles. *Bob Ansett, Australian businessman who set himself as a business rival of his father (Ansett Airlines), and suffered much business turbulence.*

Heliacal Setting Star
Being drawn into polarities, discovering that one is most successful when having to deal with opposites. Seeking a life of learning but finding that one has to defend one's ideas or one's lifestyle. *John Harrison, 17th century English inventor who developed a way of measuring longitude at sea, but struggled for recognition for his work, only receiving it at the end of his life.*

Star on one of its pivot points at the moment of birth
A lifestyle that straddles more than one culture. Talented in languages, interested in other cultures; seeking to build a bridge between disparate opinions. *Peter O'Toole, English actor known especially for his portrayal of T.E. Lawrence (Lawrence of Arabia).*

Physiological Correspondence: The vocal cords and larynx.

Ptolemy's location: The star in the head.

World Cities: Cairo, Egypt; Chongqing, Nanjing and Shanghai, China; Nagasaki, Japan; Tripoli, Libya at latitudes between 29⁰ to 33⁰ north.

Castor in paran with:

Sun: Skilled with language, a profession linked with writing and communication. A story-teller, a poet or song writer, one who loves to learn.   ♦   A speech is given, a writer is honoured. *John Lennon, The Beatles' rhythm guitarist and vocalist, and partner in the Lennon-McCartney song-writing team.*

Moon: The therapeutic use of humour, to be involved in education; a desire to bring stories to others.   ♦   To hope that everything will be all right, to disbelieve bad news. *Mack Sennett, 19th century Canadian film maker who created the Keystone Cops and developed slapstick comedy for film.*

Mercury: A skill with words and language, quick-witted, highly dextrous; the scribe, and/or the merchant, one who is good with figures.   ♦   A clever plan is revealed. *Tom Stoppard, Czech-born British playwright whose work is marked by verbal brilliance, ingenious action, and structural dexterity.*

Venus: Socially skilled, charming, and even artistic. The gifted orator or singer; to be a spokesperson for one's community.   ♦   A noteworthy speech is made. *John Keats, 18th century poet best known for his lyrical verse and his search for perfection in poetry.*

Mars: One who plans, a thinker, a solver of problems. To love puzzles, to seek intellectual challenges. To be argumentative. ◆ A focus on a person who reveals a plan. *Blaise Pascal, 17th century French mathematician whose greatest contribution is to have founded the modern theory of probabilities.*

Jupiter: A negotiator, or one who arbitrates. To deal in polarities and find successful resolutions. To have inspirational ideas about how two things can be united. ◆ Victory to the person who is decisive. *Sergey Diaghilev, early 20th century Russian arts promoter best known for fusing Russian music, art and dance.*

Saturn: The Map Maker, a person who gives shape to intellectual concepts. A pathfinder or one who can lead others to new ideas or places. ◆ A project is launched. *Chuck Berry, US singer who was one of the first to shape blues music into what is known today as rock 'n' roll.*

Uranus: To show others a new way, to be interested in the education or the ideas of the common people. ◆ A popular author, film, or cause takes the community's attention. *Andreas Marggraf, 18th century German chemist who discovered beet sugar which led to the development of the sugar industry.*

Neptune: A strong intuition, a spiritual approach to life. Sensitive to colour and design. ◆ A wave of spiritual, religious or metaphysical thinking. *John Wesley, 18th century Anglican clergyman, evangelist, and founder of the Methodist movement in the Church of England.*

Pluto: To be obsessed with an idea; to be drawn to large projects or to find one's words having far-reaching effect. ◆ A powerful orator or author takes the spotlight. *Regiomontanus, (Johannes Muller), 15th century German mathematician who revived trigonometry and developed a system of house division in astrology.*

The Node: To be associated with an idea, to link one's life to a philosophy. To embody the concept of a teacher. ◆ A breakthrough in communication technologies. *Sir Isaac Pitman, 19th century English educator who invented the Pitman system of shorthand.*

DENEB ADIGE

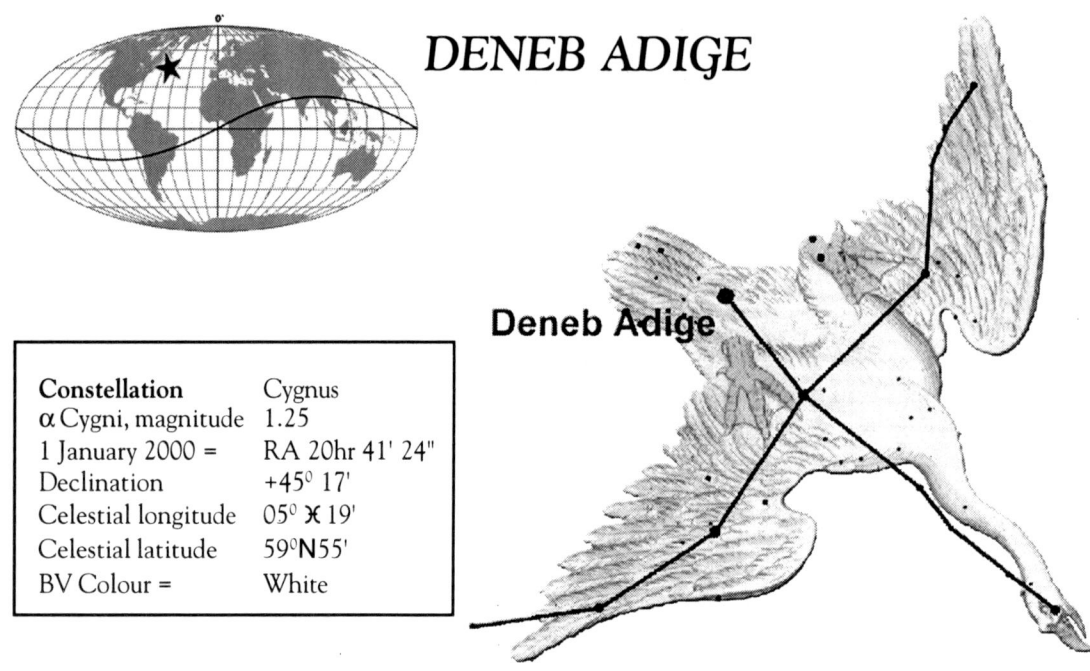

Constellation Cygnus
α Cygni, magnitude 1.25
1 January 2000 = RA 20hr 41' 24"
Declination +45° 17'
Celestial longitude 05° ♓ 19'
Celestial latitude 59°N55'
BV Colour = White

Cygnus, the Swan

The Swan, Cygnus, is one of a grouping of constellations in the northern sky consisting of three birds; the eagle, Aquila; the swan, Cygnus a vulture now renamed the Lyre, and the arrow, Sagitta. The naming of Cygnus may have originated on the Euphrates but the Greeks knew it as the swan that was Zeus in his seduction of Leda, the mother of Castor and Pollux[1]. In this myth there are echoes of an older Hindu story, involving a shamanic practice of wearing a swan-feather cloak to enable the gods to take the form of a swan. Krishna from the Hindu tradition became a swan knight through this process and the story of Zeus and Leda is thought to be a Greek update on the story of Krishna and "Lady", whose union created the World Egg[2]. In modern times we think of the swan as a graceful, peaceful bird, but it is in its nature a hostile animal, willing to battle any bird or beast that enters its space.

The principle of Deneb Adige, the shaman's star, the spiritual warrior

This is a very subtle star. It contains the strength and hostility of the swan, while at the same time it holds within its symbolism the mystic, transcendental qualities embodied in shamanistic legends of the creation of the World Egg. The symbolism of Deneb Adige can be seen in both the aggressive and the spiritual sides of a life. The Egyptians saw this star as the exit of the birth canal of Nut, the great starry sky goddess. Through her birth canal the Sun, Ra, was born anew every winter solstice. Thus, Deneb Adige is linked to the idea of the hero's journey, as a journey of actively seeking spiritual awareness, but not in a gentle manner rather in a practical hands-on way. It is the shaman's star.

Heliacal Rising Star
To seek the hero's journey, a desire to become aware. To always feel that one can take a deeper step, to feel that one has to walk the less trodden trail. *Leo McKern, Australian-born actor who worked in England and is best known for his role as Horace Rumpole, the struggling lawyer who demonstrated deep insight into human behaviour, and a biting wit.*

Heliacal Setting Star
Finding that life slowly pulls one into the path of the spiritual warrior, to learn to love philosophy, to grow in learning and knowledge. *Soko Yamaga, 17th century Japanese military strategist and Confucian philosopher who set forth the first systematic exposition of missions and obligations of the samurai (warrior) class.*

Star on one of its pivot points at the moment of birth
To live the hero's journey, a desire to be tested. *Napoleon Bonaparte, 18th century French general known as "The Little Corporal", Napoleon revolutionised military organisation and training as well as sponsoring the Napoleonic Code which became the basis for later civil law codes.*

Physiological Correspondence: The face, and one's ability to make of it a mask appropriate to one's intent.

Ptolemy's location: The bright star in the tail of the swan.

World Cities: Belgrade, Serbia; Bordeaux, Lyons and Marseilles, France; Bucharest, Romania; Milan and Venice, Italy; Odessa, Ukraine at latitudes between $43°$ to $47°$ north.

Deneb Adige in paran with:

Sun: The desire to explore – places, spiritual beliefs and ideas. The courage to act on one's beliefs. The shaman, one who touches other worlds.   ♦   News of a pioneer. *Henry Ford, American industrialist who revolutionised factory production by introducing the assembly line.*

Moon: To walk a different path from society's expectations. To go against the expectation of others in order to follow one's own beliefs.   ♦   Arrogant dismissal of the welfare of others. *Galileo Galilei, 17th century Italian who is considered to be the father of modern physics for daring to question the conventional acceptance of the principles of Aristotle.*

Mercury: An idea-magician; the poet, the actor or the shaman. Intuitive thinking, seeking an enchanted world.   ♦   A time of confusion in reporting, or a mystical or intuitive idea is put forward. *Alan Alexander Milne, English author best known as the writer of the popular children's books featuring Christopher Robin and his toy bear, Winnie the Pooh.*

Venus: The poetic soul struggling to live in the mundane world. Seeking the divine in art or music, finding one's fulfilment in the arts. ♦ Religious art or music is celebrated. *Omar Khayyam, 11th century Iranian poet who is known in the English speaking world primarily for his Rubaiyat (quatrains).*

Mars: A noble warrior, a person who acts from their principles. The desire to bring change to people's attitudes, the researcher or social activist. ♦ A noble act is reported. *Mohandas K. Gandhi, 19th century Indian statesman who overthrew English rule through a principle of non-violent resistance.*

Jupiter: Physically adept, or desiring to solve problems of the physical world. To inspire others into new ways of thinking. ♦ Problems of space, place, or land are solved. *Sir Isaac Pitman, 19th century English educator best known for developing the Pitman system of shorthand.*

Saturn: To act against the tide of society's conventions, to feel restricted by social norms, to rebel and place oneself in danger. ♦ Solutions are sought to long-term problems. *Benedict Arnold, 18th century American traitor. At the outbreak of the War of Independence - 1775 to 1783 - Arnold joined the colonial forces but acted as a spy for the English army.*

Uranus: One who can bring dreams into reality. To work towards the practical realisation of popular dreams. ♦ A time when science fantasy becomes science fact. *Guglielmo Marconi, 19th century Italian known as the inventor of radio telegraphy.*

Neptune: A persuasive individual, one who can convince others of supernatural or spiritual truths. To be gullible or have a tendency to assume the mysterious. ♦ The media is being censored, or propaganda abounds. *Joseph Smith, 19th century religious leader and founder of the Church of Jesus Christ of Latter-day Saints (Mormons).*

Pluto: To be motivated by spiritual beliefs, to believe strongly in one's own dreams, a lover of the magical or impossible. ♦ The paranormal realm takes a high profile. *Joseph-Michel Montgolfier, 18th century French balloonist who, together with his younger brother, Jacques-Etienne, was a pioneer in hot-air balloon design.*

The Node: To see the magic in daily life, to bring the unfocused into focus. To be always aware of other pathways, other ways of doing things. ♦ Mysteries are solved, a miracle happens. *Carl Ziess, 19th century German who gained worldwide reputation as a manufacturer of fine optical instruments.*

NOTES

1. Room, *Dictionary of Astronomical Names*, p.78.
2. Walker, *The Woman's Encyclopedia of Myths and Secrets*, p.963.

DENEB ALGEDI

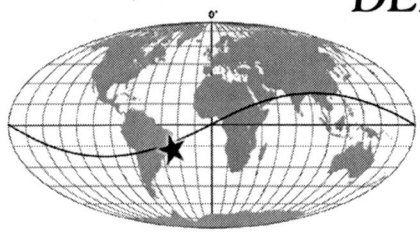

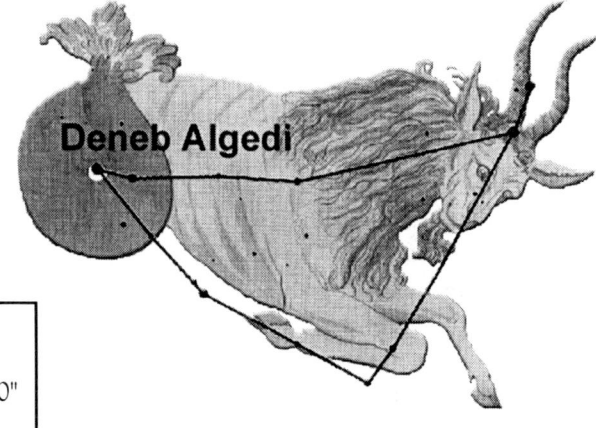

Constellation	Capricorn
δ Capricornus, magnitude	2.87
1 January 2000 =	RA 21hr 47'00"
Declination	-16°08'
Celestial longitude	23° ♒ 32'
Celestial latitude	02°S36'
BV Colour =	White

Capricornus, the sea goat

At the time when the winter solstice occurred amongst the stars of Capricorn around 3,000 to 2,000 BCE, it was known as the Southern Gate of the Sun. The Sea-Goat or Goat-Fish was also known in early Babylonian times as the god Ea, *He of Vast Intellect* and *Lord of the Sacred Eye*[1]. Ea was the protector of his people and from his place in the sky the great rivers flowed, giving life. Periodically he would rise from these waters, to teach and bring civilization to his people. Ea was considered the *Father of Light* and his celebrations, dating back to 15,000 BCE, were carried out wearing goat skins[2]. He was honoured as law giver and educator. The Greeks took this ancient god and created Pan, telling legends of how the great Pan dived into the water and developed a fish tail.

The principle of Deneb Algedi, the ancient law giver

This star is symbolic of a law-giving, justice-orientated ancient god who was seeking to bring civilisation to his people. Such a symbol continues to be reflected in the laws of the establishment, and the structure of civilisations that yield ordered societies. In paran therefore the star brings to one's chart a stabilising, authoritarian and conservative nature but always focused on what is considered by society to be best for the individual.

Heliacal Rising Star
Seeking the legal, physical or metaphysical laws that govern the world. A seeker of knowledge or solutions, endeavouring to help others in one's community. *Alessandro Volta, 18th century Italian physicist, inventor of the electric battery, the first man-made source of continuous current.*

Heliacal Setting Star
One who wants to help others through the establishment of systems; the politician or team leader. Finding leadership skills under pressure. *Dawn Fraser, Australia swimmer who was the first female swimmer to win gold medals in three consecutive Olympics; after having her own career ruined by false accusations she became a leader representing athletes' rights.*

Star on one of its pivot points at the moment of birth
One who is physically talented; a skilled artisan and a lover of nature, but a tendency for hubris. *Isadora Duncan, 19th century American dancer known for her interpretative dancing and an advocate of natural rhythm in dance.*

Physiological Correspondence: The spine – the thoracic vertebrae in the upper back.

Ptolemy's location: The tail of the goat.

World Cities: La Paz, Bolivia at latitudes between $14°$ to $18°$ south.

Deneb Algedi in paran with:

Sun: To be respected, to give wisdom. To instil in others a love of knowledge and to build a reputation for being steady and consistent within one's profession.   ♦   A time when the respected person steps forward. *Sir Hans Sloane, a naturalist whose private collection formed the basis for the British Museum.*

Moon: A story-teller, the use of story to promote greater awareness of humanity. One who is drawn to myths or stories that heal and teach.   ♦   A story captures the imagination of the people. *George Smith, archaeologist who discovered literary works from the Mesopotamian civilization, one of which was "The Epic of Gilgamesh".*

Mercury: The scholar, the one who is seen to be wise. To be known as fair in one's negotiations; to have an attitude of thoroughness in one's work.   ♦   A time when the institution of the law is in the news. *Max Wolf, 20th century German astronomer who applied photography to the search for asteroids and discovered 228 of them.*

Venus: A conventional attitude to art, or the social customs of relationships. A lover of the classics in music, film or literature.   ♦   Society's appreciation of its art. *Jane Austen, 19th* century English writer who applied common sense to apparently melodramatic situations, a technique she later developed in evaluating ordinary human behaviour.

Mars: To take the law into one's own hands, for better or for worse. A desire to make laws, or to break what one may consider incorrect laws. ♦ Times of terrorism, actions against the state. *Jesse James, American outlaw who, accompanied by his brother, Frank, became the most notorious outlaw of the American West.*

Jupiter: A desire to helping others through education; seeking to improve the spiritual or physical lives of people. The lawyer, or teacher who wants to lead by example. ♦ The reformer gains ground. *John Basedow, 18th century German educational reformer who advocated an end to physical punishment and rote memorization in language-learning in schools.*

Saturn: A person who believes in the value of persistence and hard work. A life philosophy of hard work and commitment, the need to see the results of one's efforts. ♦ Legal, safety, or security systems fail. *Ayn Rand, Russian writer noted for her philosophy of objectivism, which advocated that all real achievement is the product of individual ability and effort.*

Uranus: To have a social conscience, seeking justice for the common folk. To listen to and work for minority groups. ♦ The common law is upheld. *Sydney Nolan, 20th century Australian artist known for his paintings of the popular outlaw, Ned Kelly.*

Neptune: To be involved with environmental issues; to work in film; to be drawn to new spiritual ideas. ♦ The justice of the legal system or the law is challenged. *Sir John Bennet Lawes, 19th century English industrialist who founded the artificial fertiliser industry and the oldest agricultural research station in the world, Rothamsted.*

Pluto: Interest in the fabric of the law, to want to understand the workings of society. To wrestle with the legal system. ♦ Attacks against the law and the fabric of society. *Tony Blair, UK Labour Prime Minister (1997-2007) who oversaw the creation of an unprecedented number of new laws in the UK in his efforts to control terrorism.*

The Node: The lawyer, the educator, one whose life embodies the role of the establishment in maintaining the order of society. ♦ The law is used to maintain order. *Karl Marx, 19th century German writer who wrote the Communist Manifesto.*

NOTES

1. Black and Green, *Gods, Demons and Symbols of Ancient Mesopotamia*, p.75.
2. Jobes and Jobes, *Outer Space: Myths, Name Meanings, Calendars*, p.139.

DENEBOLA

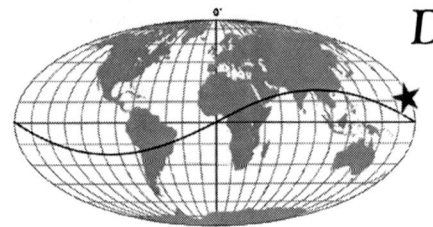
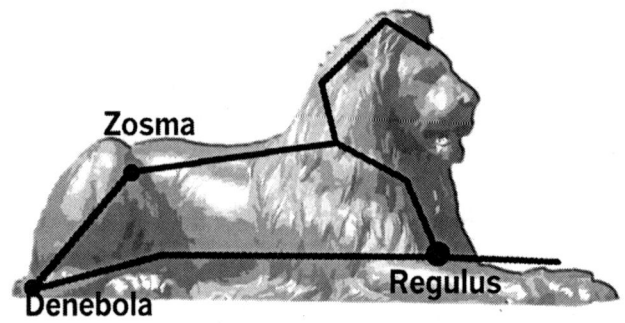

Constellation	Leo
β Leonis, magnitude	2.14
1 January 2000 =	RA 11hr 49' 03"
Declination	+14° 34'
Celestial longitude	21° ♍ 37'
Celestial latitude	12°N 16'
BV Colour =	White

Leo, the Lion

Around 6,000 to 3,000 BCE, the stars of Leo were the heliacal rising stars of the summer solstice, linking this constellation with hot summers and the longest days. This connection, occurring at the dawn of writing, linked the constellation Leo with the Sun. Recognised as a lion by the Persians, Syrians, Babylonians and Egyptians, this constellation seems to have been a lion throughout antiquity from the beginning of cultivation and civilisation. The lion was also linked to Sekhmet, the sister form to Bast-Hathor of Egyptian mythology. She was a Sphinx-lioness symbolising the Destroyer and was an active aggressor on behalf of her father's enemies[1]. She would sit beside Ra and pour forth blazing fire which would scorch and consume his enemies, or else use fiery darts to strike them from afar. Later, with the stars of Leo no longer claiming the important solstice position, the Greeks and Romans considered this constellation the Nemean Lion which was killed by Hercules as one of his labours[2]. (For more information see Regulus and Zosma).

The principle of Denebola, the tail of the lion, non-conforming

Denebola seems to be associated with the mythology of the Nemean Lion for, just as the Nemean Lion was symbolic of the goddess worship still practiced in rural areas, this star indicates in some degree "being out of step" or being out of the main stream of thought. Not conforming and living on the fringe. Denebola's presence in a chart adds an element of uniqueness, seeing the world through different eyes, holding a different philosophy and living outside of the norms of the establishment.

Heliacal Rising Star
Pursuing an alternative life. To seek a life on the edge of society, a loner, to be drawn to alternative groups. *Paul Hogan, Australian actor who gained fame through his screen character Crocodile Dundee.*

Heliacal Setting Star
To do one's best work when one steps outside of established systems. To be forced to find unusual solutions. Learning that one can achieve results by going outside of established practice. *Philippe Pinel, 18th century French physician who pioneered the humane treatment of the mentally ill.*

Star on one of its pivot points at the moment of birth
A lifestyle of struggling against conventional thinking. To clash with the establishment, or struggle to be heard; to have one's rights acknowledged or accepted. *Charles I of England, 17th century monarch who was executed after the English Civil War.*

Physiological Correspondence: The coccyx – the tailbone.

Ptolemy's location: The star at the tip of the tail.

World Cities: Bangkok, Thailand; Dakar, Senegal; Guatemala City, Guatemala; Manila, Philippines at latitudes between 12° to 16° north.

Denebola in paran with:

Sun: To be independent and to do things in one's own way. To represent the struggle for a different lifestyle, to see oneself as different from the norm of society. ♦ The alternative person takes centre stage. *George Armstrong Custer, US general who led his men to death in one of the most controversial battles in the history of the USA known as "The Battle of Little Big Horn".*

Moon: The anthropologist, an acute awareness of and interest in the different, the romantic, or the difficult lifestyles of others. ♦ A time when a society struggles with different religions or cultures within it. *Kingsley Davis, US sociologist who was the first to coin the terms "population explosion" and "zero population growth".*

Mercury: To have a different point of view on language and culture. To struggle with language, or live where one does not speak the language. One who can find an unusual business opportunity. ♦ A contra opinion gains ground. *John Dee, controversial 16th century English astrologer to Mary Tudor and Elizabeth I.*

Venus: To challenge accepted social opinions. To have unique ideas in the world of design and fashion. ♦ Society's standards are ruffled. *Anne Newport Royall, US writer who broke with convention and became the first American journalist.*

Mars: To champion the non-mainstream cause. Motivated to work with alternative causes, within or outside of the law. ◆ Actions which are designed to shock. *Yuri Gagarin, Russian cosmonaut who became the first man to travel in space.*

Jupiter: To have success with unpopular or unusual ventures. Learning valuable lessons from an unconventional mentor. ◆ Success gained by unorthodox methods. *John Flynn, Presbyterian minister who was the founder of the Royal Flying Doctor Service of Australia in 1928.*

Saturn: A person who represents alternative life choices. To willingly engage in arduous or unpopular endeavours. ◆ A minor political party speaks out. *Nostradamus, 16th century French astrologer and physician well known for his "Centuries", a collection of prophecies first published in 1555.*

Uranus: To be tolerant of others; to be accepting of the different beliefs and customs of other cultures; to live in and enjoy a foreign culture. ◆ Alternative customs are accepted. *Sir Thomas Stamford Raffles, 18th century administrator who was the founder of Singapore and responsible for the creation of Britain's Far East empire.*

Neptune: To use art to make social commentary; to drop out of society through drugs; to have strong views on alternative subjects or religions. ◆ Events produce a time of uncertainty. *William Penn, 17th century English Quaker leader who founded the Commonwealth of Pennsylvania as a refuge for religious non-conformists.*

Pluto: To want to empower those who have no voice in society. Interest in how society works. To seek alternative ways of earning a living. ◆ A time of people-power, the authority loses control. *Arthur Charles Nielsen, 20th century US researcher who developed the Nielsen rating system of television viewing.*

The Node: To be associated with working for alternative or unacknowledged groups. To link one's life with the empowerment of those who have no voice in society. To want to give a voice to the unexpressed opinion. ◆ A fashion craze. *Isaac Singer, 19th century US inventor who developed the first practical sewing machine and brought it into domestic and general use.*

NOTES

1. David P. Silverman, "Divinity and Deities in Ancient Egypt," in *Religion in Ancient Egypt* ed. Byron E. Shafer, London: Cornell University Press, 1991, p.43.
2. Grimal, *The Dictionary of Classical Mythology*, p.197.

DIADEM

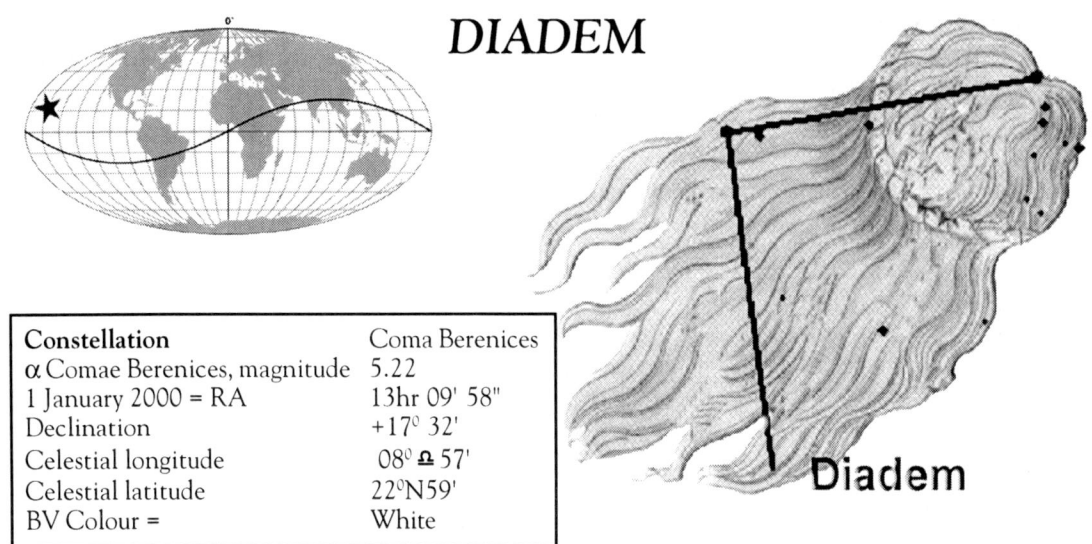

Constellation	Coma Berenices
α Comae Berenices, magnitude	5.22
1 January 2000 = RA	13hr 09' 58"
Declination	+17° 32'
Celestial longitude	08° ♎ 57'
Celestial latitude	22°N59'
BV Colour =	White

Coma Berenices, the Woman's Crown

Coma Berenices was once the tuft of the lion's tail in Leo, it was first alluded to as Ariadne's Hair or Ariadne's Crown by Eratosthenes in the *Catasterismi* [1]. The Greeks placed a date of 243 BCE on the naming of the constellation and, according to their history, the hair belonged to a woman called Berenice. The Greek story was that Berenice, sister-wife of Ptolemy III, was awaiting her husband's return from war and prayed to Aphrodite (Venus) daily for his safety. One day it came to her that if she could sacrifice something of great importance, then this would ensure her husband's safe return. Her sacrifice was her hair, traditionally amber in colour. This may seem a small sacrifice in the 20th century but a woman's hair in that period was a sign of her status and to have short hair was a form of disgrace. The hair disappeared from the altar and it was assumed that Aphrodite, so moved by the sacrifice, took the tress of hair and placed it in the heavens[2].

The Principle of Diadem, a woman's sacrifice

The star takes its name from the word diadem, a symbol of royalty worn on the head or a small crown. Diadem is thus linked to feminine strength. However, it is strength which does not seek glory or personal fame but rather belongs to the quiet workers, the people who slave for years helping or working for the benefit of a group but who never seek personal recognition or fame. At times the sacrifice that it asks may seem beyond the person's ability to give.

Heliacal Rising Star

To believe that sacrifice is a necessary component of one's life, to have a desire to serve. To accept that one will have losses in life and that life is about how one "bears" these loses. *Luc Jouret, Belgian religious leader who lead a mass suicide of his followers in 1994.*

Heliacal Setting Star
To slowly come to the realisation that one needs to make sacrifices in order to gain what one truly wants. *The Duke of Windsor (Edward VIII), in 1936 abdicated the English throne in order to marry the divorcee Wallis Simpson.*

Star on one of its pivot points at the moment of birth
To devote yourself to a cause, to live by the philosophy that the needs of the many outweigh the needs of the one, to be an example of a sacrifice. *Alexander Murray Haley, US author who is known for his semi-autobiographical account of his own family's encounter with slavery, Roots: The Saga of an American Family.*

Physiological Correspondence: The lining of the uterus, the endometrium – shed each month in menstruation.

Ptolemy's location: Ptolemy defined three stars as being in Coma Bernenices, it is unsure which he defines as Diadem.

World Cities: Bombay, India; Kingston, Jamaica; Rangoon, Myanmar at latitudes between 15° to 19° north.

Diadem in paran with:

Sun: Willing to make a sacrifice. One who undertakes a course of action, designed to benefit others.   •   A time when people make sacrifices. *Henry Morton Stanley, 19th century British-American explorer of central Africa, famous for his rescue of David Livingstone and for his discoveries in the Congo region.*

Moon: To show devotion to a cause, or group. A willingness to give of oneself to the needs of another.   •   A time for humanitarian acts. *Clare of Assisi – 12th century Italian saint who founded the Poor Clares Order. She was deeply influenced by Francis of Assisi and refused to marry.*

Mercury: One who values ideas more than money. To be non-materialistic, to work for or donate to charities.   •   The needs of the people win through. *Emily Dickinson, US poet, a shy, religious intelligent woman who earned the title of "the New England mystic".*

Venus: Appeasement, to be able to make compromises. A tendency to concur too easily, or to be unsure of one's beliefs.   •   Society makes a sacrifice. *Arthur, 1st Duke of Wellington, British Army commander during the Napoleonic Wars whose success was based on caution and understanding the needs of his troops.*

Mars: Hardship, sacrifice of oneself for others. The rescue worker, the one who tries to help.   •   A rescue occurs. *Johann Conrad Weiser, US Indian agent who arranged agreements between the Iroquois tribes and the colonial governments that respected the traditional lives of the tribal groups.*

Jupiter: A generous person, or one who uses others. To tithe and give unselfishly or to expect others to contribute to your personal needs. ♦ Old problems solved by helping a group. *Nelson Mandela, and in contrast, the Marquis de Sade whose sexual appetite gave birth to the word 'sadism'.*

Saturn: Finding opportunities in the simple mundane things of life. Interest in the lives of ordinary people, interest in the common things. ♦ A time when the establishment must make a sacrifice. *Isaac Singer, US inventor who developed the first practical sewing machine and brought it into domestic and general use.*

Uranus: To seek to be of benefit to large organizations, the public servant. To be devoted to a large and popular cause. ♦ Innocent people are sacrificed. *William James Pirrie, 19th century Canadian shipbuilder best known as the builder of the liner "Titanic".*

Neptune: Being able to make sacrifices, accepting hardship in order to allow a group or another individual to benefit. ♦ The sacrifice of many, a loss of innocence at the collective level. *Tsar Nicholas II, 19th century Russian emperor who, together with his wife and children, was massacred by the Bolsheviks after the Russian Revolution in 1917.*

Pluto: To see oneself as a part of a large pattern, to recognize the contribution of those that uphold the system without reward. ♦ A lone sacrifice that can change a nation. *King John, 12th century English monarch who, after a revolt by barons, was forced to sign the Magna Carta, which permanently changed the role of the English crown.*

The Node: The devoted worker, to not seek recognition but wish to remain in the background. A lifetime of service to an idea or another person. ♦ A time when the nameless are honoured. *Alan Turing, English mathematician who was pivotal in cracking the German Enigma code machines of WWII but later was driven to suicide because of his homosexuality.*

NOTES

1. The Catasterismi ("placings among the stars") is an Alexandrian prose retelling of the mythic nature of the constellations as they were interpreted in 1st century BCE.
2. Jobes and Jobes, *Outer Space: Myths, Name Meanings, Calendars*, p.152.

DUBHE

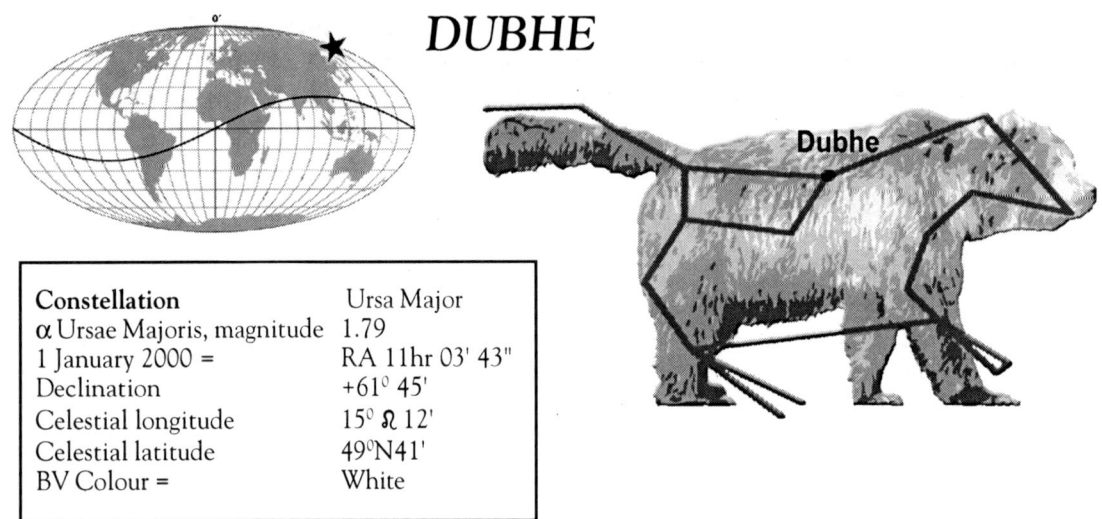

Constellation	Ursa Major
α Ursae Majoris, magnitude	1.79
1 January 2000 =	RA 11hr 03' 43"
Declination	+61° 45'
Celestial longitude	15° ♌ 12'
Celestial latitude	49°N41'
BV Colour =	White

Ursa Major, the Great Bear

The Great Bear appears in all major star catalogues since ancient times. Aratus, in the 4th century BCE, talks of an ancient tale about a bear set in the heavens because it had nurtured the infant Zeus[1]. In India the seven stars of Ursa Major were called the Seven Bears and with this constellation orbiting the point of stillness, the pole, it has associations with the giving of life. The sky bear may well be a goddess image from the Neolithic period. However, by the time of Homer she had become nothing more than the wood nymph, Callista, raped by Zeus and turned into a bear to protect her from the wrath of Artemis[2]. Probably seeking to reconcile the fact that one of Zeus' conquests was so honoured by being placed in this sacred place in the sky, the Greeks later suggested that this constellation was Artemis, the She Bear, who was said to have ruled over all the stars until overthrown by Zeus. To the native Americans the bear was seen, in the evenings, to be walking along the line of the horizon at the time of the greening (summer months) a visual phenomenon which links this constellation to the rhythm of the seasons and life on earth.

Dubhe, the ancient animal goddess, passive strength

This star, with its placement in the Great Bear, is concerned with insight, persistence, endurance and passive strength. It talks of the strength found in the feminine side of one's nature rather than in the more masculine inclination to act, it is the strength of patience, and the use of time to calmly solve problems rather than to take dynamic action. This star is about quiet strength and faith in the rhythm of life.

Heliacal Rising Star

Believing in persistence, and maintaining a pacifist position. Feeling linked to the environment, working towards the protection of the land. *Anton Apriantono, Indonesia's Minister of Agriculture (2004-) who is a researcher at the Food Science and Technology at Bogor Agricultural University.*

Heliacal Setting Star
Being captured by nature. Finding a passion for being in, or working for the environment, or with animals. *John James Audubon, 18th century American ornithologist and bird artist who when sent from his birth place in Haiti to the USA to look after his father's property, discovered a love of birds and spent several years seeking out every species of bird in America in order to catalogue them.*

Star on one of its pivot points at the moment of birth
A lifestyle which embraces a methodical approach. Able to maintain one's focus over long periods of time. To be seen as one who is linked with animals or nature. *Guicciardini, 15th century Italian historian and statesman considered the Father of Modern History, due to his use of government documents to verify his "History of Italy".*

Physiological Correspondence: The breast – the nourishment of mother's milk.

Ptolemy's location: Of the stars in the quadrilateral, the bright star in the back.

World Cities: Helsinki, Finland; Oslo, Norway; St. Petersburg, Russia; Stockholm, Sweden at latitudes between 59^0 to 63^0 north.

Dubhe in paran with:

Sun: To protect, to nurture people or ideas. To value quietness and to have great strength in maintaining your views, to be able to resist force.   •   An emphasis on the nature of parenting. *Niccolo Machiavelli, 16th century Italian who is best known as the author of "The Prince", a work which expanded on his belief that the end justifies the means, especially when the needs of the state were at stake.*

Moon: To give one's strength and support to another. Being drawn to a care-giving profession. Wanting to help others.   •   A charitable organisation is in the news. *Emmeline Pankhurst, suffragette and champion of women's suffrage whose forty year campaign culminated in British women receiving the vote in 1927.*

Mercury: To seek understanding of nature or to be interested in collecting knowledge of a people's culture or history. A lover of the fabric of life or culture.   •   A time when a place of learning is highlighted. *Charles Darwin, naturalist who established and documented the theory of evolution which eventually became known as "Darwinism".*

Venus: The healer who seeks the well-being of others; to seek to help children, a lover of things that help children.   •   Debates on public health. *Beatrix Potter, 19th century English author best remembered for her animal characters, in particular Peter Rabbit.*

Mars: The protector of children or those who are vulnerable. Motivated to heal and/or protect people or intellectual concepts. A person who creates, children or art. ◆ A time of actions fuelled by parental instincts. *Gladys Aylward, in 1930, aged 28, she spent her entire savings on a railway ticket to Tientsin in North China; there, with a Scottish missionary, she founded the famous Inn of the Sixth Happiness.*

Jupiter: The historian or philosopher success through quiet focused work. To be a collector of cultural objects, either from art or from sport, film or fashion. ◆ Acknowledgement given to the quiet achiever. *Jeronimo de Zurita, 19th century Spanish government official who is regarded as the first modern Spanish historian.*

Saturn: A persistent and determined approach to life; being able to solve what appear to be insurmountable problems. ◆ A time when the old leader holds the power. *Queen Elizabeth II, current English monarch.*

Uranus: A lover of culture, or history; the family historian, a collector of photographs. One who promotes their own culture. ◆ The community shows support for outsiders. *Satyajit Ray, film director who is credited with modernising Indian cinema and bringing international recognition to the industry.*

Neptune: A lover of art; interested in art about people; to protect art or any form of the media. A curator, a conservationist, a collector. ◆ A time when something precious is threatened. *Michelangelo Buonarroti, 15th century Italian artist whose legacy to art includes long term projects such as the ceiling of the Sistine Chapel.*

Pluto: To value land either for its beauty or for its monetary worth. To seek the wealth in the environment, whether to preserve or exploit. ◆ Land issues, land that needs protection. *John Augustus Sutter, German settler and colonizer in California whose discovery of gold on his land (1848) precipitated the California Gold Rush.*

The Node: To be involved in the safety or protection of homes, people or communities. To be a guardian, to hold something precious for others. ◆ Environmentalist in the news. *Linus Yale, 19th century American inventor, designer of the compact cylinder pin-tumbler lock that bears his name.*

NOTES

1. Aratus, "Phaenomena," p.209.
2. Jobes and Jobes, *Outer Space: Myths, Name Meanings, Calendars*, p.259.

EL NATH

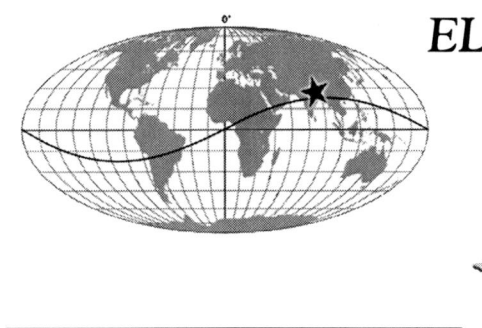
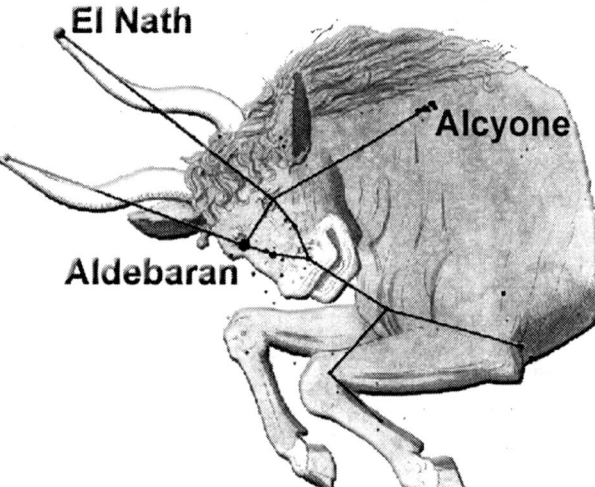

Constellation	Taurus
β Tauri, magnitude	1.65
1 January 2000 =	RA 05hr 26' 18"
Declination	+28° 36'
Celestial longitude	22° ♊ 35'
Celestial latitude	05°N23'
BV Colour =	Blue-Green

Taurus, the Great Bull of Heaven
One of the earliest and most noted constellations probably because it marked the vernal equinox from about 4,000 to 1700 BCE in the age of archaic astronomy. To the Phoenicians the bull-god was called Father of Men and was given the title of El, meaning bull. He was also known as, or linked with, Ahura Mazda, a saviour figure also known as the Bull-Slayer[1]. His worship involved a baptism of bull's blood in which the initiate stood in a pit underneath a slotted platform and was showered with the blood of a sacrificial bull slaughtered above. In later mythology, as the Bull began to slip from the equinox to make way for Aries it took on a more negative essence as shown in the Greek myth of Jason who had to tame a fiery bull in order to pass one of the tests towards claiming the Golden Fleece of Aries, the constellation that now contained the sun at the time of the equinox[2]. (For more information see also Alcyone and Aldebaran).

The Principle of El Nath, the horn of Taurus, a weapon
El Nath is the tip of the horn, the point of attack. It was viewed as the force of the Bull, thereby having power over the waters or blood of life, and thus it symbolises a great and terrible weapon. This star is associated with a potentially destructive skill that can be used to annihilate or conversely to give life – El Nath is a weapon which can be used for good or for ill.

Heliacal Rising Star
A confronting attitude, a desire to deal with real life, real issues. A philosophy that one must strive to gain the life that one desires. Abrasive but strongly focused on one's goals. *Henry Lawson, 19th century Australian author known for his work about the rough and tough Australian bush life.*

Heliacal Setting Star
Discovering one's inner resolve under pressure. A love of challenge; to develop a combative approach to life as one grows older. *Jeanne d'Arc, 15th century French saint and military commander who was inspired by God to leave her farm and take leadership of the French army to drive the English from her country.*

Star on one of its pivot points at the moment of birth
Assertiveness as a lifestyle, to confront or to suffer as a result of the cruelty of life; one who loves martial arts. *Francisco Franco, 20th century Spanish general who became the dictator of Spain.*

Physiological Correspondence: The male genitalia.

Ptolemy's location: The tip of the northern horn and the right foot of the Charioteer.

World Cities: Cairo, Egypt; Chihuahua, Mexico; Chongging, China at latitudes between 26° to 30° north.

El Nath in paran with:

Sun: To strongly and physically focus on one's goals. A crisis worker; one who can be verbally aggressive; one who can "get the job done". ♦ Times of attacks or battles. *Anne Frank, Dutch Jewish child known for the diary she kept for two years while in hiding to escape Nazi persecution.*

Moon: A fighter, or one who knows the cruelty of life. To suffer at the hands of others; to be drawn to aggressive individuals. ♦ A group suffers from the cruelty of others. *Winston Churchill, the English Prime Minister who led England through WWII and was known for his ability to rouse the people to fight.*

Mercury: The satirist, the one who comments. To be abrasive and blunt-speaking, to talk frankly. ♦ Talk of war. *Jonathan Swift, 17th century Anglo-Irish author, the foremost prose satirist in the English language ("Gulliver's Travels"), and known for his attacks against astrology.*

Venus: Taking a contra or antisocial attitude. To flaunt social customs; to resist being a slave to convention or fashion. ♦ A period when society is being challenged. *Germaine Greer, 20th century Australian feminist who wrote "The Female Eunuch".*

Mars: To take physical action even in the face of strong opposition. To be brave, or fool hardy with one's safety. ♦ An aggressive or violent act. *Neil Armstrong, first man to walk on the Moon, on 21 July 1969.*

Jupiter: Breaking new ground artistically, or as a humanitarian. To fight for one's beliefs; to clash with those of different philosophical opinions. ♦ The glorification of an aggressive action. *Martin Luther, 15th century German religious reformer whose attacks on the abuses of the clergy precipitated the Protestant Reformation.*

Saturn: Prepared to battle the establishment; a hard life, to lead the life of a battler, to struggle physically or financially. ♦ A time when a hard life is revealed. *Dylan Thomas, 20th century Welsh poet and writer known for his humorous, rhythmical and lilting writing style as well as his excessive drinking.*

Uranus: A lover of history, a military historian or collector of historical items or images. A sports fan. ♦ A new weapon, a new problem. *Isaak Babel, 20th century Soviet short-story writer noted for his war stories and Odessa tales.*

Neptune: To battle with or love nature, to live in what others may call a hostile environment, to pit one's wits against the terrain or one's family. ♦ Hopelessness, no control over emerging circumstances, acts of nature. *Herman Melville, 19th century American writer known for his masterpiece, "Moby Dick" which deals with the battle between one man and a whale.*

Pluto: To struggle to solve or overcome powerful or hidden problems. To suffer from being marginalized, to be discriminated against. ♦ Destruction, or threats in a manner not previously considered. *Louis Pasteur, 19th century French researcher who discovered that micro-organisms cause fermentation and disease.*

The Node: The fighter, the rescue worker, to be able to handle a crisis. To be good in a crisis and have the ability to help. ♦ An examination of safety systems is needed. *Henri Dunant, 19th century Swiss humanitarian who founded the Red Cross after the Battle of Solferino (1859) that resulted in 40,000 casualties.*

NOTES

1. Mary Settegast, *Plato Prehistorian, 10,000 to 5,000 B.C. Myth, Religion, Archaeology*, New York, USA: Lindisfarne Press 1990, p.112.
2. Bulfinch, *Myths of Greece and Rome*, p.153.

FACIES

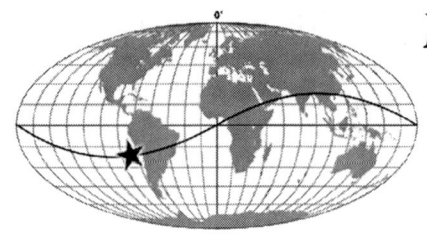
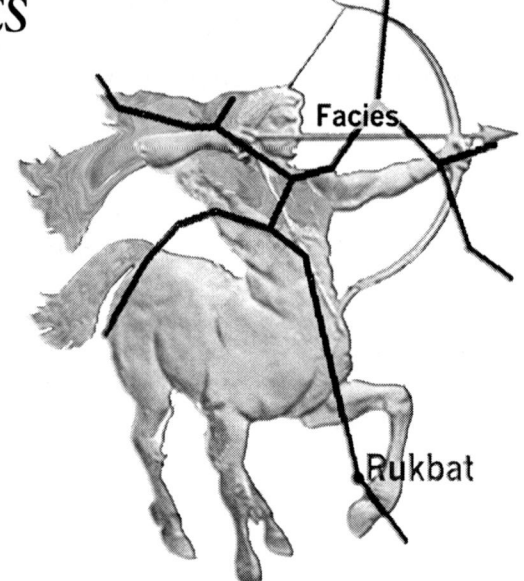

Constellation	Sagittarius
Nebula, magnitude	5.10
1 January 2000 =	
RA	18hr 36' 22"
Declination	-23° 54'
Celestial longitude	08° ♑ 18'
Celestial latitude	00°S44'
BV Colour =	White

Sagittarius, the Archer
Originating on the Euphrates with cuneiform tablets calling it the Strong One or The Giant King of War[1], this constellation was the archer god of war. To the Persians it was Kaman, to the Turks it was *Yai* and in Syria it was *Kertko*, all names signifying a Bow or Bow and Arrow[2]. The Egyptians saw it as a hand holding an arrow and Aratus called it the Wielder of the Bow[3]. The animal part of the constellation emerged in the classical period where it was called a centaur and was displayed as a threatening figure, symbolic of warriors who had mastered archery from horse back, a most feared fighting force.

The Principle of Facies, the eye of the archer, penetrating vision
Facies (a nebula) is the penetrating stare of a lethal weapon. It holds the most difficult and possibly most violent symbolism in the heavens. It represents a penetration of action that has no regard for others and a person capable of this can become a great leader or a fearsome dictator. The other side of Facies is the individual who may be the victim of the archer's stare. Facies can thus be cruel and ruthless or in a gentler manifestation, it can symbolise strong focused energy, producing someone who is a high achiever but somewhat brusque in manner.

Heliacal Rising Star
A philosophy that life is hard or unforgiving; a belief that one must focus strongly on one's goals

in order to achieve them; an expectation of being treated harshly; a self-protective attitude. *Robert Whitehead, British engineer who invented the modern torpedo in 1856.*

Heliacal Setting Star
Finding though a harsh teacher that one's best work is achieved through strong focus and determination. Finding inner strength in the face of aggression or hardship. *Nelson Mandela, 20th century lawyer who maintained continuous resistance to the British presence in South Africa and who was victorious after 27 years of imprisonment.*

Star on one of its pivot points at the moment of birth
The soldier, athlete, or aggressor; alternatively, a person who works against aggression, the antiwar protestor, or the one who is wounded by acts of aggression. *John Lennon, the Beatle who devoted his life to peace but was shot dead by a crazed fan in 1980.*

Physiological Correspondence: The eyes. The quality of one's vision.

Ptolemy's location: The nebula in the eye.

World Cities: Asuncion, Paraguay; Rio de Janeiro, Brazil at latitudes between 22^0 to 26^0 south.

Facies in paran with:

Sun: An obsessive dedication to one's goals to the point of ruthlessness. To be drawn to work with the harder, more stressful, or the unseemly, side of life; to have a prophetic vision.
• A time of terrorism. *Nostradamus, 16th century French astrologer and physician well known for his "Centuries", a collection of prophecies.*

Moon: Experiencing violence or turmoil. The sadist, or the humanitarian who wants to help children or minority groups in need.   •   To learn of wounded people, people who have been harshly treated. *Ivan the Terrible, 16th century Russian Tsar, the first formally-proclaimed Tsar of Russia whose time on the throne was defined as a reign of terror.*

Mercury: A gift of prolonged and intense mental focus. A pessimistic attitude, or one who is judged, or speaks, harshly.   •   News of aggression or harsh actions. *Arthur Miller, 20th century American playwright whose work combines social issues with personal responsibility. His best-known work is "Death of a Salesman" (1949).*

Venus: Anger at injustices, seeking a different order. A tendency to be black and white in one's judgement of social issues.   •   A time when there is a ruthless approach to social problems, or savage artistic comment. *Rene Descartes, known as the "Father of Modern Philosophy". His most famous axiom "I think, therefore I am" became a catchword of rationalist philosophy.*

Mars: Endurance, physical or mental, for good or for evil. Unswerving, even ruthless, in pursuit of personal ambition. ◆ Stories of endurance or great hardship occupy the news. *Stirling Moss, 20th century English racing car driver considered to be one of the greatest drivers in the history of the sport.*

Jupiter: Strong but potentially abrasive religious or philosophical views. An obsessive desire to learn and explore. ◆ Religious zealots, or people with emphatic one-eyed opinions, seem to win the day. *Ivan the Terrible, see Facies in paran with the Moon.*

Saturn: To be the outsider in belief or action. To be obsessive at trying to building a body of work, an idea or a physical object. ◆ An attack on the civil rights of people. *Voltaire, 17th century philosopher and writer considered one of France's greatest authors. Most of his works are polemics against the society in which he lived and thus he is regarded as a courageous crusader against tyranny, bigotry, and cruelty.*

Uranus: Gullible to fashion or trend-swings in the community, to become outraged at injustices. To seek to understand or instigate change in one's culture or society. ◆ The people move as one, mass hysteria or mass emotions. *Charles Henry Dow, originator of the Dow Jones company, which published in 1884 a compilation of the first average of US stock prices, now used as a measure of the nation's economic mood.*

Neptune: To be a victim of some form of abuse, whether physical or mental or through depleting illness. To be wary of the aggression or corruption of others. ◆ A ruthless attack on a national, or collective, symbol. *Elizabeth I, Queen of England (1588-1603) who lived in fear for her life, first from her father and later from those who did not want a non-Catholic on the throne.*

Pluto: To be a catalyst for change. A person who focuses intensely on their goals. To be at the right place at the right time. ◆ The end of one era and the beginning of another. *Event: The first manned space flight by Yuri Gagarin on April 12, 1961.*

The Node: To be seen to work against injustice or corruption, to work against the abuse of power. An advocate for minority rights. ◆ A time when society is changed by a single act. *Paul Revere, 18th century hero of the American Revolution, forever remembered for raising the alarm that the British were coming on the night of 18 April 1775.*

NOTES

1. Jobes and Jobes, *Outer Space: Myths, Name Meanings, Calendars*, p.235.
2. Allen, *Star Names Their Lore and Meaning*, p.352.
3. Aratus, "Phaenomena," p.231.

FOMALHAUT

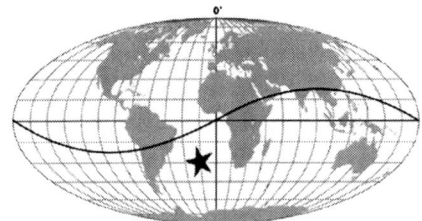

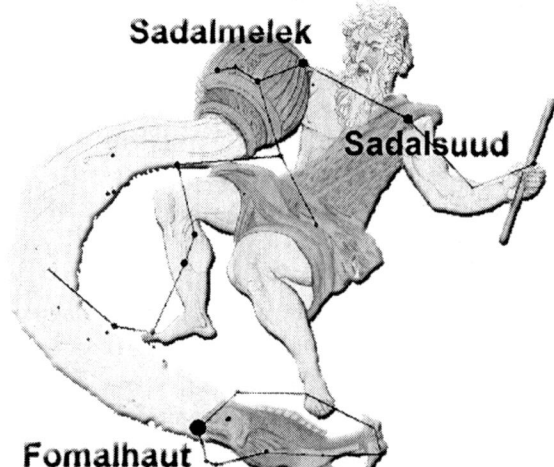

Constellation	Piscis Australis
α Piscis Austrini, magnitude	1.16
1 January 2000 = RA 22hr	57' 37"
Declination	-29° 38'
Celestial longitude	03° ♓ 51'
Celestial latitude	21°S08'
BV Colour =	White

Piscis Australis, the southern fish
Lying close to Aquarius in the part of the sky which Aratus named the Water, this is the fish that drinks the flow from the urn of Aquarius. This stream-drinking fish is an earlier symbol of life and fertility, for it was the one that carried the egg, drinking the sperm or river of life. This is also the fish in Celtic mythology that swallows a magical ring only to have it retrieved later by the story's hero[1]. Around 3,000 BCE the Persians considered its alpha star as one of the Royal Stars and called it the Watcher in the South, as it marked their winter solstice[2]. Later in 500 BCE the Greeks developed, or inherited, rituals around the heliacal rising of this constellation when they aligned temples for Demeter to its rising[3]. Always mysterious, this small constellation is symbolic of the nature of enchantment, where in one accomplishes things through a deep natural understanding of the nature of relationships, rather than the use of will power.

The Principle of Fomalhaut, the Watcher of the South, idealism or charisma
This is one of the Royal Stars of Persia and as such represents a path which contains a nemesis, a way that the individual can fall from grace. This nemesis is hubris, thus the individual must steer clear of the seduction of charisma, in themselves and others. Fomalhaut contains a touch of the mystic, a sense of magic, and is based on high ideals or lofty visions. It can bestow charisma on an individual as they seek to express the divine in art or poetry, for this star is also the bitter-sweet madness of the poetic mind challenged to remain in the physical world. This is the child stolen by the fairies who must reject the sweet non-life and fight to return to the mortal world of death and pain.

Heliacal Rising Star
One's dreams and ideals are the dreams and ideals of humanity; a life spent in admiration of great artistic gifts, or great art or literature. To emulate noble works or noble lives. *Sir Laurence Olivier, the most revered English actor of the 20th century celebrated for his charisma and profound acting skills.*

Heliacal Setting Star
Life circumstances lead one into taking a idealistic or noble stand. To learn to allow events to emerge; to find that by steering life with a gentle hand one can achieving one's goals. *Helen Reddy, Australian-born singer who was propelled to stardom after many years of struggle by her album, "I am Woman"*

Star on one of its pivot points at the moment of birth
A strong but possibly ill-founded belief in oneself; the possibility that one is living in an illusion of oneself, or to live in "another" world. To be destroyed by hubris. *O.J. Simpson, charismatic US sports star accused, and finally acquitted, of murdering his wife; the case captured popular interest with its constant clouds of confusion and misdirection.*

Physiological Correspondence: The body's histamine reaction – allergies and environmental oversensitivity.

Ptolemy's location: The star-fish's month, the same as that at the beginning of the Water.

World Cities: Brisbane, Australia; Durban, South Africa at latitudes between 27° to 31° south.

Fomalhaut in paran with:

Sun: The artist, the idealist, the charismatic person; to be vulnerable to hubris. The need to keep one's feet on the ground while one's head is in the clouds. ◆ A time of dreams, realised or lost. *Cecil Rhodes, 19th century British businessman whose empire encompassed British South Africa and who lamented that he could not also own the stars.*

Moon: To catalyse idealistic or romantic feelings in others. To have illusions about what other people need to do, or are able to achieve. ◆ A time when patriotism is stressed by the media. *Emily Post, 20th century writer who is remembered for her work on etiquette ("Etiquette: the blue book of social usage") which was first published in 1922.*

Mercury: To have an idealistic vision, or to deceive. The poet or the liar, to be persuasive with one's words. ◆ False reports, or reports based more on illusion than fact. *Vesta Tilley, 19th century English actor who was a music hall singer, comedian and the leading male impersonator of her day.*

Venus: The artist or the fanatic; seeing the magic in everyday life, or promoting ideologies. To be a dreamer. ♦ An artistic event, or a naive attitude to a social problem. *James Barrie, 19th century English author best known for being the creator of Peter Pan, the boy who refused to grow up.*

Mars: An idealistic warrior or a mystical hero; to seek or admire the path of the spiritual warrior or the potential to become a blind fanatic. ♦ The actions of a fanatic, or a dreamer, take centre-stage. *Claudio Aquaviva, 16th century Italian general of the Society of Jesus, (the Jesuits) considered to have been one of the order's greatest leaders.*

Jupiter: Charismatic, or to have a philosophical cause and a love of the classics. A love of travel to exotic or unusual places. ♦ A grand, or far-reaching vision is put forward. *Alexander Pope, 17th century English poet who was self-taught, learning Greek, Latin, French and Italian; best known for his work "Essay on Man".*

Saturn: A productive person, one who can bring to fruition their dreams or higher ideals, to be able to make things happen. ♦ The personal philosophies of a leader become political policies. *Antonie-Joseph Sax, 19th century Belgian instrument maker who invented the saxophone.*

Uranus: Sensitive to the dreams of one's culture; seeking to express, in art, words or music the desires of one's generation. Taking the commonplace and turning it into art. ♦ The expression of a desire or longing. *Jean Genet, 20th century French author known for transforming the erotic and obscene into poetical and dramatic works.*

Neptune: The inspired artist or the deceiver. To follow one's ideals or dreams without regard for the well-being of oneself or others. To be an interpreter of dreams. ♦ Ideals and dreams come undone. *Peter Tchaikovsky, 19th century Russian composer known for his magical enchanted works (Swan Lake); privately tormented by mental problems and his homosexuality.*

Pluto: To be able to make money from illusions or the virtual world. To understand that the virtual world is just as important as the physical world. To work in the media. ♦ The media distorts the news story. *Charles Babbage, 19th century English mathematician who is credited with having conceived the first automatic digital computer.*

The Node: To embrace a fantasy as a lifestyle, to live in a different world. To work in theatre or any medium that can portray alternative realities. ♦ A deception is revealed. *Jean-Eugene Robert-Houdin, 19th century French stage magician who is considered to be the father of modern conjuring.*

NOTES

1. Green, *Dictionary of Celtic Myth and Legend*, p.184.
2. Allen, *Star Names Their Lore and Meaning*, p.346.
3. Jobes and Jobes, *Outer Space: Myths, Name Meanings, Calendars*, p.320.

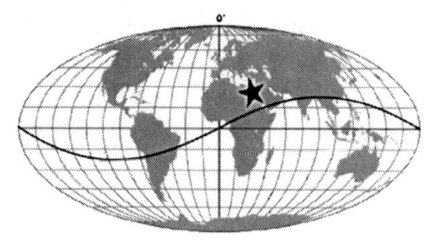

HAMAL

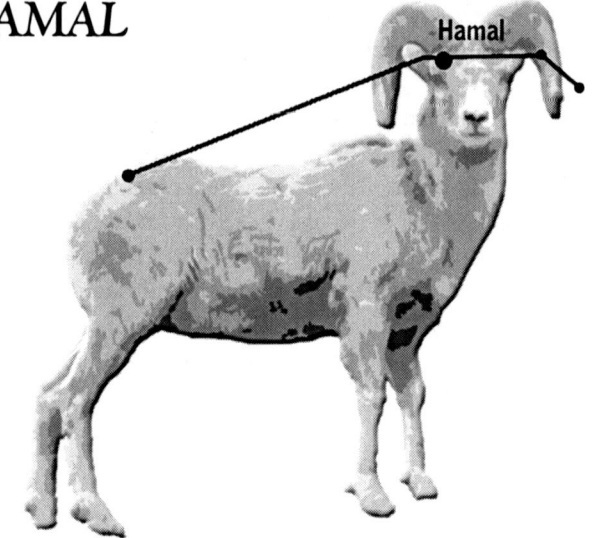

Constellation	Aries
α Arietis, magnitude	2.00
1 January 2000 =	RA 02hr 07' 10"
Declination	+23° 28'
Celestial longitude	07° ♉ 40'
Celestial latitude	09°N58'
BV Colour =	Orange

Aries, the Ram
Known as the Ram it is marked by a noticeable triangle to the west of the Pleiades. As the stars of Aries the Ram became the heliacal rising constellation for the spring equinox at around 2,000 BCE it heralded the beginning of a new god: Tammuz Daum-uzei to the people in the Euphrates, the Only Son of Life, with the emphasis on the word "only"[1]. The Israelites also came forward with their One God/monotheistic concept and spoke now of the blood of the lamb rather than the blood of the bull. The new Arian god was a solo creature who shared his glory with no-one. In this period the Egyptians moved into what is now called the New Empire which culminated with the creation of Amen-Ra, "king of the gods and lord of the thrones of the two lands" also known as "Lord of the Head"[2]. He was a new type of god for the Egyptians for he shared his glory with no other god. The Greeks adopted Amen-Ra as their Zeus and developed the story of Jason and the Golden Fleece, a fleece from the ram who saved Phrixius the son of Athamas. In gratitude the ram was sacrificed and placed in the heavens, his golden fleece hung in the grove of Ares[3].

Principle of Hamal the head of the Ram, will and determination
Hamal is a forceful star of action and it enhances any planet it contacts with the strength of independence. This may have negative or positive consequences. Hamal's presence in a chart bestows a certain strength of will and determination. This can manifest as the simple but useful ability to be focused and direct, or it can express as temper or frustration, and the inability to deal with authority figures whether within the family or within one's career.

Heliacal Rising Star
A personal philosophy of action rather than words, to automatically seek a physical solution to all problems, a lifestyle where one is willing to work hard to achieve one's dreams. *Poppy King,*

Australian business woman who while quite young, developed a cosmetic empire based on her single idea of a better lipstick.

Heliacal Setting Star
To find that one can excels when one becomes active. To discover that determination and action yield the best results. *Sally Louise Tompkins, US humanitarian was the only woman to be commissioned in the Confederate Army. With her own money, she purchased a private residence in Richmond, Virginia where she created and ran a hospital during the Civil War.*

Star on one of its pivot points at the moment of birth
A physical approach to life's problems, a lover of challenge. The adventure seeker, a love of sport. A willingness to engage in difficult problems in a practical down-to-earth manner. *Margaret Thatcher, British Prime Minister (1979-1990) known for her hard hitting and uncompromising determination to modernise Britain.*

Physiological Correspondence: The head – the cranial blood vessels which can dilate to cause headaches.

Ptolemy's location: The bright star at the base of the right horn.

World Cities: Calcutta, India; Canton, China; Havana, Cuba; Hong Kong, China; Mazatlan, Mexico; Mecca, Saudi Arabia at latitudes between 21° to 25° north.

Hamal in paran with:

Sun: Assertively following one's own path. The ability to work independently of the views of others. ♦ A time when a forceful or abrasive person is talked about. *Charlemagne, 12th century German monarch through whose enlightened leadership the roots of learning and order were restored to Medieval Europe.*

Moon: To be a popular rogue. To challenge authority but in a way that is loved, or appreciated, by others. ♦ The free spirited person or sporting hero wins the day. *Horatio Nelson, 19th century British admiral known for courageous but unconventional methods which eventually ensured the safety of Britain from invasion.*

Mercury: To think like a detective, always probing and looking for different options, willing to confronting in pursuit of information. ♦ A time of jolting news, the truth unveiled. *Albert Einstein, 19th century German scientist who discovered the relationship between matter and energy and is considered to be the father of modern physics.*

Venus: To seek different ways of relating; to be creative in a unique way, to have little regard for the opinion of others. ♦ A time of the dictator, a person who believes they know what is best for others. *Joseph Smith, US religious leader known as the founder of the Church of Jesus Christ of Latter-day Saints (Mormons).*

Mars: Skilled in physical movement; hot tempered or prone to act in haste. A person who takes physical risks or one who has to deal with violent situations.   ◆   A military event. *Marcel Marceau, considered the best mime artist of the twentieth century; his signature character was Bip.*

Jupiter: The independent, successful pioneer, or the headstrong individual. The ability to land on one's feet.   ◆   A time when the brave and reckless succeed. *Harrison Ford, US actor who specialises roles of the maverick, reckless adventurer and fortune seeker.*

Saturn: Hard physical or intellectual choices that can stir up frustration or anger. To experience a strong disciplinarian figure in one's life.   ◆   Harsh critics, and people angry. *Hugo Ball, 19th century German who was a harsh social critic and wrote an early highly critical biography of the German novelist Hermann Hesse.*

Uranus: To enjoy public events; to be motivated to work for public goals; to admire large architecture.   ◆   Strikes and industrial trouble. *Gustave Eiffel, 19th century French engineer who built the tower that bears his name, even through it was rejected by the city of Barcelona and, during construction, by the people of Paris.*

Neptune: To be a religious warrior, to have strong spiritual opinions upon which one acts. Passionate about art or music.   ◆   Upheavals over matters to do with oil or chemicals. *Annie Besant, 19th century English reformer known for her work with the Theosophical Society and for her promotion of self-rule for India.*

Pluto: Single mindedness, willing to engage in life and death issues. To be drawn towards tragic or powerful figures; to desire to explore the underworld.   ◆   A time of war. *Maria Walewska, the Polish mistress of Napoleon Bonaparte, whom he met in Poland in 1806, and again in Paris and finally Elba.*

The Node: To play the hero, to take the noble and heroic pathway with one's life. To seek the glorious rather than the mundane life.   ◆   Brave actions make the news. *Bella Abzug, 20th century US feminist and lawyer a prominent peace campaigner who was nicknamed Battling Bella.*

NOTES

1. see Magnus Magnusson, B.C. – the Archaeology of the Bible Lands, London: British Broadcasting Corporation, 1977.
2. Budge, The Gods of the Egyptians, p.174.
3. Grimal, The Dictionary of Classical Mythology, p.371.

MARKAB

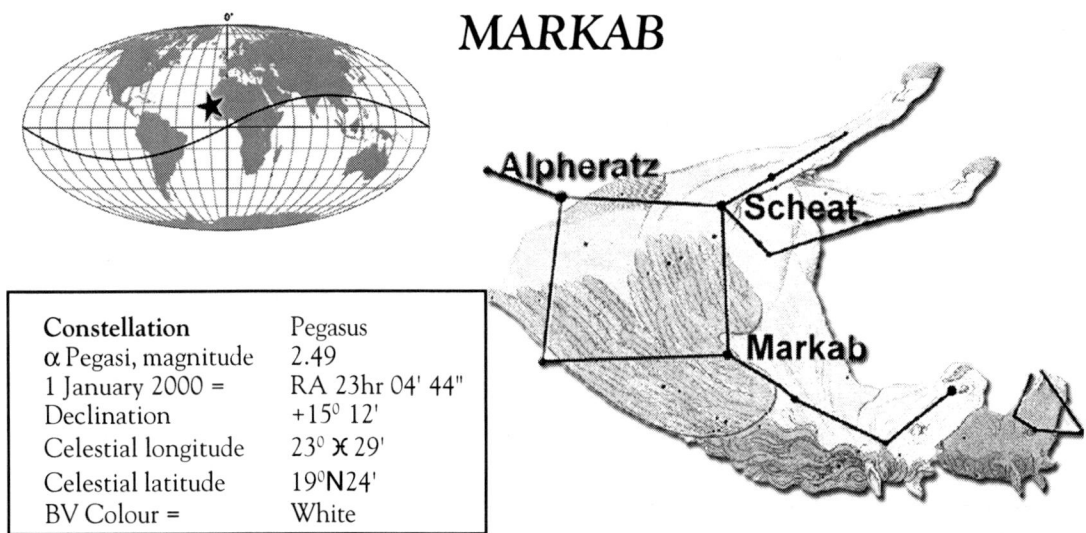

Constellation	Pegasus
α Pegasi, magnitude	2.49
1 January 2000 =	RA 23hr 04' 44"
Declination	+15° 12'
Celestial longitude	23° ♓ 29'
Celestial latitude	19°N24'
BV Colour =	White

Pegasus, the winged horse

Pegasus emerges from the neck of Andromeda and belongs to the symbolism of the sacred horse. Born with wings to show its speed, only half of this horse is shown in the sky. The Greeks saw this horse being born from Medusa's neck as she was slain by Perseus. Pegasus is also known as "I-iku" or "I-iku Star" which was the measure used in building the perfect cubed Ark of Babylon. The four main stars of Pegasus form a great square in the sky which may have been seen to reflect the importance of the number four – the four natural points in the solar year, the four compass points and the division of the world (above, below and the rising and setting points) into four sections[1]. The Hebrew god of the Old Testament, who is all-manifesting, full of action and wrath is also known by the number four. So Pegasus is considered not only as a winged horse but it is also symbolic of a great magical square - and linked to the mythological and theological concept of the number four. (For more information see also Scheat).

Markab, the saddle of Pegasus, to be stable

This star is the saddle of Pegasus and represents great solidness and reliability, a point of steadiness or the power to maintain stability under pressure. This could be a beneficial contact, giving one leadership skills and the ability to handle crises; or it could twist the other way and manifest as a certain stubbornness and a refusal to move or consider other options. If Markab is placed in a chart, it offers as a resource the power to maintain stability under pressure. To be solid and tangible.

Heliacal Rising Star
A person who stands firm for their beliefs and principles. To feel that one's beliefs are the rock of one's life. To be consistent in action and thought. *Peter Abrahams, South African writer who produced most of his work in exile as it was on the political struggles of black people, "Tell Freedom" (1954) being his most famous work.*

Heliacal Setting Star
To be forced by life events to stand up for what one believes. To act as a steady point for others at times of crisis or confusion. *Charlton Heston, US actor famous for many memorable heroic roles, and unpopular for many by giving his unflinching support to the US National Rifle Association.*

Star on one of its pivot points at the moment of birth
To build something that others can use. To have physical and mental endurance and reliability. One's actions are seeds on which further change can emerge. *William Shatner, Canadian actor who rose to fame as Captain James Kirk in "Star Trek", a role that symbolised for the collective the desire for new frontiers.*

Physiological Correspondence: The soles of the feet.

Ptolemy's location: The star in the shoulder at the beginning of the wing.

World Cities: Bangkok, Thailand; Dakar, Senegal; Guatemala City, Guatemala; Manila, Philippines; Rangoon, Myanmar at latitudes between 13° to 17° north.

Markab in paran with:

Sun: A person who is consistent in their beliefs, an unchanging person; to be seen as stubborn or strong willed.   ◆   A strong, persistent leader takes control. *Richard I, "Richard the Lionheart", 12th century English king famous for his prowess in the Third Crusade.*

Moon: To be emotionally consistent, to be unchanging in one's devotion. To seek to serve in a practical manner, the needs of others.   ◆   A time when the nobleness of volunteers is honoured. *John Kay, 18th century English inventor of the flying shuttle which helped automate the process of weaving wool.*

Mercury: To value logical argument, to build on one's knowledge. One who is respected for their ideas.   ◆   The voice of authority speaks out. *Blaise Pascal, 17th century French mathematician who is the founder of the modern theory of probability.*

Venus: Strong personal and moral philosophies. To look for firm foundations, or reasons for current social or cultural customs; the anthropologist.   ◆   Society finds solace in maintaining its customs and traditions. *Anzai Yamazaki, 17th century Japanese propagator of the neo-Confucian* *philosopher Chu His – reduced His' philosophy to a simple moral code and blended it with Shinto religious doctrines.*

Mars: To be honest and act in an open-handed way. To show great persistence and consistency over many years in striving to obtain that goal.   ♦   A time where society is asked to take a stand. *Karl Weyprecht, Arctic explorer who discovered Franz Josef Land, an archipelago north of Russia, and who advanced a successful scheme for international cooperation in polar scientific investigations.*

Jupiter: The teacher/philosopher, in sport, or in a spiritual discipline. One's small actions become the basis for much larger projects.   ♦   The wise person; the need for consistency in the law. *Betsy Ross, the 18th century seamstress who is said to have fashioned the first American flag, the Star-Spangled Banner.*

Saturn: Seeking respect by endeavouring to build reliable structures and ideas. Being cautious, overly concerned with stability, seeking to understand chance.   ♦   Safety is sought in tradition, protocol or the upholding of the law. *Blaise Pascal, 17th century French mathematician who is the founder of the modern theory of probability. See Mercury in paran with Markab.*

Uranus: To understand what is popular; to work in advertising; to be someone who can read the common mind, or fulfil a task for the community.   ♦   The reliability and consistency of the common folk is shown. *Milton Hershey, 19th century manufacturer who founded the corporation which popularized chocolate candy throughout the world.*

Neptune: Being able to deal with shifting times; being able to see the opportunities in new ideas; happy to live in a foreign culture.   ♦   Immigration, migration, a change in the make-up of society. *Benjamin Altman, founded B Altman & Co (1906) in New York, which established the idea of the stylish department store with branches in different states.*

Pluto: Seeking new social levels for oneself; happy to destroy foundations in an attempt to build anew; dealing with a people who need to build a new life.   ♦   Inventions which change the way we live. *John F. Kennedy, US president who was assassinated, many believed, for his radical attempt to rebuild American society.*

The Node: To be seen to be consistent; to be stubborn in one's ideas; or to be strong willed.   ♦   Calmness or no action is put forward as a solution. *Sir Thomas More, 15th century Chancellor of England who was beheaded by Henry VIII because he refused to acknowledge him as the head of the newly formed Church of England.*

NOTES

1. de Santillana and von Dechend, *Hamlet's Mill*, p.297.

MENKAR

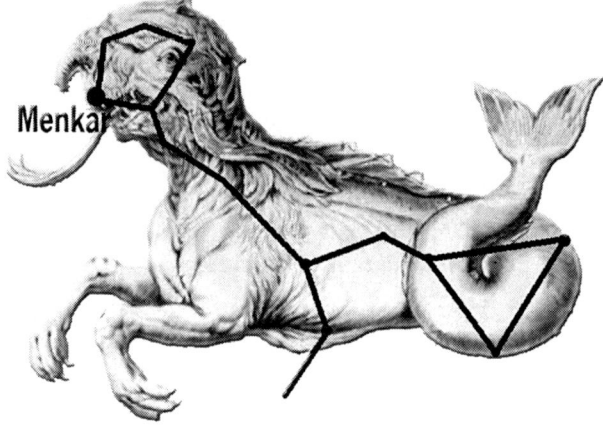

Constellation Cetus
α Ceti, magnitude 2.53
1 January 2000 = RA 03hr 02' 17"
Declination +04° 05'
Celestial longitude 14° ♉ 19'
Celestial latitude 12°S35'
BV Colour = Red

Cetus, the Whale
Over 50° in length on modern maps, the Whale reaches from the Urn of Aquarius to the edge of the constellation Eridanus, the river, crossing the equator on its way. According to the Greeks, Cetus is the sea monster who was sent to devour Andromeda; Perseus, however, saved her by using the severed head of Medusa to turn the sea monster to stone. But stories of this whale in the sky seem to predate the Greek version. Cetus has been illustrated at times with a dog's head and forelegs and with a mermaid-like tail. To us this constellation may strike more true as the freshwater mythic creature the Loch Ness monster than a marine whale in that it represents an unknown beast from the depths, instead of a gentle giant of the sea. Aratus in the 4th century BCE, referred to the constellation as: "the hateful monster Cetus"[1]. Christian mythology saw this as the whale that swallowed Jonah.

The Principle of Menkar the mouth of the whale, being open to the collective
The whale in the sky is symbolic of the human collective unconscious, for it is that which can erupt like a beast from the deep bearing, with equal probability, moments of great collective insight or chaos and mayhem. Menkar is associated with such unconscious forces in human culture and history, always physically out of sight in the depths of the human collective. This star's placement in a chart can be difficult. The sea of the collective can be a stormy one to sail, so a great deal would depend on the presence of other fixed stars in the chart. The positive expression lies in the potential to achieve something for the collective. The negative manifestation is vulnerability to becoming a victim of the collective.

Heliacal Rising Star
The nihilist, or a person who goes with the flow. To be gullible, or empathic to the unexpressed feelings around one. To have one's actions influence many. *The Marquis De Sade, 18th century French writer whose erotic writings gave rise to the term "sadism".*

Heliacal Setting Star
To be forced to deal with social issues that are not of one's making, to have famous parents or a heritage which hampers one, to seek to be anonymous. *Kahlia Chamberlain, daughter of Lindy Chamberlain, born while her mother was wrongly in prison for the alleged murder of her sister Azaria. The story of Azaria's disappearance became the film "Evil Angels".*

Star on one of its pivot points at the moment of birth
To be a leaf in the wind; glory, fame, infamy or oblivion. To have prophetic dreams, to sense or see the future; to be open to the winds of the unconscious mood of the people. To be empathic. *Indira Gandhi, first female Prime Minister of India, assassinated in 1984. She grew up in a political family, and was personally familiar with, and thus influenced by Mahatma Gandhi.*

Physiological Correspondence: The olfactory faculty – the sense of smell.

Ptolemy's location: The star at the edge of the monster's open jaws.

World Cities: Bogota, Colombia; Cayenne, French Guiana; Kuala Lumpur, Malaysia at latitudes between 02° to 06° north.

Menkar in paran with:

Sun: Great success or great loss; to be a pawn in the winds of change. To work with people who are victims, to be a victim oneself.   ♦   A time of extremes (of action or weather). *Leni Riefenstahl, brilliant German film maker best known for her documentary films of the Nazi movement, which later damaged her career in filmmaking.*

Moon: Emotionally committed to, or responsive to, the needs of the collective. One's actions have far reaching effects.   ♦   Emotions run high in the general public. *H. G. Wells, 20th century English novelist, journalist, sociologist, and historian, best known for science fiction such as "The Time Machine" and "The War of the Worlds".*

Mercury: An inspirational thinker. An uncanny nose for solving a problem or understanding what is needed. To find solutions to life problems in one's dreams   ♦   The masses speak out, the voice of the people is heard. *Samuel Morse, 18th century US inventor and painter, the inventor of Morse code and an early developer of the telegraph.*

Venus: Socially confronting, or seeking to represent others. Needing to accept and understand customs or social problems, or issues beyond your sphere of knowledge.   ♦   Society's values are challenged. *Caroline Norton, 19th century English socialite whose reputation is based on her matrimonial suits which resulted in the recognition of women's rights within marriage in Britain.*

Mars: Actions that please or jolt the collective; to be driven by hidden forces. To be vulnerable to the pressures of a peer group.   ♦   A violent act. *Adolf Hitler or in contrast, John of God, the founder of the Hospitalier Order of St John of God.*

Jupiter: Feast or famine, the fickleness of life. Success or failure based on the whims of popular support.   ♦   A time of the popular hero, the popular cause. *Napoleon Bonaparte, 18th century French general and emperor who later died in exile.*

Saturn: One's actions, or work, affecting many. To have the potential to be the embodiment of a collective issue, the beast or the saviour.   ♦   The true situation is revealed. *Alan Alexander Milne, 19th century English writer, author of the popular children's books featuring Christopher Robin and his toy bear, Winnie the Pooh.*

Uranus: A tendency to place oneself in unsettled situations. One's work involved with helping to restore order or being a harbinger of chaos.   ♦   The voice of the people calls for stability. *Andre-Jacques Garnerin, 18th century French aeronaut who was first person to use a parachute regularly and successfully.*

Neptune: To lose one's identity in a popular image; to be a fan of celebrities; to change one's name or appearance.   ♦   The appearance of a metaphysical or artistic statement from the collective. *Marilyn Monroe, US actress who lost her identity in the blonde sex symbol that she played.*

Pluto: To impose one's culture on another. To be intolerant of the differences in people, or to be subject to intolerant attitudes.   ♦   Dramatic events that rock the lives of a large number of people. *Event: The construction of the Berlin Wall, Germany in 1961.*

The Node: To be skilled at marketing, to work in advertising or selling an idea to the people, to understand what society is seeking from one year to the next.   ♦   A popular craze. *Coco Chanel, 19th century French fashion designer who revolutionized haute couture fashion by removing the corset.*

NOTES

1.   Aratus, "Phaenomena," p.235.

MIRACH

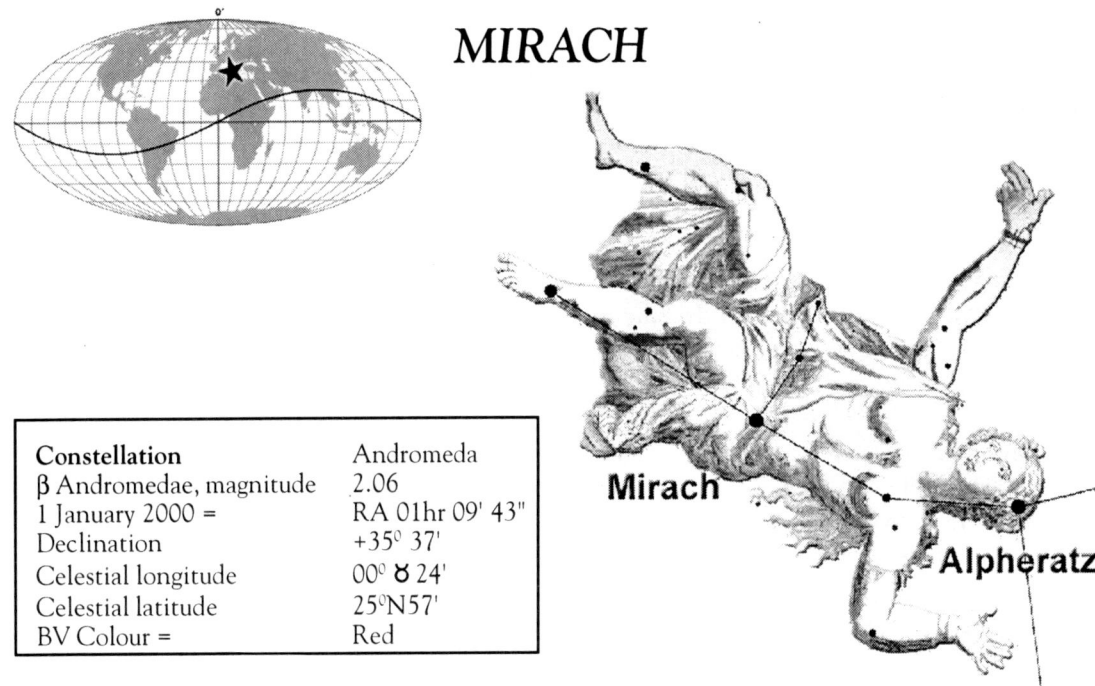

Constellation	Andromeda
β Andromedae, magnitude	2.06
1 January 2000 =	RA 01hr 09' 43"
Declination	+35° 37'
Celestial longitude	00° ♉ 24'
Celestial latitude	25°N57'
BV Colour =	Red

Andromeda, the princess

Placed just south of Draco and the two bears, Ursa Major and Minor, is the constellation of Andromeda. The Greeks saw this constellation as the figure of a princess chained to a rock, about to be eaten by the sea monster Cetus, the Whale[1]. Before the Greeks, however, she was seen as a member of the royal family which consists of Cepheus the king, Cassiopeia the queen, Andromeda the daughter or princess and Perseus the prince[2]. In this grouping Andromeda is symbolic of the young woman in a receptive position ready to take a suitor, ready to receive, rather than the chained, distressed figure of Greek mythology. Andromeda's alpha star is Alpheratz which is both the naval of Pegasus and the neck or head of Andromeda. In Greek mythology Pegasus, the winged horse, was born after his mother's head had been severed, his mother being Medusa the so-called gorgon slain by Perseus. So these two constellations of Perseus and Andromeda are mythically intertwined, both as the dynamics of the hero and a damsel in distress and as the story of two lovers. (For more information see Alpheratz).

The Principle of Mirach, the receptive feminine and indulgent

This star is connected to concepts of the young fertile virgin: receptivity, feminine power, intuition, the arts, and aesthetic inclinations. The theme of this star is to be receptive and fertile, but Mirach also has a shadow of being self-indulgent or personally obsessed. However, its presence in a chart implies that one is open to ideas, willing to be receptive. This receptiveness is more usefully thought of as fertile and productive rather than as naive or innocent.

Heliacal Rising Star
Using rapport and consensus as a personal life philosophy. Believing that increasing the beauty or harmony in one's world leads to greater fulfilment for all concerned; enjoying a sensual life. *Poppy King, Australian business woman who started a cosmetic empire based on her idea for a better lipstick.*

Heliacal Setting Star
Learning that diplomacy does work. Discovering the hard way that balance and rapport are more important then words or actions. Seeking sensuality. *Auguste Rodin, 19th century French sculptor, considered the greatest portraitist in the history of sculpture, whose work was influenced by his lustful and unbridled sensuality.*

Star on one of its pivot points at the moment of birth
To be focused on relationships, sexual or intellectual. To understand the importance of networking and being receptive to others. To be able to easily get rapport or mirror another person. *Meryl Streep, US actress renowned for her ability to "disappear" into a role.*

Physiological Correspondence: The pelvis, in particular its role in the sexual act.

Ptolemy's location: The southern star of the three above the girdle.

World Cities: Algiers, Algeria; Nagoya, Osaka and Tokyo, Japan; Teheran, Iran at latitudes between 33° to 37° north.

Mirach in paran with:

Sun: Wanting to remove the pain or ugliness from life, interested in beauty. A talent for building consensus and gaining rapport. ♦ The promotion of peace, or order, in a territory. *Horace Wells, 19th century American dentist who pioneered the use of surgical anaesthesia.*

Moon: The peace-seeking artist; or a reflective, self absorbed individual. To become emotionally distressed by ugliness or coarseness. ♦ A desire for peace; feelings of sentimentality. *John Lennon, the Beatles rhythm guitarist and vocalist renowned for his songs and peace-seeking "sleep-ins".*

Mercury: The translator, a person who builds rapport between ideas or languages. The sales person or counsellor. ♦ A time when a mediator can find the middle ground. *John Bartholomew, 19th century cartographer who revolutionized map-making by producing the geographical and contour maps of Britain which set the standard still used today.*

Venus: Beauty or the vamp; the artist, the person who knows how to use words, colour, or their own physical beauty to influence others. ♦ A time when people seek strength in harmony and order. *Joyce Hall, 20th century US business woman who founded Hallmark Cards and helped create the modern greeting card industry.*

Mars: A thrill-seeker; a person absorbed with their own needs. A person who is motivated by being receptive, one who seeks the physical stimulation of life. ◆ Gay rights, or sexual issues in the news. *Andre-Jacques Garnerin, 18th century French inventor known as the first person to use a parachute regularly and successfully.*

Jupiter: Living in a world of opportunity or an insatiable appetite for the physical world, money or people. ◆ Greed and excesses. *Marquis de Sade, 19th century French author; De Sade's erotic writings gave rise to the term "sadism".*

Saturn: A loved leader, or a person whose work is loved. The ability to understand what others need, a successful artist or negotiator. ◆ A time of restrictions. *Aubrey Beardsley, 19th century English illustrator who illustrated an edition of Malory's "Morte d Arthur".*

Uranus: The successful designer. To create images or objects which are popular in one's community. To help a group create or learn how to create better networks. ◆ The people hold their breath, in joy, or disbelief. *Herbert Austin, 19th century designer who created the Baby Austin car, which became the most popular car in Britain.*

Neptune: To be able to create an illusion; to struggle with personal relationships; to be drawn to a spiritual life or seek a union with the divine. ◆ A period when there is a false sense of security. *Leonie Adams, 20th century US poet and educator whose verse interprets emotions and nature with an almost mystical vision.*

Pluto: Breaking new ground in design or art; involved in fashion; an obsession or repulsion from sensual needs. ◆ Earthquakes; or the finding of new levels politically or geographically. *Helen Rubinstein, 19th century Polish-born European business woman who founded a cosmetic empire.*

The Node: A love of money and material goods; knowing how to work with the material world; gifted with colour and design. ◆ Stories about networks, whether of people or in virtual media. *Elsa Schaipparelli, 20th century Italian fashion designer who influenced the fashion world for 40 years, emphasizing the use of accessories and bold colour.*

NOTES

1. Room, *Dictionary of Astronomical Names*, p.57.
2. Aratus, "Phaenomena," p.221.

MIRFAK

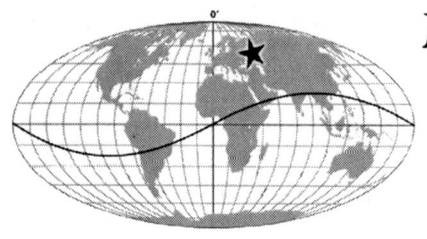

Constellation	Perseus
α Persei, magnitude	1.79
1 January 2000 =	RA 03hr 24' 20"
Declination	+49° 52'
Celestial longitude	02° II 05'
Celestial latitude	30°N08'
BV Colour =	Green

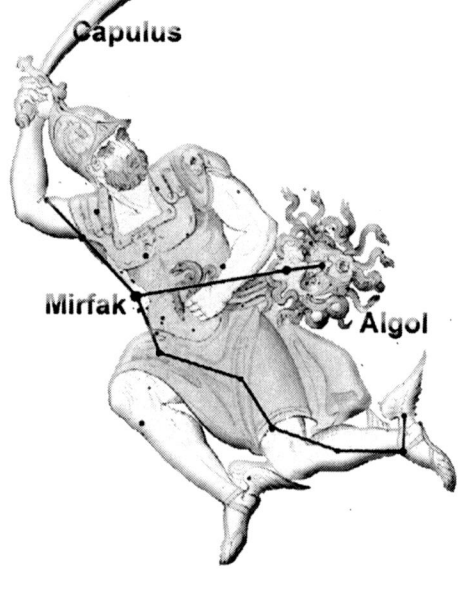

Perseus, The Young Warrior

Placed just south of Andromeda, Perseus the hero is one member of a royal family, which also includes Cepheus the king, Cassiopeia the queen and Andromeda the daughter or princess. He stands facing Andromeda with his foot on the Milky Way. Perseus can be viewed in the Greek mould as the conquering hero saving the damsel in distress (Andromeda), with his sword raised and holding his prize of Medusa's head[1]. Or we can see him as part of this natural balance, the royal family: Andromeda's suitor, young, masculine, full of male energy symbolised by his sword raised like a huge phallus, holding in his hand the head of an animal or the head of an enemy as his offering, his hunting prize or the symbol of his courage, his ability to protect or his hunting skill. (For more information see Algol and Capulus).

The Principle of Mirfak the young warrior, a love of action

This star represents the concept of the young warrior proud of his strength, his hunting and fighting abilities, and flaunting his trophy. Mirfak is young male energy. He is the hero of a thousand faces as well as the primal concept of the warrior. When active in a chart it can imply a rashness of action and a headstrong attitude to life events, or a tendency to overestimate one's own strength but also a love of the challenge.

Heliacal Rising Star

A natural desire to engage in challenge, a person who triumphs by being aggressive. A person with physical vitality but who at times is reckless. *Bryan Brown, Australian actor who gained recognition for his portrayal of Breaker Morant, a maverick Australian soldier of the Boer War.*

Heliacal Setting Star
Finding that action brings results; tending to become more reckless or challenge-oriented as one grows older; to seek the path of the spiritual warrior or to grow in aggression. *John Edgar Hoover, controversial director of the FBI for 48 years who misused his authority to challenge those who held political opinions or attitudes to which he did not subscribe.*

Star on one of its pivot points at the moment of birth
A sports-orientated person, or a person who is very physical, and always active, busy and outward going. Hot tempered or impatient. *Slim Pickens, US rodeo performer and actor who epitomized the profane, tough cowboy.*

Physiological Correspondence: The ribcage, its role as protector of the internal organs.

Ptolemy's location: The bright star in the right side of Perseus.

World Cities: Bristol and London, England; Brussels, Belgium; Frankfurt and Munich, Germany; Paris, France; Prague, Czech Republic, Vienna, Austria at latitudes between 48° to 52° north.

Mirfak in paran with:

Sun: To have vitality and enthusiasm. The sports person, an athlete, or to have a great deal of energy for one's daily life.   ♦   The enthusiasm of the warrior. A time to take action. *Edward White, the first US astronaut to walk in space.*

Moon: Thrill seeker; the lover of a good fight or challenge. The emotional need to be associated with a struggle, political, military, or on the sports field.   ♦   A popular victory. *Sam Colt, 19th century US inventor of the Colt revolver popularised in Wild West fiction.*

Mercury: To be verbally assertive; a tendency to be mentally obsessed with a problem. The smart advocate, the probing journalist, or the fanatic.   ♦   Public arguments. *James Earl Ray, whose notoriety rests on his assassination of Martin Luther King Jr.*

Venus: To be candid in personal, and public, relationships. An unwillingness to see another person's point of view.   ♦   Social niceties are ignored. *Louisa May Alcott, US writer who in 1868 achieved enormous success with the children's classic "Little Women" which drew on her own childhood experiences.*

Mars: A person who uses aggression, or raw physical energy, as an instrument of change. To have an immense store of energy.   ♦   News of an aggressive or violent action, either military or on the sports field. *David Helfgott, 20th century Australian pianist and subject of the film "Shine", renowned for his sheer physical energy.*

Jupiter: Achievement through decisive action. To function better as a loner; or to be a leader of a challenge-oriented team. ◆ A time of military action. *Arthur 1st Duke of Wellington, British Army commander during the Napoleonic Wars and later Prime Minister of Britain (1828-30).*

Saturn: To clash with others; to feel restricted. A tendency to dominate others, a strong overpowering personality. ◆ Laws are challenged. *Daniel Mendoza, 18th century English boxer who was the first Jewish heavyweight fighter and the first to use a more scientific style of boxing incorporating rapid punches.*

Uranus: A desire to work with others to improve their physical or mental well-being; involved in sports or education. ◆ Able to motivate groups. A hero is paraded. *Piet Retief, 18th century hero of the mass migration of Boers, known as the Great Trek, who sought independence from British rule in South Africa.*

Neptune: To seek to defend spiritual or new-age thinking. To champion minority causes. ◆ The spiritual warrior; or the fallen sports hero. *Michel Gauquelin, 20th century French mathematician who sort to prove the validity of astrology by statistical research but subsequent attacks from the establishment drove him to suicide.*

Pluto: Great endurance; to be able to undertake arduous tasks; to be willing to take on the long battle. A persistent, but at times fanatical individual. ◆ An exceptional act of physical bravery or recklessness. *EVENT: Pilgrims land at Plymouth Rock, America, 11 December, 1620*

The Node: To be a symbol of struggle or determination for one's family or community. To teach others how to compete or fight. ◆ News of a civil war. *Mao Tse-Tung, 20th century Chinese communist leader who developed the guerrilla tactics known as the "people's war" in civil war in China.*

NOTES

1. Bulfinch, *Myths of Greece and Rome*, p.133.

MURZIMS

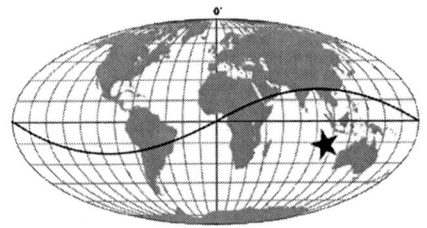

Constellation	Canis Major
β Canis Majoris, magnitude	1.98
1 January 2000 =	RA 06hr 22' 43"
Declination	-17° 57'
Celestial longitude	07° ♋ 12'
Celestial latitude	41°S15'
BV Colour =	Blue-Green

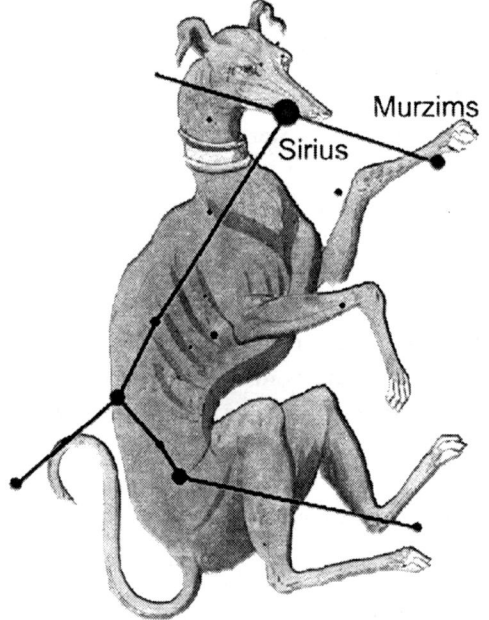

Canis Major, the big dog

Not far from the stern of the Argo lie two dogs, a large one, Canis Major, lying in the south and a smaller dog, Canis Minor, sitting above it on the equator. The Greeks see Canis Major as one of Orion's hunting dogs, sitting up in a begging position but with a watchful eye on the nearby hare[1]. But this dog was in the sky long before Aratus recorded it in the 4th century BCE. The dog was one of the first animals that humans domesticated and was seen as a guardian, both in life and in death. The Egyptians called this guard, and sometimes judge, *Anubis* and he became the god of mummification. Later Greek myths talk of *Cerberus*, the three headed dog called the Hound of Hades for he guarded the gate to Hades[2]. In the Christian mythology this role was taken over by a gentler image of Saint Peter, one who is said to sit at the pearly gates of heaven guarding and sometimes judging those who pass. (For more information see Sirius).

Principle of Murzims, the Announcer, to wish to speak

Murzims was called *The Announcer* because it rose before Sirius. This star embodies the symbolism of the dog and is associated with the concept of announcements, to make a noise, to speak out, to carry a message or to have something important to say. Unlike Sirius, the other major star in Canis Major, this is not an overwhelming star, but it will carry this "Announcer" energy into one's life.

Heliacal Rising Star
A person who lives the life of the researcher; a gossiper; or an announcer of facts. One whose philosophy of life is to find out information in order to announce it to the world; difficulties in keeping a secret. *Leopold Zunz, German historian of Jewish literature who is often considered by many to be the greatest Jewish scholar of the 19th century.*

Heliacal Setting Star
To learn the need to speak out; to find that one needs groups; the loner who comes in from the cold. To struggle to be heard. *Michael Hutchence, tragic Australian rock singer who was the main spokesperson and sexy front-man for his band INXS but struggled with his own introverted nature.*

Star on one of its pivot points at the moment of birth
An opinionated person; someone who speaks out, the politician, the professional orator or public speaker. To use words, spoken or written, as part of one's lifestyle. *Yul Brynner, Russian-born US actor who, apart from his acting roles used his voice in videos released after his death from lung cancer to speak out against smoking.*

Physiological Correspondence: Tongue, vocal cords, hyoid bone – the whole quality of the voice.

Ptolemy's location: The star at the end of the forefoot.

World Cities: La Paz, Bolivia; Tananarive, Madagascar at latitudes between 16° to 20° south.

Murzims in paran with:

Sun: The desire to make a statement. To be seen as a person who has a message; to have a vision, or a concept that needs to be shared.   ♦   A bold, or very public, statement. *John Rolfe, 16th century American colonist and husband of Pocahontas, a native American Indian princess who accompanied him back to England.*

Moon: A researcher of people, health or behaviour; a lover of biographies. Seeking to improve the welfare of others.   ♦   A time of emotional speeches. *Philippe Pinel, 18th century French physician who pioneered the humane treatment of the mentally ill.*

Mercury: The writer, the researcher and a person who speaks out. One who has the courage to explore different business ideas.   ♦   New business ideas, media ownership controversy. *Harland Sanders, US entrepreneur who is better known as "Colonel Sanders" the founder of, and whose image became the trademark of, Kentucky Fried Chicken.*

Venus: A persuasive person, a silver voice. A social conscience, and attitudes which find acceptance in a wider group.   ♦   A popular leader; a spokesperson who is well received. *Isabel*

Allende, *Chilean author whose first novel, "The House of Spirits" (1985) became a worldwide best-seller and critical success.*

Mars: Forthright in all ways of communication. One who is motivated to explore, reveal, speak the truth, find the solution, or shake out the facts.   ♦   Alarming news; news of events that causes anger. *Margaret Thatcher, who in 1979 became Britain's first woman Prime Minister.*

Jupiter: The desire to document or record events. To be drawn to exploring religion, sociology and philosophy.   ♦   Transparency, the true situation in revealed. *Thomas Francis Wade, 19th century British diplomat and Sinologist who developed the famous Wade-Giles system of Romanising the Chinese language.*

Saturn: Being able to influence others through one's words. The desire to build something tangible, with information and announcements.   ♦   A leader speaks, serious times. *George Baxter, English engraver who invented a process of colour printing (patented 1835) that allowed for the mass reproduction of paintings.*

Uranus: To love languages; to enjoy the works of popular culture; to be interested in or have an understanding of the thinking of the general people.   ♦   Popular opinion, the opinion polls. *John Russel Bartlett, 19th century American bibliographer who made his greatest contribution to linguistics with his pioneer work, "Dictionary of Americanisms".*

Neptune: Confusion with the truth; one who is an intuitive thinker; a person who has a religious message.   ♦   News or information that is not believed, or causes loss. *EVENT: Bombing of the World Trade Centre, New York, 9/11/01.*

Pluto: To explore all ways of communication; to be interested in arcane languages or codes; to seek out secret knowledge.   ♦   The words of one person, or a seemingly small event, has very powerful consequences. *Rene Descartes, 17th century French philosopher known as the "Father of Modern Philosophy". His most famous axiom "I think, therefore I am" became a catchword of rationalist philosophy.*

The Node: To be identified with a body of knowledge, to link oneself with a philosophy or code of living.   ♦   The diplomat. *Bruce Lee, US actor and martial arts expert who brought the philosophy of eastern martial arts to the west.*

NOTES

1. Aratus, "Phaenomena," p.233.
2. Bulfinch, *Myths of Greece and Rome*, p.292.

PHACT

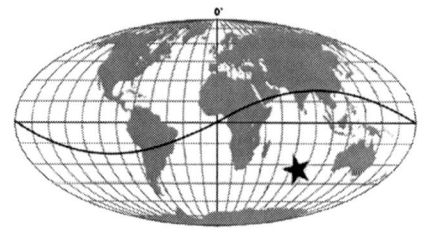

Constellation	Columba
α Columbae, magnitude	2.64
1 January 2000 =	RA 05hr 39' 40"
Declination	-34° 05'
Celestial longitude	22° ♊ 11'
Celestial latitude	57°S23'
BV Colour =	Blue-Green

Columba Noae, The Bow of the Argo or the Dove

Early works in cartography place the stars of this constellation amongst the stars of Canis Major but Royer, in 1679, cut the constellation in two, taking two stars from Canis Major and renaming them Alpha and Beta Columba Noae to avoid confusion with stars in the Argo. The two stars are Phact and Wezn.

The Principle of Phact, the Dove, to explore

This star used to be part of the Argo, on the top of the bow, crashing through the waves in uncharted waters. Phact adds the element of exploration, of seeking the unknown and of being prepared to move into situations that are unfamiliar. It can be a bold risk-taking statement or, alternatively, it can be the exploration of intellectual pursuits.

Heliacal Rising Star

To seek that which is just out of reach; to plunge into the unknown. A life which does not know caution and is willing to take risks to encounter the new. *Richard I, "Richard the Lionheart", 12th century English monarch famous for his prowess in the Third Crusade.*

Heliacal Setting Star

To find success in a foreign land or culture; to leave one's own group but then to find acceptance in another. *Stephen Hatton, 20th century Australian politician who tried to promote statehood for the Northern Territory, a largely native Australian population.*

Star on one of its pivot points at the moment of birth
A risk taker, a person who wants to explore new horizons. To have restlessness as one's shadow. Needing the "new" on a daily level. *Walt Disney, 20th century American entrepreneur who was an innovator in animation and theme park design.*

Physiological Correspondence: The neck, its function in supporting the head.

Ptolemy's location: The bright star in the Dove or on the deck of the Argo.

World Cities: Adelaide, Sydney and Perth, Australia; Cape Town, South Africa; Montevideo, Uruguay; Santiago, Chile at latitudes between 32^0 to 36^0 south.

Phact in paran with:

Sun: Headstrong, someone who does not seek or take advice; to be an explorer of places or ideas.
◆ A time of the fanatic. *Siegfried Sassoon, 20th century English poet known for his anti-war poetry, which he wrote after being awarded the Military Cross for service on the battle fields of WWI.*

Moon: The romantic adventurer, of places or ideas. A craving for that which is exciting, a thrill seeker. ◆ A romantic adventure grips popular culture. *Edward Whymper, 19th century English mountaineer and artist, associated with the exploration of the Alps and the first man to climb the Matterhorn.*

Mercury: An original thinker or a foolish mind, always seeking the new idea. The mind of an inventor, and/or the researcher. ◆ Technological breakthroughs, the advance of science in the news. *Michel Adanson, 18th century French botanist who was the first to classify plants into natural orders.*

Venus: A trend-setter in new design work, or in social attitudes. A person who is willing to live an alternative lifestyle. ◆ A fashion craze, a popular item claims the market. *John Baskerville, 18th century English printer, creator of a typeface of great distinction bearing his name and whose works are among the finest examples of the art of printing.*

Mars: Bold, daring and original, needing a challenge. A person who needs exciting situations in order to feel alive; sports, speed, sex, adventure. ◆ Fires or explosions. *Pierre baron de Coubert, 19th century French educator who is best remembered for being the father of the modern Olympic Games.*

Jupiter: The explorer, the wanderer through places or ideas. A thirst for independence and freedom, difficulty in holding to commitments. ◆ Athletic records are broken. *Matthias Zdarsky, 19th century Czech ski instructor considered to be the father of Alpine skiing, and who was probably the first regular ski instructor in Austria.*

Saturn: Taking on large and difficult projects. To be willing to take on projects where others dare not, or are unable to go.   ♦   *The actions of a loner take focus in news. Johannes Kepler, 16th century German mathematician whose years of calculation established the laws of planetary motion.*

Uranus: Willing to break new ground on behalf of one's community or one's culture. To be the first in your family to travel or to step into a different social world.   ♦   *The people seek a new law or a new government. Maria de Zayas, the most important of the minor 17th century Spanish novelists and one of the first women to publish prose fiction in the Castilian dialect.*

Neptune: One who takes a spiritual journey; to be seeking the divine. One who lives in a virtual world or suffers from delusions.   ♦   *The pharmaceutical industry, or drug laws, under question. David Sarnoff, early 20th century Talmudic scholar who later used the invention of radio to show its uses in popular culture.*

Pluto: A strong sense of personal belief, the tendency to consider one's own path to be correct for everyone.   ♦   *The act of one person empowers many. John Kellogg, 19th century American physician remembered as the father of the breakfast food industry, which he developed based on his religious beliefs and vegetarianism.*

The Node: The traveller, the one who takes journeys physically or intellectually. A tourist guide, a travel consultant, a person who shows us other places.   ♦   *A journey that changes everything. Stephen Hawking, 20th century British physicist whose work on black holes and theories of space and time have established him as the most important physicist of his time.*

POLARIS

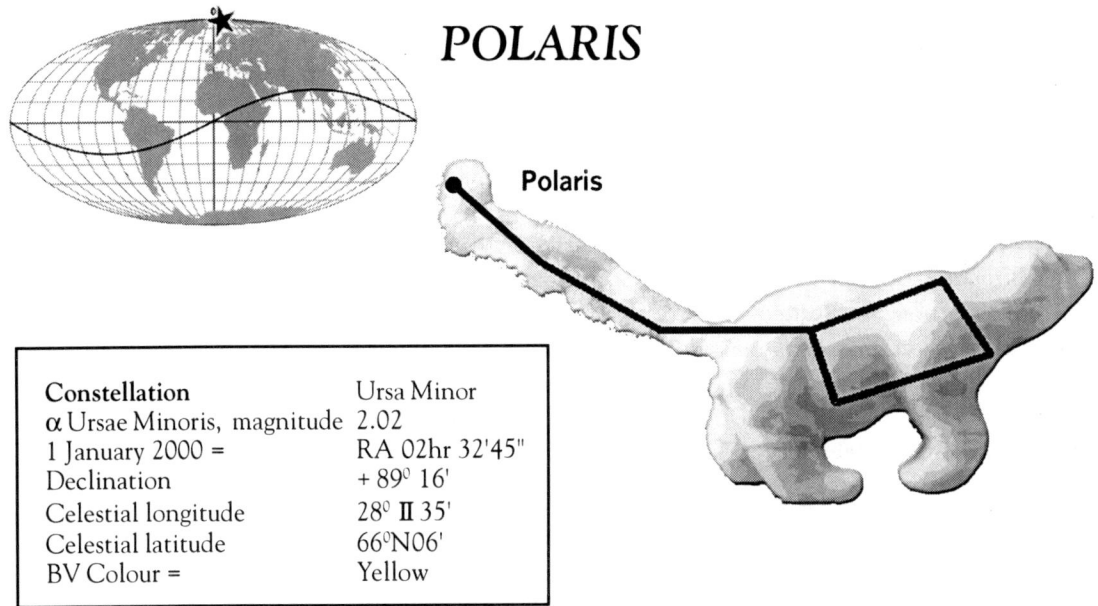

Constellation	Ursa Minor
α Ursae Minoris, magnitude	2.02
1 January 2000 =	RA 02hr 32'45"
Declination	+ 89° 16'
Celestial longitude	28° Ⅱ 35'
Celestial latitude	66°N06'
BV Colour =	Yellow

Ursa Minor, the little bear

The Little Bear was a navigational aid to 6th century BCE sailors because, along with the stars of Draco, it was near the important pole position. The Little Bear is in fact surrounded on three sides by the constellation Draco, the Dragon, and when the bright star of the Dragon, Thuban, was the pole star around 2,500 BCE, the Little Bear was considered to be the wings of the dragon. Indeed Thuban, in Draco, was the last star to occupy the north celestial pole, and Polaris in Ursa Minor now holds this position, which has been vacant in the night sky for around 4,500 years. Manilius captured the importance of this little bear, acting as a navigator and commanding the night in the 1st century CE, when he wrote: "The smaller Bear, though less in size and light, In narrower Circles she commands the Night."[1] Aratus, some centuries earlier, also sees this group of stars as one of the Bears[2], lesser than the Great Bear because its seven main stars are dimmer in appearance, and it occupies a smaller place in the heavens than Ursa Major. The constellation has also been known as a dog, with the Egyptians calling it the Jackal of Set. In this sense it has been called "the dog's tail".[3]

The Principle of Polaris, the Pole Star, to be guided by one's principles

Polaris is strongly tied to its history as a pole star, for it has been used for centuries by sailors of both sea and desert as a guide. Thus we find many layers of a path-finding symbolism associated with this part of the sky. While there is no practical method by which we can use this star when working with visual parans, as it never rises or sets but can only be used if it co-culminates with a planet, it will, nevertheless, give a flavour of the path-finder to any chart that it touches.

Heliacal Rising Star
No delineation, only possible for a birth just a few minutes of latitude south of the equator.

Heliacal Setting Star
No delineation, only possible for a birth just a few minutes of latitude north of the equator.

On its point of culmination at the time of birth
Single mindedness, strong focus. To be focused on a single pathway, to be unreceptive to other opinions or thoughts. *Jeanne d'Arc, 15th century French saint and military commander who was inspired by God to leave her farm and take leadership of the French army to drive the English from her country.*

Physiological Correspondence: The navel, the body's omphalos and centre of gravity.

Ptolemy's location: The star at the end of the tail.

World Cities: Nil cities at latitudes between 87° to 90° north.

Polaris co-culminating with:

Sun: Single mindedness, a strong focus. To devote one's life to a single passion, to maintain focus on a single goal despite all obstructions.   ♦   The time when the media is preoccupied with a single subject. *John Dee, 16th century court astrologer to Queen Elizabeth I who worked extensively in the magical arts; also Aleister Crowley, renowned 19th century English explorer of magical arts.*

Moon: Obsession with a goal. A belief that only the achievement of one particular goal can fulfil one's life. To have over zealous expectations or ambitions for those one loves.   ♦   An obsession with a celebrity's life or a single event. *Hermann Rorschach, 19th century Swiss psychiatrist who developed the inkblot test used to diagnose psychopathological illnesses.*

Mercury: Strong mental focus. To remain loyal to an idea even if others have given up. To be the fanatic or the genius.   ♦   A pivotal news story. *Bernadette Soubiros, 19th century French saint known for the visions she experienced which led to the foundation of the shrine at Lourdes.*

Venus: Single-minded ideas about relationships; a closed attitude to human sexuality and social customs.   ♦   A preoccupation with the private life of a celebrity. *Queen Elizabeth I, English monarch who reigned (1588-1603) while successfully resisting the unrelenting pressure to marry in order to produce an heir to the throne.*

Mars: Strong sexual or physical drives. A strong desire to engage physically with life, to be sexually or sensually obsessive.   ♦   The actions of fanatics. *Pedro Almodovar, film maker known* *for his provocative treatment of sexual themes. One of his most famous films, made in 1988, was "Women on the Verge of a Nervous Breakdown".*

Jupiter: The entrepreneur; a person who can see the potential in a new situation. To maintain a belief in one's ideas, to pursue a dream.   ♦   An entrepreneur is featured in the news. *Ray Kroc, US restauranteur best known as the founder of the fast-food industry and for the McDonald's chain of restaurants.*

Saturn: A builder – of ideas, of artistic works, or of expertise. To design or build, to pursue a dream into a practical expression, the inventor.   ♦   The expert is called in. *Seth Thomas, 18th century US inventor who pioneered the mass production of clocks.*

Uranus: To take a popular stance on a social problem; to be drawn to a group's opinions, to join protests or contribute monies to the action of this group.   ♦   A popular solution to social poverty or ills. EVENT: *The day of the commencement of the French Revolution: 14 July, 1789, Paris.*

Neptune: A devotional attitude to a religion, career or belief system. To seek the divine in one's life. A singular belief that gives strength to one's daily life.   ♦   A final solution presented, or a last chance that fails. *Mohandas K. Gandhi, 19th century Indian leader who advocated pacifism and the sanctity of all living things; his unshakable faith in this moral position, as the basis of resistance to an oppressive colonial regime, eventually led India to independence.*

Pluto: To be challenged on one's unshakeable beliefs. To have to face the collapse of one's ideals; to find sanctuary in the deeps of one's philosophy.   ♦   The death blow, one action that ends a situation. EVENT: *The dropping of the atomic bomb on Hiroshima on 6 August, 1945.*

The Node: A monist philosophy. To link one's life with a single path, a single God, a single vision, a single dream.   ♦   A time when only one opinion is heard. *Huey Long, 19th century US politician who was accused by his opponents of dictatorial tendencies, because of his near-total control of the state government, and his obsession with making "Every Man a King".*

NOTES

1. Manilius, *Astronomica*, 1:298-305.
2. Aratus, "Phaenomena" p.209.
3. Allen, *Star Names Their Lore and Meaning*, p.450.

POLLUX

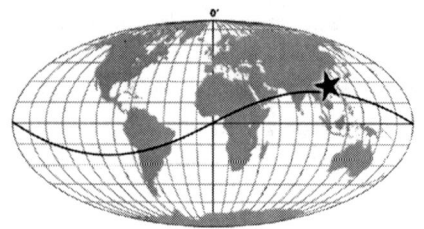
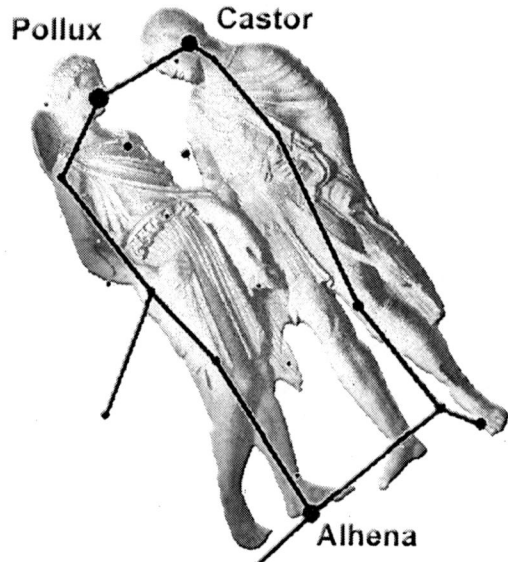

Constellation	Gemini
β Geminorum, magnitude	1.14
1 January 2000 =	RA 07hr 45'19"
Declination	+28° 01'
Celestial longitude	23° ♋ 13'
Celestial latitude	06°N41'
BV Colour =	Orange

Gemini, the Twins

Known as the twins in most ancient writings, these two companion stars and their resulting constellation embody the wonder of twins in the human psyche. Dylan and Lleu, twin powers of dark and light, were born from Arianrhod the Celtic goddess of the Star Wheel[1]. Ahura Mazda and Ahriman were God and Devil born simultaneously from Zurvan's womb in Zoroastrian mythology. In the bible it is Cain and Abel. For the Egyptians, the god of the Morning Star and light was Horus and the God of the Evening Star was his evil brother Set, who was darkness and was also connected to the never-setting circumpolar stars (Ursa Major and Draco) which the Egyptians considered to be the wife of Set[2]. To the Greeks they were Castor, linked with horsemanship, and his brother Pollux who was a boxer[3]. Such pairs represent the concept of polarity and Gemini is the most well-known heavenly pair. (For more information see Alhena and Castor).

One of the twins of Gemini, – Pollux, wisdom through painful insights.

This star is one of the twins, its brother being Castor. Both these stars are associated with the art of the story-teller, who is able to weave threads of both good and evil, overlapping the one with the other until both are changed and both are whole. So these stars are concerned with the blending of opposites and the merging of the two. With Pollux in a chart, one will have an awareness of opposites or polarity but with this star the focus will be on the shadowy or difficult side of the issues. Pollux suggests that understanding or wisdom is gained through pain or angst and that a person has a tendency to come at issues from the more problematic side, or to take the more physical approach to a situation.

Heliacal Rising Star
Life is a journey of self-discovery through the mountains and valleys of one's own soul. To be able to feel or communicate the deeps of human emotions. *Isabel Allende, exiled Chilean author whose worldwide best-selling novels are focused on human emotions and drama.*

Heliacal Setting Star
To find that one's greatest strength lies in understanding physical force, or discovering that one has an instinctive understanding of the darker or more secretive side of the human soul. *John Graham Chambers, 19th century English sportsman who devised the Marquess of Queensberry rules used in boxing.*

Star on one of its pivot points at the moment of birth
A lifestyle of exploring painful truths, intellectually or physically; to be associated with a difficult idea or a difficult physical challenge. *Evel Knievel, American motorcycle daredevil, an entertainer famous in the United States and elsewhere during the late 1960s and 70s.*

Physiological Correspondence: The ears – the auditory capacity.

Ptolemy's location: The star in the head of Pollux, the eastern twin.

World Cities: Chihuahua, Mexico; Chongqing, China at latitudes between 26° to 30° north.

Pollux in paran with:

Sun: To be considered a researcher or inventor. To choose the path of greatest challenge, greatest growth, the path that wrestles with obstacles.   ◆   The focus is on a person with different ideas. *Walter Savage Landor, 18th century English writer who is known for his work, "Imaginary Conversations", a collection of imagined interchanges between famous people in history.*

Moon: To want to bring reform or change through knowledge. To explore less popular or less mainstream styles of thinking.   ◆   Help which is needed fails to arrive. *Anne Sullivan, Helen Keller's teacher, recognised for her achievement in educating people without sight, hearing or speech.*

Mercury: Struggling with new or unusual ideas, to take the contra-argument. To brush up against the legal system.   ◆   A person in authority goes against the tide of public thinking. *Wilfred Owen, early 20th century English poet whose work is noted for its anger at the cruelty of war.*

Venus: The artisan; or living an alternative lifestyle. To be attracted towards the wounded, or the disadvantaged.   ◆   The contra-social opinion is aired. *Maria Hrabina Walewska, Polish mistress of Napoleon Bonaparte, who followed him to Paris and finally to Elba the island of his imprisonment.*

Mars: One who expresses unpopular or even dangerous opinions. To challenge others with one's words or one's physical presence.   ♦   The physical solution wins the day. *Colin Wilson, 20th century English novelist and writer on philosophy, sociology, music, literature, and the occult.*

Jupiter: Loving the pursuit of the unusual idea; or mental addiction. To be obsessive, to be addicted to a subject to the point of being blinded to other options.   ♦   The alternative idea, or person, is successful. *John Holland, 19th century Irish inventor who is known as the father of the modern submarine.*

Saturn: A person who can take a simple idea and build it into a practical application. To work with proletarian matters; teaching those who are disadvantaged.   ♦   People's lives altered by the actions of an aggressive group. *Galileo Galilei, 16th century Italian mathematician who is the father of the experimental method.*

Uranus: To express or support unpopular but essential statements about society, to be a spokesperson on alternative matters.   ♦   Repressed situations explode. *John Milton, 17th century English poet known as one of the greatest poets of the English language, due especially to his epic "Paradise Lost".*

Neptune: One who experiences difficulties due to hasty action or ill-founded decisions. To have little regard for, or feel confusion over, the rights of others.   ♦   Fire or natural disaster. *Lord Herbert Kitchener, 19th century British commander whose practice of interning women and children, during the Boer war, introduced the concept of concentration camps.*

Pluto: Methodical and painstaking research; to undertake a physical or intellectual journey knowing it will be long and hard.   ♦   The painful truth is exposed. *Michael Ventris, 20th century English cryptographer who in 1952 deciphered the Minoan Linear B script and showed it to be Greek in its oldest known form.*

The Node: To be wounded; to be associated with a form of disability though one's own body or through one's career. To suffer an injury, physically or to one's reputation.   ♦   A time which belongs to the oppressed. *Lord Horatio Nelson, 19th century British admiral who died at the Battle of Trafalgar after already losing an eye and an arm in previous naval battles.*

NOTES

1. Green, *Dictionary of Celtic Myth and Legend*, p.54.
2. Lockyer, *The Dawn of Astronomy*, p.146.
3. Bulfinch, *Myths of Greece and Rome*, p.188.

PROCYON

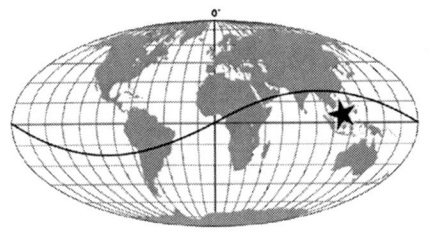

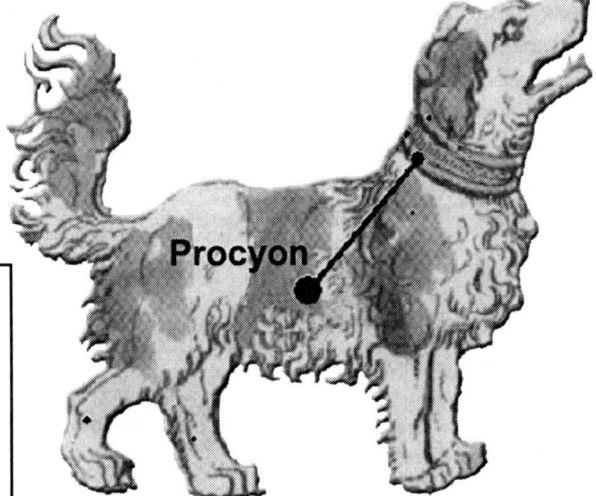

Constellation	Canis Minor
α Canis Minoris, magnitude	0.38
1 January 2000 = RA 07hr	39'19"
Declination	+05° 13'
Celestial longitude	25° ♋ 47'
Celestial latitude	16°S01'
BV Colour =	Green

Canis Minor, the little dog
Above Canis Major on the equator is a small dog called Canis Minor. The sitting dog, or small dog was used as a divine symbol in the Old Babylonian Period (2000-1595 BCE) and was associated with Gula, the Babylonian goddess of healing[1]. Around 660 BCE the Assyrian astrologer priests used a dog's image or figurine associated with a star (drawn above its head) as part of a cleansing ritual[2]. To the Greeks, Canis Minor was Orion's second hound, and it has also been called The Puppy[3]. It rises before Canis Major and thus its main claim to fame is the fact that it heralds the rising of Sirius, the brightness star in the sky apart from our sun.

The Principle of Procyon, the one that comes before, things in transition
Procyon comes before *The Shining One*, Sirius, and so can indicate a quick rise but with no real substance. With this star in a chart, there is an experience of early gains upon which one should capitalise quickly rather than rest in the expectation of their continuation. Procyon is metaphorically similar to fireworks – wonderful to watch, takes centre stage, but quickly fades. This star suggests that one needs to harvest opportunities as they emerge, for they will disappear as quickly as they arrive. Procyon is about transition, whether this takes the form of a healing crisis, drawing from the Babylonian view, or of the collapse of a faulty or ephemeral structure, drawing on the Greek idea of Procyon simply coming before Sirius.

Heliacal Rising Star
To know how to land on one's feet; to have a drive to diversify and add many options to one's life. *Jacqueline Kennedy Onassis, wife of the assassinated president JFK, and later of the shipping tycoon Aristotle Onassis.*

Heliacal Setting Star
To discover that the solution to one's problems is diversity; to succeed by constantly changing one's approach to a problem. To learn to keep one's options open. *Max Theiler, South African researcher who won the 1951 Nobel Prize for his research and development of a vaccine for yellow fever, achieved by mutating the virus through many strains.*

Star on one of its pivot points at the moment of birth
To live a changing life, to explore different lifestyles, a need to move on from one's success otherwise a life spent reliving past glories. *Dick Smith, Australian businessman who deals in electronics, food, publishing and is also an aviator.*

Physiological Correspondence: Physical fitness – must be maintained daily, or the gain is lost.

Ptolemy's location: The bright star in the hind parts of the little dog called Procyon.

World Cities: Bogota, Colombia; Cayenne, French Guiana; Georgetown, Guyana; Kuala Lumpur, Malaysia; Paramaribo, Suriname at latitudes between 03° to 07° north.

Procyon in paran with:

Sun: Exceptionally skilled, but needing to diversify this talent. The sports person; or to have skills that do not carry forward into the elder years.   ◆   A time of sporting success, or short-lived, ephemeral glories. *Edson Arantes do Nascimento, known as Pele, is considered to be the most famous athlete of his era having led the Brazilian soccer team to three victories in soccer's World Cup.*

Moon: Subject to mood swings, shifts in likes and dislikes. Difficulties in maintaining friendships.   ◆   Sudden highs or lows in people's feelings. *George W Bush, 43rd president of the USA whose approval ratings swung wildly from less than 50% at the time of election to over 85% after the World Trade Center bombing of 9/11, (11 September, 2001).*

Mercury: One who can adapt to changing situations. To have varied interests, in both intellectual and/or financial, areas, and to show great adeptness.   ◆   The completion of a time of glory, a sports champion retires. *Christopher Wren, 17th century English architect, designer, astronomer, and geometrician, considered to be the greatest English architect of his time.*

Venus: Struggling to sustain personal relationships, or society's values. A person follows fashion whims in clothing, colour, art and music.   ◆   A new fashion statement. *Alan Turing, English mathematician who was pivotal in cracking the German Enigma code machines of WWII, but later was driven to suicide because of his homosexuality.*

Mars: Stops and starts, many changes to one's career, or life path. To have many and varied activities or interests. ♦ A rash or violent act, or a sudden break-through achievement. *Leni Riefenstahl, German photographer and filmmaker best known for her documentary films of the Nazi movement.*

Jupiter: Achievements and lifestyle are based on bold, decisive action. The ability to land on one's feet in times of upheaval or crisis. ♦ Finding the unexpected solution. *Henry VIII, 16th century Tudor king of England, noted for the number of his wives and for establishing the Church of England.*

Saturn: To try to build a body of work in difficult, or changing, circumstances. To be a stabilising force at times of upheaval, crisis or emergency. ♦ A short term policy, or leader, comes to the fore. *Oliver Cromwell, leader of the parliamentary forces during the English Civil War (1642-1649).*

Uranus: To work in a changing industry; the need to be adaptable in one's social milieu; to switch profession or places of employment often. ♦ An unexpected outcome in an election or popular event. *Elizabeth Taylor, British actress known not only for her acting career but also her many marriages.*

Neptune: A vivid imagination; to be pursuing a dream. To be able to envisage something before it has begun. ♦ A new start, a new beginning, forced or otherwise. EVENT: *The sailing of the first fleet of five ships with just over 1000 people which included 750 convicts for Australia 13 May 1787.*

Pluto: An intuitive thinker; to suddenly find solutions to problems without applying oneself; to jump from one subject to another. ♦ The sudden ending of a problem, or social issue. *Eli Whitney, 18th century American inventor remembered for developing the concept of mass-production of interchangeable parts.*

The Node: To be associated with a changing attitude; to work in an area where one needs to alter one's role or actions in response to emerging events. ♦ A plan fails. *Patty Hearst, US heiress who gained notoriety in 1974 when, following her kidnapping by the Symbionese Liberation Army (SLA), she joined her captors in furthering their cause.*

NOTES

1. Black and Green, *Gods, Demons and Symbols of Ancient Mesopotamia*, p.70.
2. Simo Parpola, *Letters from Assyrian Scholars to the Kings Esarhaddon and Assurbanipal Part 1*, Germany: Butzon and Kevelaer, 1970, p.141.
3. Allen, *Star Names Their Lore and Meaning*, p.132.

RAS ALGETHI

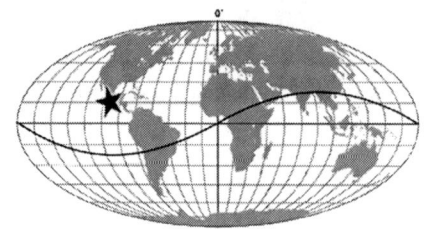

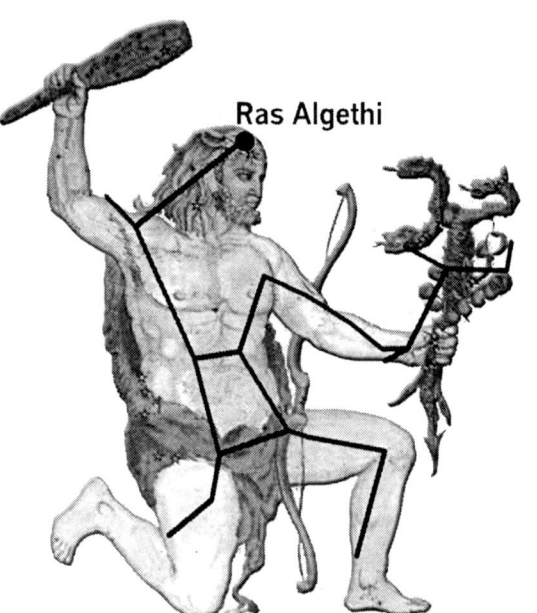

Ras Algethi

Constellation	Hercules
α1 Herculis, magnitude	3.48
1 January 2000 =	
Declination	RA 17hr 14' 37"
	+14° 23'
Celestial longitude	16° ♐ 08'
Celestial latitude	37°N17'
BV Colour =	Red

Hercules, the kneeler

Hercules is also known as The Phantom or The One Who Kneels[1]. He was also Gilgamesh, the great solar hero who seems to have been the first to encounter the whirlpool and strive for immortality[2]. The Phoenicians called him Harekhal and to the Greeks and Romans he was Hercules, the name he still carries today. Whatever his name this figure is shown as kneeling in the presence of the great Bear and the Dragon. This posture resembles the Egyptian hieroglyphic sign for a man in his correct position in society and giving service to the divine, which is that of kneeling on one knee while holding an arm upward and bent[3]. The phantom holds this posture perfectly in the part of the sky reserved for the sacred, the area of the north pole.

The Principle of Ras Algethi, acknowledging the natural order

This star is tied to the giving of honour or prayer to the gods, the instinctive attitude of humans in awe of the gods or goddesses, and is associated with the idea of the natural order of the world. To our modern mind this could be expressed as a respect for nature, a caring about the planet, a desire to have all things in their place; in short, a concern about the correct order of nature, life and the heavens. If Ras Algethi is in a chart it will indicate, via the planet to which it is linked, a sense of order or correctness, or a seeking of this order. There is a spontaneous need to submit to or honour something larger than oneself. This can give a sense of purpose to one's life, or it can be simply the adoration of another human – being a fan.

Heliacal Rising Star
To believe in natural order, to be one who looks for the simple solutions to social issues; one who can bring harmony into their family. To look to nature for life's solutions. *Samuel Alexander, 19th century Australian who was instrumental in establishing the principle of a Jewish national home land.*

Heliacal Setting Star
To find oneself having to deal with questions of ethics, morals and social justice. A growing interest in the environment or the natural world. *Gregor Mendel, 19th century Czech monk who was the first to lay a mathematical foundation for the science of genetics by working with peas.*

Star on one of its pivot points at the moment of birth
The philosopher; a person who seeks the meaning of life. A desire to honour something larger than oneself thus giving purpose to one's life. *Immanuel Kant, 18th century German philosopher whose themes were a love of nature and a belief in "goodness".*

Physiological Correspondence: One's eating habits and the effect on one's body and well-being.

Ptolemy's location: The star in the head of the Kneeler.

World Cities: Bangkok, Thailand; Dakar, Senegal; Guatemala City, Guatemala; Manila, Philippines at latitudes between 12° to 16° north.

Ras Algethi in paran with:

Sun: Seeking the natural order of life; looking for a balance in diet and life habits. A person sensitive to the environment, a lover of the natural world. ♦ The need to restore balance to a situation, laws or the economy. *John Harvey Kellogg, 19th century American who drew on his religious beliefs in originating the breakfast food industry.*

Moon: The desire to help, heal, or bring balance to others. A person who uses natural health techniques, one who seeks to prevent problems rather than try to cure them. ♦ The swing of the pendulum; people are out of balance. *Jonas Edward Salk, 20th century US physician known for developing the anti-polio vaccine.*

Mercury: Inquisitive about the nature of objects, people, or the laws of creation. The desire for just or moral dealings in one's life. ♦ A pressure point is released, with new levels thus revealed. *Gerardus Mercator, 16th century Flemish cartographer, geographer and mathematician best known for his mapping work, especially the Mercator projection which used straight lines to indicate latitude and longitude.*

Venus: Insightful in the use of money, or colour or personal appearances. A person with a broad network of friends, associations and/ or lovers. ♦ The status quo is maintained. *Theda Bara, 19th century US silent film star who was one of cinema's earliest sex symbols.*

Mars: Wanting to live by a moral code; strong principles and sense of justice. A tendency to take a simplistic view of social issues. ♦ Justice is done, what is natural and correct comes to pass. *Giovanni Pico della Mirandola, 15th century Italian philosopher known for his treatise on the enemies of the Catholic Church, which included an exposition of the deficiencies of astrology.*

Jupiter: A person who promotes a more naturalistic approach to life. To strongly believe in a particular way of living; the preacher. ♦ The need to restore balance; the need to fill a power vacuum. *Edward Taylor, 19th century English anthropologist regarded as the founder of cultural anthropology.*

Saturn: A strong personal creed; a disciplined person. A person who will not compromise their personal philosophy, one based in natural, or spiritual principles. ♦ The natural order is restored. *Sir Thomas More, Chancellor of England beheaded for refusing to acknowledge Henry VIII as the head of the newly- formed Church of England.*

Uranus: To instigate change in one's family or society's practices. To adopt new eating habits. To break away from established religions. ♦ A sudden upset in the political balance of power. *Kgnaz Semmelweis, 19th century Hungarian physician who introduced the concept of antisepsis into medicine.*

Neptune: To have one's birthright removed; to lose an opportunity which was yours for the taking; to walk away from family, power or prestige. ♦ That which is honoured, or deemed sacred, fails. *EVENT: Wall Street Crash on 29 October, 1929.*

Pluto: To be a founder or a destroyer. To want to repair what one considers to be out of balance; to seek to remove pain or severe distress. ♦ The collapse of or the birth of, a stable system. *William Thomas Morton, 18th century American dentist who held the first public demonstration of the use of ether for anaesthesia during surgery.*

The Node: To be seen as a person with a good network. A lifestyle linked to promoting a natural balance, or a spiritual path of healing. ♦ New government policies are announced. *Dorothea Dix, 18th century American whose dedication to the plight of those with a mental illness saw reforms instituted in the USA and Europe.*

NOTES

1. Aratus, "Phaenomena," p.213.
2. Jobes and Jobes, *Outer Space: Myths, Name Meanings, Calendars*, p.185.
3. W.V. Davies, *Reading the Past, Egyptian Hieroglyphs*, London: British Museum Press, 1997, p.34.

RAS ALHAGUE

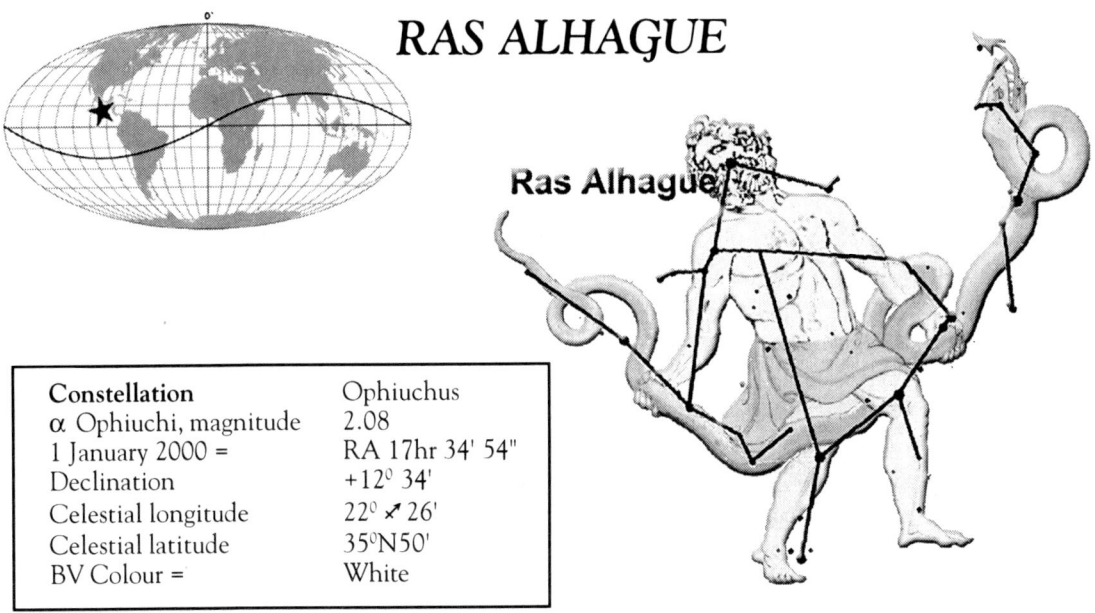

Constellation	Ophiuchus
α Ophiuchi, magnitude	2.08
1 January 2000 =	
RA	17hr 34' 54"
Declination	+12° 34'
Celestial longitude	22° ♐ 26'
Celestial latitude	35°N50'
BV Colour =	White

Ophiuchus, the Healer
The original constellation has now been broken up into two constellations: Ophiuchus, the serpent holder, and Serpens the serpent in his grasp. The serpent itself has also been divided into two sections, one on each side of Ophiuchus, called Serpens Caput and Serpens Cauda. When Scorpio lost its claws to Libra, it also lost most of its contact with the ecliptic and so Ophiuchus now cuts a larger tract across the ecliptic than the modern Scorpio. Ophiuchus was known to the Greeks as Serpentarius the Healer, who was also the god Asclepius son of Apollo[1]. He learnt the healing arts from Chiron and is usually depicted as holding a stick on which a serpent is coiled. Later, under Christian influence, this constellation became Saint Paul with the Maltese Viper[2]. The serpent was seen as a healing agent because it represented prudence, rejuvenation, wisdom and rebirth.

The Principle of Ras Alhague, the healer
The themes of this star are that of the healer, teacher, or one who is wounded. With this star in a chart one is drawn to the healing professions, or at least has a natural gift in that area. What one chooses to heal may vary and it can lead to a life in politics or other areas of "social" healing. Whatever the symbolism of this star in a person's life, the driving force of its expression is to repair that which is damaged, to heal.

Heliacal Rising Star
The healer; one who tries to bring help, through words or actions. A deep drive to seek to remedy old problems; a personal philosophy of helping one's family or friends. *Germaine Greer, Australian-born writer and scholar widely regarded as one of the most significant feminist voices of the 20th century.*

Heliacal Setting Star
To find that one is led to an place of healing, to learn the hard way about the importance of harmony and balance. To learn to heal oneself. *Madam Blavatsky, 19th century Russian spiritual leader who wrote that all religions were both true in their inner teachings and problematic or imperfect in their external conventional manifestations.*

Star on one of its pivot points at the moment of birth
To physically try and make a difference, to be proactive in seeking change. To want to repair that which is damaged, to heal. *Albert Camus, 20th century French author whose most important phrase for the future was: "All of us, among the ruins, are preparing a renaissance beyond the limits of nihilism. But few of us know it".*

Physiological Correspondence: The lymphatic system as the defender of the internal body.

Ptolemy's location: The star in the head of the Serpent-charmer.

World Cities: Bangkok, Thailand; Caracas, Venezuela; Dijibouti, Dijibouti at latitudes between 10° to 14° north.

Ras Alhague in paran with:

Sun: A reporter, interested in the stories of events and people. A career which is in some way involved with the stories of human nature.   •   A popular story or novel is released. *Kerry Packer, Australian media owner who, in the late 20th century, was Australia's richest man.*

Moon: A person who probes the hidden meanings, or sacredness, of life. The person who brings relief; the person who makes the breakthrough.   •   A human interest story inspires the population. *Neil Armstrong, US astronaut who was the first man to walk on the moon.*

Mercury: Interested in spreading, investigating, or studying methods of healing. The medical researcher, the midwife or the herbalist.   •   Health care in the news. *Marie Stopes, 19th century feminist who was a major advocate of birth control and who founded the UK's first instructional clinic for contraception.*

Venus: A person who expands the collective's options by increasing the availability of information.
• To want to help by teaching. *Karl Landsteiner, Austrian researcher who discovered the major blood groups and developed the ABO blood typing system.*

Mars: Bringing order and wisdom to difficult problems. A desire to be of benefit to others.
• Wisdom finally used to solve old problems. *Benjamin Franklin, 18th century diplomat best known for his role in the formation of the United States of America and its separation from Great Britain.*

Jupiter: A person who uses knowledge and optimism to expand the lives of others. To be a river of information for others.   • Openness and a willingness to listen delivers a solution. *Ivar Aasen, 19th century fervent Norwegian nationalist who was the creator of the "national language" called "Landsmal" later known as New Norwegian.*

Saturn: The desire to leave a legacy of knowledge or wisdom. To hand information from one generation to the next, to hold the family stories.   • The civic order needing repair. *Gerard Manley Hopkins, 19th century English poet known for the original and lyrical style of his poetry which had a significant influence on 20th century literature.*

Uranus: A person who works for the good of their community; the volunteer worker. To support charities or movements trying to bring healing to people or the planet.   • An event that brings hope, or healing, to many. *Martin Luther, 15th century German reformer whose attacks on the abuses of the clergy precipitated the Protestant Reformation.*

Neptune: A person with strong opinions, for or against, on the use of pharmaceutical drugs; to have dietary fads. To seek a spiritual lifestyle.   • Collective wisdom or science fails. *John Lennon of the Beatles, who devoted his life to peace and was an influence in the emergence of the drug culture of the late 1960s.*

Pluto: To be the researcher; to be interested in natural therapies; to be interested in the complexity of life and health.   • The wisdom of one influences many. *Louis Pasteur, 18th century French researcher who discovered that micro organisms cause fermentation and disease.*

The Node: To devote oneself to the idea of moderation. To seek balance, physically, mentally or in health.   • A time of moderation is called for. *Frances Willard, 19th century American reformer, the founder of the World's Woman's Christian Temperance Union.*

NOTES

1. Room, *Dictionary of Astronomical Names*, p.123.
2. Allen, *Star Names Their Lore and Meaning*, p.299.

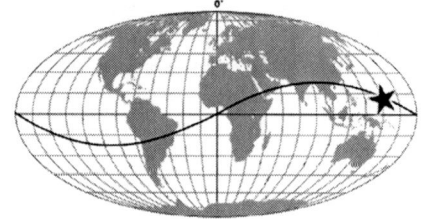

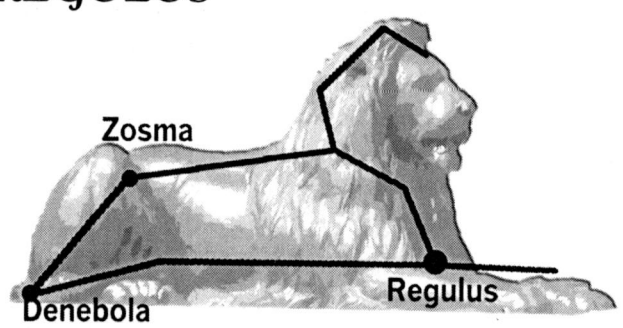

Constellation	Leo
α Leonis, magnitude	1.35
1 January 2000 =	RA 10hr 08'22"
Declination	+11° 58'
Celestial longitude	29° ♌ 50'
Celestial latitude	00°N28'
BV Colour =	Blue-Green

Leo, the Lion

Around 6,000 to 3,000 BCE, the stars of Leo were the heliacal rising stars of the summer solstice, linking this constellation with hot summers and the longest days. The earliest known use of the lion as a symbol appears to be Sekhmet, the sister form to Bast-Hathor of Egyptian mythology[1]. She would sit beside Ra and pour forth blazing fire which would scorch and consume his enemies or else use fiery darts to strike them from afar. The Nile also flooded in the period of Leo's heliacal rising and so these life-giving waters of the Nile were linked with the lion whose role was to protect the precious water. The lion's head would often be sculptured on the irrigation gates which opened to allow the Nile into the fields[2]. In this manner the Egyptians saw the Lion as a guardian of water, a belief still echoed in fountains which use a lion's head as a font. (For more information see Denebola and Zosma).

The Principle of Regulus, the heart of the lion, success but avoiding revenge

Being one of the Royal Stars of Persia, this is one of the great historical stars of the sky. The Persians saw it as the Watcher in the North and linked the star to their mythical king Feridun who, according to their stories, once ruled the entire known world. Feridun, in his old age, decided to divide his kingdom amongst his three sons. However the two eldest fell upon and murdered their younger brother in order to take his lands. This act so grieved Feridun that he took revenge upon his two elder sons and the resulting battle destroyed the kingdom[3]. The importance of this story is that it is a myth which goes beyond the military honours and success associated with Regulus. Like the other three Royal Stars, great success can be gained but only by facing a particular nemesis. For Regulus, this nemesis is revenge.

Heliacal Rising Star
A strong belief in the correctness of one's position, or path. A drive to succeed, to shine, or to move forward in one's life while needing to resist the urge take any form of revenge. *Ben Chifley, one of Australia's most influential Prime Ministers, who brought in many social reforms – against such strong resistance that it eventually led to his political demise.*

Heliacal Setting Star
To find in oneself both a natural talent but at the same time that one is subject to rumors. To succeed in the face of those who are envious of one's work or hard won position. *Sir Charles Chaplin, English actor of silent movie fame, created the "Little Tramp" and other memorable characters, but suffered at the hands of the USA's anti-communist movement and lived most of his life in exile in Europe.*

Star on one of its pivot points at the moment of birth
A person who is a natural leader; one who is able to rise above the petty squabbles of others. *Oliver Cromwell, the English civil war military commander who rose in power to become the Lord Protector of England, but whose body was defiled after death when the monarchy was restored.*

Physiological Correspondence: The heart and vascular system.

Ptolemy's location: The star at the heart called Regulus.

World Cities: Bangkok, Thailand; Caracas, Venezuela; Dijibouti, Dijibouti at latitudes between 10° to 14° north.

Regulus in paran with:

Sun: A person who holds the high expectation of others. One who receives honours and awards, but who needs to be wary of vengefulness.   ◆   A time of noble, or military, endeavours. *Marian Anderson, US black singer who was made a delegate to the UN in 1958 and received many honours and international awards.*

Moon: A natural leader who leads by love and devotion, rather than by power and authority. To be drawn to a humanitarian career and to be loved by others.   ◆   Event-driven, pride in success or anger at failure. *John of God, 16th century soldier who became a saint and devoted his life to the care of the poor and the sick.*

Mercury: To have a grand design, to inspire people with an idea. To receive recognition for noble ideas but the need to avoid revenge and refuse to be baited by gossip.   ◆   A news story concerning national defence. *Jorn Utzon, 20th century Danish architect known for his dynamic, imaginative but problematical design for the Sydney Opera House, Australia.*

Venus: A creative person who seeks perfection and needs to rise above the petty jealousies of others. To receives honours; or a diplomat. ◆ The role of the leader is questioned. *John Keats, 19th century English poet known for his lyrical verse and his search for perfection in poetry.*

Mars: A team leader; interested in sports or action-filled activities. To be able to maintain faith in one's skills. ◆ The hero wins the day. *Isadora Duncan, American dancer known for her interpretative dancing and an advocate of natural rhythm.*

Jupiter: To be involved with those who hold high office. To act with confidence, or at times to have an air of nobility. ◆ The noble hero is paraded. *Betsy Ross, 18th century seamstress who is said to have fashioned the first American flag.*

Saturn: Success through hard work; seeing the big picture and being able to bring the vision to fruition. ◆ To play the king. *Francis Scott Key, 19th century lawyer known as the author of the US national anthem "The Star Spangled Banner".*

Uranus: To be popular, to represent the common view; to hold the power in one's family or community. ◆ The people select a popular leader; or a sports person is the favourite of the crowd. *Sun Myung Moon, 20th century religious leader who was the founder of the Unification Church; his followers were known as Moonies and he was known as "Father".*

Neptune: To be an artisan; to gain success or recognition for one's craft; to be interested in design or colour. ◆ The leader fails, the king is dead. *Peter Carl Faberge, 19th century Russian designer who is considered to be one of the greatest jewellers and decorative artists of his era.*

Pluto: A deep belief in one's own ability; to be a leader at a time of crisis in one's family or community. A tendency to be obsessed with one's own success. ◆ A time of tyranny. *Horatio Nelson, 19th century English Admiral known for his courageous victories, especially at the Battle of Trafalgar which ensured the safety of Britain from invasion by Napoleon.*

The Node: To be decisive; to be associated with strong ideas or fast thinking; to be seen as the military or noble figure. ◆ A time when victory belongs to the one who acts quickly. *Manfred Baron von Richthofen, top German flying ace of World War I, known as the Red Baron.*

NOTES

1. Budge, *The Gods of the Egyptians*, p.515.
2. Jobes and Jobes, *Outer Space: Myths, Name Meanings, Calendars*, p.194.
3. P. Masson-Oursel and Louise Morin, "Mythology of Ancient Persia," in *New Larousse Encyclopedia of Mythology*, London: Hamlyn, 1984, p.323.

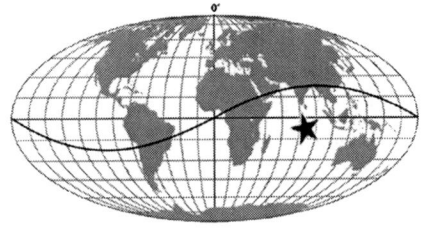

RIGEL

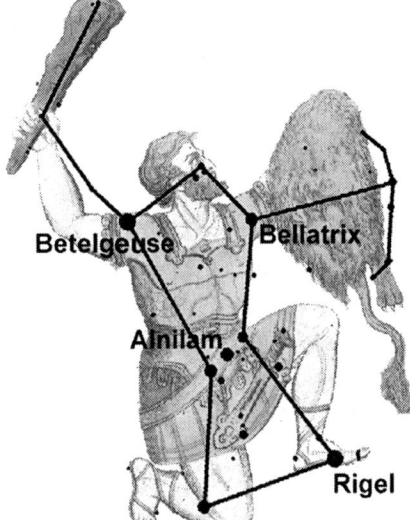

Constellation	Orion
β Orionis, magnitude	0.12
1 January 2000 =	RA 05hr 14' 33"
Declination	-08° 12'
Celestial longitude	16° Ⅱ 50'
Celestial latitude	31°S07'
BV Colour =	White

Orion, the warrior and the pharaoh

Around 6,000 BCE, Orion was celebrated and noted by the Egyptians to rise before the sun on the morning of the spring equinox. The image of this huge human-like constellation rising in the predawn light and being scooped up, as the Egyptians believed, into the fiery boat of the sun linked this constellation to the concept of a god. However, as hundreds of years went past, they noted that less and less of Orion rose before the dawn on the equinox morning. To account for these observations, the Egyptians developed the concept of an immortal god dying, slipping into the underworld and passing on his throne to his son, another bright star which now rose before the dawn equinox[1]. Therefore Orion sits on the equator and, like the constellations on the ecliptic, is subject to the hero's journey of the precession where he appears to slowly, over thousands of years, slip into the "whirlpool". (For more information see Alnilam, Bellatrix and Betelgeuse).

The Principle of Rigel, the educator, the scholar

This star is in the foot of Orion. The Egyptian's saw Orion as the pharaoh, and to be under a pharaoh's foot was to be under his protection[2]. Rigel can therefore be thought of as active and educating; a concept of forward development, not just for personal gain but, more importantly, for the gain of many. Rigel is an educator, be it in the local school, in the public sector or in any field of knowledge. It symbolises the desire to learn or to teach, to bring knowledge to others.

Heliacal Rising Star

A life spent seeking to bring order to chaos, with words or actions. A natural ability to see the patterns of life, the complexity of one's world. *Carl Jung, 20th century Swiss psychiatrist, one of the founding fathers of modern depth psychology.*

Heliacal Setting Star
A growing belief in education; to find success through sharing information; the writer, the researcher. *Henry Handel Richardson, Australian author (Ethel Florence Richardson); her most notable work was a trilogy, "The Fortunes of Richard Mahony" which offered insight into the life of an Australian immigrant.*

Star on one of its pivot points at the moment of birth
Wanting to bring structure to groups, which can lead one to be somewhat righteous and overbearing. To seek to implement one's ideas in a practical manner. A superior attitude. *Margaret Thatcher, British Prime Minister (1979-1990) known for her strong opinions on social order and a direct, even at times abrasive and overbearing, approach.*

Physiological Correspondence: The body's posture – how one stands.

Ptolemy's location: The bright star in the left foot common with the Water [of Eridanus].

World Cities: Jakarta, Indonesia; Port Moresby, Papua New Guinea at latitudes between 06° to 10° south.

Rigel in paran with:

Sun: Imposing one's will on a situation to change the natural outcome, or bring reform. A person who wishes to help others by imposing their idea of order.   •   The government decides to reform a situation. *Samuel Johnson, 18th century English lexicographer regarded as an outstanding literary figure; his best known work is "A Dictionary of the English Language".*

Moon: The metaphysician, or one who is drawn to alternative, or hidden wisdoms. A lover of books; one who seeks a mentor.   •   The focus is on a loved teacher, a wise man or woman. *Colin Wilson, 20th century English novelist and writer on philosophy, sociology, music, literature, and the occult.*

Mercury: Strong personal views; to be strong-minded or stubborn. To be an independent thinker and follow one's own philosophy of life.   •   The media having a strong opinion and trying to influence current issues. *Piet Retief, one of the Boer leaders of the Great Trek. This was the mass migration of Boers who sought independence from British rule in South Africa in the late 1700s.*

Venus: Not restrained by social opinions on ethical, relationship, or religious issues. To have little or no regard for social convention.   •   The imposing of a new social order by the authorities. *Marsilio Ficino, Renaissance philosopher and astrologer who was responsible for translations of Plato and other classical authors into Latin.*

Mars: Acting independently, a free agent. Possible difficulties with the law or with constituted authority.   ♦   Military action, or the lone, headstrong action of an individual. *Henry the Navigator, 14th century patron who enabled the advancement of cartography and naval instrumentation.*

Jupiter: To be brave physically, or with one's ideas. One who can act boldly, or even criminally, outside of conventions or the established order.   ♦   A time when the rules are broken. *Edward VIII, the Duke of Windsor, who in 1936 abdicated the English throne in order to marry the divorcee Wallis Simpson.*

Saturn: A law maker, or a law breaker. To have authority whether in one's family or in one's community.   ♦   Faith in an elected leader. *Bugsy Siegel, 20th century American gangster and crime boss who initially developed Las Vegas as a gambling Mecca.*

Uranus: To reorganise, or reform, a situation in an assertive, or even aggressive, manner. Representing others who are seeking reform.   ♦   A time of demonstrations. *Peter Lalor, 19th century revolutionary who is known for his leadership of the most famous insurrection in Australian history at the Eureka Stockade.*

Neptune: To have faith in those in authority; to look for solace in one's spirituality; to be or to seek a spiritual leader.   ♦   To march forward into confusing times, or times of despair. *Shirley Maclaine, American actress well-known for her acting, and also for her devout belief in reincarnation and extraterrestrials beings.*

Pluto: A desire to break through a "glass ceiling", to remove limitations placed on oneself or one's community.   ♦   The will of one person is imposed on society; a defiant act. *Napoleon Bonaparte, 19th century French Emperor who, apart from his attempted conquest of Europe, also reformed the French legal system.*

The Node: To be associated with a message, to link oneself with a brand, belief system or philosophical point of view; to be a life long fan.   ♦   Education systems are reviewed. *Mary Baker Eddy, 20th century US religious leader who was the founder of the Christian Science movement.*

NOTES

1. Sellers, *The Death of Gods in Ancient Egypt*, p.33.
2. Richard H. Wilkinson, *Reading Egyptian Art*, London: Thames and Hudson, 1992, p.87.

RUKBAT

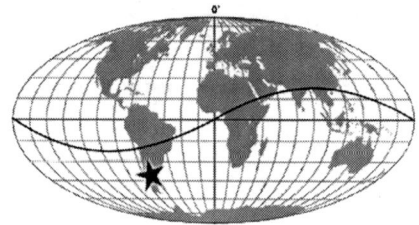

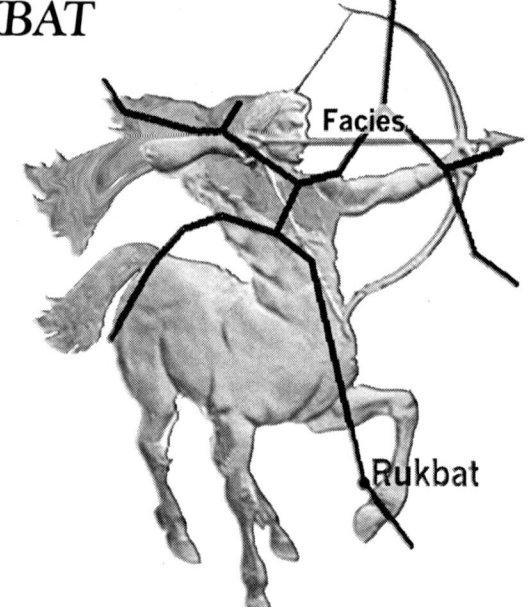

Constellation	Sagittarius
α Sagittarii, magnitude	3.97
1 January 2000 =	RA 19hr 23' 50"
Declination	-40° 37'
Celestial longitude	16° ♑ 38'
Celestial latitude	18°S23'
BV Colour =	Blue-Green

Sagittarius, the archer
Sagittarius is known as the Archer. Originating on the Euphrates with cuneiform tablets calling it the Strong One or The Giant King of War[1], this was the archer god of war. The animal part of the constellation came in the classical period where it was called a centaur and was displayed as a very threatening figure. The warrior of Sagittarius was cruel, stormy, wild and feared. Over time, as the bow was no longer considered a feared weapon, the Archer became more friendly and the centaur became the focus of the image rather than the bow. By modern times it seems to have been forgotten that, when Zeus, of Greek mythology, wanted to place Chiron in the heavens, he could not displace Crotus, the cruel, wild centaur of Sagittarius and so was forced to place Chiron far to the south in the constellation Centaurus[2]. (For more information see Facies).

The Principle of Rukbat, the steady stance of the archer
Rukbat is the foot of the archer, Sagittarius, and is the expression of steadiness, implying stability or solidness. Rukbat in a chart will add the symbolism of a "rudder" or "anchor" to one's life. This symbolism is the nature of providing a rock, a base onto which one can build or allow others to build political ideals or, philosophies; or it may be the building of the base for a family, a family home, a family hearth. This star implies a reliability and a consistency which can be a great strength, but it can also become a rigid stubbornness. From buildings to families and communities Rukbat symbolises the base from which things grow.

Heliacal Rising Star
To believe that one's life is governed by a pattern; to lead a life that is unswerving from what one holds to be the true path. *Galileo Galilei, 16th century mathematician who was imprisoned by the Church because he refused to recant on the concept of a sun-centred solar system.*

Heliacal Setting Star
To find fulfilment by providing a foundation for others to use. To work towards adding structure to people's lives or institutions, a humanitarian. *Ted Noffs, 20th century Australian theologian and social engineer who established a foundation for the care of young people, known as the Noffs Foundation.*

Star on one of its pivot points at the moment of birth
To be seen as one who provides support; to stand firm, to hold fast; a steady person in mind or body who provides a foundation for others. *Harvey Bernard Milk, an American politician and gay rights activist, who was the first openly gay man elected to a substantial political office in modern times.*

Physiological Correspondence: The ankles their role in support and balance.

Ptolemy's location: The star in the knee of the left leg.

World Cities: Wellington, New Zealand at latitudes between 38^0 to 42^0 south.

Rukbat in paran with:

Sun: To be persistent in your aims, to be unswerving in your goals. A tendency to be seen as stubborn, or uncompromising. ♦ A leader stands firm. *Matteo Ricci, 16th century Italian missionary who introduced Christianity to the Chinese empire and lived there for 30 years.*

Moon: Providing a foundation, or beginning, for the people or ideas that you love. To have loyalty and consistency as one's trademarks. ♦ Calmness is called for. *Betsy Ross, the 18th century seamstress who is said to have fashioned the first American flag, the Star-Spangled Banner.*

Mercury: A level-headed approach to life; a good head for business. A potential to become fixed in one's thinking. ♦ Big companies in the news; a focus on the steadiness of the economy. *Niccolo Machiavelli, 15th century Italian statesman who is best known as the author of "The Prince", a work which advanced his thesis that the end justifies the means.*

Venus: To be consistent, or rigid, in your social views and ideas. To hold some ideas or people as sacred; to be loyal in personal friendships. ♦ The community stands firm, the community is seen to be strong. *Shah Johan, Moghul emperor and builder of the Taj Mahal, 1632-1648, a shrine devoted to his deceased wife.*

Mars: To be motivated to provide a base for others. To build an idea, institution or object to be used as a foundation. ♦ A group makes a stand, a project is begun. *Michel Gauquelin, 20th century French psychologist and statistician who, in the 1950s, conducted statistical research on astrology.*

Jupiter: Success through a steady and thorough preparation. A person who can build on their dreams. ♦ A steady hand is needed to deal with a problem. *Howard Florey, an Australian pathologist who, in 1939, was responsible for purifying penicillin for clinical use.*

Saturn: To undertake tedious or painstaking tasks; to work with great care and precision. To being order to ideas or people. ♦ The foundations of a society are altered. *Melvil Dewey, 20th century American librarian who is the father of the Dewey Decimal System of Classification widely used in library cataloguing.*

Uranus: To support the popular cause; to be a "seed person", to start an idea that becomes popular. ♦ The people stick to the status quo. *Johannes Strauss the Younger, 19th century Austrian composer who is known as the Waltz King, for his Viennese waltzes and operettas.*

Neptune: One whose ideas are not limited by established restrictions; a person who ignores authority or dissolves structures. ♦ A solid, or stubborn, position become untenable; a structure fails. *Jules Verne, 19th century French author whose writings laid much of the foundation of modern science fiction.*

Pluto: One's actions have far-reaching effects in one family or community. To be prepared to break new ground. ♦ The opinion of one person is heard by many. *Edward Squibb, 19th century US chemist who developed methods of making pure and reliable drugs and founded a company to manufacture them.*

The Node: To associate oneself with a sports team, political party or philosophy. To be steadfast in one's loyalty to a group. ♦ The community comes out in force to demonstrate. *Martin Luther King, US activist who was one of the principal leaders of the American civil rights movement.*

NOTES

1. Jobes and Jobes, *Outer Space: Myths, Name Meanings, Calendars*, p.235.
2. Jobes and Jobes, *Outer Space: Myths, Name Meanings, Calendars*, p.146.

SADALMELEK

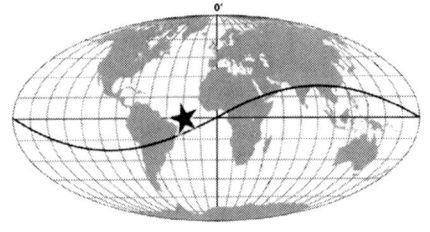
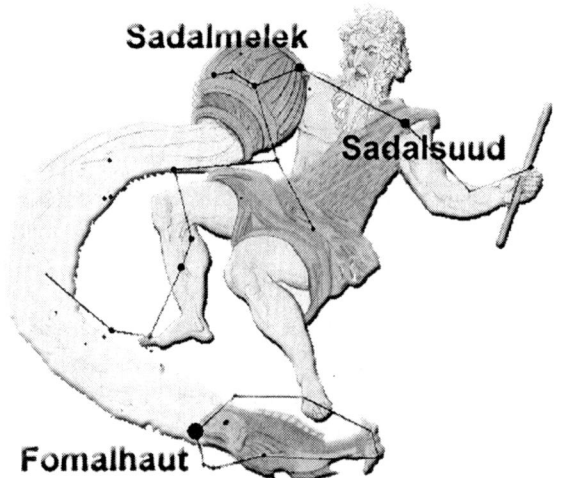

Constellation	Aquarius
α Aquarii, magnitude	2.96
1 January 2000 =	RA 22hr 05'45"
Declination	-00° 19'
Celestial longitude	03° ♓ 21'
Celestial latitude	10°N40'
BV Colour =	Orange

Aquarius, the water bearer
Around 4,000 BCE Aquarius was one of the major points of the zodiac, holding the position of the winter solstice. The Babylonians referred to this constellation as the Great One[1], and called the stars of Aquarius the "Seat of the Flowing Water"[2] and saw this as the rain which caused the great deluge of their creation myth. In Egypt, where rainfall was negligible, the Nile was and still is the source of all water. The Nile is the most predictable and reliable river in the world and every July through to October it floods, pouring life-giving water and silt over the Nile Valley floor. At that archaic time, Aquarius, during the flooding season, was the heliacal setting constellation, meaning that as the sun rose, Aquarius set on the western horizon. In this visually observable phenomenon the Egyptians saw the Water Carrier dipping his urn into the Nile, his pot displacing the water, which caused the flooding; or, more simply, that he leaned down and poured water into the Nile. Manlius also saw water flowing from his great urn, and considered it one of the sources of Eridanus, the river in the sky[3]. This constellation is linked to the river of life-giving water. He is the Great One, one of the oldest creation entities. (For more information see Fomalhaut and Sadalsuud).

The Principle of Sadalmelek, the Lucky One of the King, making one's own luck
Sadalmelek is one of a pair of stars in the constellation of Aquarius. Their names mean a form of luck, Sadalmelek being translated as Lucky One of the King, and Sadalsuud, its twin, meaning Luckiest of the Lucky. They are the shoulders, and thus the power of the Water Carrier, one of the original creator gods. Both these stars bring life and fertility and Sadalmelek, in the right shoulder, is associated with opportunities which are of one's own making. A blessing in life, for it implies the ability to water one's own ideas, to nourish one's own thinking and have the skill to coax dreams into form.

Heliacal Rising Star
An optimistic life philosophy; the expectation of continuing fruitfulness in one's life. A confident person with a good network. *Rupert Murdoch, Australian media tycoon who built his empire from humble beginnings.*

Heliacal Setting Star
To discover a fruitfulness where none was expected. To learn that one can take a difficult situation, or a small idea, and successfully build upon it. *Agatha Christie, early 20th century English mystery writer; with most of her 80 detective novels still in print she is regarded as the best-selling writer of books of all time.*

Star on one of its pivot points at the moment of birth
A person who knows the value of networking. To be able to put one's understanding of relationships and associations to practical use. *Henry Ford, 19th century American manufacturer who revolutionised factory production by introducing the assembly line for making cars.*

Physiological Correspondence: One's conscious sense of time.

Ptolemy's location: The bright star in the right shoulder.

World Cities: Belem, Brazil; Nairobi, Kenya; Singapore, Singapore at latitudes between 02° north to 02° south.

Saladmelek in paran with:

Sun: An optimistic attitude. To be a good networker; to be seen as a hub of information or social contacts.   ♦   The successful use of a connection. *Sir Conan Doyle, 19th century English author known as the creator of the famous detective Sherlock Holmes, who gathered a lot if his information from the streets of London.*

Moon: Good, or fortunate, associations; one's creative work is well received. Beneficial friendships.   ♦   The end of a drought, literally, metaphorically or spiritually; rain. *Auguste Rodin, 19th century French sculptor whose work including "The Thinker", built him a reputation as the greatest portraitist in the history of sculpture.*

Mercury: An agile and nimble person whose ideas appeal to others. An intuitive creative thinker, one who can see business opportunities where others cannot.   ♦   A time of over-confidence due to a plan considered to be invincible. *Benjamin Franklin, 18th century American known for his role in the formation of the USA, but also for the establishment of a newspaper and the idea of public services.*

Venus: A sense and appreciation of beauty. To have an eye for decoration and colour; to be able to influence others in fashion or design.   ♦   A celebrity takes the limelight. *Charles Revson, US* businessman who in 1932 founded the Revlon cosmetics empire with $300 and built it into a multinational company worth millions.

Mars: A person who makes their own luck; auspicious events follow concentrated effort. A person who can defend their opinions in the face of challenge.   ♦   The home team wins. *John Speke, 19th century British explorer who was the first European to reach Lake Victoria in East Africa, which he correctly identified as a source of the Nile.*

Jupiter: To have inspirational breakthroughs that can solve old problems. To be able to think outside of a situation and see it from a different point of view.   ♦   Acting with the establishment's support. *Albert Einstein, 20th century scientist who, in a moment of inspiration while still a teenager, conceived of the Theory of Relativity.*

Saturn: Struggling with a place to be, unable to settle and find a home. The person who finds stability uncomfortable; the explorer.   ♦   A time when paradise is lost. *Virginia Dare was the first English settler child born in the Americas, on Roanoake Island; however all 117 settlers disappeared without trace.*

Uranus: To follow or create a popular cause; to be a trend follower or a trend setter.   ♦   A time when people hope for luck. *George Eastman, 19th century American who introduced the first Kodak camera and made it a byword of popular photography.*

Neptune: A lover of films or theatre; being successful in the virtual world; living with an illusion about one's life; living in hope.   ♦   An expectation of success. *Heinrich Schliemann, German archaeologist who discovered Troy based on his belief that there was historical truth behind the Homeric legends.*

Pluto: One's actions have an impact on one's community; small events tend to blow up out of proportion; to be subject to scandal or gossip.   ♦   Chain reactions, a small event acts as a tipping point for great change. *Rudolf Valentino, Italian-born US silent screen actor whose wildfire popularity establish the concept of the cinema sex symbol.*

The Node: To be linked with an era, or a fashion a fruitful time. To align oneself with a new idea; to start something new for one's group.   ♦   A time when things, good or bad, can take root. *Elizabeth I, Queen of England (1588 to 1603), who ushered in a time of development of English literature and the arts known as the Elizabethan age.*

NOTES

1. Francesca Rochberg, *The Heavenly Writing, Divination, Horoscopy, and Astronomy in Mesopotamian Culture*, Cambridge, UK: Cambridge University Press, 2004, p.xxv.
2. Allen, *Star Names Their Lore and Meaning*, p.47.
3. Manilius, *Astronomica*, 1:272-73.

SADALSUUD

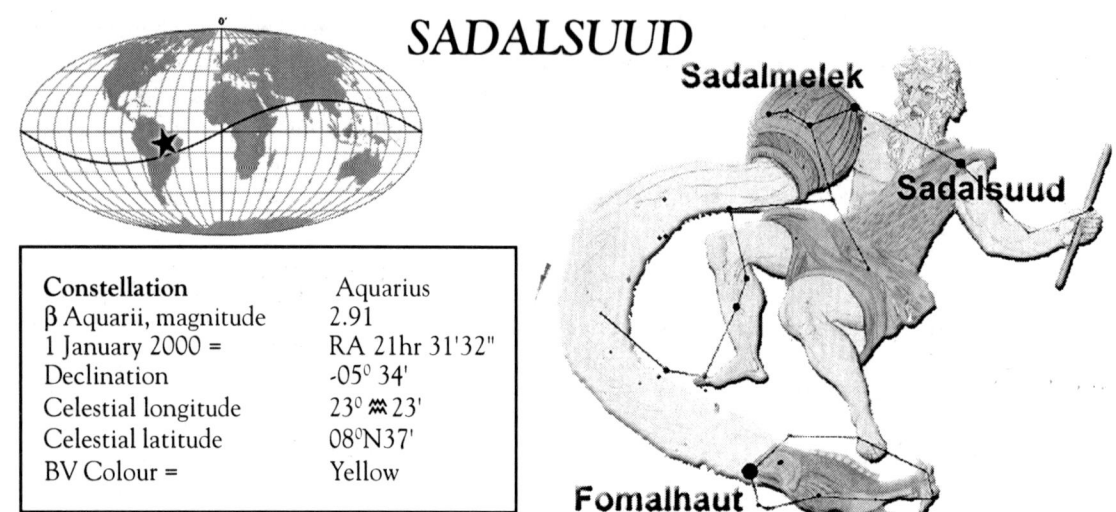

Constellation	Aquarius
β Aquarii, magnitude	2.91
1 January 2000 =	RA 21hr 31'32"
Declination	-05° 34'
Celestial longitude	23° ♒ 23'
Celestial latitude	08°N37'
BV Colour =	Yellow

Aquarius, the water bearer

Aquarius, the Great One, was seen to govern the huge cosmic sea which contains the constellations of Pisces the Fishes, Cetus the Whale, Capricornus the Sea Goat, Delphinus the Dolphin, Eridanus the River, Pisces Australis the Southern Fish and Hydra the Water Serpent. The Babylonians had different names for this constellation but one of them, linked with the fact that it was the winter solstice constellation in their era, was the God of Storms[1]. To the Egyptians he was responsible for the life-supporting flood of the Nile and he is depicted as holding a Norma Nilotica[2], a rod for measuring the rising waters of the Nile. By the middle ages he was thought of as John the Baptist[3], matching the ancient Babylonian image of a man pouring water; this period, however, saw his measuring rod replaced by a bath towel – which devolved him from a great creator god to a bathhouse servant. (For more information see Fomalhaut and Sadalmelek).

The principle of Sadalsuud, the Luckiest of the Lucky, a natural rapport

Sadalsuud is one of a pair of stars in Aquarius. Its twin, Sadalmelek, is translated as Lucky One of the King and this star, Sadalsuud, means Luckiest of the Lucky. By linking this theme of luck with the symbolism of the Water Carrier as a bringer of life-giving water and/or rain, we can think of this star as representing a bringer of good events or news. Sadalsuud is the intuitive or less conscious flow of this luck, or life-giving water. If this star is active in a chart then the area of its activity is one in which there is a natural flow, a natural rapport with situations. Some will call it luck but it is more akin to being in rhythm, being connected with an ensouled world.

Heliacal Rising Star

A person whose path is crossed by happy chance; someone who can find what they need; gifted from the rich diversity of life. *Ricardo Güiraldes, 20th century writer who was blessed with a diversity of experience in his childhood and became one of the most significant Argentine writers of his era.*

Heliacal Setting Star
To learn to let things take their own course. Developing the ability to watch for the small signals and follow the tiny leads. Learning to have faith in synchronicity. *Gene Roddenbury, the US screen writer and creator of Star Trek, which grew from a small TV series to a global phenomenon of popular entertainment.*

Star on one of its pivot points at the moment of birth
A lucky person; a person with a natural physical talent. A person who tends to land on their feet; one who can emerge from problems reasonably unscathed. *Jack London, 20th century American writer and adventurer who was one of the first Americans to make a lucrative career exclusively from writing.*

Physiological Correspondence: The circadian and other body rhythms which manage the body's cycles.

Ptolemy's location: The star to the left of the man, in his shoulder.

World Cities: Jakarta, Indonesia; Kinshasa, Congo at latitudes between 03^0 to 07^0 south

Sadalsuud in paran with:

Sun: Fortune or luck coming from difficulties. Resilience to life's ups and downs; making the best of unfortunate situations.   ◆   After a drought comes rain, literally or metaphorically. *Dame Nellie Melba, 19th century Australian opera singer who, against the odds, became a prima donna in the 1920s.*

Moon: Being able to hold onto the good feelings or things of life. To have good female friendships or relationships.   ◆   Issues of water quality or safety. *Debbie Reynolds, Hollywood actor renowned for her "good" characters, whose only Oscar nomination was for starring in "The Unsinkable Molly Brown" (1964).*

Mercury: Honest and direct in one's thinking. To have a natural flair for business dealings.   ◆   The truth is told. *George Washington, general, statesman, and first president of the United States; renowned for his honesty.*

Venus: Loyal friends, happy relationships. To be able to meet the right people at the right time.   ◆   Public works; the building of a new structure for the good of the community. *Richard Rodgers, 20th century composer who found success by forming partnerships with friends Oscar Hammerstein and Lorenz Hart.*

Mars: To enjoy a challenge; a lover of gentle conflict. A person who enjoys competing with friends.   ♦   Winning a battle; the end of a conflict. *Maurice Chevalier, 20th century French actor who starred in Hollywood films generally as the polite but persistent suitor to the leading lady.*

Jupiter: To benefit by the fortunate turn of events; the gambler. Relying on luck to help with the outcomes.   ♦   A luck event "saves the day". *Queen Elizabeth 1, 16th century English monarch who was fortunate in that her half-sister and brother both died childless, and also in that a storm destroyed the Spanish Armada which would probably have otherwise defeated England.*

Saturn: Genius or lucky; ideas and insights that are of benefit to others. To solve life's problems through timely inspiration, or fortunate turns of events.   ♦   Issues of safety and shelter in the community. *Herbert Austin, English engineer who, in 1905, opened his own car factory to produce the very popular "Baby" Austin, showing his understanding of the popular need for a small car.*

Uranus: Being able to make money; having access to the flow of energy which is life; one who benefits others by their bountifulness.   ♦   A safe place is built, or provided, for a group; sanctuary is given. *Cornelius Vanderbilt, 19th century US self-made shipping magnate whose fortune was made by carrying people across water.*

Neptune: To be subject to the fickleness of life; to find spiritual solace in uncertain times; to lack at times the needs of life.   ♦   To win or to loses, all things hang on a single outcome. *Sir Charles Chaplin, English silent movie actor, who created most famously the "Little Tramp", and personally suffered at the hands of the anticommunist movement in the US as well as UK.*

Pluto: To inherit, money or talent. To be the holder of secrets; to be the guardian of information through books or the spoken word.   ♦   Matters of safe haven, matters of sanctuary. *Bruce Lee, 20th century US martial arts master and actor who bought the secrets of the martial arts into western awareness.*

The Node: To be the source of information; to produce a great deal of work, or have it produced on one's behalf.   ♦   To be focused on children. *Pablo Picasso, Spanish artist who is one of the most prolific artists of the 20th century.*

NOTES

1. Allen, *Star Names Their Lore and Meaning*, p.47.
2. see: Elijah H. Burritt, *The Geography of the Heavens*, New York: Huntington and Savage, 1835.
3. Jobes and Jobes, *Outer Space: Myths, Name Meanings, Calendars*, p.115.

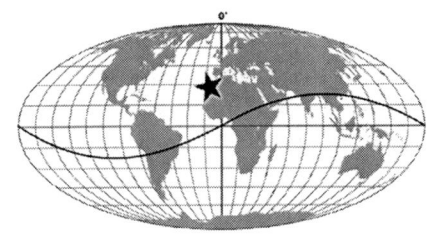

SCHEAT

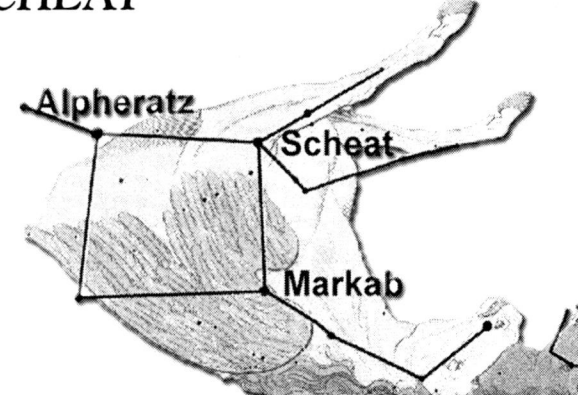

Constellation	Pegasus
β Pegasi, magnitude	2.42
1 January 2000 =	
Declination	RA 23hr 03'45"
Celestial longitude	+28° 05'
Celestial latitude	29° ♓ 22'
BV Colour =	31°N09'
	Red

Pegasus, the flying horse

Pegasus emerges from the neck of Andromeda and is the symbol of the sacred horse. Born with wings to show his speed and divinity, only half of him is in the sky: his front legs, wings, back and chest. Four stars make the Great Square which forms the body and head of the winged horse. The Greeks saw him being born from Medusa's neck at the time she was slain by Perseus. However Aratus, in the 4th century BCE, suggests that this image containing a Great Square is sacred and that it is the horse which opened the fountain of Helicon (the fountain of the muses) for humankind[1]. At the time of the ingress of the equinox into Aries, the Abrahamic monotheistic religion was also emerging and built its theology around the number four with their god being known as the Tetragrammaton. This god of the Old Testament is an "all-manifesting, full of action and wrath" god, to whom one draws near by education and learning. This concept of power and action associated with the number four has also been carried into astrology with the fourth harmonic – the square aspect, embracing these same principles. The divine Pegasus supporting the great magical square in the sky can thus be seen to embrace not only action but also the search for truth. (For more information see Markab).

The Principle of Scheat, a love of intellect, a searcher for truth

This star is part of the Great Square of Pegasus. The square, in ancient cultures, represented the intellect, the knowing rather than the unknowing. Intuition, on the other hand, was symbolised as circular. As a part of this sky-square, Scheat appears to represent the essence of intellect. Depending on the planet with which it is in paran, Scheat indicates a love of intellect and the challenge of logic in one's life, in service to the search for a truth. This star denotes a free thinking and independent person who will have a need to break with conventional thought or philosophy.

Heliacal Rising Star
To pursue a life of learning and thinking; to value intellectual challenge above all else; to have one's life devoted to a mental endeavour. *Brett Whiteley, Australian artist, one of the most revered artists of his country. His lyrical expressionism and lack of inhibition placed him at the forefront of Australia's avant-garde art movement.*

Heliacal Setting Star
To be forced out of the nest, to find success by leaving one's safe place, physically or mentally. To work in different places or in different languages. *Arthur Phillip, English naval officer who headed the First Fleet, which established the first permanent European settlement in Australia. He won great credit for his work in the new colony of New South Wales.*

Star on one of its pivot points at the moment of birth
A physically talented, or gifted, person. An individual who is associated with creating new knowledge, and/or putting such knowledge into practical use. *Albert Einstein, the German physicist known for his work in energy and matter.*

Physiological Correspondence: Motor skill and muscle memory.

Ptolemy's location: The star in the right shoulder and at the beginning of the foot.

World Cities: New Delhi, India; Cairo, Egypt at latitudes between 26° to 30° north.

Scheat in paran with:

Sun: Headstrong; an independent thinker. Pursuing one's ideas or one's version of truth without regard to the opinions of others.   ♦   A time when unusual, or independent, ideas are voiced. *Henry VIII, Tudor king of England, noted for the number of his wives and for the establishment of the Church of England.*

Moon: Challenging social conventions; free-thinking in the arts, cuisine and matters of care.   ♦   A time when social or business conventions are broken. *Peter Ilyich Tchaikovsky, leading Russian 19th century composer whose works are notable for their melodic inspiration and their orchestration.*

Mercury: The innovator, gifted with ideas, words or rhythm; far-sighted. To be able to think outside the square. To actively seek the "truth".   ♦   A brave new idea; a radical thought. *Nostradamus (Michel de Notredame), an astrologer and physician well-known for his "Centuries", a collection of prophecies first published in 1555.*

Venus: Independent ideas concerning fashion, relationships and social customs. To admire or to create leading edge art.   ♦   The social order confronted with change. *Peter Carl Faberge, 19th century Russian goldsmith considered to be one of the greatest jewellers and decorative artists of his era.*

Mars: A physically confident person; or a gifted inventor. To be brave and/or to have physical skills in sport or dance. ◆ Confident of resources, physical strength, or the military might of the nation. *Richard I, "the Lionheart", English king and monarch known for his prowess in the Third Crusade (1189-1192).*

Jupiter: The theologian or sports person who is teaching a moral code. To value education and all its institutions. ◆ A period where religious leaders speak out. *Izaak Walton, English author of "The Compleat Angler" (1653), a discourse on the joys of fishing that has been one of the most frequently reprinted books in English literature.*

Saturn: The one who records and notates. To collect, compile or compute data; a tendency to be dogmatic with one's ideas of truth. ◆ A time when the so-called experts are challenged. *Gregory Mendel, 19th century German botanist, who was the first to lay a mathematical foundation for the science of genetics.*

Uranus: The journalist or reporter; to collect information on behalf of a group or the community. To be interested bringing "truth" to a particular community. ◆ Educational, or sports, institutions come under investigation. *John Wesley, 18th century religious reformer who was the founder of the Methodist movement in the Church of England.*

Neptune: Spiritual or prophetic insights; a talent for mathematics or a lover of archaic or secret knowledge; working with cultures foreign to oneself. ◆ Spies, undercover agents, national secrets revealed. *Tycho Brahe, 16th century Danish astronomer who was famed for his accurate and comprehensive astronomical observations.*

Pluto: Strong mental focus; or adherence to a philosophy in spite of mounting opposition. To be a genius or a fanatic. ◆ A person is heralded as a genius, a discovery is made. *Thomas Sopwith, British aircraft designer famous for the military aircraft Sopwith Camel and Triplane.*

The Node: To know no boundaries, to reject anything that inhibits one. To constantly look for ways of travelling, changing or increasing one's knowledge. ◆ Limits are broken. *Peter the Great of Russia, 17th century Russian monarch who was responsible for extending Russian borders and involving Russia in Europe.*

NOTES

1. Aratus, "Phaenomena," p.225.

226   *Star and Planet Combinations*

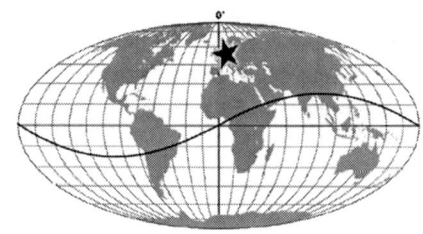

SCHEDAR

Constellation	Cassiopeia
α Cassiopeiae, magnitude	2.23
1 January 2000 =	
RA	00hr 40' 30"
Declination	+56° 32'
Celestial longitude	07° ♉ 47'
Celestial latitude	46°N38'
BV Colour =	Orange

Cassiopeia, the Queen

Placed just south of Draco and the two bears the constellation of Cassiopeia is a member of the royal family, which consists of Cepheus the king, Cassiopeia the queen, Andromeda the daughter or princess and Perseus the prince. The Arabs called these stars The Lady in a Chair, although earlier writings talk of it as The Hand Stained with Henna, the red hand reflecting the practice of women of power tattooing their hands with henna[1]. The Egyptians placed the shape of this constellation, as well as the rest of the celestial royal family, on their seals. It would seem, therefore, that the major theme of this group of stars is one of female sovereignty, initially placed next to the king in balance but thrown into a state of punishment when that balance was lost. This loss of balance is shown in the Greek claim that Cassiopeia had committed a crime of vanity and in punishment for this crime she was chained to her chair and set in the sky to orbit around the pole for eternity[2]. The Christians named her Mary Magdalene and at other times Deborah[3].

The Principle of Schedar, the Queen, to have dignity

This star is the symbol of the queen, the natural ability to command respect through wisdom. This star represents the ability to take a leadership role based on the feminine model which incorporates intuition and mysticism, just as the masculine model incorporates strength and focus. This star represents a strong woman who exudes dignity, and rules by the power of her respectability and honour. With this star in a chart, one can rely on their instinct to always function with propriety, to know that dignity is the source of one's power.

Heliacal Rising Star

A life spent leading, or seeking, a noble cause. To lead a group with dignity; to believe that honour and decency are the foundations of one's life. *Che Guevara, 20th century Marxist revolutionary, medically trained scholar who was so moved by the poverty of the Cuban people that he decided to help* establish a Marxist government there. He has, since his death, been effectively deified due to his noble appearance and sentiments.

Heliacal Setting Star
To learn slowly that dignity and justice produce the desired results. To discover that one's greatest hope for success lies in discourse towards agreement rather than the use of force. *Indira Gandhi, Prime Minister of India who maintained her position by using populism; the use of discourse to propagate ideas which try to appeal to "the people" by setting up a dichotomy between "the people" and "the elite".*

Star on one of its pivot points at the moment of birth
Strength in one's dignity; assuming respect from others. To be seen as someone who grows in respectability through the propriety of their position or actions. *Camilla Parker-Bowles, long term mistress and second wife of Prince Charles of England.*

Physiological Correspondence: One's physical sense of balance.

Ptolemy's location: The star in the breast of the Queen.

World Cities: Aberdeen, and Glasgow, Scotland; Belfast, Northern Ireland; Copenhagen, Denmark; Moscow, Russia; Newcastle-on-Tyne, England at latitudes between 54^0 to 58^0 north.

Schedar in paran with:

Sun: To want to help or lead people; to wish to maintain dignity in one's family or community. To have an aura of respectability whether it is deserved or not. ♦ The people, or an exalted woman, act with dignity. *Annie Besant, 19th century reformer who is best known for her work with the Theosophical Society as well as her promotion of self-rule for India.*

Moon: A noble, religious or spiritual soul. To be from a family of noblewomen, or to seek such people as friends or colleagues. ♦ Respect and dignity are on display. *Mohandas K. Ghandi, 20th century Indian leader, reared by his mother in a moral environment that advocated pacifism and the sanctity of all living things.*

Mercury: A person of principles, a natural honesty in all business dealings; to seek classical or spiritual education. ♦ The truth is upheld; a person speaks with dignity. *Edith Stein, Carmelite nun, philosopher, and spiritual writer who was executed by the Nazis because of her Jewish ancestry and is regarded as a modern martyr.*

Venus: To support another, friend or partner, with quiet dignity. To lend one's credibility to a cause or an idea; to treat all people with dignity. ♦ Society undertakes to act with dignity. *Abraham Lincoln, 19th century US president considered the president who established the high standard of honour and dignity of the presidential office.*

Mars: A noble warrior with the potential for blind dedication to a cause. To believe that one's cause is noble, to act with an air of nobility. ♦ A time when a leader seeks the moral high ground. *Margaret Thatcher, Britain's first woman Prime Minister (1979-90) who was known for her noble if sometimes arrogant demeanour.*

Jupiter: A person who values the past, the historian, or the fundamentalist. One who seeks solutions to today's problems by looking to the past. The family historian. ♦ A time when history is used to justify a decision. *Esther Van Deman, 20th century American archaeologist and the first woman to specialize in Roman archaeology. She established criteria which advanced the study of Roman architecture.*

Saturn: To strive for dignity in one's work. To build a body of work which others will respect. To act with dignity; to act in what is considered a noble cause. ♦ A person is honoured for their life's work. *Frederic-Auguste Bartholdi, French sculptor who in 1886, created the Statue of Liberty in New York Harbor.*

Uranus: A person who is a natural leader in their community or family; the one in a group who is respected for maintaining the dignity of others. ♦ The popular leader; the people's king or queen emerges. *Martin Luther King, 20th century American activist who emerged as the leader of the civil rights movement.*

Neptune: A person who is drawn to the goddess in any of her many forms. To idolize or admire women; or to struggle with the role of the feminine in one's life. ♦ Something, or someone, noble is lost. EVENT: *The fall of Constantinople on 29 May, 1453 to the Ottomans. The city was the jewel in the crown of the Christian Latin Eastern Empire.*

Pluto: A person who gains respect and gives others respect through the arts, history or through being a spiritual writer. The family or community historian who gives the group respect. ♦ The dignity of one person shines through. *Pinyin Su Dongpo, 11th century, one of China's greatest poets who was also an painter and calligrapher.*

The Node: A person who earns respect for physical endeavours; the athlete or one who admires the perfection of the human form and its physical abilities. ♦ A woman is honoured. *Pele, Brazilian soccer player of the late 1950s and 60s who is considered to be the most famous athlete of his era.*

NOTES

1. Allen, *Star Names Their Lore and Meaning*, p.144.
2. Robert Graves, *The Greek Myths*, Vol. I, London: Penguin, 1960, p.51.
3. see: Julius Schiller, *Coelum Stellatum Christianum*, 1627.

SIRIUS

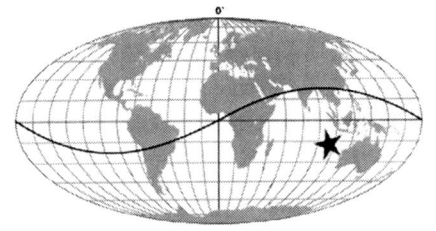

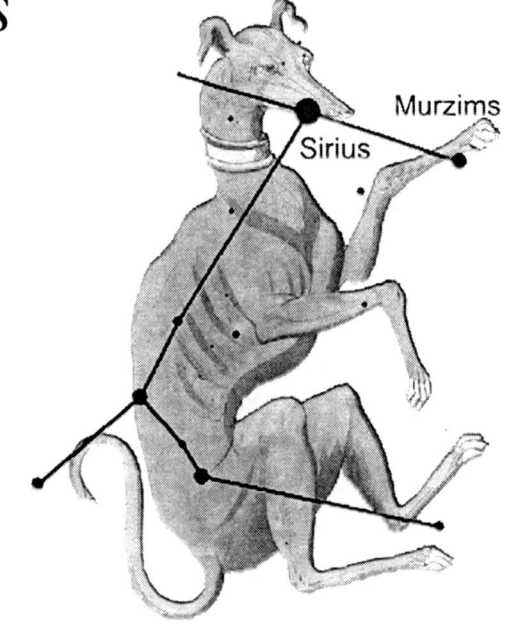

Constellation	Canis Major
α Canis Major, magnitude	-1.46
1 January 2000 =	RA 06hr 45'10"
Declination	-16° 43'
Celestial longitude	14° ♋ 05'
Celestial latitude	39°S36'
BV Colour =	White

Canis Major, the greater dog

Not far from the stern of the Argo lie two dogs, a large one, Canis Major, lying in the south and a smaller dog, Canis Minor, sitting above it on the equator. The Greeks see Canis Major as one of Orion's hunting dogs, sitting up in a begging position but with a watchful eye on the nearby hare[1]. But this dog was in the sky long before Aratus recorded it in the 4th century BCE. The dog was one of the first animals that humans domesticated and was seen as a guardian, both in life and in death. The Egyptians called this guard, and sometimes judge, *Anubis* and he became the god of mummification. Later Greek myths talk of *Cerberus*, the three headed dog called the Hound of Hades for he guarded the gate to Hades[2]. For the Celts, a faithful hound continued its service after death by being buried beneath the doorstep so it could continue guarding the family; this later led to the custom of carrying a new bride over the step so that the guardians would encounter her as a resident rather than an intruder[3]. (For more information see Murzims).

The Principle of Sirius, the Scorcher, the quest for immortality

Apart from the sun, Sirius is the brightest star in the sky with its magnitude of -1.43. The Egyptians called this brilliant white star *The Shining One* or *The Scorcher*. It was linked to the life-giving rising of the Nile and in that capacity it was also called *The Nile Star*. Sirius, with its dominant sky visual, and its closeness to Orion, itself seen as the god or pharaoh, was considered to be Isis, the wife of Osiris, and in this relationship along with its brightness, it has always been associated with great and/or sacred deeds. Sirius struggles at a personal level as it seeks to link small personal actions to great sacred moments, to find the sacred in the mundane actions of daily life, and in this process the individual can be sacrificed to the greater expression.

Heliacal Rising Star
Thinking of one's own life as a part of something bigger; devoting oneself to the noble cause. An awareness of the importance of the moment. To seek to live with the gods. *Neil Armstrong, the first man to walk on the moon, and his famous line as he stepped on the surface of the moon: "One small step for a man, one giant leap for mankind"*

Heliacal Setting Star
A person who finds that they have to defend a cause even at the expense of their own personal needs. To passionately follow a vocation in the promotion of a social concept. *Germaine Greer, 20th century Australian academic who has devoted her life to the rights of women and minority causes.*

Star on one of its pivot points at the moment of birth
To be touched by the gods; to have a sense of the divine, and be seeking perfection in one's work. To struggle with the expression of one's passions. *David Helfgott, 20th century Australian concert pianist who has struggled with mental health and is the subject of the film "Shine".*

Physiological Correspondence: The sweat glands – the body's cooling system.

Ptolemy's location: The brightest star in the face [of the dog] called Sirius.

World Cities: La Paz, Bolivia at latitudes between 14° to 18° south.

Sirius in paran with:

Sun: A person who can be sacrificed to the larger need; a vocation which overrides the normalness of one's life. To be swept up in emerging events.   ♦   The potential for great and immortal events to emerge. *Horatio Nelson, early 19th century English admiral known for his courageous victories culminating in the Battle of Trafalgar where he died but saved the nation and became immortalised in English culture.*

Moon: A desire to create a lasting monument to a loved person; to give one's own energy to a loved one; to seek the success of another.   ♦   A martyr; a person mourned by the common folk. *Shah Jahan, Moghul emperor and builder of the Taj Mahal (1631) which he built for and dedicated to his wife after her death.*

Mercury: Skilled with language or ideas. Drawn to work in large communications projects or business ventures.   ♦   A publication, or the words of a person, have far-reaching repercussions. *Paul Julius Reuter, 19th century German publisher and founder of the first news agency which still bears his name.*

Venus: The poet, the artist or the talented musician. To look for divinity within one's relationships.   ♦   Migration, immigration, new beginnings. *John Milton, 17th century poet known as one of the greatest poets of the English language due principally to his epic "Paradise Lost".*

Mars: Dedication which leads to brilliance; strong powers of concentration. The expert; brilliance within a narrow field. ◆ Heat, politically, socially, or even meteorologically. *Alexander Alekhine, Russian chess master who won the world championship in 1927 and defended it successfully for nearly 20 years.*

Jupiter: Inspirational in artistic, architectural or athletic endeavours. To suddenly achieve a result well beyond one's dreams. ◆ A successful project, which sets new standards. *Sir Christopher Wren, 17th century architect, designer, astronomer, and geometrician, the greatest English architect of his time.*

Saturn: To be a founder of an institution; an idea that goes from strength to strength. To lay a foundation stone for others in one's family or community. ◆ Immortality; a leader or a concept becomes exalted. *Alfred Deakin, Australian prime minister (1903-4, 1905-8, 1909-10) and one of the architects of federation.*

Uranus: A person who wants things to be larger than life. To be in awe of the monumental, to consider that bigger is better. ◆ A time of awe and wonder. *William James Pirrie, 20th century ship builder who built the ill-fated liner "Titanic". He controlled the largest ship building firm in the world.*

Neptune: The mathematician, the person who sees divinity in numbers or geometry; to seek immortality through one's work or one's children. To have a strong awareness of time. ◆ Events are written into history. *Charles Babbage, 18th century English mathematician who conceived the first automatic digital computer.*

Pluto: An obsession with details; stripping something down to its basic parts. Reshaping ideas or philosophy in order to build afresh. ◆ A time of invasion or the breaking up of a community. *Isaac Newton, 17th century English mathematician whose work on motion and gravity laid the groundwork for the scientific revolution.*

The Node: The traveller, a person who is driven to explore both places and ideas. One who pushes past accepted limits. ◆ An endeavour is announced. *Ralph Baldwin, US astrophysicist known for charting the Moon's surface. He wrote "The Face of the Moon" in 1949 which proved that the moon hand been hit by meteorites.*

NOTES

1. Aratus, "Phaenomena," p.233.
2. Bulfinch, *Myths of Greece and Rome*, p.292.
3. Walker, *The Woman's Encyclopedia of Myths and Secrets*, p.136.

SPICA

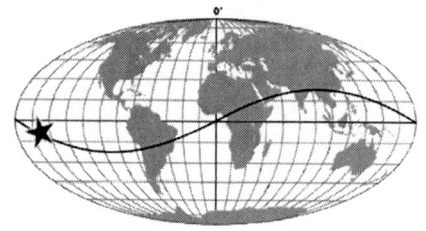
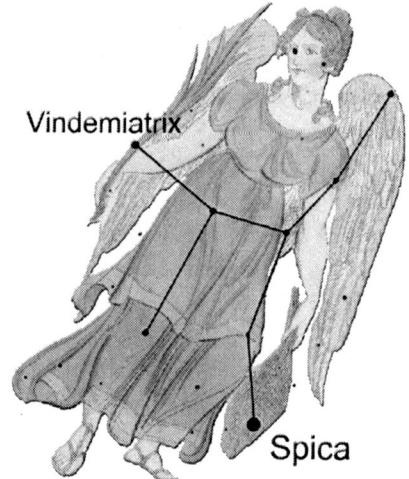

Constellation	Virgo
α Virginis, magnitude	0.98
1 January 2000 =	RA 13hr 25'11"
Declination	-11° 10'
Celestial longitude	23° ♎ 50'
Celestial latitude	02°S03'
BV Colour =	Blue-Green

Virgo, the virgin

This goddess in the sky was probably part of the original six zodiac constellations and is considered by some astronomers to have been formed as a constellation over 15,000 years ago at the time the spring equinox occurred in this part of the sky[1]. The Egyptians saw her as another image of the thousand-named goddess Isis, wife of the dead Osiris and mother of the god Horus. She was seen as holding a wheat sheaf in her hand seeds of which she dropped to form the Milky Way, reflective of her Babylonian name of "The Farrow"[2]. She ruled the summer solstice about 6,000 BCE. The Golden Age was said to have ended when this figure no longer governed the solstices. To the Arabs she was Al Adhra al Nathifah, the Innocent Maiden, she was also known as the Pure Virgin and the Chinese knew her as the Frigid Maiden, which looks like an unkind literal translation from the Chinese. By the time of Christianity she had become Mary holding the Child[3]. (For more information see Vindemiatrix).

The Principle of Spica, a gift from the goddess, to be gifted

The star is in the wheat sheaf in the hand of the goddess, and thus can be considered a symbol of her gifts to humankind. Originally these gifts included the knowledge of cultivation; however, in present times, this knowledge is no longer venerated - nevertheless Spica is still the symbol of knowledge and insight. The star is not connected with any particular field or profession but rather shows the potential for brilliance. Spica is a gift of brilliance, an innate talent, skill or ability which is out of the ordinary. The word "gifted" applies to strong Spica people and whatever this star touches it will illuminate in some way.

Heliacal Rising Star

A person who can excel in a particular area; to have a gift, physical, emotional or intellectual, which one uses on a daily basis level. Wanting to use one's talents for the greatest possible good. *Sir Christopher Wren, 17th century architect, designer, astronomer, and geometrician, the greatest English architect of his time.*

Heliacal Setting Star
To discover natural skills as one grows older. To find that one functions best when under mental pressure, to willing undertake the learning of new skills in order to deal with a problem or block. *Morris West, Australian author noted for such best-sellers as "The Devil's Advocate" (1959) and "The Shoes of the Fisherman" (1963) who spent the early part of his life in religious orders.*

Star on one of its pivot points at the moment of birth
Being very talented; having a gift that can bring joy to others. One who enjoys sports or visual arts and/or performance. *Martina Navratilova, Czech-born tennis player considered by some to be the greatest woman player of the 20th century.*

Physiological Correspondence: The faculty of memory.

Ptolemy's location: The star in the left hand called Spica.

World Cities: Darwin, Australia; Port Moresby, Papua New Guinea at latitudes between 09° to 13° south.

Spica in paran with:

Sun: A talented person; to admire those who excel in their profession; a tendency to be a fan but the need to claim this gift for oneself.   ♦   A bright idea, a new solution. *Wolfgang Amadeus Mozart, 18th century Austrian composer considered to be one of the greatest composers of all time.*

Moon: A person who embraces new technology: one who enjoys tools. To put one's faith in the future; a lover of science fiction or science fact.   ♦   The hope that new technologies will save the day. *Annie Oakley, 19th century US sharp-shooter thought by the people of her day as a "brilliant", talented and skilled woman.*

Mercury: Success through putting forward new ideas. To have a curious and hungry mind.   ♦   A new business, a bright idea is reported. *Johannes Kepler, 16th century German mathematician whose life work proved the error of Aristotle and Plato's model of the cosmos.*

Venus: A master of getting one's needs met, a persuasive personality. To draw gifted people into one's network of friends.   ♦   A time of propaganda or spin-doctors. *Alfred Bernhard Nobel, engineer and industrialist who invented dynamite and other explosives but is better known for his institution of the Nobel Prizes in 1901.*

Mars: A designer, or one who plans, plots, draws or performs. A person who understands how to use space.   ♦   A time when well planned intelligent action wins through. *Regiomontanus (Johannes Muller), 15th century German mathematician who was responsible for the revival of trigonometry, as well as an astrological house system.*

Jupiter: A person who goes beyond the recognised limits of their field. The researcher, the explorer, the inventor, or the athlete. ♦ An event beyond people's expectations. *Jean Baptiste Anville, 17th century cartographer who greatly improved the standards of map-making. Whenever possible he adjusted measurements to astronomically determined positions.*

Saturn: To be the prime mover of an idea, a founder, an originator. To willingly take the long hard path in order to achieve one's goals. ♦ A time when a measured response is needed. *Charles Macintosh, Scottish chemist who is best known for his invention in 1818 of a method of waterproofing garments.*

Uranus: A person who is a networker; being seen as the self-made person; coming from a hard or poor background and rising in society. A popular person. ♦ A new idea takes people's fancy. *Joseph Priestley, 18th century British theologian known as the discoverer of oxygen as well as the inventor of soda water. He was a sickly child from a poor background but in adulthood taught himself chemistry.*

Neptune: A person who loves mythology and/or fantasies; interested in esoteric knowledge. One who brings the unreal into reality. ♦ A plan fails, an illusion is broken. *Frank Lloyd Wright, 19th century US architect and writer, the most abundantly creative genius of 19th century American architecture.*

Pluto: A person seeks the "right" answer; to be seen as someone who is a problem solver; to have high expectations of oneself. ♦ An idea or invention that grabs people's imagination. *Sir James Murray, 19th century English lexicographer who was the first editor of what is today known as 'The Oxford English Dictionary'.*

The Node: To be drawn to new ideas, new fashions, to be linked with a new popular invention or object. ♦ To have one's career enmeshed with the new. *Prospero Alpini, 16th century Italian botanist who is credited with introducing coffee and bananas to Europe.*

NOTES

1. Lockyer, *The Dawn of Astronomy*, p.404.
2. Rochberg, *The Heavenly Writing, Divination, Horoscopy, and Astronomy in Mesopotamian Culture*, p.xxv.
3. Allen, *Star Names Their Lore and Meaning*, p.464.

SUALOCIN

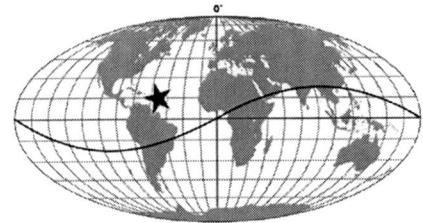

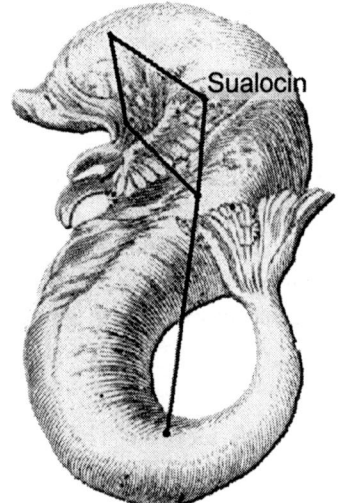
Sualocin

Constellation	Delphinus
α Delphini, magnitude	3.77
1 January 2000 =	RA 20hr 39' 36"
Declination	+15° 55'
Celestial longitude	17° ♒ 22'
Celestial latitude	33°N01'
BV Colour =	Blue-Green

Delphinus, the Dolphin

The Dolphin is a small constellation next to Aquila the Eagle in the northern hemisphere. It is placed in the sky in an area which Aratus, in the 4th century BCE, called the Water. The Dolphin has maintained its present form and shape for thousands of years and there are many different stories associated with it, all with the common theme of helpfulness and playfulness. The Greeks also saw the constellation as The Sacred Fish while Manilius calls it "The Pride of Sea and Sky, in each revered"[1]. The Christians continued with the theme of the Fish, linking it with the early symbol for Christianity. In contrast to this the Arabs saw this constellation as The Riding Camel, the ship of the desert[2].

The Principle of Sualocin, the dolphin, intelligent playfulness

This is the alpha star of the Dolphin and represents a kind of intelligent playfulness, but at the same time a certain mastery, or at least confidence of mastery, of one's environment. With Sualocin in a chart, it will add a touch of natural talent or consummate skill to the planet it touches. Its symbolism is focused in curiosity about, as well as intuitive knowledge of, one's space and environment. This star speaks of a native talent in an area where others may flounder.

Heliacal Rising Star

To lead a life full of action and freedom; to strive for mastery in a particular field, but to do so with humour. A love of the sea; a love of the clown. *Sarah Ryan, Australian Olympic swimmer who won relay medals at three consecutive Olympics 1996-2004 and is remembered for her colourful fingernails.*

Heliacal Setting Star
To find that one's hobby can become one's major life work. To discover fulfilment in one's recreation that is missing from one's career. To discover a natural talent in oneself. *Michael Faraday, 19th century English inventor who discovered electromagnetism and built an electric motor. He was trained as a bookseller and although Faraday received little formal education and knew little of higher mathematics, he was one of the most influential scientists in history.*

Star on one of its pivot points at the moment of birth
To have an artist's eye, to have an understanding of space and form, to be able to work with space and the flow of energy physically, virtually or spiritually. To have acting skills, to play with a role or image. *Cary Grant, Archibald Alec Leach was an English-born American film actor noted as perhaps the foremost exemplar of the debonair leading man, handsome, virile, charismatic and charming.*

Physiological Correspondence: The skin – its elasticity and sensitivity.

Ptolemy's location: The northern star in the western side [of the dolphin].

World Cities: Dakar, Senegal; Guatemala City, Guatemala; Kingston, Jamaica; Manila, Philippines; Rangoon, Myanmar at latitudes between 14^0 to 18^0 north.

Sualocin in paran with:

Sun: Physically talented, vital and alive. A person who has wit, or is a trickster with a sleight-of-hand approach to life. ♦ The talented long-shot takes centre stage. *Sir Charles Chaplin, 19th century silent film actor, writer, director and producer renowned for his genius with physical comedy.*

Moon: Good networker, helpful friends, and a popular person. A tendency to be overly dependant on one's natural talents. ♦ To be optimistic that an idea or an endeavour will be successful. *Elvis Presley, one of the most popular US rock and roll singers of the 20th century.*

Mercury: Playfulness with truth and facts, a different way of seeing the world. A lover of puzzles and mental challenges, or a clever wordsmith. ♦ Entertainment, theatre and the circus, popular amusement. *Hans Christian Andersen, 19th century Danish children's writer regarded as one of the world's great story-tellers.*

Venus: An artistic eye with colour, design or performance. To be socially skilled and use sexual charm. ♦ Public works of art, in focus. *Marilyn Monroe, US actor and one of the greatest sex symbol and screen idols of the 1950s and 60s.*

Mars: One who can motivate others; a person who can sell an idea and exudes mastery of the territory. ♦ A time when experts are believed. *Charles Henry Dow, 19th century founder of the Dow Jones company which in 1884, published a compilation of the first average of US stock prices.*

Jupiter: Bending the rules, intellectually or legally; to be spontaneous even with the law. A love of gambling and a tendency to take too much risk.   ♦   A time of excess. *Bugsy Siegel, 20th century US gangster and crime boss who initially developed Las Vegas as a gambling Mecca.*

Saturn: The eccentric, the one who acts or thinks differently. To hold very different attitudes and beliefs but still be a part of the mainstream world.   ♦   A break with tradition, a shift in establishment thinking. *Kenneth Grahame, 19th century Scottish writer whose classic children's story "Wind in the Willows" was initially ridiculed as it was one of the first works to anthropomorphize animals.*

Uranus: To be a maverick; to be popular in one's community or subculture. A person who enjoys socializing but struggles with issues of commitment.   ♦   A sudden surprise; the underdog succeeds. *Radclyffe Hall, early 20th century English writer who is best known for the novel "The Well of Loneliness", the publication of which caused a scandal due to its lesbian theme.*

Neptune: The artist, the designer. One who has an imagination and dreams of wealth, spiritual wholeness or glory.   ♦   A time of illusion. *Michelangelo Buonarroti, 15th century Italian painter, sculptor, poet and architect whose grand artistic vision is displayed notably in the ceiling of the Sistine Chapel.*

Pluto: To seek to extend the senses, spiritually or physically. To be interested in the micro and/or the macro worlds.   ♦   People are taken by surprise. *Alexander Graham Bell, 19th century Scottish inventor who invented the telephone, but was also called "the father of the deaf" due to his work to help the deaf.*

The Node: A person who loves, or is associated with, movement; one who needs freedom and space.   ♦   The adventurer takes centre stage. *Nikolaus Otto, 19th century German engineer developed the petrol powered four stroke internal combustion engine which was the first practical alternative to steam power.*

NOTES

1. Manilius, *Astronomica* 1:346.
2. Jobes and Jobes, *Outer Space: Myths, Name Meanings, Calendars*, p.167.

THUBAN

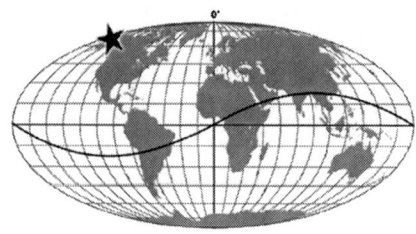

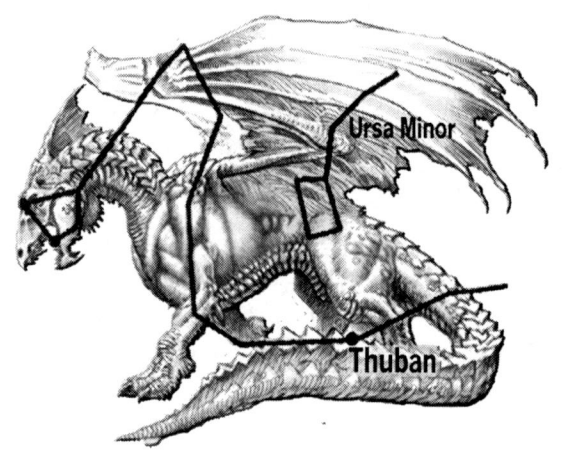

Constellation	Draco
α Draconis, magnitude	3.65
1 January 2000 =	RA 14hr 04'21"
Declination	+64° 22'
Celestial longitude	07° ♍ 28'
Celestial latitude	66°N21'
BV Colour =	Blue-Green

Draco, the Dragon
Throughout the ages this constellation has been seen as a snake, a dragon or a serpent. It was seen by the Babylonians as Tiamat the Great Dragon or horned snake[1] when it occupied a much larger space in the heavens encompassing the two Bears. Since the time of the Greeks it has been depicted without wings, for the stars of the Little Bear were originally known as the Dragon's wings, giving Draco the well known western mythological image of the dragon. With Draco's stars being the pole stars from about 4,500 BCE to about 2,000 BCE, the mighty celestial dragon was seen to guard the greatest treasure of all, the forever still point of the pole. The dragon never slept because it never set, thereby suggesting that this is also the creature which is the hundred-eyed non-sleeping dragon which guarded the golden apples in the Garden of Hesperides of Greek mythology[2]. Apples were also the dragon's treasure offered to Eve in the Christian Garden of Eden and in Celtic mythology the image of the dragon was used to protect that which was sacred[3]. However, by the time of the Arthurian legends, the dragon was seen as the protector or guardian of only material treasure - that of gold and jewels.

The Principle of Thuban, the dragon who guards, to hoard or guard
Traditionally the dragon guards the great treasure of the pole, but in modern times the dragon's treasure has degenerated into the world of physical treasures. Thuban, its alpha star, carries this symbolism and is associated with the control of this "treasure", or this symbolism can be interpreted as the jealously-guarding, hoarding creature of the Arthurian legends. If forming a paran to a chart, it will indicate issues around giving and sharing and a fear of exhausting one's resources.

Heliacal Rising Star
A person who is aware that they are protecting a treasure, to guard something important be it an idea, a cultural tradition or a physical object. *EVENT: Battle of Ayacucho, Peru 9 December, 1824.*

It was the battle that sealed the independence of Peru, as well as the independence of South America from the Spanish.

Heliacal Setting Star
To learn to value what one has; to protect one's lifestyle, both spiritual and physical. *Country: Sultanate of Oman, the small oil-rich nation on the south-east coast of the Arabian Peninsula which is currently ruled by a benefic absolute monarch who returns its wealth to the people and the country's infrastructure – date of independence 23 July 1970.*

Star on one of its pivot points at the moment of birth
A lifestyle of collecting, gathering or hoarding. To guard something precious for others or to be a miser. *J. Edgar Hoover, Director of the FBI of the United States for 48 years who collected and hoarded dossiers on any person he considered could be radical or subversive.*

Physiological Correspondence: The body's natural tendency to store nutrients without limit.

Ptolemy's location: The bright star in the fifth knot known as the pole star in about 3000 BCE.

World Cities: Reykjavik, Iceland at latitudes between 62° to 66° north.

Thuban in paran with:

Sun: One who finds, collects, or gives a treasure. To instinctively collect information or things, the need to avoid meanness with your knowledge or resources.   ♦   A national treasure receives attention. *Pablo Picasso, 19th century Spanish artist who is the only artist whose works were hung in the Louvre while he was still living. He created a variety of styles in art as well as the unique treasure of his vast body of work.*

Moon: The miser, or the philanthropist; awareness of the imbalance of wealth in society. The need to give, and the fear of not having "enough" is a major theme of life.   ♦   Government's use of money in the news. *Benjamin Altman, 19th century US merchant who collected paintings and sculptures and then bequeathed his collection to the Metropolitan Museum for all to enjoy.*

Mercury: A profession concerned with the organising, collecting, and even guarding of information, the historian, or a librarian. To collect, decipher and organise facts.   ♦   National secrets, spies and security matters. *Hermann Göring, Nazi general who was one of the Nazi plunderers of art from occupied Europe.*

Venus: Prone to jealousy and avarice in personal relationships; a lover of the diversity of life. An insatiable sexual appetite.   ♦   Protecting society's values and culture. *Arthur Miller, 20th century US playwright renowned for his sexual exploits.*

Mars: The need to defend one's property. A fear of losing the necessary material needs of life, a tendency to be over protective of one's resources.   ♦   To go to battle, to fight for property or rights. *Eli Whitney, 19th century American inventor of the cotton gin but also known for his suppression of growing hemp instead of cotton, to the long-term detriment of the environment.*

Jupiter: A person who can be a river of knowledge or information. The more knowledge, learning and information one give to others, the fuller one's own cup of life becomes.   ♦   Full disclosure, a time of no secrets. *Nicholas Culpeper, 17th century English physician who was one of the leading voices in the use of herbs in western medicine.*

Saturn: One who holds onto power. The need to learn to let go of power, to resist the temptation to dominate others.   ♦   The dictator, a strong but dictatorial person. *Abd-ul-Hamid II, 19th century Sultan named "The Great Assassin" as his reign was notable for his cruel suppression of revolts in the Balkans.*

Uranus: To hold a narrow point of view, to be rigid in one's opinions, to be blinkered to emerging issues.   ♦   A focus on that which belongs to the people, the collective wealth of the nation. *Samuel Seawell, 17th century English judge who was one of the judges in the Salem witchcraft trials in which 19 people were accused and condemned to death.*

Neptune: To create illusions of security; to work in the entertainment or virtual worlds. A lack of security around home and/or family.   ♦   The wish for a safe house; or false security and lost treasures. *Johnny Weismuller, American Olympic medal winning star swimmer who played the role of Tarzan, a "noble savage" who had been abandoned in a jungle as an infant and reared by apes.*

Pluto: To understand money, to be able to build financial resources or manage them for others. A stock broker, a banker, a community treasurer.   ♦   Worry about money, a robbery, a theft. *William Arthur Fadden, Australian Prime Minister and Treasurer responsible for "horror budgets" in the 1950s.*

The Node: The collector, one who knows and understands how to use their resources, the accountant, the bookkeeper.   ♦   A time when careful plans are revealed. *Boris Spassky Soviet chess master, world champion from 1969 to 1972.*

NOTES

1. Black and Green, *Gods, Demons and Symbols of Ancient Mesopotamia*, p.177.
2. Guerber, *The Myths of Greece and Rome*, p.129.
3. Green, *Dictionary of Celtic Myth and Legend*, p.195.

TOLIMAN

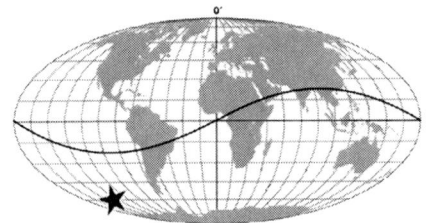

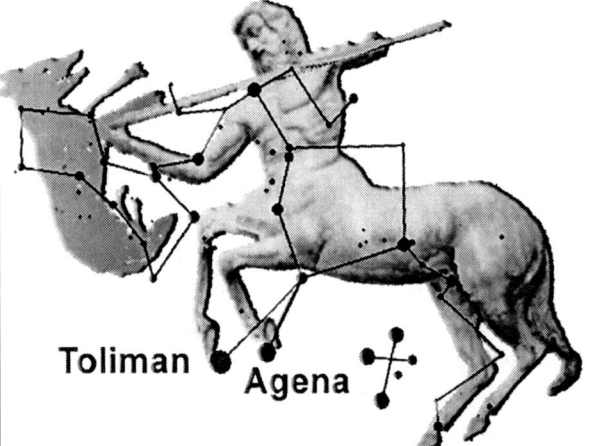

Constellation	Centaurus
α1 Centauri, magnitude	-0.01
1 January 2000 =	
Declination	RA 14hr 39'34"
Celestial longitude	-60° 50'
Celestial latitude	29° ♏ 28'
BV Colour =	42°S36'
	Yellow

Centaurus, the Centaur Chiron

Centaurus the Centaur, Lupus the Wolf and Ara the Altar are a group of three constellations that are entangled in a story of worship and devotion[1]. The Centaur is a large constellation covering an area between 30° to 60° of southern declination and is said to be holding Lupus, the wolf, in his out-stretched hand. He is thought, by both the Greeks and the Arabs, to be making his way to Ara, the Altar to make a sacrifice. He is considered to be either Chiron or Pholos, both famous centaurs in Greek mythology. The stories of Chiron and Pholos are intertwined - one being immortal but receiving a mortal wound, the other being mortal and in helping Chiron is wounded and dies. Zeus then tried to place Chiron in the sky near the place of Sagittarius but, due to the ferocity of the Archer, failed and was forced to place Chiron deep in the southern sky. (For more information see Agena).

The Principle of Toliman, the right foot of the Centaur Chiron, the teacher

This is the centaur, Chiron, who is going to the Altar to make a sacrifice. Chiron is a healer and a teacher but he carries a wound. Toliman being on the foot of the great tutor, like Rigel on the foot of Orion, indicates that the star's meaning is connected to matters of learning and education that expand one's world view. In a chart this star will be concerned with some cause or issue that needs to be corrected or healed, either privately or collectively, and one will seek to heal the problem through education, or teaching.

Heliacal Rising Star

The Teacher, one who brings knowledge to others. To believe that the path forward is one of learning, education and organisation. A tendency to be dictatorial. *Mao Tse-Tung, was the leader* of the People's Republic of China (PRC) from its establishment in 1949 until his death in 1976; through his "five year plans" and Cultural Revolution, he tried to reorganise China.

Heliacal Setting Star
To discover from experience that strong opinions may not be correct; to learn from life's lessons to be open to other ways of proceeding. Wisdom in one's elder years. *Azaria Chamberlain, The infant who was killed by a dingo in the Australian desert. The media attack on her parents became a landmark case on the errors and damage of mass opinions fuelled by the press.*

Star on one of its pivot points at the moment of birth
To be associated with cultural issues; the love of different cultures or a tendency to be xenophobic and fearful of other cultures. *Paddy Ashdown, 20th century British politician noted for his gift as a polyglot, to speak many languages.*

Physiological Correspondence: The bones of the feet.

Ptolemy's location: The star at the tip of the right foot.

World Cities: Nil at latitudes between 58° to 62° south.

Toliman in paran with:

Sun: To expand the world of others. To be a teacher or the perpetual student. ◆ A time when the voice of the people is forcibly expressed. *Charles Sturt, Australian explorer whose expedition down the Murrumbidgee and Murray rivers (1829-30) is considered to be one of the greatest in Australian history.*

Moon: A person who leads others by their passion and beliefs. A passionate, vocation-driven person. ◆ The people take action based on religious, or cultural, beliefs. *Mao Tse-Tung, a Marxist and a founding member of the Chinese Communist Party (1921).*

Mercury: Dedicated to spreading information. One who is dedicated to the truth, who passionately pursues the answers. ◆ A time where people's emotions are stirred. *Nelson Mandela, first president of South Africa in 1991 and a leading activist who spread his campaign message while being held in captivity.*

Venus: Questioning people's principles, to be argumentative if one believes there are falsehoods. ◆ Society's values and beliefs, are challenged. *Jayaprakash Narayan, an Indian freedom-figher, who in 1932 was imprisoned for participation in the civil disobedience movement against British rule in India.*

Mars: A persistent personality. To be a rebel or activist fuelled by one's own strong beliefs. ◆ A strong hand used by the authorities. *Bao Dai, the son of Emperor Khai Dinh, was the last emperor of Vietnam (1925-1955); he sought to reform and modernize Vietnam but was unable to win French cooperation.*

Jupiter: To seek recognition for one's plans or ideas. To build success through finding the positive in life events. ◆ The direct or noble person is victorious. *Anthony Fokker, a pilot and aircraft pioneer who produced over 40 different types of aircraft during World War I.*

Saturn: The politician: a person who seeks social justice within the framework of the establishment. To seek to help others by working within an instituted framework. ◆ Non-conservative political parties gain the power. *U Thant, Burmese academic, and third General Secretary of the UN, 1961-1971; he was a devout Buddhist, and critical of both the US and Russia whose actions threatened world peace.*

Uranus: A lover of education; a researcher of the common people; the anthropologist. ◆ Changes to the public education system. *Colleen McCullough, 20th century Australian author and neuroscientist. The depth of historical research in her Roman novels earned her a Doctor of Letters from the Macquarie University in 1993.*

Neptune: To build alternative education systems; to be interested in alternative knowledge; to work in the arts. ◆ Corruption or confusion in education or health. *Satyajit Ray, 20th century Indian film maker who is credited with modernising Indian cinema and bringing international recognition to the industry.*

Pluto: To have strong opinions which can blind one's judgment. To become a crusader for an idea. ◆ An outspoken person attacks the system. *William Arthur Fadden, Australian Prime Minister for only 40 days (1941); renowned for his strong personal opinions on social order and his desire to outlaw some political parties.*

The Node: To be associated with a political idea, to link oneself with a manner of education or governing system. ◆ A strong leader emerges. *Achmen Sukarno, 20th century Indonesian statesman whose support for the growth in the power of the military resulted in General Suharto taking control and heading a dictatorial regime.*

NOTES

1. Aratus, "Phaenomena," p.241.

244 *Star and Planet Combinations*

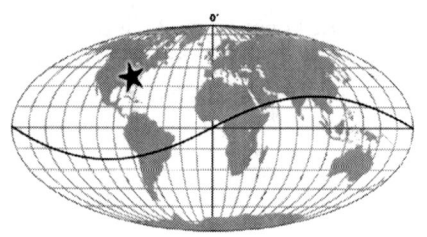

VEGA

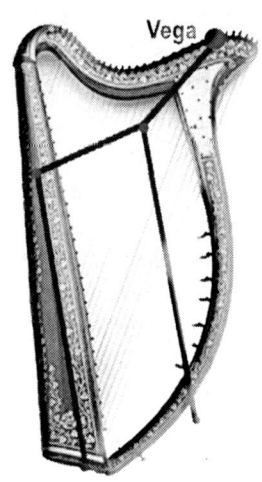

Constellation	Lyra
α Lyrae, magnitude	0.03
1 January 2000 =	RA 18hr 36'54"
Declination	+38° 47'
Celestial longitude	15° ♑ 18'
Celestial latitude	61°N44'
BV Colour =	White

Lyra, the Lyre

This constellation, although carrying many different names through history has generally had the common thread of a musical instrument. The Greeks thought of it as the Lyre of Orpheus. This lyre was made from a tortoise shell by the infant Mercury and later given to Orpheus by Apollo[1]. Aratus called it the *Little Tortoise*, explaining how Hermes used the animal to create the first Lyre[2]. Pliny called it the Harp-star. The Anglo Saxons and Celts knew it as a harp and later saw it as "Talyn Arthur", the Hero's Harp. The Christians called it King David's Harp and later, totally out of step with the tradition of the constellation, named it the Manger of the Infant Saviour[3]. In India this grouping was also linked to the vulture and at times in the desert of Arabia it was the Great Swooping Eagle, in contrast to the constellation of Aquila which was the Great Flying Eagle. Up to a few centuries ago it was also known as the swooping vulture which held a lyre in its beak. In this guise as a harp-carrying vulture it was the third Stymphalian Bird.

The Principle of Vega, the lyre, enchantment

Vega is a most beautiful and bright star and, through its mythological association with Orpheus, is linked to enchantment and divine spells. The myth of Orpheus is that of a musician whose music could tame the wildest of animals and in this tradition Vega captures the enchantment of spell-binding music. When in paran to a planet it symbolizes a creative, mysterious skill which can be used for artistic, spiritual expression or in a negative reading as a tool of deception. Its presence will bestow charisma and the suggestion that one has been touched by the other world.

Heliacal Rising Star

The poetic soul seeking the magic of life; one who wants to understand life and the complex interplay between all things. *Max Theiler, South African a virologist, whose work produced a vaccine for yellow fever and also laid a foundation for understanding how to make vaccines for viruses.*

Heliacal Setting Star
To discover in oneself creative skills and a love of the arts; to explore the creation of magic; to attempt to reach for other worlds in one work or hobbies. *Giacomo Torelli, 17th century Italian military engineer who was the developer of theatre machinery and techniques which provided the basis for modern theatrical devices.*

Star on one of its pivot points at the moment of birth
To have charisma, to be a strong influence on others. To represent or be associated with a magical or "other world" type individual. To admire the mystical. *Clint Eastwood, 20th century US actor whose fame comes principally from his roles as the mystical or "other worldly" cowboy.*

Physiological Correspondence: The body's need to sleep and to dream.

Ptolemy's location: The bright star in the shell called the Lyre.

World Cities: Algiers, Algeria; Ankara, Turkey; Athens, Greece; Beijing, China; Lisbon, Portugal at latitudes between 36° to 40° north.

Vega in paran with:

Sun: Seeing the magic in life; touching another world. Devotion to another world; music and the arts, or a strong spiritual life. ♦ A charismatic leader or cause. *Antonine Frederic Ozanam, 19th century Italian scholar and founder of the Society of St Vincent de Paul. His faith led him to a belief in the religious need for charity.*

Moon: A compassionate leader; someone who cares. To be focused on humanitarian issues. ♦ High expectations; seeking a saviour. *Maria Montessori, 19th century Italian educator whose system of education is based on a child's creativity and natural willingness to learn, as well as the right to be treated as an individual.*

Mercury: A visionary with a very persuasive voice and/or charismatic ideas. To be interested in the secrets, fantasy writing or the mythology of different cultures. ♦ Euphoric news, or news that cannot be believed. *Claude Vaugelas, 16th century French grammarian who played a major role in standardizing the French language.*

Venus: The artist, and visionary or one who supports different ideas about new social orders. Unrealistic expectation of others, leading to disappointment in an idea or person. ♦ A celebration of the arts, a charismatic person takes centre stage. *Michelangelo Buonarroti, 15th century Italian painter and sculptor who has had a major influence on western art.*

Mars: An imaginative, inventive person; or too idealistic. Not allowing the limitations of others to restrict one's creative ideas. ♦ The glorification of an invention, or a hero. *John Kay, 18th century inventor famed for the invention of the flying shuttle which helped automate the process of weaving wool.*

Jupiter: Obsessive problem solver; or obsessed with a grand idea. To be obsessed with grand schemes. ♦ Illusions about who has the power; dreams obscure reality. *Pierre Larousse, 19th century encyclopaedist who created the "Grand Dictionnaire" in 1863. His works were imbued with his love of knowledge and his desire to disseminate information even if unconventional.*

Saturn: A dominating person who can hold onto power. To wield authority over others by the weight of one's personality and/or powerful connections. ♦ The old warrior, the old hero. *Francisco Franco, 20th century Spanish military ruler who overthrew the democratic republic in Spain in 1939 and ruled Spain until his death in 1975.*

Uranus: A person who brings a touch of enchantment into everyday life. One who is trusted and loved for their openness or honesty, to hold a trustworthy position. ♦ A focus on a popular leader; being loved by the masses. *Hans Christian Andersen, 19th century Danish writer, one of the world's most loved story-tellers.*

Neptune: To seek revelations, to look for inspiration in one's daily life. A lover of nature and one who is always seeking that which is "real". ♦ Propaganda, the incorrect use of a leader's influence, or position. *Joseph Smith, 19th century US founder of the Mormons based on his own religious revelation gained while walking in woods as a teenager.*

Pluto: The magician; one who can produce moments of awe in any medium, from pyrotechnics to art and buildings. ♦ A time of awe and wonder; inspirational events. *Frank Lloyd Wright, 19th century US architect and writer, the most abundantly creative genius of American architecture.*

The Node: The dreamer, the inventor, one who is associated with or devoted to a particular vision of the future. ♦ A spectacular event is held. *Franz Baader, 18th century German mystical theologian who was the founder of modern ecumenical activity as he had the vision of using Christian alliances in Europe to avoid the recurrence of large scale conflict.*

NOTES

1. Manilius, *Astronomica* 1:324.
2. Aratus, "Phaenomena," p.229.
3. see: Julius Schiller, *Coelum Stellatum Christianum*, 1627.

VINDEMIATRIX

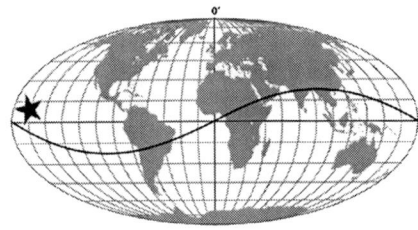

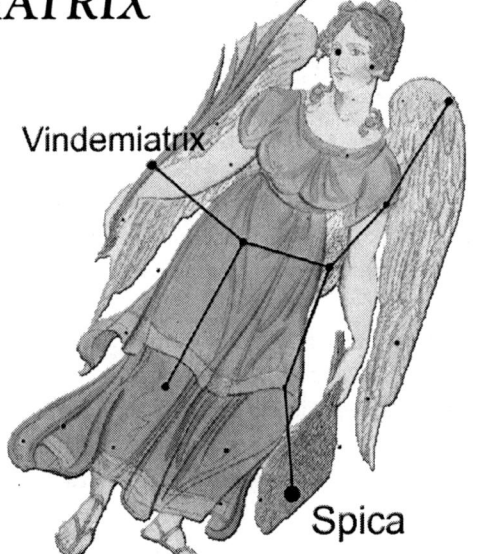

Constellation	Virgo
ε Virginis, magnitude	2.83
1 January 2000 =	RA 13hr 02'10"
Declination	+10° 58'
Celestial longitude	09° ♎ 56'
Celestial latitude	16°N12'
BV Colour =	Orange

Virgo, the virgin

The earliest expression of Virgo was around 2,900 BCE with the construction of the Sphinx, believed to be a celebration and adoration of the two zodiac signs (Virgo and Leo), through which the sun travelled at the time of summer and the harvest[1]. The Sphinx, it is suggested, had the head of the great harvest goddess and the body of a lion. The Egyptians/Greeks drew Virgo on the Denderah zodiac, larger than she is now and with no wings, but clearly a goddess. To the Greeks she was Demeter, goddess of the harvest, who withdrew herself and her seasons from the earth when Pluto abducted her daughter[2]. They also saw her as Erigone, a maiden who became so distressed at the ways of the human race that she hanged herself. By the time of Christianity she had become Mary holding the Child. (For more information see Spica).

The Principle of Vindemiatrix, the Gatherer, to collect and gather

The name Vindemiatrix means Grape-Gatherer, for it was said to be the heliacal rising signal to harvest the grapes. Even after precession removed Vindemiatrix from this important calendar time, the Greeks and Romans maintained her identity as the Grape Picker. Vindemiatrix, connected with the time of harvest, therefore implies a time of action, a time to pick what one has sown. This star will not force its mark onto a life, like the great Spica or one of the Royal Stars. However, it will indicate that one is a collector or gatherer. Art collectors, stamp collectors, people who gather facts or things, are the expression of this star.

Heliacal Rising Star
A life philosophy of completing projects, a person who sees solutions by collecting data, a person who seeks to complete collections. *Sir Donald Eckersley, 20th century Australian agricultural expert involved with the improvement of farming practice by better integration of marketing and business practices.*

Heliacal Setting Star
To discover that solutions can be found in collections of data; to learn the value of keeping records; one's own collected information brings one success. *Florence Nightingale, 19th century English reformer who instituted the practice of maintaining records for patients and drugs.*

Star on one of its pivot points at the moment of birth
To work hard to bring things together, objects ideas or people; to be a networker, one who unites. An organised person, tidy, with a structure to their lives. *Giuseppe Garibaldi, 19th century Italian patriot who is considered the Italian national hero as he personally led many of the military campaigns that brought about the formation of a unified Italy.*

Physiological Correspondence: The kidneys – the renal system.

Ptolemy's location: The northern star called Vindemiatrix.

World Cities: Djibouti, Djibouti; Panama City, Panama at latitudes between 08° to 12° north.

Vindemiatrix in paran with:

Sun: The one who gathers information, things or people. To bring order to collections, to see patterns of meaning.   •   People gather together, an event that unites. *Blaise Pascal, 17th century French mathematician, the founder of the modern theory of probability.*

Moon: A watcher, of people or events. A deepening interest in people or animals.   •   A human interest story takes the headlines. *Charles Perrault, French writer best known for his collection of stories for children first published in French in 1697 "Tales of Mother Goose" (Contes de ma me're l'oye).*

Mercury: A person who measures; a collector of data. An excellent memory, and a talent for handling large amounts of data.   •   A long running news story with many spin-offs. *Christian Thomsen, Danish anthropologist who, in 1819, developed the three part system of labelling pre-history - Stone, Bronze and Iron Ages.*

Venus: Interested in the culture and lives of other people. An observer and a commentator of social customs.   •   A polarization based on social rank, class or nationality. *Leo Tolstoy, Russian novelist whose publication of "War and Peace" in 1865 established him as the pre-eminent Russian author of his day.*

Mars: A thirst for knowledge or information; a lover of research. To be a teacher, or a researcher. ◆ War, or conflict, between different cultural ideas. *J.K. Rowling, 20th century British author of "Harry Potter" who has used her influence to encourage children to read.*

Jupiter: To gather others around an idea, a teacher. To be one who joins clubs or cults; to be a leader of a group centred on a particular idea. ◆ A gathering of people for the common good, or under a common banner. *Joseph Smith, 19th century US reformer who founded the Church of Jesus Christ of Latter-day Saints (Mormons).*

Saturn: Exploring, or collecting information in order, over many years, to implement new systems. To feel blocked or suppressed in collecting new knowledge. ◆ Social, or political, order is challenged; information is suppressed. *Johannes Kepler, 16th century German mathematician whose years of calculation resulted in the laws of planetary motion.*

Uranus: Interested in people and a collector of stories. Looking for information in places or objects which have been forgotten or abandoned. To have a tendency to seek the pot at the end of the rainbow or to be over-optimistic in looking for a windfall. ◆ The desire to gather and hoard; treasure-hunting. *EVENT: Californian Gold Rush, the first major gold strike in North America occurred at Sutter's Mill, near the Sacramento River in California, on 24 January, 1848.*

Neptune: An interest in sacred art; one who collects or explores esoteric knowledge. ◆ What has been collected in the past is vulnerable to loss. *Nostradamus, 16th century French astrologer and physician well known for his "Centuries", a collection of prophecies.*

Pluto: One who is relentless; a person who pursues a goal at whatever price. To be persistent in one's endeavours. ◆ A cyclone, literally or metaphorically. *Oliver Winchester, 19th century US manufacturer of weapons who developed the Winchester rifle thus popularizing the idea of a self-loading and repeating rifle.*

The Node: To align oneself with a structure; to be drawn to those who bring order. To look for the missing piece of a puzzle. ◆ News about food supplies. *Michel Adanson, 18th century French botanist who was the first to classify plants into natural orders, before Linnaeus.*

NOTES

1. Lockyer, *The Dawn of Astronomy*, p.404.
2. de Santillana and von Dechend, *Hamlet's Mill*, pp. 424-26.

250   *Star and Planet Combinations*

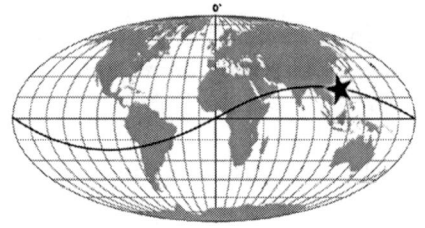

ZOSMA

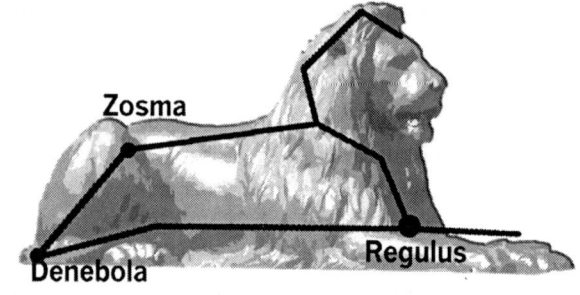

Constellation	Leo
δ Leonis, magnitude	2.56
1 January 2000 =	
RA	11hr 14'06"
Declination	+20° 31'
Celestial longitude	11° ♍ 19'
Celestial latitude	14°N20'
BV Colour =	White

Leo, the Lion

Around 6,000 to 3,000 BCE, the stars of Leo were the heliacal rising stars of the summer solstice, linking this constellation with hot summers and the longest days. However, as Leo moved from its summer solstice position and the Egyptian culture declined, it began to lose its importance and by 243 BCE it had lost the tuft of its tail to the constellation Coma Berenices. With the stars of the lion no longer claiming the important solstice position, the Greeks and Romans called the constellation the Nemean Lion which Hercules killed as one of his labours[1]. Later the Romans imported the symbol of the lion into Britain where it was portrayed on their coins as a lion led by a woman. They saw the Virgin and the Lion as two constellations wed together not only physically but also mythologically. She was known in Britain as the "Lady who Ruled Lions" and became a symbol of early divinity. By the early Middle Ages the lion was being used as a symbol of sovereignty in Britain and by the 12th century was the only animal shown on Anglo-Norman shields[2]. To the Christians this constellation was the lion that Daniel faced in its den. (For more information see Denebola and Regulus).

The Principle of Zosma, the back of the lion, victimisation

Zosma is the place on the back of the Nemean Lion where it was crushed by Hercules. This myth is a symbol of the point in Greek and Roman mythology where the older, goddess-centred beliefs were extinguished. Zosma itself is not feminine but belongs rather to those whom the established order makes powerless, whether directly of indirectly. Generally it does not belong in the charts of the rich and famous, unless they fall from grace. The planet in a chart that is tied to Zosma will suffer. It may be through naivety resulting in a victimized situation, or it may be reflected in the work of a social worker or care-giver. This is not a star of glory and fame but rather of the invisible work of dealing with the victim, either in oneself or in one's work.

Heliacal Rising Star
Independent; to prefer death to servitude to a hated or passionless career. To value one's personal freedom, above all else, whether emotional, spiritual or physical. *Country: Papua New Guinea, 16 September, 1975 (independence). The majority of the population live in traditional societies and practice subsistence-based agriculture.*

Heliacal Setting Star
The "wounded healer"; learning that helping others also helps oneself. To fight against that which disempowers an individual or a group. *Mary Wollstonecraft, 18th century English writer, noted as a passionate advocate of educational and social equality for women.*

Star on one of its pivot points at the moment of birth
The victim; the person who feels persecuted; to be associated with helping people; to seek a better life for oneself or for others through the idea of being "saved". *Billy Graham, 20th century US preacher considered the world's most popular and successful preacher.*

Physiological Correspondence: The lumbar spine – the lower back.

Ptolemy's location: In the back of the Lion.

World Cities: Bombay, India; Veracruz, Mexico at latitudes between 18° to 22° north.

Zosma in paran with:

Sun: To receive, or cause, suffering. Struggling with the mentality of the victim, either in oneself or others.   ◆   A group of people are the innocent victims of a senseless act. *King John, 12th century English monarch who lost almost all English possessions in France and who was forced, after a revolt by barons, to sign the Magna Carta.*

Moon: The pacifist or the warmonger - to hate, or enjoy, the suffering of others. To be sympathetic to the pain of others.   ◆   Concern for victims of crime, or natural disasters. *Robin Williams, an actor whose lead role in films like "Good Morning Vietnam" (1987) "The Fisher King" (1991) and "Awakenings" (1990) established him as a character-actor specialising in empathy and compassion.*

Mercury: To be concerned with the difficulties of others. A financial advisor or one who helps those with financial problems.   ◆   The underdog wins; victory to the little people. *Grandma Moses, US folk painter known for her simple and ingenuous painting style portraying rural life in America at the turn of the 19th century.*

Venus: Depression; a difficulty with self-esteem. To feel alienated from society; struggling with coping with one's role in society.   ◆   Racism; a group suffers because of their race or creed.

Marlon Brando, US actor who, despite early acting acclaim, suffered from depression and became increasingly more difficult to work with.

Mars: To work in impossible, or extremely difficult, circumstances. To work hard in an area where one gains little reward. ♦ A person, or a group, is victimised. *Mary Tudor, 16th century English monarch known as Bloody Mary for her persecution of Protestants, as she struggled unsuccessfully firstly to produce an heir and secondly to return England to the Catholic faith.*

Jupiter: The Angel of Mercy; to have compassion. One who helps empower others. ♦ The weak and victimised are assisted to become strong. *Kate Barrett, 19th century American physician who directed the rescue-home movement for unwed mothers in the United States.*

Saturn: A minority leader; or a person who grows in pessimism. To help those the establishment has abandoned. ♦ A simple thing causes tragic consequences. *Vincent de Paul, 16th century French saint who worked for the wellbeing of the peasantry and for education and training of a pastoral clergy.*

Uranus: To represent a contra position; to like the unusual or the surprising; to be aware of the needs of other people. ♦ A controversial, or upsetting outcome. *Hiram Revels, 19th century US politician who was the first African-American elected to the US Senate.*

Neptune: Looking for answers to life's problems in spiritual, religious or esoteric practices. A person who restores objects, or ideas. ♦ The loss of culture, the loss of history, the loss of objects that are precious to the collective. *Emily Balch, American leader of the women's movement for peace during and after World War I.*

Pluto: To promote the plight of the common person. To be victimised by political opinions or racial acts. ♦ A nation mourns, or a nation is victimised. *Sir Charles Chaplin, English silent movie actor who created the "Little Tramp" but suffered at the hands of the USA's anti-communist movement and lived most of his life in exile in Europe.*

The Node: To prefer the common things; to be in rapport with the masses; to be a pacifist. ♦ Suffering in one's own community. *Sri Aurobindo, 20th century Indian mystic who renounced nationalism and politics for yoga and Hindu philosophy.*

NOTES

1. Guerber, *The Myths of Greece and Rome*, p.125.
2. Allen, *Star Names Their Lore and Meaning*, p.254.

ZUBEN ELGENUBI

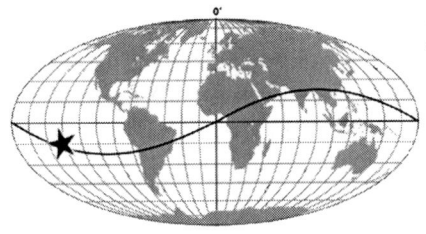
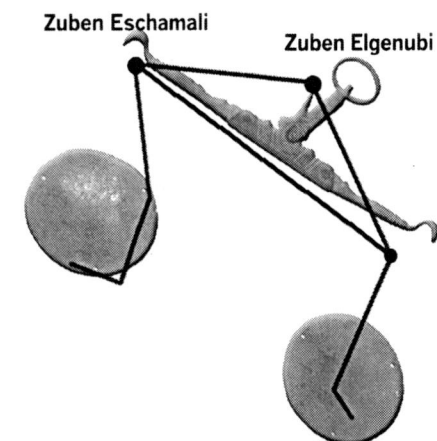

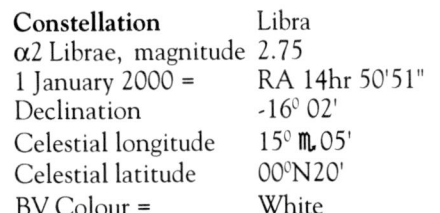

Constellation	Libra
α2 Librae, magnitude	2.75
1 January 2000 =	RA 14hr 50'51"
Declination	-16° 02'
Celestial longitude	15° ♏ 05'
Celestial latitude	00°N20'
BV Colour =	White

Libra, the claws turned to scales

The Claws of the Scorpion became known as The Scales around the time of the Greek and early Roman empires. Before this, however, the Babylonians associated these stars with judgment and kingship, linking them not only with the planet Saturn but also with the power to give bountifulness to king and country[1]. Other images see the stars as a lamp held by the Scorpion, a type of light and dark symbol linked in more recent times to the ancient yin/yang symbol of the I Ching. It was through the claws of the scorpion that the sun passed as it moved into the southern hemisphere and thus into the winter period, the time of less light. (For more information see Zuben Eschamali).

The Principle of Zuben Elgenubi, the southern pan, the volunteer

One of a pair of stars, its twin being Zuben Eschamali. The word *zuben* means claw, as the pans of Libra were originally the claws of Scorpio. Both of these stars have a common theme, which is to be strongly involved in social reform or social justice. This star, Zuben Elgenubi, symbolises higher ideals than its northern partner, for in its meaning the prime motive is not personal gain but rather to benefit the group. This star is associated with reform and it will resist the temptation for personal gain or power. Its presence in a chart will involve one in groups, whether they are concerned with national reform, politics and the law, or are simply hobby, or social, groups.

Heliacal Rising Star

To spend one's life trying to improve the quality of life for all. An instinctive need to lead or be involved with others who are actively seeking to help society. *Piet Retief, 18th century Boer leader of the Great Trek. This was the mass migration of Boers who sought independence from British rule in South Africa.*

Heliacal Setting Star
To find one's voice only if one is forced to use it. To be a reluctant authority or leader. Understanding what is needed to help others in crisis. *Robert Peary, 19th century US explorer who is acknowledged as the leader of first expedition to reach the North Pole.*

Star on one of its pivot points at the moment of birth
An unselfish person, who gives of their time or funds; a person who is a fund-raiser; one who helps. *Christopher Reeve, US actor who played Superman and later became a quadriplegic, after which he continued his work with the homeless but also worked tirelessly in the promotion of medical research.*

Physiological Correspondence: The hands and wrists.

Ptolemy's location: The bright star at the end of the southern claw.

World Cities: La Paz, Bolivia; at latitudes between $14°$ to $18°$ south.

Zuben Elgenubi in paran with:

Sun: A person with a social conscience. Someone who is a volunteer and works for a social cause.
* A time of salvation; a leader is sacrificed. *Mary Baker Eddy, 19th century American founder of the Christian Science movement.*

Moon: A person who wants to give aid to others; to work with women or children. A person who works to help friends.   • Emotions focused on the common good, or the spiritual needs of society. *Benjamin Spock, 20th century American paediatrician whose books changed the way western culture raised its children.*

Mercury: A spokesperson for a group, or a body of knowledge. To be interested in cycles and patterns.   • The drafting of new laws for the safety of the people, or commerce. *Gustave Eiffel, 19th century French engineer remembered for building the tower that bears his name.*

Venus: Manipulating the social order for better or worse. To be attracted towards relationship with people who are from a minority group.   • A time when volunteers are needed. *H G Wells, 20th century English novelist and sociologist known for science fiction such as "The Time Machine" and "The War of the Worlds", the latter of which convinced many people that the world was being invaded by Martians.*

Mars: Actively involved with the quality of other people's lives. To be willing to work hard for the improvement of something in one's community.   • People helping people help themselves. *Milton Hershey, US business man who in 1903 founded the corporation which helped popularize chocolate candy throughout the world; at the time it was considered a boon for the quality of people's lives.*

Jupiter: A humanitarian who looks for the big solution. Wanting to improve a situation by increasing general knowledge about the subject.   ◆   Humanitarian issues take the focus. *Alfred Adler, 19th century pioneer psychiatrist who introduced the concept of the inferiority complex.*

Saturn: A designer; a person who lays down parameters, or sets standards, for others. To wish to set standards by which others can measure.   ◆   A charity foundation is called into question. *Elsa Schiaparelli, 20th century Italian designer who influenced the fashion world for 40 years by emphasising the use of accessories and bold colours.*

Uranus: Seeking to help society improve its health or education; or seeking a new society to help improve one's family's health or education.   ◆   Migration, immigration, people seeking a better lifestyle. *John Robinson Pierce, 20th century US inventor who was the father of the communications satellite, seen as a global benefit.*

Neptune: A person who helps brings magic to the earth, to introduce it to others. One who is drawn to fantasies or one who can be delusional.   ◆   People in awe of unfolding events; disbelief or wonder. EVENT: *First manned space flight, Yuri Gagarin was the first man in space on Apr. 12, 1961.*

Pluto: To be prepared to become emotionally involved in the plight of others; to be empathic to people's needs.   ◆   The people seek a utopia. *Joseph Sturge, 18th century English Quaker, pacifist, and political reformer, who was important as a leader of the antislavery movement.*

The Node: An eye for fashion; to admire that which brings harmony or beauty to society.   ◆   Good works or beautiful works in the news. *Cesar Ritz, 19th century Swiss hotelier who founded the Paris hotel "The Ritz" which became a byword for elegance and luxury.*

NOTES

1.   Hunger, *Astrological Reports to Assyrian Kings*, p.24.

ZUBEN ESCHAMALI

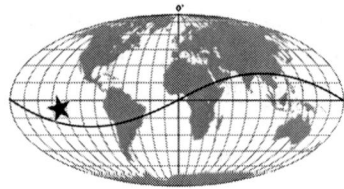

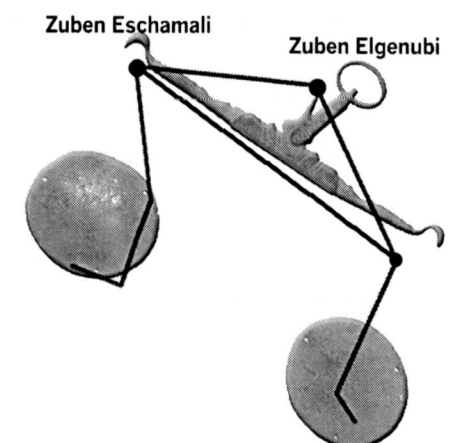

Constellation	Libra
β Librae, magnitude	2.61
1 January 2000 =	RA 15hr 16' 59"
Declination	-09° 23'
Celestial longitude	19° ♏ 22'
Celestial latitude	08°N30'
BV Colour =	Blue-Green

Libra, the claws turned to scales
The scales and the journey into the underworld are a theme in Babylonian and Egyptian theology, where the souls of the dead passed though a doorway into the Hall of Judgement and were tested and weighed on a great scale[1]. The Romans also associated Libra with judgment or justice, as they saw this part of the sky as their goddess, Astraea (Virgo), who held the Scales (Libra) in her hands[2]. This image is still used today to represent the law and courts. So whether we see these stars as the scales of justice in Virgo's hands or the claws of the Scorpion carrying souls through the gateway to the after-life, the themes of judgment and/or justice are the essence of this part of the sky. (For more information see Zuben Elgenubi).

The Principle of Zuben Eschamali, the northern pan, the professional helper
One of a pair of stars, its twin being Zuben Elgenubi, with each star representing one of the pans of the scales of Libra. However, this star, Zuben Eschamali, is also one of gatekeepers to the underworld for as the Sun passed by this star it entered the winter or darker period of the year. Like Elgenubi it is involved in matters to do with social reform or social justice, but it has a more self-interested agenda, seeking to help, but as a profession, in a way that improves the helper's personal power or financial situation. This star is not the tireless volunteer but rather the tireless social worker or benefactor who has opinions and seeks wages or social position from their work.

Heliacal Rising Star
A natural desire to help, using one's own knowledge or social influence. A profession which aids others. *John Flynn, 20th century Australian missionary who is remembered as the founder of the Royal Flying Doctor Service of Australia which he established by drawing on his position within the Presbyterian Church.*

Heliacal Setting Star
Finding that the only way to improve one's own position is to help improve the position of others. Forming mutually supportive relationships. *Peter the Great of Russia, 17th century ruler who was responsible for extending Russian borders and involving Russian in Europe.*

Star on one of its pivot points at the moment of birth
A team player, a person who can work in a group for the common good. To seek to improve a group by getting them all to work in a more cooperative fashion. *Sir Jack Brabham, Australian racing car driver who was the first driver in history to be knighted for services to motor sport.*

Physiological Correspondence: The nails – fingers and toes.

Ptolemy's location: The bright star at the end of the northern claw.

World Cities: Port Moresby, Papua New Guinea at latitudes between 07° to 11° south.

Zuben Eschamali in paran with:

Sun: The ability to influence society through one's work. Seeking a role in one's local community. ♦ Leaders come under observation; leaders are empowered. *Claude Vaugelis, 16th century French grammarian who played a major role in standardizing the French language of literature and of polite society.*

Moon: To feel responsible for social, or ecological, problems. A profession in economics; or simply handling the financial affairs of family members. ♦ Self-interest outweighs consideration for the group. *Albert Camus, 20th century Algerian-French philosopher whose contribution to philosophy was his idea of the absurd, demonstrated, in his work, as the result of our desire for clarity and meaning within a world that offers neither.*

Mercury: Imposing one's views on others. One's desire for good mixed with one's belief about what is correct for others. ♦ Biased philosophies impact on the media or markets. *Charles Taze Russell, 19th century US founder of the International Bible Students Association which eventually became the Jehovah's Witnesses.*

Venus: To feel strongly about what is right and what is wrong. To have strong opinions about fashion, social customs or acceptable behaviour within society. ♦ Social customs are challenged. *Sir Thomas More, 16th century Chancellor of England who was beheaded by Henry VIII because he refused to acknowledge him as the head of the newly formed Church of England.*

Mars: A disciplined, and ambitious, individual. To have a strong motivation towards becoming a successful member of the establishment with rank and power. ♦ A person will claim, or take, power. *Kerry Packer, 20th century Australian media owner who was, before his death, Australia's wealthiest man.*

Jupiter: Kingship; to be the recognised leader in one's profession. To excel at one's craft; to gain recognition for one's work. ♦ *The polished politician is successful. Jean Henri Riesener, 18th century French designer, the best known cabinet maker during the reign of France's Louis XVI.*

Saturn: To choose the hard, or less trodden, path for one's career. To gain recognition within the establishment. ♦ *A time when the nation's needs outweigh those of the individual. Helen Magill White, educator who was the first woman in the United States to earn a Ph.D. degree in 1877.*

Uranus: To be interested in politics; to seek to understand what drives society and what fuels moods, fashion and fads. ♦ *Power to the people; the people have their say. EVENT: The onset of the American War of Independence, the initial skirmishes between the British Army and American patriots, 19 April, 1775.*

Neptune: To be idealistic about a political idea, to idolise a leader; to be the subject of other people's high expectations. ♦ *Loss or despair in a group due to the selfish actions of a minority. Marilyn Monroe, US actress, model, Hollywood icon, and sex symbol who was in the end destroyed by the extremes of her life.*

Pluto: A person who can inspire others towards a desired goal; to be able to motivate others to do one's work. ♦ *A person is given, takes, or claims, power. EVENT: The bombing of Pearl Harbour by the Japanese, destroying the US Pacific fleet 7 December, 1941.*

The Node: To link one's life with a social need. To work in an area where one becomes well known in one's community. ♦ *A focus on the welfare system. Pierre Larousse, who is famous for publishing a body of educational and reference works of 19th century France which bear his name.*

NOTES

1. Budge, *The Egyptian Book of the Dead*, pp.351-2.
2. Allen, *Star Names Their Lore and Meaning*, p.270.

SOURCES

Al-Biruni. (1934). *The Book of Instruction in the Elements of the Art of Astrology*. Translated by R.Ramsay Wright. London: British Mus.

Allen, Richard Hinckley. (1963). *Star Names Their Lore and Meaning*. New York: Dover Publications, Inc.

Anonymous of 397. (1993). *The Treatise on the Bright Fixed Stars*. Translated by Robert Schmidt. Berkeley Springs, WV: The Golden Hind Press.

Aratus. (1989). "Phaenomena." In *Callimachus, Hymns and Epigrams Lycohpron, Aratus*. Cambridge: Haravard University Press.

Armstrong, A.H. (1938). "The Gods in Plato, Plotinus, Epicurus." *The Classical Quarterly* 32, no. 3/4: 190-96.

Baily, Francis (1843). "The Catalogues of Ptolemy, Ulugh Beigh, Tycho Brahe, Halley, Hevelius..." *Memoirs of the Royal Astronomical Society* Vol. 13.

Bierlein, J.F. (1994). *Parallel Myths*. New York Ballantine Books. .

Black, Jeremy, and Anthony Green. (1992). *Gods, Demons and Symbols of Ancient Mesopotamia*. London: The British Museum Press.

Bowman, Marion. (1991) "Phenomenology, Fieldwork and Folk Religion." Paper presented at the BASR Conference, Oxford, UK.

Brady, Bernadette. (1998). *Brady's Book of Fixed Stars*. Maine, USA: Samuel Weiser, Inc.

Budge, Wallis E. A. (1967). *The Egyptian Book of the Dead*. New York: Dover.

———. (1969). *The Gods of the Egyptians* Vol. I. New York: Dover.

Bulfinch, Thomas. (1979). *Myths of Greece and Rome*. New York: Penguin.

Burnett, Charles. (1996). *Magic and Divination in the Middle Ages*. Aldershot: Ashgate Publishing.

Burritt, Elijah H. (1835). *The Geography of the Heavens*. New York: Huntington and Savage.

Cairns, Hugh, and Bill Yidumduma Harney. (2003). *Dark Sparklers, Yidumduma's Aboriginal Astronomy*. Merimbula, Australia: H.C.Cairns.

Campion, Nicholas. (2000). "Babylonian Astrology: Its Origin and Legacy in Europe." In *Astronomy across Cultures: A History of Non-Western Astronomy*. Edited by Selin.H, 509 - 53. Amsterdam: Kluwer Academic Press.

Cicero, Marcus Tullius. (1979). *De Senectute, De Amicitia, De Divinatione* Translated by William Armistead Falconer. New York / London: Harvard University Press / William Heinemann Ltd.

Davies, W.V. (1997). *Reading the Past, Egyptian Hieroglyphs*. London: British Museum Press.

de Santillana, Giorgio, and Hertha von Dechend. (1977). *Hamlet's Mill*. Boston: Non-pareil.

Dunand, Francoise, and Christiane Zivie-Coche. (2004). *Gods and Men in Egypt, 3000 BCE to 395 CE*. London, UK: Connell University Press.

Ebertin, Reinhold. (1940). *The Combination of Stellar Influences*. Tempe, USA AFA.

Frankfort, Henri. (1948). *Ancient Egyptian Religion*. New York: Columbia University Press.

Gain, D. B. (1976). *The Aratus Ascribed to Germanicus Caesar*. London: Athlone Press.

Graves, Robert. (1960). *The Greek Myths*. Vol. I. London: Penguin.
Green, Miranda J. (1992). *Dictionary of Celtic Myth and Legend*. London: Thames & Hudson.
Grimal, Pierre. (1986). *The Dictionary of Classical Mythology*. Translated by A. R. Maxwell-Huslop. Cambridge: Blackwell Reference.
Guerber, H.A. (1991). *The Myths of Greece and Rome*. London: Harrap.
Guirand, F. (1965). *Egyptian Mythology*. New York: Tudor.
Hunger, Hermann. (1992). *Astrological Reports to Assyrian Kings*. Helsinki Helsinki University Press.
Jobes, Gertude, and James Jobes. (1964). *Outer Space:Myths, Name Meanings, Calendars*. New York: Scarecrow.
Jones, Alexander. (1999). *Astronomical Papyri from Oxyrhynchus*. Vol. Volumes 1 and 2. Philadelphia, USA: American Philosophical Society.
Kepler, J ed. (1609) *Astronomia Nova*. 1992 ed. London: Cambridge University Press., 1609.
Kunitzsch, Paul. (1989). *The Arabs and the Stars*. Northampton: Variorum.
Kunitzsch, Paul, and Tim Smart. (2006). *A Dictionary of Modern Star Names*. Cambridge, USA: Sky Publishing.
Lesko, Leonard H. (1991). "Ancient Egyptian Cosmogonies and Cosmology." In *Religion in Ancient Egypt*, edited by Byron E. Shafer, 88-122. New York: Cornell University Press.
Lockyer, Norman. (1892). *The Dawn of Astronomy*. Kila, MT: Kessinger.
Magnusson, Magnus. (1977). *B.C. - the Archaeology of the Bible Lands*. London: British Broadcasting Corporation.
Manilius, Marcus. (1977). *Astronomica* Translated by G.P.Gould. Cambridge: Harvard University Press.
Masson-Oursel, P., and Louise Morin. (1984). "Mythology of Ancient Persia." In *New Larousse Encyclopedia of Mythology*, 309 - 25. London: Hamlyn.
McCafferty, Patrick, and Mike Baille. (2005). *The Celtic Gods - Comets in Irish Mythology*. Stroud, UK: Tempus.
Parpola, Simo. (1970). *Letters from Assyrian Scholars to the Kings Esarhaddon and Assurbanipal Part 1*. Germany: Butzon and Kevelaer. .
Plato. (1997). "Republic." In *Plato Complete Works*, edited by John M. Cooper. Cambridge: Hackett Publishing Company.
Plotinus. (1992). *Plotinus, the Enneads*. Translated by Stephen MacKenna. New York, USA: Larson Publications.
Ptolemy, Claudius. (1993). *The Phases of the Fixed Stars*. Translated by Robert Schmidt. Berkeley Springs, WV: The Golden Hind Press.
———. (1998). *Ptolemy's Almagest*. Translated by G.J. Toomer. New Jersey, USA: Princeton University Press.
———. (1969). *The Tetrabiblos*. Translated by Ashmand. J. M. Mokelumne Hill, USA: Health Research.
Reiner, Erica. (1999). "Babylonian Celestial Divination." In *Ancient Astronomy and Celestial Divination*, edited by N.M Swerdlow, 21– 37. London MIT Press.

Rochberg-Halton, Francesca. (1989)."Babylonian Horoscopes and Their Sources."In *Orientalia*. Rome: Pontificium Institutum Biblicum.

——— (1988). "Elements of the Babylonian Contribution to Hellenistic Astrology." *Journal of the American Oriental Society* Vol 108, no. No. 1: 51 - 62.

Rochberg, Francesca. (1998). *Babylonian Horoscopes*. Philadelphia, USA: American Philosophical Society.

———. (2004). *The Heavenly Writing, Divination, Horoscopy, and Astronomy in Mesopotamian Culture*. Cambridge, UK: Cambridge University Press.

——— (1999). "Review Of: *The Concept of Fate in Ancient Mesopotamia of the First Millennium: Towards an Understanding of Simtu* by Jack N Lawson." *Journal of Near Eastern Studies* 58, no. 1: 54-58.

Room, Adrian. (1988). *Dictionary of Astronomical Names*. New York: Routledge.

Sellers, J.B. (1992). *The Death of Gods in Ancient Egypt*. London: Penguin.

Settegast, Mary (1990). *Plato Prehistorian, 10,000 to 5,000 B.C. Myth, Religion, Archaeology*. New York, USA: Lindisfarne Press

Silverman, David P. (1991). "Divinity and Deities in Ancient Egypt."In *Religion in Ancient Egypt*. Edited by Byron E. Shafer, 7 - 87. London: Cornell University Press.

Thorndike, Lynn. (1923). *The History of Magic and Experimental Science*. Vol. II. New York: MacMillan.

Valens, Vettius (1993). *The Anthology Book I*. Translated by Robert Schmidt. Berkeley Springs, WV: The Golden Hind Press.

Walker, Barbara. (1983). *The Woman's Encyclopedia of Myths and Secrets*. San Francisco: HarperSanFrancisco.

Walker, C.B.F. (1989). "A Sketch of the Development of Mesopotamian Astrology and Horoscopes." In *History and Astrology*., edited by Annabella Kitson, 7-14. London Uwin Paperbacks.

Wilkinson, Richard H. (1992). *Reading Egyptian Art*. London: Thames and Hudson.

Other books by The Wessex Astrologer

The Essentials of Vedic Astrology
Lunar Nodes - Crisis and Redemption
Personal Panchanga and the Five Sources of Light
Komilla Sutton

Astrolocality Astrology
From Here to There
Martin Davis

The Consultation Chart
Medical Astrology
Wanda Sellar

The Betz Placidus Table of Houses
Martha Betz

Astrology and Meditation
Greg Bogart

Patterns of the Past
Karmic Connections
Good Vibrations
Judy Hall

The Book of World Horoscopes
Nicholas Campion

The Moment of Astrology
Geoffrey Cornelius

Life After Grief - An Astrological Guide to Dealing with Loss
Darrelyn Gunzburg

You're not a Person - Just a Birthchart
Declination: The Steps of the Sun
Paul F. Newman

The Houses: Temples of the Sky
Deborah Houlding

Temperament: Astrology's Forgotten Key
Dorian Geiseler Greenbaum

Astrology, A Place in Chaos
Bernadette Brady

Astrology and the Causes of War
Jamie Macphail

Flirting with the Zodiac
Kim Farnell

The Gods of Change
Howard Sasportas

Astrological Roots: The Hellenistic Legacy
Joseph Crane

The Art of Forecasting using Solar Returns
Anthony Louis

www.wessexastrologer.com

Lightning Source UK Ltd.
Milton Keynes UK
UKOW03f2130130115

244419UK00001B/18/P